The
Insurrection in Mesopotamia, 1920

Lt. Gen. Sir Aylmer Haldane.

The Insurrection in Mesopotamia, 1920

BY

LIEUTENANT-GENERAL
SIR **AYLMER L. HALDANE**
G.C.M.G., K.C.B., D.S.O.
AUTHOR OF 'HOW WE ESCAPED FROM PRETORIA,'
'A BRIGADE OF THE OLD ARMY'

"*'Tis true, they are a lawless brood*"

The Naval & Military Press Ltd

Published by

The Naval & Military Press Ltd
Unit 5 Riverside, Brambleside
Bellbrook Industrial Estate
Uckfield, East Sussex
TN22 1QQ England

Tel: +44 (0)1825 749494

www.naval-military-press.com
www.nmarchive.com

In reprinting in facsimile from the original, any imperfections are inevitably reproduced and the quality may fall short of modern type and cartographic standards.

PREFACE.

WITH the exception of a few additions here and there, most of which are in the final chapter, this account of the 'Insurrection in Mesopotamia' was written at Baghdad between June and September 1921. I take this opportunity of expressing my cordial thanks to Group-Captain A. E. Borton and Flying Officer A. P. Ledger, Royal Air Force; to my Aide-de-Camp, Lieutenant S. Grehan, and others, for the photographs which illustrate the pages that follow.

A. HALDANE.

LONDON, 31st *May* 1922.

CONTENTS.

	PAGE
PREFACE	v
I. FROM COLOGNE TO BASRAH	1
II. FIRST IMPRESSIONS	8
III. AFTER THE ARMISTICE	19
IV. STORM CLOUDS	35
V. THE FIRST EXPLOSION	39
VI. BAGHDAD TO TEHERAN	45
VII. MILITARY ENCUMBRANCES	57
VIII. STATISTICS AND OTHER MATTERS . . .	64
IX. THE OUTBREAK AT AND RELIEF OF RUMAITHAH	73
X. THE DISASTER TO THE MANCHESTER COLUMN .	91
XI. ALARUMS AND EXCURSIONS	104
XII. THE OPERATIONS AT HILLAH	124
XIII. THE RETREAT FROM DIWANIYAH . . .	128
XIV. THE RECOVERY OF THE HINDIYAH BARRAGE .	140
XV. THE OPERATIONS NORTH-EAST OF BAGHDAD .	152
XVI. THE RELIEF OF KUFAH	176
XVII. EVENTS IN THE RIVER AREA . . .	193
XVIII. THE RELIEF OF SAMAWAH	214
XIX. THE OPERATIONS NORTH OF BAGHDAD . .	231
XX. THE OPERATIONS IN NORTH PERSIA . .	250

CONTENTS.

XXI. THE DISARMING OF THE TRIBES	256
XXII. THE REOPENING OF THE EUPHRATES VALLEY ROUTE	277
XXIII. A MARCH ACROSS THE SHATT-AL-HAI	285
XXIV. CONCLUSION.	298

APPENDICES

I. ORDER OF BATTLE.	315
II. ADVENTURES OF OFFICERS	320
III. RESPONSIBILITY OF OFFICERS	324
IV. STRENGTH OF TROOPS IN MESOPOTAMIA AND PERSIA	325
V. LETTER FROM THE CAPTAIN OF THE "GREENFLY"	326
VI. TRIBES WHICH PARTICIPATED IN THE INSURRECTION	328
VII. MEMORANDUM REGARDING DISARMAMENT	329
VIII. BRITISH, INDIAN, AND ARAB CASUALTIES	331
IX. NOTES ON ARAB WARFARE, WITH TWO DIAGRAMS	332
X. DEMANDS FOR REINFORCEMENTS	343
XI. STATEMENT OF COMBATANT REINFORCEMENTS RECEIVED FROM INDIA	344

INDEX	345

ILLUSTRATIONS.

LIEUT.-GENERAL SIR AYLMER HALDANE	*Frontispiece*	
KUT, LOOKING DOWN-STREAM	*Facing p.*	8
KUT, LOOKING UP-STREAM	,,	8
TEL AFAR—POLITICAL OFFICE	,,	42
TEL AFAR—FROM THE EAST	,,	42
TAK-I-GIRRAH PASS	,,	48
KARIND CAMP	,,	48
ZAKHO VILLAGE	,,	50
ZAKHO CAMP	,,	50
TAK-I-BOSTAN	,,	52
MANJIL PASS—SOUTHERN ENTRANCE	,,	52
SHAIKH SHA'ALAN ABU	,,	74
RUMAITHAH—BUILDINGS DEFENDED ARE WITHIN WHITE LINE	,,	76
RUMAITHAH—POLITICAL SERAI	,,	76
CAMP OF MANCHESTER COLUMN FROM SOUTH-EAST OF BRIDGE LOOKING TOWARDS MOUNDS	,,	100
BIRS NIMRUD	,,	100
BLOCKHOUSE NO. 19, BAGHDAD	,,	112
TYPICAL MESOPOTAMIAN SCENERY (ONE MILE EAST OF BAGHDAD)	,,	112
THE FIRE OF 3RD AUGUST—BAGHDAD	,,	122
PART OF HINAIDI CANTONMENT, LOOKING EAST	,,	122

ILLUSTRATIONS.

DIWANIYAH AND CAMP	*Facing p.* 130
BRIGADIER-GENERAL CONINGHAM'S COLUMN BETWEEN IBN ALI AND GUCHAN	,, 130
JARBUIYAH BRIDGE, LOOKING DOWN-STREAM	,, 134
JARBUIYAH POST, 4TH AUGUST 1920	,, 134
HINDIYAH BARRAGE FROM THE WEST	,, 142
HILLAH FROM THE SOUTH-EAST	,, 142
BRIDGE AT MUSAYIB FROM LEFT BANK	,, 144
BRIDGE AT TUWAIRIJ FROM RIGHT BANK	,, 144
BRIDGE OVER DIYALAH RIVER NEAR BAQUBAH	,, 154
BAQUBAH—RAILWAY STATION IN FOREGROUND	,, 154
BLOCKHOUSE AND REGULATOR OF RUZ CANAL	,, 164
SHARABAN—QISHLAH OR OLD TURKISH BARRACKS IN FOREGROUND	,, 164
TABLE MOUNTAIN	,, 166
QURAITU RAILWAY STATION	,, 166
KHAN NUQTAH	,, 170
BAGHDAD FROM THE SOUTH-WEST	,, 170
KUFAH FROM THE SOUTH-EAST, 4TH OCTOBER 1920. (BUILDINGS HELD BY GARRISON ARE SHOWN WITHIN WHITE LINES)	,, 178
BLOCK OF BUILDINGS HELD AT KUFAH BY 108TH INFANTRY. (DEFENCE VESSEL "FIREFLY" ON THE LEFT)	,, 178
THE CLIFF WHICH GIVES IRAQ ITS NAME	,, 186
KARBALA FROM THE EAST	,, 186
BASRAH FROM THE WEST	,, 194
NASIRIYAH, LOOKING UP-STREAM	,, 194
KHIDHR RAILWAY STATION ON BASRAH-BAGHDAD SYSTEM	,, 196
BALAD RAILWAY STATION ON BAGHDAD-SAMARRAH SYSTEM	,, 196
SAMAWAH RAILWAY STATION AND CAMP	,, 204
SAMAWAH—THE DISABLED ARMOURED TRAIN	,, 204

ILLUSTRATIONS.

FATHAH GORGE, LOOKING UP-STREAM	*Facing p.* 234
SAMARRAH FROM THE EAST	,, 234
COUNTRY NEAR SHERGAT	,, 236
MOSUL FROM THE EAST	,, 236
ASSYRIAN WARRIORS	,, 240
ARAB LEVIES	,, 240
ARBIL FROM THE NORTH-WEST	,, 246
KIRKUK FROM THE WEST	,, 246
NAJAF FROM THE EAST	,, 264
ANNOUNCEMENT OF TERMS OF SURRENDER AT NAJAF	,, 264
DEFENCE VESSEL "BLACKFLY"	,, 270
TYPES OF MESOPOTAMIAN BOATS	,, 270
QALAT SIKAR	,, 288
SHATTRAH	,, 288

MAPS AND PLANS.

TEL AFAR	41
THE ADVANCE TO RUMAITHAH	85
CAMP OF MANCHESTER COLUMN	99
ACTION NEAR JARBUIYAH	136
HINDIYAH BARRAGE	144
CANAL HEAD DEFENCES NEAR TABLE MOUNTAIN	167
OPERATIONS ROUND HILLAH	183
KUFAH GARRISON	188
SAMAWAH	207
ACTION AT IMAN ABDULLAH	281
GENERAL MAP OF MESOPOTAMIA AND PART OF PERSIA	*at end*

The Insurrection in Mesopotamia, 1920.

CHAPTER I.

FROM COLOGNE TO BASRAH.

THE reductions which inevitably follow in the wake of every great war brought to an end my connection with the VIth Corps, which I had commanded in France and Germany for over three years; and, on the 4th November 1919, I regretfully bade adieu to the British Army of the Rhine and took my departure for London.

The prospects of early re-employment for any one of the rank of lieutenant-general seemed remote, as, after the Armistice, all appointments which were vacant or held by temporary commanders had been filled by men chosen from generals whose corps or armies at the front had been abolished; and a term of half-pay was the vista which extended in front of me. However, an inquiry made at the War Office on the subject of future prospects of employment elicited the opinion—for it was nothing else—that something might "turn up," and a subsequent interview which I had with Mr Churchill, who was then Secretary of State for War, did not tend altogether to dispel that hope.

The term of half-pay proved to be briefer than anticipated, and on the 21st December one of the members of the Army Council mentioned to me that he believed that I was about to be offered the command in Mesopotamia. Ten days later I sent my acceptance of that appointment to the Military Secretary, from whom in the meantime I had received the customary communication.

Throughout the war my attention, like that of many of us on the Western Front, had been concentrated on the problem which faced us there, to the exclusion of much that was taking place in, what were called colloquially, "side-shows." The occurrences in Mesopotamia, including General Townshend's successful application of the principles of war and the capture of Baghdad by General Maude, were, of course, known to me; but the details of their campaigns, which had absorbed so many troops to the disadvantage of the decisive theatre in which we were engaged, as well the geography and character of the country in which they had been waged, were in no way familiar to me. Indeed I must confess to feeling little interest in either, for the impression that our commitments, there and in other countries far distant from the heart of the great struggle, were unsound and could lead to no decisive result, was predominant in my mind, and only grew stronger with the course of time.

Besides congratulations on my new appointment, I was the recipient of more than an equal number of condolences; and although no official hint was breathed that Mesopotamia might prove to be something other than the proverbial bed of roses, I had many private warnings which induced me to believe that those flowers would not be unaccompanied by their usual crop of thorns. I was resolved, however, that, large and exposed to external attack and internal disturbances as was the area of which I was soon to be the civil and military head, I would leave no stone unturned to hand it over undiminished on the termination of my appointment. Little did I then realise how six months later we should be fighting with our backs to the wall, with insurrection rife throughout the greater, and that the most thickly-populated, part of the country, and face to face with the very problem which had occupied my thoughts before leaving home. But let me not anticipate!

During the weeks which preceded my departure I endeavoured to acquire some first-hand information regarding the country whither I was shortly to be bound, but the diversity of views which were ungrudgingly poured forth to my expectant ears, some favourable, others the exact reverse, served to exemplify the truth of the adage, "tot homines, quot sententiæ." According to some the synonym for paradise was Mesopotamia, and their one desire seemed to be to return to that land of bliss; while others—the majority—wavered between lukewarmness and execration, with an inclination to the latter, partly repressed no doubt out of consideration for my feelings. Sir John Cowans —alas! no more—who I knew had paid a short visit, as also had Sir John Hewett, to this supposed Garden of Eden, both exceptional men and blessed with powers of observation and deduction far beyond the average, gave me some useful hints; but I think the opinion of the former might best be summed up in an unquotable dictum of the British soldier, which he repeated for my benefit. Finally, I came to the conclusion that the evidence of my own eyes would provide the only satisfactory method of solving the mystery of Mesopotamia, with its climate, insects, and the many peculiarities with which it was credited, and I turned my attention to the usual preparations which one has to make on leaving the United Kingdom for a time.

For perusal on the voyage to Basrah the energetic researches of Messrs Hatchard provided me with quite a respectable number of books, new and second-hand, whose contents covered the period of the late campaigns and the earlier history of the reputed Cradle of Mankind. A revised version of the Bible, with notes, published by the Oxford University Press, was by no means the least valuable of the literary possessions which I took with me.

A few days before the date fixed for my departure I was bidden to report myself at the War Office, where Mr Churchill, with great lucidity and pleasing power of expression, held forth to me for twenty minutes on the necessity for drastic reductions in the garrison of my future command, the expense of which had become an intolerable burden to the British taxpayer. Being one of that suffering class, I found myself in full sympathy with all he said on the subject, and undertook to do my utmost to carry out the policy which he so clearly enunciated. Until, however, I could examine the problem on the spot, where I suspected it would assume a very different aspect from that presented by the Secretary of State—as he stood with his back to a blazing fire, his hands in the pockets of his trousers and his coat-tails resting on his forearms, while I, all ears, sat facing him in a comfortable arm-chair—I felt that an expression of my views, beyond a general assent, would be of little value, and refrained from uttering it.

Some delay occurred—which I did not regret—in securing passages for myself and my aide-de-camp, Lieutenant S. A. J. Grehan, M.C., Royal Artillery, who had served in the VIth Corps with me, which I understood was due to the lack of restrictions regarding the travel to the East of persons other than those on business bent. Indeed, on reaching India I found that there was considerable feeling on this subject, as many officers and others, who during the war had been forced to remain in the East, now met with great difficulty in transferring themselves, and in many cases their families, to the United Kingdom.

Having a few days to spare I left London on the 9th February to visit some friends near Cannes, and on the 15th sailed from Marseilles, where my aide-de-camp met me, on board the P. & O. *Devanha*. Among the passengers was His Highness the Agha Khan, with whom I had some interesting talks about Mesopotamia. His view was that we would have been wiser not to have occupied the country further inland than the junction of the Tigris and Euphrates at Kurna, and that the Arabs should be interfered with as little as possible, and left to work out their own salvation in what might be described as small republics. The *Pax Britannica*, which we insisted on introducing wherever we went, regardless of local conditions, and which does not wink at lawlessness, would, if enforced by Indian

Civil Service officers, who were accustomed to work in
settled districts, assuredly land us sooner or later in trouble.
The French, he remarked, in Morocco tolerate a good deal
of lawlessness, and affairs there are carried on quite successfully. Our system of government involved a large
garrison, and was consequently costly. He considered
that the methods followed by Sir Robert Sandeman in
Baluchistan were suited to Mesopotamia. He did not like
the idea of native levies, and favoured the judicious bestowal
of " baksheesh," to which both Arabs and Kurds—and not
they alone—are susceptible. At that time I had no con-
ception of the system on which we governed Mesopotamia,
for it had not been possible to get much information regarding it, but the wisdom of some of his remarks forcibly
recurred to me a few months later.

On reaching Bombay on the 2nd March I found a telegram from the Commander-in-Chief, Sir Charles Monro,
inviting me to stay with him at Delhi so as to have the
opportunity of meeting my predecessor in Mesopotamia,
Sir George MacMunn—then Quartermaster-General in India
—and other officials who were concerned with the administrative arrangements for the Indian troops who were
shortly to come under my command.

I had not been in India since the outbreak of the South
African War in 1899, when I resigned my appointment as
aide-de-camp to the Commander-in-Chief, the late General
Sir William Lockhart, in order to accompany my regiment
to the scene of operations. During the first tour he made
after his appointment we had visited Delhi, and although
the place itself had not suffered any notable changes, its
inhabitants seemed to be less well disposed than formerly,
while a considerable number had adopted as head-dress
the fez in place of the pugaree. The brief glimpse which I
now had of India made me think that much of the glamour
which had formerly pervaded it was gone for ever, and that
the time was not far off when it would cease to be a desirable
residence for the Sahib. Those of the sepoys across whom
I came seemed to be unchanged and loyal as of old, but
there was an indefinable something about the Delhi popu-

lace which I did not like, and which pointed to their having laid aside their manners when they changed their head-dress. Besides a brief interview with the Viceroy, Lord Chelmsford, who looked tired and over-worked, and a visit to a sitting of the Legislative Council, I enjoyed the advantage of going with Sir Edwin Lutyens over the ground where New Delhi was just beginning to emerge and rise above the level of the surrounding plain.

But what interested me most of all were the famous Ridge and other spots, reminiscent of Mutiny days and Mutiny heroes. During my visit twenty years earlier my duties as aide-de-camp had naturally restricted my freedom to go wherever I pleased, and I now took full advantage of my leisure, and spent many hours wandering over the historic ground, and picturing to myself the scenes which had been enacted there.

I had purposed remaining at Delhi for two or three days only, but several things combined to prolong my stay. On the 10th March I bade farewell to my kind host and hostess, and reached Bombay on the 12th. Here I and my aide-de-camp were obliged to remain in the second-rate Taj Mahal Hotel, with its first-class prices, until the 14th, when the vessel, a British India ship, the *Chakdina*, of 1580 tons burthen, which was to carry us to Basrah, sailed. On board were drafts for Indian units, and some ten young officers of various branches of the Service and the Royal Air Force.

The voyage up the Persian Gulf has so often of late years been described, and is so devoid of interest, that I will spare my readers any mention of the five and a half days which in this case it occupied. On the 20th March we woke to find ourselves at the bar which is formed at the mouth of the Shatt-al-Arab, the river which conveys the combined waters of the Tigris and Euphrates to the sea. The view of the low-lying coast, with its background of date-palms, and the muddy water all around which soiled the pale green of the sea, inspired no admiration, and was at best a picture such as I had nowhere else encountered. The outlook struck me as particularly dreary, but as we entered the river, after crossing the bar a few hours later, the dark masses of palm-trees in serried lines, springing from the ground which lay some feet below the level of the river, added some interest to the view. As we steamed up-stream we passed the works of the Anglo-Persian Oil Company at Abadan, near the mouth of the Karun river, and an occasional brick building, of almost palatial dimensions, the dwelling presumably of some local notable ; and at 3.30 P.M. reached Basrah, where on landing I was received with the ceremonial customary on the arrival of a new General Officer Commanding-in-Chief.

CHAPTER II.

FIRST IMPRESSIONS.

THE first thing which struck me as we approached Basrah from the sea was the size of that place, which exceeded by far anything that I had pictured regarding it. From a broad water-way, bordered by date-palms, surroundings which conveyed nothing to prepare the mind for a total change of scene, one found oneself suddenly steaming up a busy thoroughfare, flanked on one side by what appeared to be miles of wharves and overlooked by buildings, some of which, judging from the flags that floated over them and the blue-garbed figures in their vicinity, were evidently used as hospitals. Indeed, we seemed to have arrived on the outskirts of a miniature Liverpool, the creation of which had not only provided for the necessities of the vast force which overcame the Turks, but had prepared for a development of the country such as might not be attained for half a century. As I drove about Basrah on that afternoon and during part of the following day, I began to realise the Augean task before me of reducing to reasonable dimensions a Base which covered some twenty square miles of ground, and which threatened to lock up far more troops than I had any intention of sparing for its safety. Nor was this all, for some months later it came to my knowledge that twenty-two miles above Basrah at Nahr Umar another port existed which had been developed during the war, in order to relieve the congestion at the former place. Two deep-sea wharves and eighteen large barge jetties, as well as quarters for the Inland Water Transport and other personnel, had been constructed here.

Kut, looking down-stream.

Kut, looking up-stream.

FIRST IMPRESSIONS

On the 21st, at 4 A.M., accompanied by Brigadier-General P. O. Hambro, my Brigadier-General in charge of Administration, who had joined me at Basrah and was ever ready with an answer to my numerous questions, I proceeded upstream on board a comfortable stern-wheeler, and reached Amarah two days later. The time of year was that of the flood season, and for miles on either side little was to be seen but a vast expanse of water, fringed far away to the east by the mountains of the Pusht-i-Kuh. I pictured with sadness our troops plodding their way along the river bank in the first mad scheme to capture Baghdad. Never could a march have been performed with surroundings less inspiring, for even Xenophon, when he began his long retreat to the shores of the Black Sea, had fortunately arrived at that part of Mesopotamia where the scenery, as one moves northwards, grows daily somewhat more pleasing to the eye. It may, of course, be said that soldiers are not concerned with scenery, and certainly, when engaged in fighting, there is little time to pay attention to the pictorial impressions of nature on the senses whether beautiful or not. When, however, peace replaces war, the effect of one's surroundings undoubtedly adds to or detracts from the popularity of one's quarters, and in respect of external attractions Mesopotamia comes a long last compared to any portion of the globe in which I have so far been.

The next place of note we reached was Kut Cantonment, for the town of Kut-al-Amarah is about two miles up-stream of the military station. Time did not then permit of my visiting that spot of tragic memory, but later on I did so on more than one occasion, and brought back with me for the Imperial War Museum portions of our howitzers which had been destroyed before surrender. Like other scenes of fighting in Mesopotamia, its interest is considerably diminished by the flatness of the country, which allows little to be seen of it from the deck of a river steamer; and I soon came to the conclusion that the best way to gain a bird's-eye view of a Mesopotamian battlefield is from an aeroplane, as the outline of the trenches held by either side can generally be traced.

The remainder of the journey to Baghdad was effected by rail, the distance by land being half of that by water. The engine-driver must have wished to impress me on this my first experience of Mesopotamian railways, for we covered the hundred odd miles in the record time of four and a half hours, during which the irregularities of the road were displayed in the severe jolting to which we were subjected. It was dark when the special train by which I travelled reached Hinaidi station, which lies a few miles south of Baghdad city. On the platform I was met by the senior military officers and several other officers, and also by the Acting Civil Commissioner, Lieut.-Colonel (now Sir Arnold) Wilson; and, after exchanging greetings with them, I proceeded to my house, which had been successively occupied by all British generals in chief command in Mesopotamia, as well as by the German general, Von der Goltz.

I spent the first few days after my arrival in taking stock of the situation, and soon realised that to hold and maintain order in a country which my predecessor had reported to be in a volcanic condition, with the number of troops at my disposal, was not going to prove an easy task.

The area to be secured was considerable. From Basrah to Zakho, my most northern post, the distance as the crow flies is roughly five hundred and fifty miles, or from Fao on the sea, sixty miles more, and is practically the same as that from Albu Kamal on the Upper Euphrates to Enzeli on the Caspian Sea. These distances are, however, very far from representing the actual length of the routes which have to be passed over when moving from north to south or from east to west, by river, road, or rail, and at least one-third must be added to the figures given. But to the Englishman, accustomed to travel at home over perfectly laid railroads, the mention of the total distance would fail to convey any idea of the time required to move troops from one point to another in Mesopotamia or from that country to Persia. From Baghdad to Enzeli not less than six weeks are occupied on the march; while from Basrah to Mosul, owing to indifferent

railway personnel, inefficient rolling-stock, and other
causes, happily now in some degree remedied, anything
up to a fortnight has to be allowed.

I may mention here that for purposes of command
and administration, Mesopotamia, for some time before
my arrival, had been divided into three areas, called the
River, 17th and 18th Division Areas. The River Area extended roughly as far north as a line from Kut to Nasiriyah, both places inclusive, but later Kut was excluded from this area. Next came the 17th Division Area, which included the Upper Euphrates region, Kirkuk, and South Kurdistan within our borders, and some twenty miles of the railway line towards Mosul. The 18th Division Area comprised the remainder of Mesopotamia, and ran as far north as Zakho.

The infantry units in these areas—whose limits corresponded with those of the three vilayats or administrative districts—were distributed as follows :—

In the River Area : guarding the Base, some Turkish prisoners, the Lower Tigris and the Euphrates valley railway line of communication, were three Indian battalions.

In the 17th Divisional Area : there was a brigade in each of the three sub-areas of Hillah, Kirkuk, and Ramadi.

In the 18th Divisional Area : there was similarly a brigade in each of the three sub-areas of Mosul, Tekrit, and Baiji.[1]

At Baghdad and Mosul were the pioneer battalions of the two divisions, and at the former place for garrison duties were two Indian units.

The above-given distribution is only approximate, since, for instance, in order to assist in guarding Turkish prisoners at Baghdad, a battalion from each of the three sub-areas of Hillah, Tekrit, and Kirkuk had to be maintained at the Capital.

As regards the important but somewhat dry statistical subject of the strength of the troops at my disposal, I shall leave that matter alone until their insufficiency to meet

[1] See Order of Battle, Appendix I.

the situation that arose became more prominent. It will suffice here to say that, on my arrival at Baghdad and after making several extended tours, I found that a large proportion of the British infantry was practically untrained, and that through many men having been withdrawn for temporary duty with departmental services, which were much undermanned, the infantry battalions to which they belonged were in a similar condition. Within a few days of reaching Baghdad I reduced the number of officers and men on guard and other duties there by the equivalent of one battalion, and orders were issued for reductions in the same respect to be made at other stations. This action at once raised an outcry such as usually follows any change, but no attention was paid to it.

The vast amount of stores in the country, ordnance and other, required that British soldiers should be placed in charge, and in spite of all precautions for their safety, the extent to which peculation was carried on almost defies belief. I hesitate to mention the rough figures which were given to me when I inquired into the subject, and which were used as an argument against the diminution of guards and piquets; but better and more effective methods were shortly introduced to replace those which had proved inadequate. From my inquiries I learned that the extensive thefts, which surpassed anything I had met before on active service, mostly occurred during the transit of goods from Basrah to Baghdad and beyond, when exceptionally favourable opportunities presented themselves to the railway robber. The country Arab, who possesses almost no worldly goods, and who in the endeavour to repair that omission was ready to accept considerable risks, was held mainly responsible; but from fuller and later knowledge I have reason to believe that the blame was not always with justice laid at his door, and that the saddle should have been put upon another horse. It is a comparatively simple matter with first-class personnel, ample supervision, and a good detective service to reduce losses to a minimum, though one's experience in France and Belgium after the Armistice showed how difficult it was

FIRST IMPRESSIONS 13

to eliminate the railway thief. But in a country where the personnel was by no means the best and was inadequate for the demands made upon it, where no railway police was in existence, and where climate, inclination, and surroundings all tended towards the slack performance of duties, it is not surprising that the total repression of pilfering, both on the lines of communication and at stations where troops were quartered, was impossible of attainment. Ali Baba and the forty thieves had flourished in or near the region where I now found myself, but the summary methods of Morgiana were no longer permissible, or perhaps the light-fingered gentry might have been exterminated.

But I have dilated further than I intended on the practice of thieving in Mesopotamia under the favourable conditions of active service—a subject, however, of great importance to the British taxpayer—and must add a word regarding the fighting troops.

We were at this time engaged in operations on the Upper Euphrates, which had been in progress for some months between Dair-al-Zaur and Ramadi, and which absorbed a mixed brigade, leaving me with no mobile reserve at Baghdad. Between that place and Mosul it is true there was another similar force, which was intended, if required, to proceed to Persia, where the Bolshevik invasion, though threatening, had not yet developed. The transfer of that force, I may mention, would leave indifferently protected the route between Baghdad and Mosul. Disturbances in the neighbourhood of the latter place, where there were already some signs of unrest, and on the borders of Kurdistan, were pointed out to me as likely to occur during the summer or autumn months.

My intention had been as soon as possible to visit every part of Mesopotamia, inspecting the troops there, and later in Persia, so as to see whether any reduction was possible, and satisfy myself that the garrisons, more particularly those which were small and isolated, were secure. On the 27th March, three days after reaching the headquarters of my command, I began my peregrinations, returning to Baghdad from time to time for a few days to transact such business as had accumulated in my absence. During three months I covered by rail, river, car and air, nearly six thousand miles, and only desisted when I had seen almost every garrison and found that the excessive heat of the summer made travelling for several days in succession, more especially by rail, almost unendurable. Besides visiting the greater part of Mesopotamia, I managed to go as far as Teheran, in order to see the ingoing and outgoing British Ministers, and take part with them in a conference on certain matters.

During my several journeys, which were accomplished without incident, three things struck me more particularly : (a) the distances, not so much measured in miles as by the time taken in moving from place to place; (b) the absence of any defensive arrangements ; and (c) the insecurity of the troops throughout the country on account of the length and inadequate protection of the lines of communication.

As regards the first of these points, I had early experience of the difficulty of moving at speed from one point to another, or indeed of moving at all in certain conditions. On my way to Sulaimaniyah, in Southern Kurdistan, where, owing to its height, 2825 ft. above sea-level, it was proposed to send some British troops from Kirkuk for the hotter months, heavy rain fell at Bazian Pass, some twenty-five miles short of my destination. Movement forward or backward was impossible, whether by motor-car or horse, and for three days I was forced to remain the guest of the hospitable commander of the little detachment, Major Adler of the 113th Infantry, and only succeeded in getting back to Kirkuk by the aid of coolies using drag-ropes, who hauled us over the more difficult places on the route, for road I cannot call it. This would by no means have been a solitary incident had I not on later occasions been guided by those who, with some reason, posed as weather prophets, and abstained from starting on a journey when the atmospheric phenomena seemed likely to prove unfavourable. Until one has paid a visit to Mesopotamia and passed a winter and a summer there, one is inclined to treat as travellers' tales the difficulties of getting about the country; but in no part of the world where I have been can movement become more quickly difficult or indeed impossible for a time than, after a fall of rain, on the slippery argillaceous soil of that country. I had, after my experiences with the Japanese Army in Manchuria in 1904-5, imagined that nothing could exceed the difficulty of transport in summer over its rain-sodden plains, but the ground there was free from the clay which is mixed with the sand of Mesopotamia, and the latter country has not the advantage of being frost-bound for several months each year, when nature makes movement, even across broad rivers, easy. Except a concrete road some six miles long at Basrah, which was constructed during the war, and, though costly, has been invaluable, and a stretch of metalled track which runs for a short distance from Mosul towards Shergat, roads in the European sense do not exist. The alluvial soil of the Tigris delta, which begins some seventy miles north of Baghdad, and the cost of bringing stone from a distance for road construction, will for a long time be an obstacle to movement during the season which is most favourable for military operations. In fact the country is unsuited to mechanical transport of all kinds, except that species which moves after the fashion of the Tank; and either railways or roads, costly as they are, are essential if movement from place to place and the carriage of stores and merchandise are to be assured. When spring comes floods make their appearance, double the strength of the river current and inundate large areas, thus causing breaches in the railway lines and confining communication in places to boats. Truly the longer one stays in Mesopotamia the more surprises it provides; and I shall have occasion later to refer to some of these which came when least desired.

As regards the last two points which struck me on my travels—the absence of defensive arrangements and the long unguarded lines of communication—I assumed that the ordinary military precautions had not been considered necessary owing to the prevalent idea among the British residents that our administration was popular and that internal troubles on a large scale were not to be expected. That I was not altogether correct in my assumption, and that there must, some time earlier, have been anticipations of an outbreak, I learned later, when my staff unearthed a War Office telegram, dated the 4th November 1919, in which was given the strength of the quite considerable force which, in the event of a general rising of the Arabs and Kurds, was regarded as the minimum necessary for the security of the country. I was not content to leave things in the highly unsatisfactory state in which, in the event of a rising, they would be, and on my return on the 7th April to Baghdad from one of my earliest tours, I ordered immediate steps to be taken to defend all isolated localities and provide for the requirements of their garrisons in all respects. I may here mention while on the subject of defence that, finding the aerodrome at Baghdad to be open to access to any one who chose to enter night or day, I made it secure with blockhouses and barbed-wire, a precaution which during the insurrection prevented an attempt to burn down the sheds with their highly-inflammable contents. I viewed the insecurity of the long lines of communication with some apprehension, for it was certain that, should disturbances arise, they would offer an irresistible bait to the Arabs. Indeed, shortly after my arrival in the country, their propensity for railway destruction had been displayed at certain points on the line north of Baghdad. The total length of the communications, along which travelled the supplies and other requirements for the troops in Mesopotamia and Persia, amounted to no less than 2622 miles, of which 910 miles were road, 856 rail, and a similar number river. It was evident that to guard these lines throughout their length would absorb far more than the troops already at my disposal, while even to protect all of the more vital portions was impracticable.

This brings me again to the question of the distribution of the garrison of Mesopotamia, prior to my taking over the command, and the reasons, so far as I could ascertain,

FIRST IMPRESSIONS

on which that distribution was based. Generally speaking, I should say that the system adopted by the Turks, our predecessors, who governed the country on lines altogether different from ourselves, was followed, and garrisons were placed at the principal towns and in areas where the presence of troops, no matter how small in number, would have the effect of restraining any tendency to disorder. In fact the troops were placed with the object of maintaining peace in the country and allowing such conditions to prevail as would facilitate the payment of revenue, and would insure, as far as possible, the safety from marauding bands of the wayfarer and his goods. The general outlook and my ignorance, for a time, regarding Mesopotamia, its people and administration, did not tempt me to make a radical change in the disposition of the troops. To have done so might in all probability have caused the smouldering fire of rebellion to blaze forth. Here and there I made some small alterations, but at any hint of an intention to remove a detachment, the civil administration, not perhaps unnaturally, were up in arms, and as the necessity for a change, though desirable, was not indeed absolutely urgent, I postponed action in the matter until such time as I should feel surer of my ground, and hoped that the efforts to maintain peace which were being made would not prove unavailing.

One thing which I must mention here, and which came to my notice not long after I landed at Basrah, was the way in which the question of the distribution of water dominated the whole situation in Mesopotamia, and the possibility of utilising that fact for strategic purposes was constantly present in my mind. Besides the system of canals and regulators and the great Hindiyah Barrage, the Arab, as in Egypt and other countries, employs for drawing water for his crops lifts which are worked by animal or manual labour and pumps whose motive power is oil. It struck me that the latter, which without oil would cease to function, might serve as an additional means of securing a hold over rebellious tribesmen, and more especially as a check on damage to the railroads by which much of the material necessary for the construction and working of these pumps was carried. I had great difficulty in getting any precise information on this, I imagine, somewhat complicated subject, and as there were too many other pressing matters to be dealt with, I postponed further inquiries. When, however, the insurrection broke out I was able to put in practice some of my ideas, but for several reasons they did not then prove as efficacious as I still think, with more study of the question, it would be possible to make them.

CHAPTER III.

AFTER THE ARMISTICE.

BEFORE dealing with the immediate causes of the insurrection, it is necessary to revert to the events in Mesopotamia which succeeded the signing of the Armistice. At the conclusion of that agreement with Turkey there is no question that British prestige throughout Iraq [1] was higher than it had ever been before. The situation, from a military point of view, was all that could be desired. The First Army Corps, after a rapid and successful advance up the Tigris, had captured at Shergat, Ismail Haqqi, with his force of eleven thousand men and fifty guns; and Mosul, protected by only one regiment and a few disorganised fugitives, who had escaped from the disaster further south, lay at our mercy. The Third Army Corps had occupied Altun Keupri on the Lesser Zab; and the 15th Division, which was operating on the Upper Euphrates, after successfully enveloping the 50th Turkish Division practically entire, had its advanced troops at Hadithah on the Aleppo Road.

Apart from these local victories, brilliant and impressive as they were, day after day brought news of further gains in Syria. Jerusalem was in our hands, the last Turkish line of resistance had crumbled, and an avalanche of cavalry, with dusty infantry pressing on its heels, had

---

[1] The boundaries of Iraq are approximately—north, Balad to Fallujah; west, Ramadi and west of Karbala and Najaf to Nasiriyah; east, undefined; south, a horizontal line drawn south of Nasiriyah. The word Iraq in Arabic means cliff, and refers to a kind of cliff or bluff which runs roughly along the western border, and which is very noticeable when approaching Mesopotamia from the desert.

captured the whole Turkish Army, and was riding in triumph through the streets of Aleppo and Damascus.

In Europe, Bulgaria and Austria had accepted the terms of the Armistice dictated at the pleasure of the Allies, and the turn of Germany was soon to follow. The British Fleet had passed the Dardanelles, and Constantinople had fallen, while our forces in North Persia were at Enzeli, on the Caspian Sea.

These facts were widely known and appreciated by the people of Iraq, who, with their own eyes, had seen on the Tigris the mighty fleet of river boats and the endless columns of troops which pressed forward north, east, and west. It was neither their desire, nor did they possess the strength, to question the actions of a Power backed as it was by overwhelming force.

It was hardly surprising that, flushed as they were with success, those who directed affairs in Iraq should have hurried on to complete their victories. The terms of the Armistice practically left it open to us to take possession of such places as we wished; and in consequence Mosul, Zakho, Amadiyah, Rowanduz, Arbil, Sulaimaniyah, and Tel Afar were occupied, while on the Euphrates Anah and Dair-al-Zaur were taken under our administration. The communications to most of these places were long and difficult, and the Political Officers who were entrusted with their administration, and were backed by a show of force or by locally enlisted levies or police, performed their mission and enforced their orders largely by relying on the prestige which our troops had won.

The signing of the Armistice had opened the door for the employment in the Political Service of numbers of officers who, during the operations, could not be released for that purpose from their military duties. These officers, who, almost without exception, had no experience of the work that would be required of them, were added to the civil administration, and were stationed in outlying districts such as Shattrah, Qalat Sikar, Diwaniyah, and Afaj; while at headquarters the administrative work was mainly controlled by members of the Indian Civil Service. These latter, who had had varying periods of experience of Indian methods, and some of whom were men of great ability, were accustomed to a settled and highly centralised form of administration, and one which is noteworthy for its fondness for regulations and red tape. The Sudan Civil Service, whose methods are more elastic, and to whose officers more initiative seems to be granted than in India, provided four officers of experience and capacity, all of whom had the advantage of knowing Arabic well. The remaining officers of the civil administration of Iraq were principally recruited from Territorial Force officers who joined at the Armistice, and were demobilised in due course. As these officers laboured under the disadvantage of having no previous acquaintance with the country and no knowledge of its people or experience of administrative work, they were employed as Assistant Political Officers, but in some cases as Political Officers.

It will thus be apparent that the majority of the members of the civil administration which was set up to rule the country after the Armistice could have little exact knowledge of the people they were called upon to govern, and had to acquire from day to day the experience necessary for the smooth execution of their duties. It is evident, therefore, that the directing influences from administrative headquarters were based in the main on past Indian experience, the result being that a system came into existence which was far too rigid, and one to which the people not only were not accustomed, but for which they were wholly unprepared. Indeed I have sometimes thought that if the inhabitants, who had known Turkish methods of assessing crops, had remembered the tale of Sinbad the Sailor—himself a native of Basrah—they might have felt that the Old Man of the Sea, in the form of red tape, had come back to hold them in his toils. The exact collection of revenue, in particular, became a fetish, and the reports and returns which were called for were so numerous that in normal times an officer in his endeavour to cope with them was tied to his office, when he would have been better employed in touring the district in his charge.

That the task to be undertaken by this scratch and somewhat incongruous team of civil and military officers, some of the former experts in their own line, the latter tyros almost to a man, was one of exceptional difficulty will be clearer when the nature of those to be governed and administered is understood.

Within the territories which were in our occupation at the time of the Armistice are the following classes of Arabs :—

1. The Badawin (Bedouin), who are pure nomads, proud of their descent, by nature independent, and with fixed and jealously-guarded traditions as to hospitality, treatment of strangers and questions of chivalry, which include particularly the giving or refusing quarter to an enemy. With these nomad tribes we were little concerned; and although they inhabit the borders of Iraq they are inclined to avoid conflict with even indifferently-disciplined troops, confining any hostile enterprise to raids against communications.

2. The half-settled Arabs, of whom certain sections cultivate the land, and others pasture their flocks with the Badawin in the desert during the winter and early spring. The tribes to which these Arabs belong vary as to the dependence which can be placed upon them, for some have strictly adhered to the traditions and principles of the pure Badawin, while others are to be relied on in diverse degree, a few being quite untrustworthy. As an instance of the different treatment to be expected at their hands, I may here mention two separate cases which occurred during the insurrection, in one of which two officers of the Royal Air Force, who fell into the hands of a section of the Bani Hachaim, were murdered; and in the other, two officers of the same corps, who landed in the Bani Hassan country, were comparatively well cared for, and finally sent into our lines (see Appendix II.) Among such people it is essential for the administrator to know the personality of the shaikhs and the comparative reliability of their tribes—those whom he can trust, and those who are fickle.

3. A third class are the settled cultivators, who comprise

the vast majority of the tribes of the interior of the country,
and who include the Marsh Arabs or dwellers in the swamps
of the Tigris and Euphrates. The latter are generally
regarded as quite untrustworthy, while the characteristics
of this class in general resemble those of their half-settled
neighbours.

4. The last type which must be mentioned are the Effendi
in the towns—that is to say, the settled townsmen—a class
which prior to and after the Armistice received but scant
attention. Their importance was probably measured by
the opinion held of their power to cause trouble, and that
was regarded as being so problematical as to be unworthy
of consideration.

These townsmen may be divided into three sub-classes :—

(i) The landed proprietors, whether Muhammadan, Christian, or Jew, whose houses during the war had in many
cases been taken as billets. Such a course was recognised
by them as inevitable ; but as time went on and the
Armistice became a thing of the past, ill-feeling was engendered through the fact that their house property was
still being utilised, and at rentals considerably below the
market rate. That such should have been the case was
directly attributable to the fact that the question of the
strength of the permanent garrison of the country, on
which depended the initiation of the building programme,
which would have gradually relieved the grievance, was
undecided. But besides the soreness that was created
owing to the small profits which were derived from the
post-war tenant, it is to be feared that a more potent cause
of ill-feeling lay at the door of the policy which was pursued of supporting the tribal shaikh and the cultivator
against the landed proprietor. In some districts this procedure was more marked than in others ; but the result
generally was that the tribesmen acquired an exaggerated
idea of their own importance, including an amused contempt for the administration, while the land-owner, besides
being exasperated, was filled with alarm and dismay. I
will quote one story which came to my knowledge after
the insurrection, which bears out what I have just stated.

A case occurred in a certain district where a tribesman asserted that the title-deeds of a landlord had been obtained by the help of bribery some years earlier. In many cases such an assertion would have sufficed for the landlord to be ejected and the matter decided in favour of the tribe concerned. Yet, even if the tribesman's contention had been true, the landlord held his freehold title-deeds, registered in the Ottoman Courts, and dated many years previous to our occupation. The officer to whom it fell to deal with the matter rightly refused to have anything to do with the case, which in this instance was, on the face of it, fraudulent. After hearing the refusal, the petitioner laughed and said, "Sahib, you are right. It is a put-up case, but so and so (mentioning names) were successful in their cases, and I thought I might as well have a try, as it is always well to get something for nothing!"

(ii) The Effendi class, by which are meant former officers of the Turkish administration and officers of the army. Of these a number were employed under the civil administration, but hundreds remained out of work, eking out a miserable existence by selling such property as they possessed or mortgaging their houses. Where pensions were given they were on a scale which was totally disproportionate to the increased cost of living.

(iii) The ordinary townsmen—merchants, shopkeepers, artisans, &c.—some of whom were affected by the seizure of their houses as billets, by the great rise in prices, and lastly, by the imposition of a ten per cent house tax, which is still regarded as an unjust and oppressive measure.

Such then were the various elements, rural and urban, whose customs in the case of the former have for centuries remained practically unaltered, which a scratch administration undertook to fashion into the Indian mould. When one looks back at the magnitude of the task which was then undertaken by the Acting Civil Commissioner, Lieut.-Colonel A. T. Wilson, one cannot help feeling that, even if the results fell short of what was anticipated—because the system was too far in advance of that for which the country was prepared—the bitter criticism to which he has been subjected was undeserved. According to the Arab metaphor applied to our administration, there are two ways of leaving a house—one by the stairs, the other by jumping from the roof—and the method chosen, the quicker but more dangerous, was the latter. It seems probable that if, in conformity with the intentions of the Allies, an indigenous government, somewhat on the lines of that which exists as I write these lines, had been set up soon after the Armistice, the aspirations of the people would, in the main, have been satisfied, and the large army of malcontents, more especially those of the Effendi class, would have had less excuse to mix themselves up in the numerous political intrigues which helped to cause the insurrection of 1920. But it must be remembered that there are those —and they embrace a considerable section of the population —who are accustomed to and prefer an alien government, and our own experience in other countries did not encourage the adoption of the indigenous form. Be that as it may, I must now resume the narrative, and endeavour to show what followed when the army was reduced, and the system of administration, getting a firmer hold upon the country, became more rigid daily and *pari-passu* more efficient.

On the 30th November 1918 a communication was sent to all Political Officers by the Acting Civil Commissioner requiring them to obtain the opinion of the people as to the establishment of a single Arab State under British tutelage. Should the inhabitants concur in the advisability of forming the future Iraq State, they were to be required to express their views as to placing it under a titular Arab head, and make suggestions as to who the Amir should be. The inquiries made in accordance with the instructions contained in this communication led to acrimonious discussions throughout the country, and the vast majority asked for an indigenous form of government under an Arab ruler. There is little doubt that the majority said what they thought would please the Government, as is the way with all Orientals, more especially because, at the time the opinion was given, there were many troops in the country.

As time went on the people of Iraq, more especially the Effendi class, began to show signs of impatience. They, like others, had been sounded as to what form of government they desired, and, longing as they were to escape from the state of straitened means and genteel poverty in which they found themselves, the delay seemed to them interminable. As month succeeded month and the consummation of their hopes was still deferred, some turned their minds to political intrigue, indulging in it according to the dictates of their individual ideas. Others went over to the Turks, and helped to swell the ranks of their Army ; while Syria, where the Amir Faisal, the son of King Husain of the Hidjaz, was established as a practically independent ruler, absorbed a goodly number. Of these Iraquis many were Faisal's best officers, on whom leading positions in the army and administration were bestowed. In the eyes of the Syrians such preference was not unnaturally distasteful, and the cry of "Syria for the Syrians !" arose.

Meanwhile the Iraqui officers in Syria were well informed as to events in their own country, with which they were in constant communication, and the state of feeling prevailing there. Their conclusions were that the time was approaching when the opportunity would be favourable for creating in Mesopotamia a condition of affairs similar to that existing in Syria, and that the moment had arrived when action towards that end was necessary. Thereupon they deliberately started a campaign of propaganda, designed to secure, if not the independence of Iraq, at least suitable positions for themselves and their friends. The chain of communication ran from Syria to their relatives and friends in their mother-country. These, in turn, spread propaganda, some of it markedly skilful, among the tribes, in which they were enthusiastically helped by the Ulama or Shiah religious leaders (literally "men of knowledge") of Karbala and Najaf, and, to a lesser degree, by those of Kadhimain, who are Persians and of the same branch of the Muhammadan religion as that people.

Fortune favoured them, for they succeeded in obtaining

the support of the Ulama, who are, by nature as well as
by heredity, inclined to intrigue. But something had
appeared on the horizon which stirred their inmost feelings,
and made them cast to the winds all thoughts of modera-
tion or discretion. This was the, now defunct, Anglo-
Persian Agreement. They had seen in Mesopotamia the
then current British ideas of what a mandate and self-
government meant, and felt gravely suspicious as to our
real intentions regarding Persia's future, fearing that should
it become a British dependency, the same fate would overtake their own country. This at all costs they were determined to prevent, and, from their point of view, they had
every reason for trying to embarrass and disturb our position in Iraq. It has been said that the insurrection, which
was now not far from breaking out, was due to a plot
hatched in other quarters, but the evidence thereof is not
convincing; and my own opinion is that the Arab rising
was the direct result of intrigue which originated in Syria,
and fell on soil which was ready to receive it. How far
the Persian emissaries who visited Karbala, Najaf, and
Kadhimain were influenced by Bolshevik promises or suggestions it is impossible to say. It may be noted, however,
that the fact of the occupation of Enzeli by the Bolsheviks
shortly before the outbreak in Iraq seems to support in
some degree the contention that their intrigues were a
contributory cause of the trouble that befell us.

I have now shown not only how but why the Syrian
and Iraq extremists were able to secure the support of the
leading religious elements in the country. It remains to
examine the means by which they obtained the armed
assistance of a large number of tribesmen, and why those
tribesmen helped their cause.

The tribes of Iraq, although, generally speaking, they
may be described as eager, fierce, and impetuous, are not
given to showing fanatical instincts when they are likely
to come into contact with a power or strength superior to
their own. Easily roused as they undoubtedly are, before
rising they give due weight to two considerations : the
amount of loot likely to be obtained, and the nature of

opposition probably to be encountered. The settled Arab of Mesopotamia has no fanciful notions as to dying the death of a hero, such as are associated with the Ghazi of Afghanistan or the Arab of the Sudan. The mainspring of his actions comes from no exalted source, but from the hope of getting plunder, more especially if it can be obtained with a minimum of risk to life or limb. Indeed, as a rule, no oratory, no matter how impassioned, would arouse him to the point of joining issue with the troops of a civilised power unless in the background he could see something more profitable than mere patriotism. No ! he is cast in clay of a distinctly material mould, and possesses a temperament which is keenly acquisitive. But even his rule admits of exceptions, and in the summer months of 1920 his somnolent patriotism was to some extent aroused. The seeds of Sharifian and religious propaganda fell on fertile soil, and, ultimately germinating, produced a rich crop of armed insurrectionists. The reasons for his attitude on this occasion were various, but it may be said without fear of contradiction that his patriotism and his courage grew as our troops gradually left the country after the Armistice. There is a saying among the tribesmen—the synonym of our proverb " Seeing is believing "—that the brain of the Arab is in his eyes, a statement which is almost literally true. He believed what he actually saw, and failed to realise that the river steamers, ocean-going vessels, and trains which took our troops away could, equally readily, bring them back. Indeed, it has come to my knowledge that, since the rebellion, certain men of education who were implicated in it and who seem since to have acquired some power of deduction, have declared that " India is too near." By this they mean that, even if the last insurrection should be only the forerunner of other risings, the tribesmen can never have a real chance of success.

But the propaganda which had so strong an influence was not confined to one form in particular. Agitators were at hand who were ready to turn to account every item, no matter how insignificant, that could help the cause they had at heart. The weak points of the officers entrusted with the administration, to which I have referred, were exaggerated. Some of them, not unnaturally, failed to appreciate the fact that the life led by many of the tribesmen was on a level only with that to be found on the North-West Frontier of India, and that their mental outlook was not far removed from that of savages. Others knew little of the language, and were obliged to have recourse to the medium of interpreters, than which few expedients could be more unfortunate for a good understanding. Then again, the youthful officers carrying out administrative duties were not, in some cases, aware that the Arab, like other Orientals, requires much time in coming to the point, and that only patience will reward the listener. Abruptness, too, and lack of courtesy, and making visitors dance attendance before seeing them, were strongly resented, more especially by men of standing and advanced in years. But the two things which the tribes disliked more than any other were the forced labour which they were required to furnish for making or repairing flood banks or for other public works, and the alteration in the method of assessment and collection of land revenue, to which I shall now refer. As regards the former cause of discontent, the Turks in their day had been careful to consult the local shaikh or shaikhs concerning any new scheme, taking care to point out the benefits that would be likely to accrue. The result was that labour was forthcoming in due course, and the scheme proved satisfactory. On the other hand, the method followed by our administration was to demand labour, whether the people themselves wanted the new works or not. No doubt in theory this was right—though I have heard of works which, as predicted by the Arabs who were employed on them, did not have the desired effect—and it may have been essential to build flood banks for the protection of cultivated areas. Nevertheless, this was regarded as oppression, whereas a good flood, even if it ruined a large cultivated area, was accepted with equanimity as being a manifestation of the hand of God.

As regards the question of crops, for purposes of greater efficiency and more exact collection of the Government share, a survey of all standing corn was made in certain districts. In Turkish times the yield had been roughly estimated by eye, and the Government took a one-fifth share in kind. The new method, combined with the fact that we took the Government share in cash, was regarded with suspicion. In feudal times, in England, had a crowd of surveyors and agricultural experts been let loose on the fields, it can easily be imagined that they would have run the risk of being accused of blighting the corn, and would have been burnt for witchcraft.

But one factor certainly which did more than anything else to encourage the tribes to unite against us was the outcome solely of our system and our methods. I refer to the settling and discouragement of blood-feuds, the effect of which bridged over century-old squabbles, and created unity among the rebellious Shiah tribes. Unfortunately, too, intensive propaganda and the mistake we made in not adopting repressive methods earlier, threw for a time the Sunni townsmen and the Shiah country-folk together, an amalgamation which approximated to the miraculous.

For the benefit of those who may care to know the origin of the gulf that separates these two sects, I give an extract from the 'Handbook of Mesopotamia.' "The division between Sunni and Shiah is based primarily on political theory. The Sunnis regard as legitimate successors of the Prophet the first three Caliphs who ruled as heads of the Moslem community, whereas the Shiahs hold that they and all the Caliphs who followed them were usurpers, the rightful succession lying in their view with 'Ali, the cousin and son-in-law of the Prophet, and with 'Ali's descendants. 'Ali himself, who was assassinated at Kufah; his son Hassan, who is said to have been murdered at the instigation of the Caliph Mo'awiyeh at Medina; and above all, Husain, the second son of 'Ali, who with his followers was slain at Karbala by the troops of Yazid, Mo'awiyeh's successor, are venerated by the Shiahs as martyrs and as semi-divine. These persons, in the sentiment if not in the theory of the Shiahs, almost take precedence of the Prophet himself."

By the discouragement then of these feuds, enemies, such as the Bani Hassan and Fatlah, were brought together and combined to oppose us. Had the blood-feud been allowed to continue, such a state of affairs would have been impossible, as may be seen at once by examining the methods of the Turks. Under their system, which reminds one of that recommended by Machiavelli to Lorenzo the Magnificent, the blood-feud was encouraged, not only between tribe and tribe, but between sections and subsections of a tribe. The fruit of this régime was that a comparatively small force would suffice to bring to order a recalcitrant tribe or section, with the certainty of such a force receiving the support of other sections or tribes. The co-operation of the tribes in carrying out this policy was assured by the fact that the payment of revenue was deliberately allowed to remain in arrears. When therefore it became necessary to coerce a certain section, other sections were called in to help, and promised in return remission of their revenue, an equal amount being extracted by the Government from the recalcitrant section. The military advantages of pursuing such a course, apart from ethical considerations, are undeniable, and I have been told by a leading inhabitant of Baghdad that, under the Turkish system, 25 per cent more revenue was collected from land cultivation than has been secured by our own more righteous procedure.

Another difference between the methods followed by the Turks and ourselves was that they strove by all means to weaken the authority of the shaikhs and deal rather with the individual than through the headman. We, on the other hand, seem to have acted on the Sandeman system, of which the Agha Khan spoke to me with approbation on the voyage to Bombay. Whether that system has proved altogether satisfactory I am not prepared to say. It demands the utmost care in the choice of shaikhs, who in some cases are inclined to abuse their power and enrich themselves at the expense of their followers, and in consequence when trouble arises, like Trades Union leaders at home, they fail to control those followers. It is not surprising that certain of the paramount shaikhs in Mesopotamia, to whom was paid money due for tribal labour on public works and which they were trusted to distribute, found the temptation beyond their power to resist, and failed to do so. The rank and file in consequence, deprived of the price of their labour, grew discontented, and so helped to bring about the insurrection of 1920. Had more direct dealings with the tribesmen been adopted, it is possible that they might have escaped the rapacity of their chiefs and had no reason for complaint; for, as stated above, our system of taxation falls more lightly on the cultivator than it did during the Turkish rule.

From April or May 1919, propaganda directed from Syria was poisoning the minds of the inhabitants of Iraq, but more especially those of the Lower Euphrates tribes. As the end of the year approached the time seemed opportune for furthering the cause by some overt, and, if possible, dramatic stroke. Should success attend some action of this nature, the cause in Iraq proper would be materially helped, and in any case the intentions of the British Government as regards that country would be disclosed. A point on the Upper Euphrates, Dair-al-Zaur, some three hundred and twenty miles from Baghdad, far away from adequate support, where the Political Officer's force consisted only of a couple of armoured cars and a few Arab levies, was chosen for the scene of action. The plan of the irreconcilables was well thought out. A certain Ramadhan al Shallash, who had formerly served in the Turkish Army, and later in the Sharifian service, a member of the Albu Sarai section of the Aqaidat inhabiting the country in the vicinity of Raqqa, was selected as a suitable agent. He had the reputation of being an irresponsible firebrand, and in addition was the proud possessor of a celluloid nose, so skilfully designed as to defy detection, which he wore to conceal the loss of his own by disease. His mission was to raise his own tribe and capture Dair-al-Zaur, while the Sharifian government, disclaiming all responsibility, but hoping to profit by his action, would be ready to express regret that they possessed no power to control him. The scheme fell out as arranged, and Dair-al-Zaur was captured on the 13th December 1919.

The question of the moment then became, "What will the British Government do in the matter ? " Nothing was done; the insult was accepted, and from that time the subsequent rising in Iraq was, in the opinion of some, a matter of absolute certainty. They foresaw that the general opinion far and wide would be that if the Aqaidat —a base-born tribe of no fighting reputation—could expel the British at their pleasure, how much more easily would the more warlike inhabitants of the Lower Euphrates be able to achieve the same result. As, a few months later, the loss of some vessels on that river and the defeat elsewhere of a detachment of British soldiers were exaggerated and recounted to the credulous tribesmen as the rout of the British Fleet and Army, so the incident at Dair-al-Zaur was one admirably suited to furnish the desired propaganda.

Worse, however, was to follow, and after Albu Kamal was evacuated by us, the Lower Euphrates tribes must have purged themselves of any doubt that may have lurked in the minds of the pusillanimous among them, that they were not fit to match themselves against our arms.

I do not propose to touch upon the question of whether the reoccupation of Dair-al-Zaur was practicable or not. Could this, however, have been promptly done and shortly after handed over in proper form to the Arab Government, the subsequent trouble at Albu Kamal and Anah would have been avoided. I might even hazard the opinion that the subsequent rising in Iraq would never have taken place.

The disastrous results of weakness were evident to our friends among the Arabs; and Fahad Beg, or, to give him his full title, Fahad Beg ibn Hadhdhal, the chief of the Amarat section of the Anizah tribe, who stood loyal to us throughout the later insurrection, prophetically remarked in February 1920 to an officer of my staff : " Whether you believe it or not, if you do not reoccupy Dair-al-Zaur you will have a rebellion on the Lower Euphrates within six months." After reoccupation, this trivial town on the river bank, so important when later events are considered, could have been handed back to the Sharif or not as seemed advisable; but the main thing was to show our power to reoccupy the place, and our determination not to accept with misplaced Christian meekness the insult offered to us.

CHAPTER IV.

STORM CLOUDS.

THE propaganda described in the preceding chapter, which was soon to lead to strife, went steadily on underrated and unchecked. The leaders of the nationalist party in Baghdad poured forth, at the *mauluds* or meetings held in the mosques on Friday nights,[1] more and more inflammatory speeches, which were applauded by crowds of excited listeners. The time was now approaching when the tribesmen, free for some months from the labours of agriculture, could turn their minds to fight and plunder. Already north of Baghdad, besides disturbances amongst the Surchi on the borders of Kurdistan, several raids had occurred on the Upper Euphrates and between Shergat and Mosul, and a goods train had been derailed south of Shergat, which led to the issue of an order directing night-running to cease on that line for a time. There was nothing, I was informed, much beyond the normal in the occurrences that were taking place or threatening. The police reports were lurid, but no worse than they had been for many months. Indeed my own impression at this time was that the danger of revolt was not as serious as on the surface it seemed to be, and I felt hopeful that the efforts of the Political Officers and the presence of the troops throughout the country would carry us over the dog-days without the incidence of trouble.

To attempt to gauge the situation on one's own account with no previous knowledge of the Arab or acquaintance

[1] So far only as the Muhammadans are concerned. Their day begins at sunset, thus making our Thursday night the Muhammadan night of Friday.

with his language would have been vain, and the information laid before me from time to time, though on the whole it pointed towards a rising, was so variable that the reliance which I learned to place on it was small.

During my numerous tours I had met, when possible, the local Political Officers, so that not only might I hear their views, but by personal acquaintance be in a position to judge up to a certain point how far their reports in time of trouble were likely to be temperate or exaggerated. But such interviews were brief, and I have so often seen men bend under the weight of responsibility in times of stress, who were like lions when no enemy was near, that I hesitated to put faith in my first impression. I could give instances of innumerable cases where the information of one day was falsified by that of the morrow, but I will confine myself to two only, as they came from sources whence they might have been least expected.

On the 3rd June, two days before I left to inspect the troops in Persia, the Acting Civil Commissioner wrote to me that so far as he could judge there was likely to be serious trouble in the country during the next two months, the threatening areas at present being Nasiriyah, Najaf, and perhaps Diwaniyah. On the same date he visited Hillah, and saw the Political Officers and shaikhs of that area, and on the following day told me what the latter had said. It amounted to this, that according to their view the source of all possible trouble was to be found in Baghdad, and they pressed him to arrest the instigators. They themselves were ready to guarantee that quiet would obtain on the Lower Euphrates, and had no intention of being influenced by the Mullahs who were trying to rouse the tribes. About a month later, when I was at Sar-i-Mil, I had a letter from Baghdad from a friend who was constantly interviewing, and had a very extensive circle of acquaintances among the best-informed Arabs, including those of the nationalist party. The letter was dated 1st July, the day after the rebellion may be said to have begun, and contained the following sentences: "The bottom seems to have dropped out of the agitation, and most of

the leaders seem only too anxious to let bygones be bygones.
I have many heart-to-heart interviews!"

I mention these two instances to show the great difficulty experienced, even by such admitted experts as the writers of these letters were, in extracting the truth, or what is believed to be the truth, from the Arab. Like the patriarch Jacob's eldest son, he seems to be "unstable as water," and his thoughts and actions are extremely difficult to foresee.

The only result of the Acting Civil Commissioner's visit to Hillah, so far as I was concerned, was to make me decide not to bring to Baghdad from the Kirkuk area a battalion which I had intended to transfer to the Capital as a reserve until the brigade on the Upper Euphrates—my normal reserve —could be brought back. I was not disposed still further to weaken the troops in the northern vilayat, as I had already despatched, under orders from the War Office, two British battalions by motor-lorry to Kasvin; while two Indian infantry units and some artillery, which were stationed between Baghdad and Shergat, were under orders to follow. The landing of the Bolsheviks near Enzeli on the 18th May and our withdrawal to positions covering Kasvin, the alarm created in Teheran, and the appeals for reinforcements, had led me unwillingly to arrange for the movement of these additional troops, but the order for their actual movement had not gone forth.

Kasvin is distant from Quraitu, the end of the Baghdad-Persian Frontier railway, three hundred and sixty-four miles, and the position held by our troops in front of the Bolsheviks was about one hundred miles further north, so that if once reinforcements were parted with, their return could not be counted on under a month. Fortunately, as it turned out, and in spite of the outbreak of trouble in another quarter, I resolved to go to Persia and judge for myself as to the state of affairs in that country from a military point of view, and I shall never regret having adhered to my determination, in spite of influences to the contrary.

Before, however, I left Baghdad, a report, not very clear at first, of an incident at Tel Afar, which lies about thirty-six miles west of Mosul on the Nisibin road, had arrived, and as it was unquestionably connected with the eventual rising further south, I reserve an account of it for the following chapter.

CHAPTER V.

THE FIRST EXPLOSION.

ON the 26th May reports were received which definitely established the presence at Fadghami on the Khabur river of a so-called Sharifian force. Its strength was estimated by the intelligence staff at Mosul to amount possibly to one thousand men, but the half of that number was regarded as nearer the mark. With this force was an attendant tribal following of slightly greater strength than the higher figure suggested for the Sharifian troops. The plan of the leader of the latter, who was thought to be Jamil Pasha, who had signed propaganda letters to the tribes as "Commander of the Northern Iraq Forces," was believed to be to advance on Mosul in conjunction with a tribal movement from the north and another on Shergat from the Euphrates. By the end of May further reports, but of a more alarmist nature, came from Zakho, to the effect that Turkish troops were in motion in the Kurdish tribal area north of that place, and about the same time propaganda from Turkish sources became more pronounced. Mosul itself was growing more and more disaffected, and nightly meetings of those who secretly favoured the nationalist movement, but who took care jealously to guard their proceedings, were held.

The country, however, appeared generally to wear its normal aspect, and although the Assistant Political Officer at Tel Afar sent word to the effect that the small local tribes were firmly convinced of the early coming of an Arab Government, the vicinity of that place was particularly peaceful. On the morning of the 4th June information arrived that the Assistant Political Officer of Tel Afar, who had spent the previous night with a local Arab shaikh, was a prisoner in the hands of a raiding party of the Shammar, a nomadic tribe, who were accompanied by a Sharifian representative. The same party, so far as has been ascertained, pushed on, and reached Tel Afar early on the same date.

That town of ten thousand inhabitants is picturesquely situated on four knolls, which stand two on each side of a deep gully, whence rises a stream which supplies the inhabitants with water. The houses are solidly built of stone and a kind of cement known as "juss" (juice), and include the bungalow of the Assistant Political Officer, his office, and the barracks of the gendarmerie, which occupy the summit of one of the knolls on the northern side of the gully. The approach to the barracks from the gully traverses a narrow lane between houses, and so steep is the ascent that except for a car in perfect running order it is difficult. It may be said that for a heavy car such as an armoured-car, the town itself constituted a veritable death-trap—a fact which was well known to the commander of the light armoured motor-battery, and which was specially referred to in the orders issued by him on the 3rd June. On that date, telegraphic communication between Tel Afar and Mosul being cut, the only aeroplane serviceable at the latter place was ordered to proceed *viâ* Tel Afar to the affected area, with instructions to drop a message, containing all information obtained, on the section of armoured-cars which had already proceeded in the same direction. The aeroplane having dropped this message on the cars, which were then six miles east of Tel Afar, flew over the town at 9 A.M., but observed nothing of an unusual nature. The observer next noticed a large party of mounted men approaching the town from the north-west, and about two miles from it. This information was dropped on the section of armoured-cars, which by this time had reached the south-east corner of the town, the spot whence they were subsequently salved, and the aeroplane returned to engage the horsemen. Almost immediately it received a shot

THE FIRST EXPLOSION

through the petrol-tank, and had to make a forced landing about one mile from the town, narrowly escaping capture. Though the pilot reported that he had seen the crews of the armoured-cars standing in the vicinity of their vehicles, their position from the first raised grave doubts as to their safety.

What occurred in the town will probably never be exactly

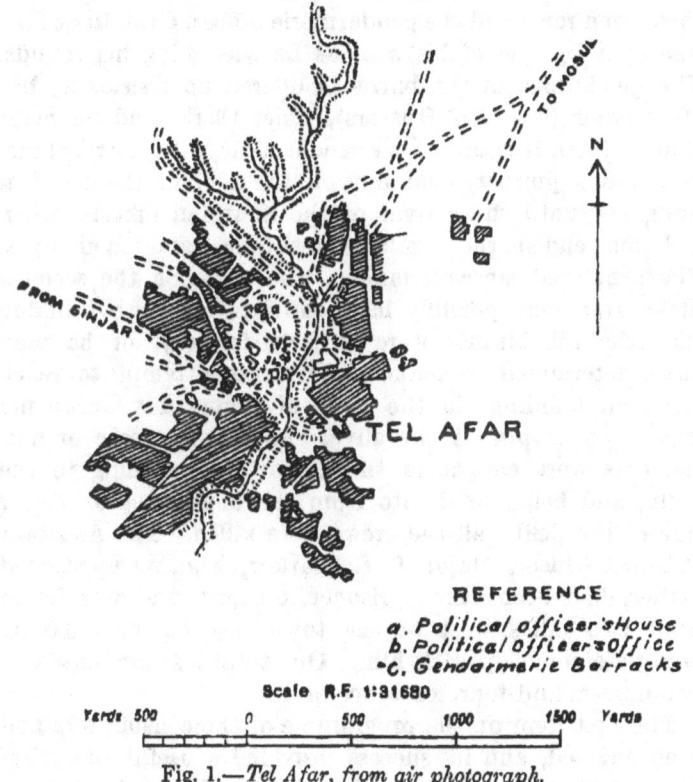

Fig. 1.—*Tel Afar, from air photograph.*

known, as only the native servant of the armoured-car commander escaped alive; but from reports, fragmentary and in many points contradictory, the sequence of events was probably somewhat as follows :—

A meeting of all the local notables had been held in the town on the night of the 2nd/3rd June, which was ad-

dressed by an ex-Turkish army officer, who stated that a
large Sharifian concentration was approaching, and invited
his auditors to co-operate either by joining the confederation personally, or seizing Tel Afar in the Sharifian interest.
 Thereafter all the local aghas or notables left the town
with the intention of joining the approaching forces, but
changed their minds and returned. Early on the morning
of the 4th a party of tribesmen arrived, whereupon the
townsmen rose, and the gendarmerie officer, Captain Stuart,
was shot by one of his men as he was going his rounds.
The gendarmes in the barracks offered no resistance, but
Mr Lawlor (late 7th Hussars), Chief Clerk, and Sergeant
Walker (13th Hussars) of the gendarmerie, with one machine-
gun and a gunner, held out on the roof of the political
bungalow until the arrival of the Sharifian officers, when
a bomb ended their gallant resistance and their lives.
The armoured-car commander, who came on the scene a
little later, may possibly have run into the town thinking
that the inhabitants were entirely friendly, or he may
have determined to make a desperate attempt to reach
the civil buildings in the hope of saving any occupants
who might happen to be alive. Be that the case or not,
the cars were caught in the narrow lane leading to the
gully, and being fired into from the house-tops on either
side of the defile, all the crews were killed. The Assistant
Political Officer, Major J. E. Barlow, who, as mentioned
earlier, had been taken prisoner, escaped, and was found
dead two miles west of the town, his pursuers having
doubtless come up with him. Our total loss amounted to
two officers and fourteen other ranks.
 The first item on the programme of the conspirators had
been enacted, and its success provided a useful advertise-
ment, besides a well-watered well-stocked base for further
operations. The rising in the city of Mosul, where for three
days there was great excitement, hung fire, however, though
a large section of the inhabitants, who looked to some decided move on the part of the Syrian Government, were
quite prepared, if opportunity offered, to resort to extreme
measures. Subordinate officials of the civil administration,

Tel Afar—Political Office.

Tel Afar—From the east.

in the execution of their duties, were greeted with such boastful taunts as " Wait until after Ramadhan (the great Muhammadan fast) and you will see what will happen." " They (the British garrison at Mosul) will be going in two days ; why do they want to register our arms now ? "

In pursuance of the plan already outlined, efforts were made by the leaders to rouse the tribes in the vicinity and to the south of Mosul. All arrangements for supplies made by us with local contractors failed, and hired transport carrying requirements for out-stations, such as Dohuk and Zakho, was looted or disappeared. The necessary steps were taken to prevent the rising in or a raid on the chief city of the vilayat, and to guard the line of communication against marauders.

It had been arranged at Mosul, as at several other stations in Mesopotamia, that mobile columns were to be ready to take immediate action when the circumstances demanding it arose ; and as Tel Afar provided a definite objective, not always easy to find in the country of the two rivers, one of the columns, under the command of Lieut.-Colonel G. B. M. Sarel, 11th (K.E.O.) Lancers, consisting of one hundred and fifty sabres, five hundred rifles, a section of 18-pr. guns, with the necessary subsidiary services, moved out and reached a point on the Tigris ten miles above Mosul on the evening of the 5th June. The appearance of this column came as a complete surprise to the insurgents, and it will suffice to say that it engaged in a skirmish with some twelve hundred horsemen, who fled before the fire of the guns and the bullets showered upon them from aeroplanes. On the 9th June it reached Tel Afar.

The arrival of troops at that place, where punitive measures were promptly taken, had an immediate effect in cooling the ardour of the disaffected inhabitants of Mosul. On the line of communication several convoys had been attacked, some with considerable determination, and a raid on Baiji had been driven off. These minor movements, intended no doubt to synchronise with disturbances of a more general nature, were countered everywhere, and the result had a further pacifying effect. On one occasion at this time a squadron of fifty sabres of the 11th Lancers, under Brevet-Lieut.-Colonel D. E. Robertson, when on patrol near Quiyarah, discovered three hundred mounted Arabs hiding in a dry river-bed, who no doubt intended to ambush the daily convoy which would pass near by their lair. He at once attacked, but the enveloping tactics of the insurgents, who outnumbered him by six to one, compelled a gradual retirement towards Quiyarah. When near the cart-track leading to that place a havildar (sergeant), with twenty men of the 1/39th Garhwal Rifles, who had just arrived as part of a draft from India, and who were marching with the daily convoy, hearing the firing, promptly moved towards it. The squadron now counter-attacked, assisted by the skilfully-led small party under the havildar, and driving off the Arabs inflicted on them casualties exceeding forty killed, themselves losing two Indian officers and nine Indian other ranks killed, and three Indian other ranks wounded. I mention this affair as the small party of horse and foot engaged belonged to two units whose gallantry in action repeatedly came to my notice, and who on several occasions, during the insurrection and before it when they were engaged, distinguished themselves. There are strong grounds, too, for thinking that the Arabs were led by Nijris al Q'aud, himself one of our most elusive and troublesome opponents on the Upper Euphrates.

During the remainder of June, though minor disturbances took place on the line of communication south of Mosul, no serious outbreak occurred, proof that the prompt action which had been taken to suppress the first signs of insurrection had discouraged those who, better advised, would have waited and struck simultaneously with the tribesmen further south.

CHAPTER VI.

BAGHDAD TO TEHERAN.

Soon after my arrival in Mesopotamia I had planned to visit Persia, as, in the opinion of those I consulted at the War Office before leaving home, it seemed to be the region where active operations were more likely to occur than anywhere else in my command. Apart from my desire to see a country which was new to me, several considerations made me anxious to go there as soon as possible. Among these were the importance of studying the ground, with a view to ascertaining where and for how long a hostile advance, should it take place, could be delayed. Distances in Persia, a country in which there are as yet no railways, are great. From Quraitu, at the head of the railway from Baghdad, to Enzeli is five hundred and fourteen miles, and the route crosses two passes, both not less than 7500 feet high, so that the transfer there of troops from Mesopotamia is, as explained before, a matter of several weeks' duration. The winter, which would not be upon us for several months, is usually severe, and troops, once over the passes and at Kasvin and beyond, could neither be reinforced nor withdrawn till well on in spring. Another consideration, which was even more important than that of reconnaissance, was how far I ought to meet the calls for reinforcements, which I had received from the Brigadier-General Commanding the North Persian Force, and which were strongly backed by Sir Percy Cox, the British Minister at Teheran. I had already, as mentioned, on the 24th May, under orders from home, despatched two battalions of British troops, by motor-lorry from Karind in Persia, where I had sent them for the summer months, to Kasvin, where their transport would arrive by march-route a month later. Like other British units, these two were weak and full of young soldiers, and together could only put six hundred rifles in the field. The effect, however, of the arrival of British troops would undoubtedly be exaggerated, and they would probably be followed shortly by two Indian units and some guns.

I have already given my reasons for regarding my visit to Teheran as of importance, and to my regret I had been obliged several times to defer it: once for over a month owing to a visit of officers from Egypt in connection with the proposed garrisoning of Mesopotamia by the Royal Air Force; and again by the arrival of the Shah from Europe on his way back to his own country. And now, just as all preparations had been made along the whole route to Teheran, came the incident at Tel Afar. Pressure from the civil side was strong against my leaving Mesopotamia at such a time, and the news that had so far arrived was of the vaguest. As, however, there were ample troops in and near Mosul to deal with a rising of the tribes of an even more extensive nature than in the present instance seemed probable, and as I had full confidence in the commander on the spot, I telegraphed my approval of the action which he proposed to take, and started for the Persian border.

In order to understand the military situation in Persia when I visited it, it is necessary to refer briefly to what had occurred there some three weeks earlier. The troops at that time consisted of the 36th Indian Mixed Brigade of four battalions, the greater part of the Guides Cavalry, " A " Battery Royal Horse Artillery, and a pack battery, the whole under the command of Brigadier-General H. F. Bateman-Champain; besides three battalions under the command of Colonel J. H. F. Lakin, who was in charge of the long line of communication. Both these officers had engineers and other services attached to their forces. The headquarters of the brigade were at Kasvin, where the reserve was, and the remainder of the force was disposed between that town and Enzeli, which was also occupied.

As will be seen by what follows, the situation at this time would appear to have been governed more by political than military considerations. The War Office instructions as to the policy to be followed were clear and sufficiently comprehensive. They laid down that the rôle of our troops was to be that of an outpost which, if attacked in position, would fall back to the main line of resistance. In doing so every means at disposal would of course be utilised to delay a Bolshevik advance; and it was suggested that full use should be made of the favourable ground at the Manjil Pass. One of the first things which I did on reaching Baghdad in March 1920 was to study these instructions, and direct the General Officer Commanding the troops in North Persia to work out in detail the arrangements for a withdrawal should that course become necessary. On the other hand, as it was desirable, if possible, to avoid embroiling Persia in hostilities, it had been settled between His Britannic Majesty's Minister at Teheran and the General Officer Commanding that, in the event of an attack, the latter would, before joining issue, endeavour to parley with the Bolshevik commander. As to the actual occurrences, they may be compressed into a small space.

At 5.15 A.M. on the 18th May the garrison at Enzeli awoke to the sound of bursting shells, and though at first the noise was attributed to another cause, it was soon realised that the Bolsheviks were firing from their ships. An hour and a half later the bombardment, if it deserves that name, slackened, and shortly afterwards a report came that a landing east of the town had taken place. Next it was heard that a force of some size had moved across our line of communication to Resht. Meantime an effort had been made by Brigadier-General Bateman-Champain, who chanced to be at Enzeli, to get in touch with the Bolshevik commander, which, being effected, an armistice was eventually arranged, and the terms offered by him were accepted. These consisted in the handing over to the Bolsheviks of the Volunteer Fleet and munitions, as well as other Russian property at Enzeli, in consideration for which the garrison would be at liberty to withdraw unmolested—a movement which was effected by midday on the 19th, with the loss of a quantity of stores and the personal effects of officers. It may be mentioned that the Bolshevik commander, with typical disingenuity, expressly stated that his sole object was to appropriate the fleet, and that once this was accomplished he would sail for Baku, as he wished no harm to the Persians. Nevertheless, at the time that I was on my way to Teheran the Bolsheviks were still in occupation of the neutral port of Enzeli, had pushed south of Resht, and were a few miles only from the Manjil Pass, which was held by our outposts.

Early on the morning of the 6th June the train by which we travelled reached Quraitu, which is a few miles across the Persian border, whence I, Brigadier-General Stewart, my Chief Staff Officer, and Lieutenant Grehan, my aide-de-camp, after a short halt, proceeded by car to Karind. There we lunched, and then resumed the journey to Kermanshah. As the car ran over the one hundred and six miles which we covered from the railhead, I noticed three strong rearguard positions, besides many other places, where the advance of an enemy could be delayed. At two points on this route—the steep and rugged Tak-i-Girrah Pass and the defile east of it to Sar-i-Mil—the scene was singularly picturesque compared with the deadly monotony of the Iraqian plain; but the absence of trees, except in the neighbourhood of towns such as Kermanshah and Hamadan, and the generally arid nature of the country, seemed to falsify the tales and poems which one had heard and read of Persia. The season of wild flowers was practically over, and those that still could bear the growing fierceness of the sun's rays were limited to hollyhocks and a few other plants of a less ostentatious nature.

The condition of our cars, after our previous day's climb to Kermanshah, which lies 3520 feet above Quraitu, compelled a halt of one day, but I grudged this short delay the less as numerous matters required to be discussed with

Tak-i-Girrah Pass.

Karind camp.

Colonel Lakin, with whom and his wife we stayed. Moreover, there are some noted rock carvings at Taq-i-Bustan, dating back to the sixth century, and these we visited on the afternoon of the day following our arrival. While there a Persian hillman performed the feat of climbing up the almost precipitous face of a cliff, which, beyond a crack here and there, showed no indication of anything that would support even a bird. Sometimes he would feign to miss his foothold and then recover it, and the whole performance, besides making one feel hot all over, roused the thought that the expected largesse which was handed to him when his feat was safely accomplished would only encourage him one day to break his neck.

On the 8th we pushed on to Hamadan, one hundred and three miles further into Persia, passing the famous rock tablets at Bisitun with their trilingual inscriptions. Some distance further on we turned sharply to the left of the road, and escorted by a wild-looking crowd of armed and mounted retainers, made our way to the house of Prince Muhammad Vali Mirza, brother of Prince Firuz Mirza, the late Persian Foreign Minister and cousin of the Shah, who had kindly invited us to lunch with him. Here we met the rather notorious Prince Sarim ud Daulah, who was on his way to Kermanshah to take up the Governor-Generalship of that place and province, and who, through a change of Prime Ministers, found himself a year later languishing in prison. Most Persians of the upper classes talk French, and as both of these had been educated abroad one had not to go through the meal in silence or communicate through the awkward medium of an interpreter. I may here mention that about a year later our host appeared in Baghdad, having fled from Persia on horseback, fearing the imprisonment which a few months before had befallen both his father and brother as the result of the same change of Prime Ministers to which I have just referred.

On reaching Hamadan we were most kindly entertained by Mr Wright, the manager of the branch of the Imperial Bank of Persia there, and his wife; and the following day we resumed our travels.

At Hamadan I found a telegram from Colonel A. T. Wilson, informing me that an attack in force by Turks on Zakho, one of our outposts seventy miles north of Mosul, was expected—but which did not take place—and urging me to withdraw the troops there. At the same time the probability of an early rising among the Arabs was indicated. After reflecting upon the situation I decided to order the two additional battalions, which had been warned to be ready to reinforce the troops in Persia, to stand fast, and to keep two batteries at Karind, where they had already arrived with a similar object. At that place they were well situated to move wherever required, and had the advantage of a cooler climate than that of Mesopotamia. I directed the General Officer Commanding the 18th Division to make the necessary preparations for withdrawing from Zakho, in case orders to that effect should be sent; but on hearing from him that more harm would result by leaving than by remaining, withheld the order for the movement. The Acting Civil Commissioner evidently thought the situation was serious, for he pressed me to send all married people, civil and other, to India. To have done so would have involved a most trying journey by rail and river, followed by a voyage through the Persian Gulf, during perhaps the worst month of the summer, to be followed by a train journey in India. Such a proceeding, which must have led to mortality among the children, who were numerous, was out of the question, and not for a moment to be considered. It was also suggested to me that unless Tel Afar were razed to the ground and Dair-al-Zaur bombed, Mosul might have to be given up. As regards Tel Afar, I knew that punishment was being meted out to its inhabitants, and a little later a detachment was posted there, which kept the town in order; while, desirable as it might be to bomb Dair-al-Zaur, that place was beyond our borders.

On the 10th, after a drive of sixty miles that soon grew wearisome through the continual changes of speed and the bumping when crossing ruts in the most indifferent road, we reached Teheran. There I stayed with the new British Minister, Mr H. Norman, a friend of many years' standing.

Zakho village.

Zakho camp.

Soon after my arrival Sir Percy Cox showed me a copy of what seemed to me to be a telegram of an alarmist nature regarding the situation in Mesopotamia, which had been sent to London by the Acting Civil Commissioner. As the situation showed no signs of marked change since my departure from Baghdad, and as I had no reason, judging from the affair at Tel Afar and the operations on the Upper Euphrates, to suppose that a combination of tribes was to be feared, I telegraphed to the War Office that I was satisfied with the number of troops which I had at my disposal, and that so far as I could judge no cause existed for uneasiness.

Of Teheran itself I saw little, being occupied with other matters than sight-seeing; but the following afternoon Lady Cox drove me to Gulahek, the summer residence of the diplomats, which is five miles from the capital. Although only six hundred feet higher, its climate is quite different, being fresh and many degrees cooler, probably because it is nearer to the Elburz Mountains, of which the pyramid-shaped Demavand, the highest point, 18,600 feet above sea-level, is visible on clear days. I had intended to leave Teheran on the 11th, but was constrained to stop for a largely-attended dinner party which the Persian Prime Minister, His Highness Vosuq ud Daulah, was to give on the evening of that date. The following day we returned to Kasvin, where we had stayed with General Bateman-Champain and his wife on our way through on the 9th.

Next morning at 5 o'clock, in company with Brigadier-General Stewart and Majors I. Burn-Murdoch and F. P. Macintyre, the last two being officers on the staff of Brigadier-General Bateman-Champain, we left Kasvin, and proceeded to the outposts in the Manjil Pass. The road after leaving Kasvin runs due north-west for about twenty-four miles over a fairly level plain, and then drops steeply, winding down till it meets the Yazbashi Chai, which it crosses. The route now follows the left bank of that stream until it joins the Shah Rud, which it likewises crosses, and which, near Manjil, swells to a river of respectable dimensions, known as the Safed Rud. On reaching Manjil, which is some three thousand feet lower than Kasvin, we proceeded first to the camp of the 2nd (K.E.O.) Gurkha Rifles, commanded by Lieut.-Colonel E. H. Sweet. After breakfasting and seeing the British and Gurkha officers, of whom some of the latter had served with me in the Tirah Campaign in 1897, we went up a low gravelly hill which dominates the camp. From this point a good view is obtained of the entrance to the narrower portion of the pass, which is completely overlooked by the much higher features on both sides. A little north of this hill an iron bridge carries the road over the Safed Rud, which joins the Caspian between sixty and seventy miles further on. We were fortunate in the weather, for it is said that only about once a month does Manjil escape the annoyance of a powerful wind, which whistles through the gorge from dawn till dusk, and covers everything and every one with dust. After taking a good look round we walked down to the bridge, which was prepared for demolition, and crossing it proceeded for a short way by car till we came up with a portion of a sapper and miner company. The men were busily engaged in preparing the road for destruction at several points where it overhangs the river, so that, if blown away, much rock-cutting would have been necessary in order to allow of the passage of troops and transport. The car was steered past the obstacle with very few inches to spare, and we ran down a gentle declivity till the village of Rudbar, eight miles beyond Manjil, the extreme point held by a patrol of the Guides Cavalry, was reached.

Looking north along the gorge-like valley, which is shut in on either side by rugged hills which rise to over three thousand feet above the road, I was vividly reminded of the Chitral valley between Kila Drosh and Gumbaz, and the Kunar river, which runs between these places. Although the scene before me was of a less impressive nature, it seemed that at Rudbar we had reached the point where the character of the ground would shortly change, the bare and rugged rocks gradually giving place to woods, and the country transforming itself, as one who knows it well has

Tak-i-Bostan.

Manjil Pass—Southern entrance.

said, to something resembling parts of Devonshire. Except, however, when viewed from an aeroplane, the ground two miles north of the village was then a closed book to the British, and after asking the vedette whether he had seen anything and receiving a reply in the negative, the motor was turned round, and we ran back to Manjil.

The undoubted strength of this cleft in the Elburz Mountains, along the greater portion of which we had travelled, struck me forcibly. According to Napoleon, mountains rank second among the obstacles most difficult to be overcome by armies in their march; and here in the Elburz, faced by troops few in numbers and scarcely worthy of that name, we had at hand what would suffice to delay for weeks, if not for months, a hostile advance on Kasvin. Moreover, on the spot was a well-known Gurkha battalion with great traditions dating from pre-Mutiny days, the very troops to carry out the idea in my mind. I therefore instructed the commanding officer to arrange to begin his defence as far northward as possible, preferably advancing, so as to deceive the enemy, rather than retiring; to explore every track on the steep mountain-sides, and note the spots whence the valley and the road were commanded; besides many other points too numerous to mention.

On my return to Kasvin I reiterated my orders to the brigade commander, who, like the commander of the Gurkhas, seemed rather less enthusiastic than I was as regards what I had seen.

I began the next day by inspecting the Guides Cavalry, which was commanded by an old friend, Colonel A. C. Stewart; and "A" Battery R.H.A., smart as ever, under Major Van Straubenzee, who did good work in the field a few months later. Then came the turn of the infantry—the 1st Battalion Royal Berkshire Regiment, the 2nd Battalion York and Lancaster Regiment, and the 1st Battalion Royal Irish Fusiliers—all glad to be away from the heat of Mesopotamia. The last of these units I had known at Ladysmith in 1899, and it had been one of the four battalions under my command in the 10th Infantry Brigade in 1914; but only two of the officers—the Adjutant, Captain

M. J. W. O'Donovan, and the Quartermaster, Major T. E. Bunting—and a few N.C.O.'s and men remained who had served with me. Later in the day the brigade commander took me to tea with the Governor of Kasvin on the upper verandah of his well-built house, which is surrounded by a charming garden. Here I met Sirdar Intizar, Commander-in-Chief of the troops in Azerbaijan, who surprised me by his force of character, which is unusual in his race.

Shortly before dinner Commodore D. Norris, R.N., arrived from England on his way to Teheran. He had been given the now somewhat fantastical task of reorganising a non-existent Persian Navy, for the operations of which the requisite sea was equally nebulous. Some months later he passed a week with me at Baghdad on his way back to England, to take up, I hope, some more tangible naval work, for he struck me as a forceful, well-read, and broad-minded officer.

Before leaving Kasvin I arranged that the artillery which I had ordered up should not go beyond Karind, and that, to help in dealing with the raids in the Mosul vilayat, two squadrons of the 35th Scinde Horse should proceed from Baghdad to Shergat as soon as they were replaced by the remainder of the regiment from Diwaniyah. The place of the latter would in turn be taken by two squadrons of the 37th Lancers from Ahwaz, a town at the south-east corner of Mesopotamia, which the Shaikh of Muhammarah, during a visit I paid him, had agreed to take charge of, provided I got him some mountain guns and rifles.

The telegrams from Baghdad had, during the last two days, shown that affairs in Mesopotamia were normal, or at any rate that there was no immediate cause for alarm. I was anxious therefore to proceed to Zinjan, a hundred miles north-west of Kasvin, where I had a battalion and some other troops, and towards which two platoons of the 1/67th Punjabis, who had been withdrawn from their isolated position in Tabriz, were marching. Zinjan was important as being on the route by which the Bolsheviks might try to turn the Manjil Pass. Between it and Kasvin was a track by means of which Hamadan could be reached and the troops in Kasvin, should they hold on too long, be cut off. But as a cable had been sent from Baghdad to the India Office by the Acting Civil Commissioner, which led to the War Office asking me to explain my absence from my headquarters, I decided to forgo my trip, which would have required two days, and on the 14th June began the journey back to Mesopotamia.

On the way, a few miles out from Kasvin, we breakfasted at the aerodrome with Flight-Lieutenant F. L. Robinson, a pilot of great skill and resolution, who had been missing at the time I arrived at Brigadier-General Bateman-Champain's headquarters on my journey to Teheran. He gave me an account of the adventures which he and Major Burn-Murdoch, one of my companions during our visit to Manjil, had shared. They had left the aerodrome on the 7th June on a R.E. 8 machine, with the object of reconnoitring the country in the Zinjan area, as a report had been received of an intended Bolshevik advance on that place. All went well until, when flying at an altitude of nine thousand feet, the engine began to splutter, and the machine lost height rapidly. The possibility of making a safe landing was most unpromising, as below was a stream in flood, and on either side were precipitous mountains rising to nine thousand feet. Indeed, Major Burn-Murdoch had already told me when I met him on the 13th that to land without a serious crash seemed to him impossible. But Robinson is a man of strong nerve and great skill in the air, and he succeeded in bringing the machine to the ground, or rather to the water, for it landed in the middle of the stream. The officers knew that they were in a country of doubtful friendliness and one hundred and four miles from home; but a few days later, after some unpleasant experiences with the inhabitants, they reached Kasvin, having burned the machine, which it was obviously impossible to salve.

After passing another night at Hamadan with the Wrights, who, it grieves me to say, have since lost there one of their small twin boys, we continued our journey to Kermanshah. There I was interested to meet Major T. E. Hammond, who in 1907 won the Stock Exchange walk to Brighton and back, and had covered at the Stadium one hundred and thirty-one miles in twenty-four hours. Though very far above my form as a pedestrian, we agreed that if later a chance came we would tackle the rugged mountain facing Kermanshah, one ascent of which he had already made.

Next evening found us at Quraitu, whence, after a hot night journey, we reached Baghdad, where the inhabitants were more gaily clad than usual owing to the Muhammadan festival of the Id-ul-Fitr, which takes place on the termination of the fast of Ramzan or Ramahdan.

During the morning I discussed affairs with the Acting Civil Commissioner, who maintained that unless the troops in the country were at once reinforced from India the administration could not be carried on. As I had no reason then to fear a combination of the tribes, having no idea that our system of Government deliberately tended towards such an end, and as I was convinced that the London Temple of Janus would never open its gates until, to put it vulgarly, " the fat was in the fire," I continued to maintain an optimistic attitude. Moreover, as I have already pointed out, I did not place great faith in the reports that came in steadily and voluminously, and if even for a time we lost the Euphrates railway, it could be regained ; while as a line of communication the Tigris river, which could not be tampered with, would still remain. Indeed, should the tribes be foolish enough to cut the railway line, the extremists in Baghdad, who were greatly responsible for the unrest in the country, would, with the population, be the earliest sufferers, for all our steamers on the Tigris would be required to feed the troops. In such a case the extremists would have good reason to put pressure on the tribes, provided, as shortly occurred, the whirlwind they were about to raise did not get beyond control. Any thought of obtaining an addition to my troops was limited by the knowledge that I was expected in the autumn to effect a reduction of a brigade of infantry and two regiments of British cavalry, provided I could get rid of several encumbrances, which I shall now proceed to mention.

CHAPTER VII.

MILITARY ENCUMBRANCES.

SOME of the troops under Brigadier-General F. E. Coningham, who had been engaged for several months in the Upper Euphrates area, had by now begun their long march back to Baghdad. These, when they arrived, would give me a useful addition to my small reserve there, and I had arranged also to withdraw one battalion from the Kirkuk area—the 45th (Rattray's) Sikhs—whence it could be spared, and make there other small reductions in garrisons. But no sooner did I make savings in one direction than my hand was called upon to go into my pocket again. The Acting Civil Commissioner was now asking for a detachment to hold Tel Afar, which is rich, and offered a tempting revenue, and proposed in return to dispense with troops at Zakho, where for a long time no tribute had been raised. The question of revenue was, as usual, uppermost, for credit or discredit depended on success or failure in its collection. As Major-General Fraser, who commanded the 18th Division in the Mosul vilayat, held strong views about giving up Zakho, with which I agreed, I went to his headquarters by air on the 21st June, returning on the 22nd, and being piloted by Flight-Lieutenant F. Nuttall, one of our best pilots and mechanics, who, I regret to say, crashed and was killed in Persia a few weeks later. The result of my visit was that arrangements were made to garrison Tel Afar, and as both the Political Officer, Colonel Nalder, a most efficient and knowledgeable officer, and General Fraser were strongly opposed to giving up Zakho, which might lead to fresh trouble on the border, I agreed to maintain the little garrison there.

During my brief absence from Baghdad the civil administration had, with the help of troops and armoured-cars, which were sent to Karbala, arrested ten out of thirteen men who had been conspiring against the Political Officer, and sharing in an agitation which was in progress there. These arrests were, I imagine, somewhat belated, more particularly in the case of one of them ; and it seems probable that if, even at the eleventh hour, the chief agitators had been seized and hanged or otherwise appropriately dealt with, the insurrection which was now at hand would not have taken place. In such matters it is impossible to speak with certainty, but I heard some months later of one shaikh of importance who, with tears in his eyes, had pressed when in Baghdad that such action should be taken, as otherwise he would find himself, having no quarrel with the Government, in the unenviable position of being forced to take up arms against us, so as to save his life at the hands of his tribe. I fully sympathised with men who were placed in so difficult a position, and later did my best to have them treated leniently.

I had previously tried to get rid of one of my encumbrances, the 14,036 Turkish prisoners, a number of whom had succeeded in escaping, and were roaming about the country, no doubt doing nothing which would tend towards its pacification. I now once more took up the matter, but it was inevitable that they should remain on my hands for some time longer.

Besides these prisoners, there were the camps of the Assyrian and Armenian refugees, a military encumbrance, of which I shall have more to say later on, which cost our country £90,000 a week. The question of their repatriation was a thorny one and difficult in the extreme to solve, and as far as could be judged there was no prospect of their immediate departure to their former homes or elsewhere. It was easy to foresee that in the event of an extensive rising these refugees, amounting in all to fifty-seven thousand of all ages and sexes, would become a considerable cause of anxiety.

But a far greater one lay in the large number of British

women and children in the country—the families of officers, non-commissioned officers, and men, not to speak of the wives of Political Officers and others who were scattered about the country, in some cases in places where only levies formed the garrison. So far as I was able to ascertain, the number amounted to five hundred and fifty-one women and three hundred and seventy-seven children.

It may here be of interest to touch upon the question of the presence of the British women and children, as the matter is one which during the insurrection caused a good deal of comment in the Press at home, some of it extremely ill-informed.

So far as I have been able to ascertain, the idea of allowing the wives and children of officers to come to Mesopotamia was first considered in the spring of 1919. In the Mesopotamian Expeditionary Force there were then a number of officers, chiefly among those quartered at Baghdad and Basrah, who had been separated from their families throughout the whole course of the war, and who saw little or no prospect of obtaining leave from the country in the near future. These officers, who remind one in an inverse sense of the mountain and Muhammad, were naturally anxious to solve the difficulty by obtaining permission for their wives to join them, and the latter, it may be assumed, desired to bring the lengthy separation to an end. The country at this time was to outward appearances quiet, and that a little more than a year later it would become unsafe throughout its length and breadth was not foreseen.

The first reference home regarding this domestic matter took the somewhat unromantic but solid form of an assertion to the effect that the Director of Works had been authorised to begin making arrangements to provide furniture for ladies coming to Mesopotamia in the autumn. What occurred in the interval I do not know, but there was the usual delay in getting a reply. This is explicable by the fact of the necessity of referring a matter, which involved the expenditure of a considerable sum of money, to several branches of the War Office.

On the 30th June, however, one of these branches, other

than the one concerned with furniture or finance, telegraphed that the provision of passages for wives of officers, as well as those of other ranks, was under consideration, and views from Mesopotamia on the subject were solicited. It was pointed out that it appeared, from a letter which had been received from the Inspector-General of Communications at Basrah, that permission had already been accorded to wives of officers to proceed to Mesopotamia, but no sanction for this procedure had been given by the Army Council. This led to further exchanges of telegrams, and by September 1919 the matter had gone so far that the War Office was told that families could be accommodated in camps, and that a hill-station was available in the Persian hills where those among them who would not or could not go to India during the hot weather could be located. The War Office, commendably anxious for the welfare of the married families, seem to have had a little suspicion of the scheme, for, on the 20th September, the General Officer Commanding-in-Chief was informed that the Army Council would not give permission for families to accompany or follow units in which their husbands were serving, without a clear and authoritative statement that good and sufficient accommodation for the whole twelve months of the year was available both for officers' families and those of other ranks.

From Mesopotamia came the reply that excellent family camps had been arranged by units for all ranks until April, when families would move to a camp in the Persian hills. Some unit commanders and other more senior officers disliked the idea of the families coming to the country, but their wishes in the matter were not consulted or were overruled. Thus the families began arriving in Mesopotamia in January 1920, and after staying for a few weeks in camp at the various stations where British troops were quartered, moved to Karind, in the Persian hills, in April.

The question of the desirability of allowing families of married soldiers, as distinct from those of officers, to come to a country such as Mesopotamia is one on which I hold a strong opinion, and which differs from that of my predecessor, who had left the country before my arrival. I have the advantage of actual experience on the subject, as when he left the married families had not arrived. My opinion, though it is much strengthened by the abnormal occurrences of last year, is based on the fundamental unsuitability of Mesopotamia as a place of residence for white women and children. The country, unlike India, is devoid of all the ordinary amenities of life, and possesses no hill-station—unless by the favour of the Shah of Persia. I will not dilate further on this matter, as my official opinion with my reasons for it are recorded at the proper place.

I cannot speak too highly of the arrangements which were made for the comfort and wellbeing of the families before I came to Mesopotamia. No complaint ever reached my ears, and I think there was no cause for any, though trivial points came up, all of which were rectified at once. Before leaving England I happened to hear of the project for sending married families to the country to which I would shortly be bound, and the idea was most repugnant to me. In the spring, however, when a telegram came to me from India inquiring whether I would care to retain there for the summer months the families who were then arriving in that country *en route* for Mesopotamia, I declined. My reasons were that I was new to the country, and did not, any more than my predecessor, consider that the local unrest, which was then but slight, would reach dangerous proportions; and I realised what a bitter disappointment it would be if, at the eleventh hour, I concurred in the continued separation between man and wife. In fact, the matter had gone too far, and I felt bound to accept a scheme of which I strongly disapproved.

Not long after I reached Baghdad the families began moving to Karind, which I had twice visited with General Hambro, my senior administrative staff officer, who had been responsible for the arrangements for their comfort there and elsewhere.

The hill-station, which is not in any way comparable to the Indian hill-stations, where the families were to pass the summer, as well as certain troops, mention of whom has previously been made, is situated on the north side of a valley which is enclosed on both sides by high hills whose sides are in places precipitous. The valley averages about five thousand feet above sea-level, and opens out at Sar-i-Mil, where it is less than a mile in width, to from five to six miles near its eastern end, sixteen miles towards Kermanshah.

The hills rise gently from the plain, and the débris from them forms the principal component of the surface soil of the valley, through which outcrops of rock penetrate here and there. The soil generally on the slopes is very absorbent, and so keeps the surface dry. In spring and early summer the valley is tinged green by grass and herbaceous plants. Here and there are wild flowers, such as anemones and poppies, which give the scene, at those seasons only, a somewhat pleasing aspect.

Near the little town of Karind, where water is available, fruit-trees, vines, vegetables, and grain grow freely. In other parts of the valley small plants shrivel up and die from drought under the heat of the summer sun. Except for a few trees near Karind there is nothing of that nature beyond a belt of bushes and shrubs, chiefly stunted oak, which lines the borders of the valley, and climbs some little distance up the hills.

The climate proved healthy, and would undoubtedly have been more so had there been quarters for the occupants to live in, more or less free from dust, in place of tents, the temperature in which sometimes rose to 94 degrees Fahrenheit.

Sar-i-Mil, which I have mentioned, and which is about four miles from Karind, was selected as a Headquarters camp. It is a few hundred feet higher than Karind, and, like that place, escapes the scourge of the malarial mosquito, although three-quarters of a mile west of it the inhabitants are infected by that pest.

To Sar-i-Mil the greater portion of my staff had already gone, while representatives of the several branches remained at Baghdad. It was intended to give the officers and clerks in turn a change of air, and as this was the first attempt to open a hill-station for the force, I proposed myself to inaugurate it. And here I may mention one of the peculiarities of Mesopotamia, which is that, unlike every other station of the British Army, there are no facilities either for leave in the country or for creating a sanatorium for those who are sick or convalescent, or whom it is desirable to spare the great heat of the plains. In 1920 we utilised Karind in Persia, which was flattered with the name of "hill-station," but the reduction of troops made the guarding of the route there impossible in 1921. Consequently those quartered in Mesopotamia must either wait until they have been long enough in the country to entitle them to take leave to the United Kingdom—an expensive journey in these days—or go through the Persian Gulf and back, at the hottest season of the year, and travel across India to the hills at a time when train-journeys are best avoided. With regard to sick, convalescent, and certain others, as it would obviously be dangerous to transfer them home or to India during the hot weather, they are obliged to bear as best they can the heat of the country, which enjoys, in the towns at any rate, a fictitious reputation for cool nights.

Before leaving Baghdad I told the Acting Civil Commissioner that, if there were any matter outside the ordinary routine work with which my staff who were left there were incompetent to deal, I could be at that city in a few hours by aeroplane, as a landing-place close to my camp in the hills had been arranged, or, if he preferred it, he could come to me.

I make no secret of the fact that I disliked the idea of remaining at Baghdad throughout the hot weather, where it was not easy, except for an hour or two in the late afternoon, to obtain sufficient exercise to preserve health. On the other hand, Sar-i-Mil was only a short distance from Karind, where there were troops of all arms and excellent ground for training, which would afford plenty of occupation outside office hours.

On the night of the 24th June I left Baghdad for Sar-i-Mil, which I reached next day, and where neither I nor my staff were to remain for long, since the threatened insurrection was at last on the point of breaking out.

CHAPTER VIII.

STATISTICS AND OTHER MATTERS.

I REGRET that, for a proper appreciation of much that follows, it is unavoidable that amongst other matters the somewhat dry subject of figures should be touched upon. The exposition will be as brief as possible, and details relegated to an appendix (No. IV.); but the misconception in the public mind at home as to the fighting strength of the forces in Mesopotamia demands an explanation.

At the time that the outbreak occurred the troops under my command, exclusive of those in Persia, in transit, and sick (who amounted approximately to 4800 British and 8000 Indian), numbered in round figures 7200 British and 53,000 Indian soldiers, or, in all, some 60,200 men. In the grand total are included 3000 British and 23,000 Indian troops, who were employed on non-combatant duties in various departmental services, and whose numbers, as in the case of guards, had been cut down as low as possible. To have reduced them still further, desirable as it was, would have been to accept unjustifiable risks, and amongst other things encourage peculation on an even more extensive scale than that from which we suffered. Appeals for the provision of regular departmental personnel had, owing to recruiting difficulties at home, been made in vain; and, unsatisfactory as it was to find over a third of one's combatant force locked up where their services, though necessary, were useless in the field, the situation had to be accepted.

Besides the total of 60,200 combatants, there was in Mesopotamia an almost similar number of Indian followers, of whom only 5500 formed what are called regimental establishments. The balance consisted of the personnel of Labour Corps, the Inland Water Transport, water-supply stations, electric-lighting and ice-making establishments, and dairy-farms. But the last and largest total amounted to 80,000 souls, all of whom were also rationed by the army. These included the prisoners of war and the refugees already mentioned, and those, over and above true military personnel, who were employed in civil and quasi-civil occupations.

And at this point I must mention that, although the civil administration had relieved the army of the railways throughout the country, there were many establishments which were properly their concern, but the charge of which they were not in a position to undertake. Some of these I have enumerated above, and of them, with the exception of the Inland Water Transport, which had obviously to retain its military character whilst the danger of a rising threatened, I would gladly have washed my hands. But even it had a civil as well as a military purpose, for a large number of additional vessels had to be kept in commission to carry out the work of distribution of nearly nineteen hundred tons a week of all natures of oil, which included fuel oil for railways and power-houses, paraffin for the commoner type of internal-combustion engines, and petrol for aviation and motor-cars. It may create surprise among those who read the preceding sentences to learn that a British Army should be so immersed in concerns which in most countries are controlled either by private enterprise or the local government. But Mesopotamia under the Turks had almost none of the requirements of a modern army, and it had needed the ability and energy of my several predecessors since 1914, not to mention the purses of the British taxpayers, to build up the elaborate system whereby the army may literally be said to have "run the country."

This fact has, I think, been overlooked in some degree by those who have hurled charges of extravagance in military administration in Mesopotamia. War at best is an expensive luxury, and when waged in such a distant country by a modern army the bill must necessarily be a heavy one. However, I am not concerned to defend such charges, and can only speak regarding my own period of command, when rigid economy, not to say frugality, was enforced.

I have already stated the fact of the inability of the civil administration to assist in the matter of relieving the army of what was a civil burden, and I was anxious, as soon as the necessary knowledge came into my possession, that commercial firms should share in the spoil, provided always that military requirements—and of this I was not satisfied—were met. But the insurrection intervened, and this important matter had to be deferred.

Before I leave this subject I would interpolate, although perhaps somewhat prematurely, what occurred later with regard to it, when the country, after the insurgents had submitted, returned to normal conditions.

In January 1921 the British Chamber of Commerce in Baghdad addressed to the High Commissioner a memorandum in which they expressed the opinion that the heavy military expenditure then being incurred in Mesopotamia was largely avoidable. They stated that in great part the expenditure was not directed towards the legitimate needs of the combatant force necessary to provide for the security of the country and the elaboration and completion of the scheme of self-government already inaugurated. In particular, the Chamber instanced as examples of unnecessary expenditure the Inland Water Transport, the Electrical and Mechanical Section, the Labour Directorate, the Department of Military Works, and the Mechanical Transport Department. In conclusion, the Chamber expressed the fear that the intolerable cost of the army in Mesopotamia would lead to its withdrawal under pressure of public opinion in England, and that such action would be disastrous to long-established British interests in Mesopotamia and the future of British trade in the country.

This memorandum was forwarded to me by the High Commissioner, with the suggestion that representatives of the civil administration and of the army should meet

STATISTICS AND OTHER MATTERS 67

representatives of the Chamber of Commerce and discuss the points at issue. In reply I stated that I cordially welcomed the proposal, and expressed my entire agreement with the Chamber of Commerce on the general question of the desirability of rigid economy in army expenditure. I added that I was ready to examine any suggestions which the Chamber of Commerce might put forward, in the hope that ways of reducing the cost of the army in Mesopotamia, without impairing its efficiency, might be discovered.

As a result of this memorandum a joint conference took place on the 15th February. It then at once became evident that the Chamber of Commerce had failed to appreciate many of the factors in the problem which the military administrative staff had to solve. For example, in reply to their contention that the mercantile shipping on the Tigris could have carried all military stores at considerably less cost than the Inland Water Transport, it was explained that during the summer of 1920, when the influx of troops to deal with the Arab insurrection caused demands for river transport which the Inland Water Transport had great difficulty in meeting, a contract to deliver two hundred tons of cargo per week at Kut-al-Amarah was let to the largest shipping firm on the Tigris—in fact the only firm which had any considerable fleet. At this time the Inland Water Transport was delivering over one thousand tons daily at Kut. The firm in question failed completely to carry out this contract, its deliveries only amounting to seventy-eight tons per week over several months. The manager of the firm in question was one of the representatives of the Chamber of Commerce at the conference, and while admitting the complete failure of commercial shipping to carry a small fraction of the army requirements in tonnage, he could offer no explanation.

As an instance of the wastefulness of the Military Works Department, the representatives of the Chamber cited the large brick-kilns erected by the army, and pointed out that the expenditure could have been avoided, and bricks obtained more cheaply by local purchase. The cost of bricks from the army kilns as worked out by the Command

Accountant came to Rs. 80 per thousand at Baghdad and Rs. 40 per thousand at Basrah. On the other hand, the local supply is very limited, the bricks are of bad quality, and the cost is Rs. 120 per thousand. When prior to the establishment of army kilns efforts were made to purchase a quantity of bricks in the local market, the price at once rose to Rs. 240 per thousand.

A further instance of waste put forward by the Chamber was that of the money spent on roads in the proposed cantonment at Hinaidi, which, they contended, were on a scale beyond any probable requirements. These roads were constructed by Turkish prisoners who could not be employed as general labourers, and would otherwise have had to be kept in idleness.

A discussion regarding other departments in which the Chamber contended great economies could be effected disclosed conditions similar to the examples given above.

After a very full, frank, and amicable discussion the representatives of the Chamber of Commerce admitted that they had entirely failed to grasp the problems which General Headquarters had to solve, complicated as they were by uncertain and often complete changes of policy, and they admitted their inability to substantiate their criticisms.

It may be observed, and I still refer to a time subsequent to the insurrection, that the army has made strenuous efforts for months to get the Civil Government or some commercial syndicate to take over and run the large electric power-plants at Basrah and Baghdad, which are the sole source of supply of electric power for those places. Their efforts so far have been fruitless.

Charges of waste in connection with Persia and the evacuation of the British force in that country are sometimes made. The force in Persia, as already mentioned, had its headquarters at Kasvin, the length and difficulty of communication with which have been described. The expense of transport on this route in consequence was enormous, for to carry one ton from Kasvin to Quraitu cost approximately Rs. 1000 (£60 to £120, according to

STATISTICS AND OTHER MATTERS 69

the value of the rupee). It is obvious, therefore, that at so prohibitive a price there were few stores which it would not be a saving to the British public to destroy or give away on the spot rather than incur the cost of bringing them back to Mesopotamia to swell the accumulation of surplus stores in that country.

But to resume. After the reductions which I was forced to make from the fighting troops, the balance that remained amounted to 4200 British and 30,000 Indian troops, which consisted of units many of which were much below strength in men and weak in officers. I had in addition five batteries of armoured-cars, of which one battery was stationed in Persia, the others being distributed at Mosul and on the line of communication between Baghdad and that place, at Baghdad, and on the Euphrates line. These batteries were manned by men borrowed from infantry units, and the cars were old and much the worse for wear, a number being always unserviceable. The personnel only sufficed to man two or three sections in each battery, and seldom could more than four cars from each battery be employed at one time. The cars at Baghdad were of a heavy type, and unsuitable for use except on good roads, a fact which limited their employment to the area of the town and its immediate vicinity.

I had heard of the successful employment in Egypt of this form of military vehicle, and undoubtedly the armoured-car has its uses in certain countries; but I soon learned that in Mesopotamia its employment even in dry weather, for in wet weather it is useless, was strictly circumscribed. In cultivated areas such as the Middle Euphrates, the Diyalah district, and the vicinity of the Tigris, the numerous canals and irrigation channels, most of which are unbridged, or if bridged are only so for light traffic, make movement difficult and often impossible. Moreover, the Arabs had learned from experience that the pneumatic tyres are the Achilles' heel of the cars, and by directing their fire at those spots they had found that they could by a successful shot place the car and its occupants at their mercy. Soon after my arrival in Mesopotamia I had telegraphed home for a supply of "tanks," for which the country seemed to be entirely suitable, but was informed that none was available, and that there was little prospect of any being provided for several years.

As regards the Royal Air Force, when hostilities began there were two squadrons in the country, the 6th and 30th; but of these there were only three flights at Baghdad, and the personnel of one flight was on its way from Anah on the Upper Euphrates. At that time three-fourths of the 30th Squadron were detached to Bushire on the Persian Gulf, Kasvin in Persia, and Mosul, two hundred and fifty miles north of Baghdad.

With the above-mentioned forces a country with a square mileage nearly thrice that of England, exceeding that of the United Kingdom, and only a little less than that of the Transvaal and Orange Free State Colonies combined, had to be garrisoned and administered. But a reference to superficial measurements or the study of a small-scale map conveys little to the ordinary mind, and what I have earlier stated as to the distances and the time taken to cover them will perhaps give a better idea of the task that lay in front of me.

At this time I had not learned that deductions based on my own well-arranged train journeys were misleading. Although the existence of several railways might lead to the supposition that troops in Mesopotamia can be moved from point to point with speed, this, as I have already hinted, is in fact not the case, owing to the insufficient and inefficient rolling-stock and lack of adequate European personnel for rapid and smooth transit. With the exception of a few miles here and there where embankments are built up, the permanent way—and this is so almost entirely in the case of the Euphrates valley railway—is laid practically on the ground level, and lies on earth and not on metal. Travelling is therefore slow, and made slower by the fact that the locomotives, either by the heat of the country or for other reasons, are compelled to stop every few miles of their run to take in water, a process lasting many minutes. Moreover, some of the Indian drivers are ill-disciplined and a source of trouble, and the stationmasters appear to have little or no authority over them, or are afraid to exercise it.

As an instance I may quote the experience of a passenger on the Basrah-Baghdad mail train, which is typical of what occurs, and whose testimony is unimpeachable. The train in question was nine hours behind its scheduled time, and had reached a wayside station, where, after standing for about ten minutes and displaying no indications of moving, the stationmaster was asked what the prospects were of the journey being resumed. Although the line ahead was admittedly clear, he seemed to think that there was nothing surprising in the delay, and replied that the train would shortly move on. At the same moment the long-suffering passenger, happening to look towards the front of the train, saw the driver get down from his engine with a bucket in his hand. This vessel he proceeded to fill with hot water, and then, deliberately and in full view of the public, and making a free use of soap, bathed himself from head to foot. This process took some time, and the driver when remonstrated with retorted that there was no one else on the spot but himself who could drive the engine, and threatened to keep the train standing as long as it suited his convenience. At length, having completed his ill-timed ablutions, he consented to perform his duty, and the line, being reported clear, the train again moved on.

Such delays as these were soon to be aggravated by the insurrectionists, who tore up the line, cut off Baghdad from Basrah by the Euphrates route, and made it impossible for rolling-stock which operated from the former place, where there were no workshops, to undergo either periodical repairs or any that became necessary through the exigences of the insurrection. Indeed, for some months the railway situation was exceedingly serious, not to say almost desperate, and the conduct of operations became difficult, for there were times when not a single locomotive was available at short notice to haul a train with urgently-needed reinforcements. In a country with a temperate climate, provided with a good system of roads and with water available at regular intervals, suspension of movement by rail for a time, though inconvenient, would not create insurmountable difficulties. In Mesopotamia, however, there are areas where, unless the river line be followed or water for the troops is carried on trains, a procedure which necessitates the protection of the line at frequent intervals, their march becomes a practical impossibility.

But the task of guarding so large a country with so limited a force did not end here, for numerous deductions had still to be made from my troops, who, nominally regarded as two divisions, represented in reality little more than one. In addition to garrison duties throughout the country, guards amounting to a brigade were required for the Turkish prisoners, while the safety of the British women and children, numbering over nine hundred souls, and of the Assyrian and Armenian refugees, had to be ensured. At this juncture, too, the Mixed Brigade, which normally would constitute my only reserve at Baghdad, was still in the Upper Euphrates area, but, as mentioned, was in part in process of withdrawal to the Capital.

Thus on the 1st July I had at my disposal as a mobile force some 500 British and 2500 to 3000 Indian troops, of which a battalion only was in a position to reach the Middle Euphrates area within twenty-four hours.

CHAPTER IX.

THE OUTBREAK AT AND RELIEF OF RUMAITHAH.

THE first few days after our arrival at Sar-i-Mil were uneventful, and no disturbing news passed over the wires from Baghdad; but the calm was not to be of long duration, for on the 30th June an incident, trivial in itself, lighted the fire of insurrection on the Middle Euphrates.

The scene of the trouble was the little town of Rumaithah, with some two thousand five hundred inhabitants, which stands on both banks of the Hillah branch of the Euphrates, about twenty-eight miles above Samawah. Its houses, which are mostly built of mud or sun-dried bricks, are scattered among gardens and date-groves. The circumstances which led to the outbreak were as follows :—

On the 25th June, Lieutenant P. T. Hyatt, the Assistant Political Officer at Rumaithah, had reported to the Political Officer of his division, Major C. Daly, that a long outstanding agricultural loan, some Rs. 800 (at that time about £100), owed by the shaikh of the Dhawalim section of the Bani Hachaim, had to be collected, and he was directed to arrest and send the defaulter to Diwaniyah. At noon on the 30th the man, Sha'alan Abu by name, was sent for, and after the necessity for payment had been explained to him, he was detained for the evening train to Diwaniyah. At 4 P.M. the retainers of the shaikh, however, took the law into their own hands, and following an example set about two weeks earlier at Samawah, fired at the political office, killed the Arab guard; and released Sha'alan. The remainder of the police ran away, and left the Political Officer alone.

On the 25th June Major Daly had heard that the Dhawalim tribe had their flags out—showing that they considered themselves to be at war with the Government—but he decided that the wisest course was to proceed with the arrest of the defaulting shaikh. That the outbreak was not purely local may be inferred from the fact that on the 1st July the railway line south of Rumaithah was torn up in several places, and a bridge destroyed. On the same date, too, a reconnoitring train from Samawah, manned by a few sepoys of the 114th Mahrattas, under Major Kiernander of the railway service, who, as well as Flying Officer G. C. Gardiner, was a passenger travelling from Basrah to Baghdad, became engaged with a large number of insurgents, and with difficulty succeeded in returning whence they came. North of Rumaithah more railway cutting was in progress, but the rising still retained its local character.

Troops, exceeding in number those sent to deal with a disturbance of a more threatening character which eighteen months earlier had been successfully quelled, were, at the urgent appeal of the Assistant Political Officer, at once despatched to the scene from Samawah. Two platoons of the 114th Mahrattas (fifty-six rifles) arrived by rail at 3.45 P.M. on the 1st July, whose commander, Lieutenant J. J. Healey, was informed by Lieutenant Hyatt that the country was very much disturbed, and a general rising of the tribesmen might be expected. Next day one company (less half a platoon) of the same regiment came from Diwaniyah, which raised the strength of the garrison of Rumaithah to one hundred and forty rifles. During the night the civilians were moved into the Political Serai, a two-storied brick building which is on the left bank of the river, and commands at some fifty yards' distance the approach to the bridge of boats, beyond which, on the other bank half a mile away is the railway station. All rations that were available, which included enough for

Shaikh Sha'alan Abu.

OUTBREAK AT AND RELIEF OF RUMAITHAH

seven days for one hundred Indian soldiers, were also placed in the Serai.

On the 3rd July a company of another unit, the 99th Infantry, under Captain H. V. Bragg, which had been despatched from Hillah on the 2nd and had left Diwaniyah at 3.30 P.M. next day, arrived, and brought with it some railway personnel. This company had had an adventurous journey, during which a wooden bridge that had been burned down by the insurgents was repaired, while the Arabs interfered by firing heavily from the surrounding villages, causing some casualties among the troops and working party.

On arrival at Rumaithah, Captain Bragg, being the senior officer, assumed command of the garrison, and with his own company occupied two Arab khans or caravanserai, one on each side of the village, while the 114th Mahrattas and the non-combatants remained in the Serai. The troops at the disposal of the commander amounted to four British officers and three hundred and eight other ranks, together with two British officers and one hundred and fifty-three railway personnel and sixty Indians—in all, five hundred and twenty-seven. The task of providing food for this small force, which had only some two days' rations with it, soon became a cause of anxiety.

On the 4th the first signs of the coming siege showed themselves, when it was noticed that the Arabs were constructing a trench system north-west of the town, and carrying out regular reliefs—an indication that ex-Turkish Army officers were probably in control. On this date, complaints having reached the Assistant Political Officer that the occupants of the village of Albu Hassan, which is about one and a half miles south-east of Rumaithah, had taken to looting the bazaar at the latter place, and were terrorising the inhabitants, it was decided that a reconnaissance through the bazaar in the direction of the seat of the trouble should be made. In consequence, the two platoons of the 99th Infantry, whose advance was covered by fire from the top of the two khans held by the 114th,

proceeded to carry out this mission under Lieutenant
Marriott of the former regiment, who was accompanied
by the Assistant Political Officer. The latter urged the
subaltern not to be bound by the letter of his orders, but
burn the hostile village before he returned to camp. This
rather rash advice was to prove costly, for, owing to some
delay in getting the men to advance, the Arabs, numbering
it is said from fifteen hundred to two thousand, began
arriving from every side. The two platoons were over-
whelmed, forty-three being reported missing, or most likely
killed, while one British officer, one Indian officer, and fourteen Indian other ranks were wounded. The usual result
of a set-back, small as this one was, occurred. The townspeople and the tribesmen in the neighbourhood became un-
mistakably hostile, and opening fire on the khans from all
quarters of the village, killed six men and wounded fourteen
others. This led to the withdrawal of every one to the
Serai, to which building the 114th fought their way along
a wall-enclosed road over a distance of one hundred and
twenty yards, escaping with the loss of two men wounded.
The question of food, with the inhabitants openly hostile,
now became prominent, as also that of ammunition, which
was running short, and medical requirements, which were
entirely lacking. Raids were therefore planned and carried
out on the bazaar, which consists of a narrow street roofed
with reed matting, some two hundred and fifty yards long,
running across the village from east to west with the usual
ramifications. Here are numerous diminutive shops,
typical of such Eastern marketing centres, the majority
of which are owned by dealers in grain and vendors of
other food-stuffs. These raids succeeded to the extent of
securing supplies sufficient for the garrison for a few days.
As the process of getting water for the garrison in the
Serai from the river was attended with considerable risk,
and three men had lost their lives in doing so, wells were
dug which, though only ten feet deep, furnished a sufficient
supply for the besieged. The ammunition difficulty had
been reported by heliograph through Samawah to Baghdad,

Rumaithah—Buildings defended are within white line.

Rumaithah—Political Serai.

OUTBREAK AT AND RELIEF OF RUMAITHAH

and could only be overcome by attempting to drop a supply in boxes from aeroplanes. This was tried on the 8th, when aeroplanes arrived and dropped three boxes. One box fell into the river, another among date-palms a hundred yards from the Serai, and the third reached its goal but fatally wounded a Naik (L/Cpl.) of the 99th Infantry and an Arab prisoner. Through the bravery of Mr E. W. L. Harper of the railway service, who had already distinguished himself at the repair of the burnt bridge and in the withdrawal from the village on the 4th, and who went out with two men, the box that was dropped into the river was recovered. That which fell into the date-palm grove was secured by Sepoy Hardat of the 99th Infantry, who had to climb three walls seven to eight feet high under the fire of the insurgents, and approach to within fifty yards of the houses held by them.

By the 12th, although a sortie by the 99th Infantry secured some food, supplies were again running short. A raid on a large scale, in co-operation with bombing aeroplanes sent from Baghdad, was organised, the results of which were highly satisfactory, and may be said to have saved the situation and gained time for a force to effect the relief of the garrison. On this occasion two platoons of the 114th Mahrattas acted as covering party, while the remainder of the garrison, except a small piquet, furnished with bags, tins, and blankets, collected sufficient food for twelve days, consisting of half a ton of grain, besides some sheep and chickens. The covering party were equally successful in another sense, and killed twenty inhabitants with no loss to themselves.

Meanwhile orders had been issued for a small column to proceed to Rumaithah, and by the evening of the 6th July the force, which was accompanied by a train carrying ammunition, food, and water, had reached a point about six miles north of its destination, after meeting with considerable opposition and being much delayed through the necessity of repairing the railway line and removing trucks that had been derailed.

The column was composed as follows :—

Commander—Lieut.-Colonel D. A. D. M'Vean, D.S.O.
37th Lancers (one squadron).
45th Pack Battery [1] (one section).
45th (Rattray's) Sikhs.
99th (Deccan) Infantry (H.Q., and five platoons).
Thirty Kurdish Levies.

On the 7th, directly the advance began, the insurgents appeared in large numbers, which were estimated at from three thousand to five thousand men, and opened a heavy fire from the bed of a dried-up canal which lay at right angles to the line of advance of the column. A gallant attempt was made to break through and reach Rumaithah, but the small force was greatly outnumbered, and the tribesmen began closing in and working round its flanks. Lieut.-Colonel M'Vean, with his small force isolated and his communications with Diwaniyah, thirty-two miles to the north, only lightly guarded, now found himself in a precarious situation. Fortunately his resolution and courage did not fail him at this crisis, and he wisely decided to break off the action, in which the safety of his force was becoming jeopardised. By 11 A.M., taking advantage of a dust-storm, he was able to withdraw, and had gained a start of a mile before his retirement was discovered. Then the Arabs hurried after him, and fighting went on until dark, when the column halted. On the following day Imam Hamzah, eighteen miles north of Rumaithah, was reached, where for the present the force remained. The casualties in proportion to the numbers engaged had been heavy, amounting to—

Killed.	Wounded.
British officer, 1.	British officer, 1.
Indian other ranks, 47.	Indian other ranks, 166.

As it seemed possible as early as the 3rd July that more

---

[1] During the insurrection the change in nomenclature from mountain to pack artillery occurred. The latter term has been followed throughout the narrative.

OUTBREAK AT AND RELIEF OF RUMAITHAH

troops might be required, should the situation on the Middle Euphrates not improve, I had ordered the reserve battalion (45th Sikhs)—whose operations have just been described—to be replaced from the 18th Division, and on the 4th warned Major-General Fraser to hold the garrison of Tekrit in readiness to move by rail to the capital. Troops were not available for guarding the railway communications throughout their length, but on the 4th July all important bridges were ordered to be guarded.

On the 7th July I proceeded from Sar-i-Mil to Baghdad, and on the following day heard of the failure to relieve Rumaithah. Aware that any reverse, no matter how slight, would at once be grossly exaggerated by the tribes, I telegraphed on the 8th to the War Office (repeating the telegram to Army Headquarters, India) requesting that an infantry brigade and a battery of field artillery (howitzers) might be held in readiness for despatch to Basrah (see Appendix X.). I was informed in reply, to my dismay, that the force I desired could not embark before the end of July. When I thought of our rapid mobilisation at home in 1914 I felt something more than disappointment at the delay that must elapse before help could come from India, but I understood later that shipping had to be taken up and men recalled from leave.

On the 8th July, too, the 87th Punjabis of the 18th Division, who were guarding Turkish prisoners of war, were replaced by some sappers and miners, and were sent to Hillah, the 1/116th Mahrattas of the same division from Tekrit being ordered to replace that battalion at Baghdad.

Major-General Fraser was also directed to send to Baghdad from Tekrit the headquarters of the 55th Infantry Brigade, one battery Royal Field Artillery (howitzers), two Indian battalions, and certain details. The British battalion of that brigade, the 2nd Battalion Manchester Regiment, was ordered to be held in readiness to follow, which it did as soon as trains were available, and both it and the 2nd Battalion Royal Irish Rifles,[1] which had arrived from

---

[1] This unit was later rechristened the Royal Ulster Rifles, but its old nomenclature has been followed in the narrative.

Karind, moved to Hillah. The 1/10th Gurkha Rifles were at this time marching from the Upper Euphrates to Fallujah *en route* for Baghdad, whilst the 86th Carnatics, who had arrived from India in relief, were sent to Hillah, and the 13th Rajputs on their way to the base were detained at Baghdad.

On the 10th July the last of the units at Karind, the 1st and 7th Dragoon Guards, were ordered to move to Baghdad, leaving at the former place to guard the married families a composite detachment of young British soldiers.

The movements stated above were demanded by the urgent necessity of relieving the garrison at Rumaithah, the state of whose food supply and ammunition was uncertain, and who were reported as unlikely to be able to hold out for more than a few days. Some delay was, however, inevitable, as the movement of the necessary troops had to be carried out by rail during one of the hottest months and over the narrow-gauge Euphrates valley railway, the capacity of whose vehicles is not equal to that of the normal gauge. This delay was accentuated by the shortage of rolling-stock and the lack of foresight in certain quarters, which led to the disregard of a well-known military canon, that of not concentrating troops or supplies too far forward. Thus trains from Baghdad, which should have gone no further south than Hillah, where the advanced depot was ordered by General Headquarters to be formed, were recklessly pushed on to Diwaniyah, fifty-two miles nearer Rumaithah. This procedure led to a considerable delay in returning rolling-stock required for the movement of troops, and caused supplies to be collected too far to the front, which, as will presently be seen, had a malign influence later on.

Meantime the garrison of Rumaithah had reported to Samawah by heliograph that their rations would only last till the 12th July, and that the food obtained by local raids was exhausted. It was in consequence of this report that the action already mentioned was taken. A raid by nine aeroplanes was carried out on the following day, when it

OUTBREAK AT AND RELIEF OF RUMAITHAH

was arranged that the garrison should force their way into the bazaar, and endeavour there to supplement their stores. The raid was successful, and information came back that rations and forage sufficient to last until the 23rd July had been secured. There now seemed every prospect that, despite the delays which had occurred, the relieving force could reach Rumaithah before lack of food had compelled a surrender and the massacre that would almost certainly follow. That force, which was placed under the command of Brigadier-General F. E. Coningham, commanding the 34th Infantry Brigade, who for several months had been engaged in the operations on the Upper Euphrates, consisted of—

37th Lancers (one squadron),
97th Battery R.F.A.,
132nd (How.) Battery R.F.A. (less one section),
45th Pack Battery,
61st Coy., 2nd (Q.V.O.) Sappers and Miners,
2nd Bn. Royal Irish Rifles (51st Infantry Brigade),
45th (Rattray's) Sikhs (52nd Infantry Brigade),
87th Punjabis (55th Infantry Brigade),
99th (Deccan) Infantry (less one company) (34th Infantry Brigade),
1/116th Mahrattas (55th Infantry Brigade),
1/10th Gurkha Rifles (51st Infantry Brigade),
17th Machine Gun Battalion (two sections),
besides details.

The column, it will be seen, was made up of units from four brigades. They did not all even belong to one division, and two only formed part of Brigadier-General Coningham's former brigade (the 51st Infantry Brigade), which he had just handed over on proceeding to Hillah. This organisation, though unsound, was unavoidable, not only because, to save time, the troops nearest at hand had to be used, but because, as I have already said, my reserve brigade, which normally would have been at Baghdad and available to proceed as a whole on any operation required, was, except for one battalion, still on the Upper Euphrates.

The communications of the force which was to carry out the relief could not be held in such strength as to make them safe. Troops for the purpose were not available to guard at close intervals the line from Hillah to Diwaniyah and further south towards Rumaithah, nor was the line from Baghdad to Hillah, sixty-four miles in length, held by troops at any point. Even if it had been possible to provide the necessary posts, the mere supply by a single-line railway of food, water, and materials for making defences put such arrangements at that time out of the question. The General Officer Commanding the 17th Division arranged that the seventy miles from Hillah to Imam Hamzah, where the 45th Sikhs still remained, should be organised in double-platoon posts two to four miles apart. For this purpose two battalions had to be used, and their detachments were frequently but unsuccessfully attacked. Such protection was, of course, inadequate, and marauding parties under cover of darkness made numerous raids on the line between the posts and tampered both with it and the telegraph wires.

At this time it was evident that the operation which was about to be carried out was of an extremely hazardous nature, and that even if successful, which was uncertain, the risk would still remain. I was committing practically all the mobile force on which I could lay hands, without denuding to danger point other areas, to an undertaking which involved its transfer to a distance of one hundred and fifty miles from Baghdad, with ill-guarded communications and with every prospect that those tribes which had not risen or which bordered the line of march would do so before the Rumaithah garrison could be extricated. The fact, too, of the failure of the first attempt to relieve Rumaithah and the certainty that the *moral* of the insurgents around that place must, by that failure and the consequent delay, have risen, was not calculated to encourage optimistic hopes regarding the coming operation. Indeed there was a prospect of the force being cut off, and having to fight its way back to Hillah during the hottest season of the year, while embarrassed by almost insurmountable food and water difficulties. The operation, naturally, was not one that commended itself to the divisional general, who shortly moved his headquarters to Diwaniyah, and though obliged to maintain an optimistic attitude, my secret sympathies lay with the view he took. I did not then know Brigadier-General Coningham, whom I had not met, but had I done so and had I known his qualities as a leader, any misgivings which I felt regarding the outcome of the operation or the scratch nature of the column would have been greatly lessened.

These misgivings and the gradual extension of the area of disturbance prompted me on the 15th July to ask for the despatch, as soon as possible, of the troops which I had demanded on the 8th, and I added a request that a full division might be held in readiness. On the 18th July, from motives of economy, I qualified my earlier telegram in so far as to suggest that the remainder of the division should not be embarked until demanded. This suggestion unfortunately led to a misunderstanding which was later rectified, as the War Office, assuming the whole division would not be required, countermanded all but my demand made on the 8th July.

By the 16th July the relief column was concentrated within sixteen miles of Rumaithah. Some of its units were weak, the 2nd Battalion Royal Irish Rifles and the 1/10th Gurkha Rifles being only equivalent in strength to one battalion, while the 45th Sikhs had recently been engaged and had suffered loss. A train accompanied the force on which were carried reserve ammunition, water, rations, and medical requirements. As, however, circumstances might arise which would make it impossible to move the train forward with the column, all army transport carts that could be spared had been collected at Diwaniyah, and on them were loaded two days' reserve rations for the whole force, one day's food and an emergency ration being carried by the men.

It was known that there was a fair number of wounded in Rumaithah, and for these and others that might result from the operation for relief, arrangements had to be made. The addition of the train increased considerably the length of the column, and as it marched parallel to the railway track it was highly vulnerable. The train, however, was indispensable—indeed without it the operation was not a feasible one, except at the cost of a delay which would have imperilled the lives of the precariously supplied garrison. As the country over which the column moved is open, it might be supposed that its length could easily have been curtailed. Owing, however, to the frequent ravines which crossed the line of march, the passages over which were confined to narrow bridges unsuitable for two carts abreast, no shortening was possible.

For a brief space it almost seemed as if the tribes in the vicinity of Rumaithah, owing to the approach of the relief force, the earlier aeroplane action, and the activities of the garrison, would come to terms. The Assistant Political Officer, Lieutenant Hyatt, had heard about the 17th July that the shaikhs wished to see him, and had arranged a meeting, at which Sha'alan and another headman were present. They evidently desired to come to terms, and were told that any one who resisted the troops marching on Rumaithah would be destroyed. This led to an agreement that Lieutenant Hyatt, who acted throughout with courage and good sense, should visit the Political Officer of the division, and, subject to their following his advice, do his best to reduce their punishment. In consequence he proceeded next day, under an Arab escort, to join General Coningham, the commander of the column, who agreed to see the shaikhs if they cared to come to him, and promised them safe-conduct. Unfortunately the meeting could not be arranged, and the force continued its march.

On the 19th July it approached the spot where the first attempt to relieve the Rumaithah garrison had failed, being greatly belated in its march owing to the necessity of repairing the railway line. The insurgents' main position, which was not at first discovered, was some two hundred yards in front of an embankment which was held as a second line, both positions being directly across the line

OUTBREAK AT AND RELIEF OF RUMAITHAH 85

of march of the column. Its strength lay in the fact that it consisted of a series of dried-up canals which ran parallel to one another, while several villages on their banks were so situated as to enfilade them. But since the unsuccessful attack of the 7th July the ground had been strengthened by trenches which were dug in front of the canals and the villages, and were skilfully hidden in the scrub—further

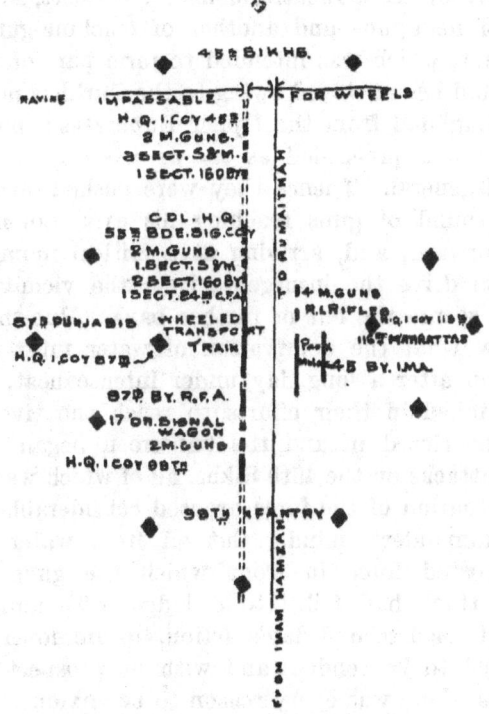

Fig. 2.—*The Advance to Rumaithah.*

evidence, if there had now remained doubts, that among the leaders of the insurgents were Arab ex-officers of the Sultan's army. The canal banks themselves were seen to be held by groups of tribesmen, whose numbers were estimated at not less than five thousand, and who were scattered along a front of three thousand five hundred yards.

At 1.10 p.m. General Coningham's guns opened fire and

the infantry advanced, but suffered from the heavy enfilade fire which came from the left; and when the assault was made three and a half hours later by the two leading battalions—the 45th Sikhs and the 116th Mahrattas—it failed to dislodge the insurgents, who held their ground tenaciously.

Another hour passed, when fortunately the 1/10th Gurkha Rifles arrived, under Lieut.-Colonel H. L. Scott, as well as a section of field-guns and another of machine-guns. This detachment, which was intended to form part of the main column, had been delayed owing to the Gurkhas not having reached Baghdad from the Upper Euphrates; but on the 18th they had proceeded as far as Diwaniyah with the divisional general. Thence they were pushed on at once; and the sound of guns reaching his ears, Colonel Scott pressed forward, and, arriving at a critical moment, was ordered to drive the insurgents from the vicinity of the river and secure the left or further bank. But the tribesmen knew what the deprivation of water must mean to the column after a long day under intense heat, and the Gurkhas failed in their efforts to reach the river.

As night closed in and the tribesmen began to make repeated attacks on the 45th Sikhs, all of which were driven off, the situation of the force aroused considerable anxiety in its commander's mind. Cut off from water, with a strongly-posted force in front which the guns and an infantry attack had failed to dislodge, with ammunition insufficient for a second day's action, an unknown number of wounded to be tended, and with no prospect of reinforcements, there was every reason to be anxious.

But situations are seldom so grave as they appear to be, and General Coningham was not the man to falter because outward appearances looked black. He was in communication with Diwaniyah, whence a train with water, ammunition, and medical dressings was despatched during the night, and reached the column at 8.45 A.M. on the 20th.

On that date the 1/10th Gurkha Rifles, supported by one section of the 97th Battery, R.F.A., one machine-gun section, and the 37th Lancers' Hotchkiss troop, began operations at dawn. By 6.15 A.M. three platoons of Gurkhas, the water reaching to their armpits, had crossed to the left bank of the river on a front of five hundred yards, driving back the Arabs, who suffered from the Lewis-gun fire directed on them. Soon after the Gurkhas had established themselves on the left bank of the river, patrols of the 45th Sikhs reported that the main position, which had defied all efforts on the previous day, was unoccupied, a fact which was confirmed by aeroplane. The practice of leaving under cover of night ground which had been held tenaciously during the day was, I believe, a noticeable feature of the tactics followed by the Turks in the earlier fighting in Mesopotamia, and that this procedure was repeated on the present occasion by the tribesmen, made assurance doubly sure that some of those who had served with the Turkish Army were now leading them.

By 6.45 A.M. three battalions of infantry were established in the position, and a quarter of an hour later an aeroplane reported that many Arabs had been seen in the villages four miles to the south, while others were holding some small ravines three miles from Rumaithah. Another party of from six hundred to a thousand strong was stated to be moving to the north-west of the ground which our troops occupied, and entrenchments were seen in course of construction on the left bank of the river. But the ammunition had by this time arrived, the animals had been watered, and the cavalry having moved south at half-past eight, all was ready for a further advance.

The 116th Mahrattas were left to guard the train and transport until the railway track, which had been badly damaged, was repaired, and General Coningham moved forward without opposition. At 3.45 P.M. word came that the cavalry had entered Rumaithah thirty-five minutes earlier, on receipt of which news all motor-ambulances were sent there, and some thirty of the more seriously wounded were evacuated to the train.

The relief operation had cost General Coningham's force three British officers and thirty-two Indian other ranks killed, and two British officers and one hundred and fifty

Indian other ranks wounded, while the casualties of the Rumaithah garrison during their sixteen days' investment totalled approximately one hundred and forty-eight all ranks, killed, wounded, and missing.

While credit is due to all who shared in the operation, Brigadier-General Coningham imputed its satisfactory outcome mainly to the valour and dogged determination of the 45th Sikhs under their gallant colonel, notwithstanding the heavy losses which befell them, especially in Indian officers and non-commissioned officers; and to the dash of the 1/10th Gurkha Rifles, who, in spite of the depth of the river—a serious obstacle for soldiers of their small stature —established themselves on the far bank.

Through the Political Officer I intimated to the insurgents that their severely wounded would receive treatment if taken to Samawah, as I felt that the tribesmen had been misled by their religious and other leaders, and that having effected the relief of Rumaithah hostilities might possibly be brought to a conclusion, provided those implicated in the local rising submitted. A month later, in order to regularise the position as regards any Arabs that might be captured, I issued an order that the usual laws and usages of war were to be observed, but that a clear distinction was to be made between those who fell into our hands in action and those who behaved in a treacherous manner.

The news of General Coningham's success lifted a weight from my mind, as the situation in several other areas was becoming threatening, and tribesmen numbering thirty-five thousand were now in arms against us. The defeat of the insurgents at Rumaithah would give a moment's breathing space, and would strengthen the hands of those tribal leaders who were striving to keep in check unruly members.

Unfortunately, desirable as it was to leave a garrison at Rumaithah of a strength sufficient to dominate the country round about, and one whose line of communication was safeguarded, neither the situation elsewhere nor the troops available made such a project possible. The relief force must be withdrawn without delay to be employed nearer

Baghdad, for until my man-power was increased the distance from the Capital at which operations could be safely carried out had to be kept within strict limits.

On looking back many months after the events above narrated and reviewing the situation in a calmer atmosphere, the more convinced I feel that, had a single unit less been used to save Rumaithah, failure with consequences of the gravest nature would have resulted.

The Arabs who had been engaged against both relief columns were well armed, extremely mobile, and ready to take considerable risks where loot was the reward. It was evident that they were directed by skilled brains, well versed in the power of the modern rifle, as well as in the limitations and weak points of our modern army. Their dispositions for defence had been skilful, and there was evidence of considerable cunning in the selection of time and place to interfere with water supplies, and with the railway and the line of march. Fortunately their ammunition supply was limited, and as each round costs them an appreciable sum, a target was seldom engaged unless the chance of hitting it was good. Like all semi-savages, they had shown themselves particularly bold when following up a retiring force, and were to be trusted to display marked skill in taking immediate advantage of a fault in dispositions.

In the march to and from Rumaithah General Coningham had adopted either a square or a diamond formation, which served to guard the transport, and was largely used in later operations. For the benefit of other commanders who had not the advantage of his experience, I caused to be drawn up by him and Lieut.-Colonel Scott of the 1/10th Gurkha Rifles, who earned a bar to his D.S.O. on the 20th for the gallant way in which he helped to save the situation, some notes which will be found in Appendix IX.

The question of taking a train with the column had been carefully considered. It must necessarily lead to tying troops to the railway, and so hampering their freedom of manœuvre, and when the line was found to be broken halts to effect repairs would be unavoidable. All these disadvantages were considered to be outweighed by the advantage that would result from possessing the power of evacuating casualties, carrying medical comforts, water, and supplies, as well as furnishing a mobile hospital for exhausted men or those who fell victims to heat-stroke.

On the morning of the 21st July, after marching into the town with a representative column, which included the 2nd Battalion Royal Irish Rifles, the 1/10th Gurkha Rifles, some Royal Artillery and Royal Engineers, the evacuation of the garrison was carried out, and the whole force fell back to the ground where it had fought two days before.

On the 22nd, after more delay owing to a locomotive breaking down, the force moved northwards at 5.30 A.M., the Arabs keeping at a respectful distance, but opening fire on three sides. About two hours later, under cover of a dust-storm, a large party of tribesmen fell upon the rearguard, which was formed of the 87th Punjabis. The disorganisation which ensued, and which disturbed the formation of the 45th Sikhs, was increased by the cavalry, who, without warning, galloped through the rearguard so as to clear its front. For a brief space the column was in great danger, more especially as its commander could see nothing for the dust; but three companies of the 2nd Battalion Royal Irish Rifles, under Lieut.-Colonel A. D. N. Merriman, were hastily despatched to restore the situation and re-form the rearguard, while the train and transport moved on to the midday halting-place. After this affair the Arabs, who have a preference for fighting within their own tribal boundaries, ceased to harass the column, which was assembled at Diwaniyah by the 25th July.

CHAPTER X.

THE DISASTER TO THE MANCHESTER COLUMN.

My intention, which had been communicated on the 19th to Major-General Leslie, who commanded the 17th Division, was to send a column of two battalions of infantry and other arms from Hillah to Kifl as soon as possible after Rumaithah was relieved. These troops would be followed by others from Diwaniyah; and the relief of the detachment of the 108th Infantry at Kufah, which I had declined to strengthen to the equivalent of a battalion on the appeal of the Political Officer, and which included some smaller detachments from other places whence they had fortunately been withdrawn in time, would be undertaken. The fact of having a garrison at Kufah was, as in the case of most detachments, a disadvantage from a military point of view, as, should it become invested, its relief would interfere with initiative. The town itself lies thirty-three miles south of Hillah, and for twenty-one miles of that distance a two-feet six-inch gauge railway ran as far as Kifl; but the line had only a small quantity of rolling-stock, and was of comparatively little use for military purposes. On every account I was anxious to remove the garrison to Hillah, but that procedure, undesirable at first for political reasons, soon became impossible on military grounds. To have done so would have removed a restraining influence upon the city of Najaf, and would certainly have hastened the hostile intervention of the tribes on this section of the Euphrates. Moreover, so long as the operations for the relief of Rumaithah were in progress, the withdrawal of the detachments would have uncovered, though at a considerable distance, one flank of the line of communication which was vital to the relief column. Kufah affords a good example of the difficulties that arise where military and political interests clash, or do so in part, for in this case there were advantages and disadvantages from both points of view in having a garrison there. The Political Officer, I have noticed on many occasions, and I refer to the soldier qua-political, seems to lose all sense of military principles soon after he joins the civil administration—assuming that he knows them —although the self-same principles apply to administrative, diplomatic, and military affairs. If permitted, he would like to scatter broadcast the forces, often small in number, which are available for the maintenance of order. In fact he sees no harm in being weak everywhere and strong nowhere. He seems to overlook the fairly obvious fact that isolated troops generally require large forces to rescue them if they become beleaguered, and relies on his political prestige and acumen, such as they may happen to be, to effect their release from a dangerous situation before it becomes quite hopeless. I would warn those who may have to deal with situations such as arose in Mesopotamia in 1920, to be on their guard, for they may expect to receive daily, sometimes oftener, urgent appeals to send troops here, there, and everywhere, which, it is represented, will achieve by their presence what an army later could not do. Sometimes a response to these appeals—and I do not for a moment doubt their *bona fide* nature, though there were cases where the necessity for help was exaggerated, or proved to be so owing to the temperament of the individual who applied for it—would help to stave off greater trouble. They must, however, be treated with discrimination, and with the motto *festina lente* in one's mind.

As early as the 11th July the stationmaster at Kifl had reported that attacks on the railway station, permanent way, and telegraphs were probable, and on the same date the railway authorities ordered the staff of the line to withdraw, arrangements, however, being made to run such trains as were required. Next day, at the instigation of

DISASTER TO MANCHESTER COLUMN 93

the Political Officer at Hillah, the staff returned to Kifl ; but on the 23rd the station was attacked, and the staff captured, and a train which had left Hillah on the morning of that date was stopped by the Political Officer and ordered to return, the line then being definitely abandoned.

Three days earlier Kufah was known to be practically invested, and on the morning of the 23rd I told the General Officer Commanding the 17th Division, who had come to Baghdad to see me, that the situation was far from satisfactory, and that the mixed column, which I had arranged should proceed to Kifl, must be increased by two battalions, these being furnished from the troops of the Rumaithah Relief Column. I impressed on him, as I had before done in writing, the urgent necessity which existed for concentrating at Hillah, with the utmost speed, all troops which were south of that place, excepting possibly the detachment which, if circumstances should develop satisfactorily, I might decide to leave at Diwaniyah. It had been my intention to operate against the Dagharah tribes which inhabit the country immediately east of Diwaniyah, and which had given much trouble by frequently cutting the railway line. The situation, however, did not permit of time being spent on what was really a subsidiary operation while the seat of the evil still remained untouched.

At this time there were at Hillah, which is some sixty miles from Baghdad, and was the base for operations undertaken in the direction of both Rumaithah and Kifl, two squadrons of the 35th Scinde Horse, the 39th Battery R.F.A. (six guns), a sapper and miner company (less one section), a portion of a bridging train, three companies of the 2nd Battalion Manchester Regiment, and one company of the 32nd Sikh Pioneers.

On the 23rd Colonel R. C. W. Lukin, the officer commanding, was very strongly pressed by Major Pulley, the Political Officer of the division, to send a detachment from the small garrison in the direction of Kifl. Every argument that could be adduced was brought to bear, more especially the usual one that a show of force would keep the wavering tribes in order, and that those who had already taken the field in the area near Hillah were, so far, few in numbers. Under the circumstances, and in view of the expected early arrival of troops from Diwaniyah, a force, commanded by Brevet Lieut.-Colonel R. N. Hardcastle, moved during the afternoon to a point some six miles south of Hillah. The force in question, which was known as the "Manchester Column," was composed as follows :—

> 35th Scinde Horse (two squadrons).
> 39th Battery R.F.A.
> 2nd Battalion Manchester Regiment (less one company).
> 1/32nd Sikh Pioneers (one company).
> 24th Combined Field Ambulance (one section).

The telegram approving of the movement, which was sent by the divisional general, laid down that the night camp of the column was to be entrenched, and that no further move towards Kifl was to be permitted.

So far no actual harm was done, for even if a sudden rising of other tribes took place, the detachment would be within reach of Hillah, whose garrison, it must be noted, were, owing to its absence, quite inadequate to defend that place against attack.

A question which, when the proposal to detach the small column was first mooted, would seem to have caused some doubt among those arranging the move, was that of water. The route which it was to follow is usually well supplied with that essential, but the first regular halting-place is not at six miles' distance but a good deal further off. Two Assistant Political Officers had been sent to make inquiries, which seem to have satisfied all concerned when on their return they reported that there was an ample supply for men and animals. On reaching the camping ground,[1] however, the commander of the column found, and reported to Hillah through the medium of an officer of the Irrigation Department, that the water in the wells was brackish, and that the animals would not drink it, but that there was a good supply at a distance of rather

[1] See Fig. 7, page 183.

DISASTER TO MANCHESTER COLUMN

over a mile. Normally there should have been plenty of water in the Mashtadiyah canal, a branch of the Amiriyah canal, both of which were in the vicinity of the camp. But the low level of the Hillah branch did not allow of water entering those two canals.

Meanwhile the Political Officer at Hillah was again bringing strong pressure to bear on the commander of the garrison to push the column, which had been despatched that afternoon, further towards Kifl. The arguments employed included an anticipated early attack on the Hindiyah Barrage, the generally critical situation in the district, and the disturbing reports which had arrived from Assistant Political Officers, who could no longer remain in safety at their posts. All these indications of further trouble pointed to the urgency of striking a blow which would discourage a rising on the part of the neighbouring tribes, doubtless a perfectly sound political conclusion. It was alleged, as an inducement to despatch the little column nearer Kifl, that the tribesmen on either side of the route were entirely friendly, and in case of an advance on our part might be trusted to keep the road and railway open behind the force. Last and most cogent was the assertion that hesitation to send the troops forward might drive the friendly tribes into the arms of the insurgents.

The upshot was that the commandant at Hillah ordered the column to advance at dawn next morning to the spot mentioned as possessing a water supply, and telegraphed at 12.15 A.M. on the 24th to the divisional general for approval of the action proposed. The telegram did not reach Divisional Headquarters at Diwaniyah till about 8.30 A.M. that day, by which hour it was assumed that the column must have reached or be near its destination. As will be seen, this was not so, but on the assumption that the march had begun as ordered at dawn and had proceeded in a normal manner, the permission that had been asked for was given.

It should here be mentioned that, in the order for the further move, Lieut.-Colonel Hardcastle was told that he was to act as the advanced guard of a force. In addition, the order stated, "If opposed by large hostile forces, you will avoid becoming so involved as to necessitate reinforcements, and should occasion arise you will fall back on the position you now occupy." The reference to the rôle of the force being that of an advanced guard evidently referred to the original idea of eventually sending a strong column to Kifl. The commandant at Hillah, however, had presumably not yet been informed of my order that, owing to the altered situation, that column was to be twice as large as was at first intended.

Before describing the further movements of the column, it should be mentioned that after the insurrection several shaikhs and others were tried before military courts for participating in the rising, and from the proceedings of one of these courts some information regarding the occurrences on the 23rd and 24th July may be gleaned.

On the former date Shaikh Ibrahim-as-Samawi of the Khafajah tribe, who was tried on a charge of "War rebellion," found guilty, sentenced to death, and reprieved, accompanied the column to its camping-place, and on arrival there was permitted to spend the night at his home. Water being the urgent question of the moment, the Assistant Political Officer, Captain Tozer, was that evening searching for a supply, and while so engaged met several small bands of tribesmen carrying arms. On inquiring whither they were bound, they stated that the shaikh in question had ordered them to assemble in order to protect their lands from a possible attack by the Shamiyah tribes, whose country lies further to the south, and who, it will be remembered, had raised their war banners on the 14th of the month.

Next day on meeting Ibrahim-as-Samawi, Captain Tozer asked him at what place he had ordered the concentration of his fighting men. Thereupon the shaikh denied all knowledge of what his followers had stated, and alleged on his trial that early the same morning he had made a tour of his sarkals or leaders of small tribal groups and warned them that troops were coming into their country and were not to be molested.

During the 24th the shaikh remained with the column

except for two hours about noon, when he appears again, somewhat unwisely, to have been allowed to absent himself. At 5 p.m. the Assistant Political Officer went to see the commander of the column, and before doing so gave orders that the shaikh was not to leave the camp. When he returned an hour later he found that he had gone.

How far this shaikh acted in a treacherous manner is difficult to say, and at his subsequent trial he was acquitted of the charge, though found guilty on another count. On that occasion he explained that he left the camp when the attack began, as, being in Arab dress, he feared that if recognised with the British he would be murdered by his men. The fact, however, of his denial of all knowledge of the concentration of his retainers as reported by them, and of his twice asking for leave to go to his home and finally quitting the camp contrary to orders, seems to justify the charge of treachery which was brought against him, and which for lack of evidence could not be proved. It is reasonable to conclude that he took advantage of the knowledge which he had gained on the 23rd as to the strength and composition of the column to call up his followers; and, armed with the further information acquired on the 24th regarding the camp and disposition of the force, profited by Captain Tozer's absence to escape and share in the attack.

The information of the second advance reached my headquarters on the 24th after it had taken place, and caused me much disquietude of mind, for I felt that nothing in my power could avert what, at the best, would mean a fight, the issue of which would be extremely doubtful. A general warning had been sent out earlier to guard against incurring the risk of a reverse, no matter how small, at a time when the least success on the part of the insurgents would add materially to their numbers in the field; and now, at a moment when General Coningham's force was still far south of Hillah, the tribesmen, who are quick to recognise mistakes, were being given an opportunity which they could hardly fail to see.

It has been mentioned that on reaching their camp the

animals with Lieut.-Colonel Hardcastle's column would not drink the water, which was brackish. In consequence they were not watered that afternoon. Next day at 4.45 A.M., under the guidance of an Assistant Political Officer, they were led to the watering-place on the Nahr Shah canal, and got back at 8.15, having satisfied their requirements, after a march of several miles. The delay in their return was mainly due to the impossibility of watering at one time a large number of animals owing to the steep banks of the canal, and the numerous dried-up canals and irrigation channels which had to be crossed in single file. Although, before leaving Hillah, it was recognised that a march at this season would be most trying, no special arrangement for carrying water, beyond what was in the water-carts and men's water-bottles, was considered necessary.

At 9.15 A.M. the head of the column moved off and reached the Rustumiyah canal at 12.45 P.M., all ranks being much affected by the great heat, especially the Manchester Regiment, of whom sixty per cent were so exhausted as to require, in the opinion of the medical officer with the column, a complete rest for twenty-four hours.

A troop of the 35th Scinde Horse was now sent to reconnoitre towards Kifl, the single minaret at which place overlooks the date-palm groves which border it, and is clearly visible from the banks of the Rustumiyah canal.

The troops meanwhile settled down in their camp, which was sited to the east of the road in the angle formed by it and the canal, a post of observation being placed on a mound a short distance to the west. The spot chosen for their resting-place was artificially strong, and had the advantage of a plentiful supply of water close at hand. On three sides of it were bunds or artificial banks a few feet above the ground level, which served on the southern side to retain the Rustumiyah canal, a water-channel about ten feet broad, while on the east was an irrigation cut of lesser width. The protection on the third side, which bordered the road, consisted of a dry ditch with a low bank on both sides of it. Beyond this side to the west,

DISASTER TO MANCHESTER COLUMN

and making an acute angle with the road, outside the perimeter selected for the camp, runs a line of mounds, or what seem to be the remains of the bank of an ancient canal, of which all other traces have disappeared. From their highest point, about ten feet above the plain, they offer an extensive view in all directions; and as they dominate the site of the camp their occupation in case of a possible attack was an obvious precaution. Only the fourth side

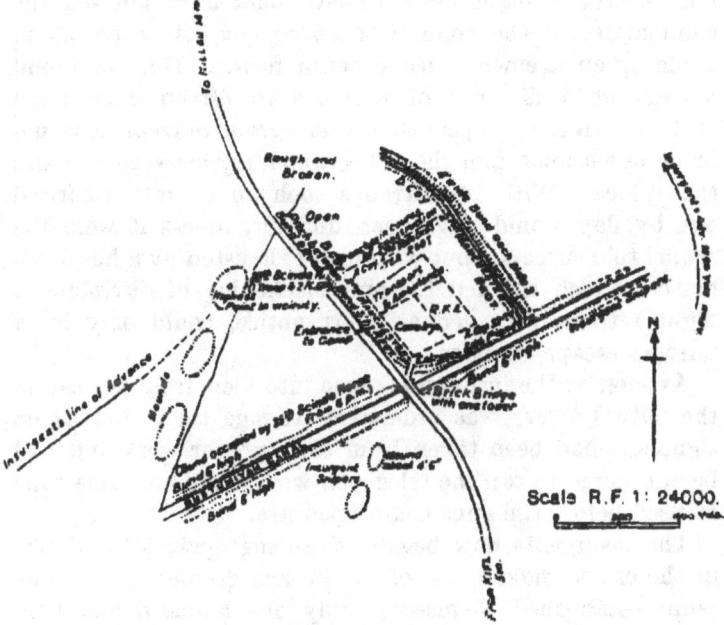

Fig. 3.—*Camp of Manchester Column, 24th July* 1920.

of the perimeter required attention, a work which was left till the cool of the evening.

The field of fire was good in all directions except on the northern side, where, owing to camel-thorn and the remains of disused irrigation channels, the ground becomes somewhat broken about three hundred yards from the trenches held by the troops.

At 5.45 P.M., when the work of digging trenches along the northern side had just begun, the reconnoitring cavalry reported that the insurgents were advancing from the direction of Kifl. The first information received gave the hostile numbers as ten thousand men, distant only two miles. A few minutes later these figures were modified to only five hundred, but it is probable that the actual number of tribesmen present did not exceed three thousand. An earlier and distant reconnaissance by the whole of the cavalry as far as Kifl, only five miles south of the camp, might have brought news which would have allowed the commander of the column to carry out his orders as to avoiding engagement with superior forces. He now found himself at a distance of fourteen to fifteen miles from Hillah, with the prospect that a retrograde movement would bring down upon him the tribes which lay between him and that place. With fresh troops such an operation carried out by day would have been difficult, unless it were the sequel to a success; but with men exhausted by a hot day's march, which had led to some slackening of discipline, a night retreat, arranged at short notice, could only by a miracle escape disaster.

As soon as the insurgents came into view from the camp, the 39th Battery was ordered to engage them, but as its signallers had been taken from their proper work and had been ordered to tap the telegraph wire to Hillah, some time elapsed before the guns could open fire.

The insurgents now began advancing against the flanks of the camp, making use of the broken ground, and at one point established themselves only one hundred and fifty yards from the perimeter.

At 7.50 P.M., while fire was being exchanged by both sides, the two Assistant Political Officers with the column informed Lieut.-Colonel Hardcastle that if the force remained where it was, all the Arabs between it and Hillah would have risen by the following day, and added that those who were now opposing them would continue to do so, while others would push on and capture Hillah. Neither the Political Officers nor the commander of the column was probably aware that within a few hours that place would be reinforced by troops from Diwaniyah,

Camp of Manchester Column from south-east of bridge looking towards mounds.

Birs Nimrud.

whence they were being moved northwards as rapidly as
railway conditions would permit. Their counsel, however,
had its effect, for a few minutes later, when it was nearly
dark, the several commanding officers were sent for, and the
situation was explained in the presence of the Political
Officers, who corroborated what was said, and emphasised
the necessity for an immediate retreat. The outcome of
the conference—or, as it might be more correctly called,
council of war—was that the force was ordered to withdraw
in half an hour. One company of the Manchester Regiment was to act as advanced guard with another on either
flank, so as to keep the tribesmen clear of the transport,
which was to be at the head of the column. In rear would
come the 39th Battery, escorted by the company of the
32nd Sikh Pioneers, and last of all, as rearguard, two
squadrons of the 35th Scinde Horse.

At 8.40 P.M. the leading company of the Manchester
Regiment moved off, and shortly after the transport,
which was close in rear, stampeded. A scene of great
confusion followed, the vehicles dashing through the troops,
who became scattered into small groups; while the Arabs,
making for the transport animals, cut down some of them
and their drivers with knives. By the gallant efforts of a
few, among whom was the adjutant of the regiment, Captain G. S. Henderson, an officer of well-known courage,
who lost his life and won a posthumous Victoria Cross, the
road was cleared, and the guns coming into action held
the Arabs off. But in the darkness and the general disorder
that prevailed a portion of the Manchester Regiment lost
its way, for the road, a little-used track, does not follow
the railway line, but twists and turns, and being overgrown with scrub, is only recognisable with difficulty after
sundown. Those who went astray fell into the hands of
the Arabs, some to be killed, while others who were made
prisoners were eventually released.

The heavy loss in horses due to the Arab fire greatly
impeded the action of the artillery and cavalry. The
former fought with their traditional courage in conditions the most difficult imaginable, and the 35th Scinde

Horse, keeping the insurgents at bay, guarded the rear, and helped by several charges to open the way for a withdrawal, which was successfully effected. The officers of the 39th Battery, more especially Lieutenant B. L. De Roebeck, who for his gallantry received the immediate reward of a bar to his Military Cross, and Major H. E. Connop of the 35th Scinde Horse, both of whose British squadron leaders were wounded, behaved like heroes, and it is to their fine example and the discipline of those under their command that a complete disaster was averted. Among other gallant soldiers who distinguished themselves during the events of this night were Sergeants Albert Victor Deering, D.C.M., and Earnest Hinxman of the artillery, and Sergeant John Willis, 2nd Battalion Manchester Regiment, the first winning a bar to the Distinguished Conduct Medal, and the other two the medal itself.

As might have been expected from the predictions of the Assistant Political Officers, the march of the remnant of the force to Hillah should have been hampered by the action of the tribes around that place. The Arabs, however, did not pursue to any distance, their attention being doubtless diverted by the thought of loot, and the troops reached Hillah on the 25th.

The night retreat which had ended so disastrously had cost us twenty killed, sixty wounded, and three hundred and eighteen missing, and many transport vehicles and animals. Of the three hundred and eighteen reported missing, only seventy-nine British and eighty-one Indians became prisoners with the Arabs. Of the former one died in captivity, while among the latter were a few Indian soldiers taken at Samawah and at other places. Thus the net loss in killed on the 24th was little short of two hundred. One gun, an 18-pr., fell into a deep canal during the night retreat, and, despite gallant efforts to recover it, had to be abandoned.

This unfortunate affair could not have occurred at a more inopportune moment. From the outset the prospect of any advantage being derived from sending out so small a force was more than doubtful. No one with the column had knowledge either of Arab warfare or the country, and it is probable that the commander did not fully appreciate the general situation and the rocks that lay ahead of him. If, as was apparently intended, the force was meant merely to show itself and avoid fighting, it was much too heavily burdened with transport, and moreover tents were carried. But apart from details, which sufficiently condemn the operation, the two main faults lay in the continued movement on the 24th towards Kifl and the night retreat, which was doomed to bring disaster in its train.

CHAPTER XI.

ALARUMS AND EXCURSIONS.

SUNDAY, the 25th July 1920, was a day I shall not easily forget. I had been out early, and on my return about 8 A.M., Brigadier-General J. H. K. Stewart, who lived next door, came to see me. This officer, who was the senior General Staff representative at General Headquarters, had passed some four years in Mesopotamia, and his intimate knowledge of the country and its inhabitants, his sound judgment and good sense, were particularly valuable to me during the Arab rising. He produced a telegram to the effect that the detachment of the Manchester Regiment and other troops had been engaged and had been routed; and a little later news came that the remnant had arrived at Hillah, where an attack was thought to be imminent. It was clear that the occurrence on the Kifl road would have a marked effect everywhere on the situation; and as the telegram announcing the disaster had unfortunately not come from Hillah in cipher, wildly exaggerated statements, which it was impossible to discount, were soon flying broadcast about Baghdad. The news was followed in due course by the information that all tribes in the vicinity of Hillah had risen, as well as others whose hostility would add to the insecurity of the railway line to Diwaniyah.

I had already decided to withdraw the troops from the latter place, as a report had reached me that the Rumaithah shaikhs, who had shown indications of submitting, had come under the influence of the Shamiyah tribes who had broken out on the 14th. It appeared therefore neither necessary nor desirable to hold Diwaniyah any longer. At that place, as already stated, were assembled practically all the troops available for active operations, and the urgent need for concentrating at Hillah, fifty-three miles to the north, without losing a moment, was now stronger than ever.

I directed Major-General Leslie, who had proposed coming to see me at Baghdad regarding the intended operation towards Kufah, to proceed at once to Hillah and organise the defence of that place. I also reiterated the orders regarding the rapid concentration there of all troops from the south, and directed the Jarbuiyah bridge over the Hillah branch of the Euphrates, a post of vital importance on the railway line, to be made specially secure.

On the 15th July, in order to be in a position to add still further to my reserve, I had warned the troops on the Upper Euphrates to be prepared at short notice to assemble at Fallujah, where they would be within reach if required. Our forces in that area were, comparatively speaking, small, but as they included a cavalry regiment—the 5th Cavalry—and, owing to the lengthy line of communication, a considerable amount of transport, the question of forage for the animals was growing serious. Indeed the situation was rapidly becoming such that a decision would have to be taken between an investment on the one hand and a forced retreat to Baghdad on the other. Needless to say, either of these alternatives would have had the worst possible effect throughout the country. Fortunately at this juncture an arrangement was come to with the Dulaim tribe, whereby their head, Shaikh Ali Sulaiman, in return for a subsidy, undertook to garrison Hit until such time as it could be reoccupied. Both he and Fahad Beg ibn Hadhdhal, Shaikh of the Anizah, as well as his son Mahrut, stood loyal to the Government throughout the insurrection, and later on received rewards for their good services at so critical a time. Our troops, thus assisted, remained at Ramadi and Fallujah, care being taken that they were provided with sufficient supplies to maintain themselves for several weeks in case of interruptions on their line of communication.

I may here add that it has recently come to my knowledge that the Muntafiq confederation had their eyes glued to what was going on in the Dulaim area, and had the latter tribe wavered for a moment in its allegiance, nothing could have prevented the former, who, like the sword of Damocles, hung over me for many weeks, from throwing their formidable weight on the side of the insurrectionists. Had this occurred, Baghdad might easily have become a besieged city. Moreover, an outbreak of the Muntafiq would probably have induced two other important tribes—the Bani Lam and Bani Rabia—to rise; and as these border the Tigris, my last and only line of communication would have been imperilled. The great service rendered by Ali Sulaiman in rallying his tribes to the British and so warding off a danger, the extent of which it is difficult to measure, has been neither forgotten nor unrequited. His firm attitude was maintained in the face of many of his relations and adherents, who were bitterly opposed to the policy which his foresight and the wise counsel of the local Political Officer, Major Eadie, led him to pursue, and for several months his life was in imminent danger.

The general situation at this time was so menacing that on the 26th July, in addition to the ten battalions which were understood to be coming as reinforcements from India, I pointed out to the War Office that a second division might be required; and on the 30th added that it should be mobilised. Following this request, it may here be stated that at later dates, as the situation continued to develop in an unfavourable manner, I asked for and was furnished with three British and seven Indian battalions. Besides these troops, a battery of horse artillery, a brigade of field artillery, five companies of engineers, some medical and other units, and an Air Force Squadron were added to my force (see Appendix XI.).

The total combatant troops of all arms which came from overseas were as follows:—

        British officers, 323.   British other ranks, 3093.
        Indian officers, 302.   Indian other ranks, 13,200.

ALARUMS AND EXCURSIONS

and of auxiliary services :—

    British officers, 46.   British other ranks, 107.
    Indian officers, 40.   Indian other ranks, 4094.

As it has been stated in public more than once that two divisions were sent as reinforcements to Mesopotamia to assist in dealing with the rising, I take this opportunity of pointing out that the war establishment of a division in Mesopotamia at the beginning of the insurrection was as follows :—

    British officers, 386.   British other ranks, 3376.
    Indian officers, 278.   Indian other ranks, 13,636.

or a grand total of 17,676. Thus the figures which represented the strength of a *single* division were only 3529 less than the reinforcements—the so-called *two* divisions—sent to join my force. It is only fair to add, however, that drafts from India to bring up to strength some of my weak units arrived as follows :—

    British officers, 587.   British other ranks, 723.
    Indian officers, 127.   Indian other ranks, 6745.

This last set of figures represents little more than the normal reinforcements to replace wastage and casualties, and moreover, it includes a considerable number of officers and men who were recalled from leave.

I should add that the Government of India accepted the patriotic offer of Lieut.-Colonel His Highness The Maharaja Sir Jagatjit Singh Bahadur of Kapurthala to furnish a battalion of Imperial Service infantry, which did useful service in sharing with other troops the responsibility of guarding the Base, and later joined in the field operations.

On the 26th July the Commander-in-Chief in India telegraphed offering to relieve me of a considerable number of Turkish prisoners—an offer which, subject to War Office approval, I gladly accepted. Eventually these prisoners were shipped direct from Basrah to Constantinople, the last contingent sailing on the 15th August. In order to ensure the safe custody of these prisoners, who were distributed in several localities as working parties, the greater part of a brigade of infantry had been absorbed, but by concentrating them a reduction in strength was effected.

I now decided to dispense entirely with regular guards and replace them with armed labour. Gradually the Director of Labour, Colonel F. B. Frost, to whose energy the credit for the execution of the scheme is due, trained some two thousand five hundred volunteers from Indian Labour Corps, a few of whom had had military experience. These men were regularly attested for a period of six months, and when not required for guarding prisoners, did useful service in certain blockhouses on the lines of communication and in guarding depots and other establishments.

I should here draw attention to the fact that the existence under the Military Authorities of Labour Corps was due to the inability of the civil administration to obtain coolies from India, owing to certain objections made by the Indian Government, which were not pressed where the army was concerned. The introduction of Indian labour had been found necessary during the earlier fighting in Mesopotamia, owing to the scarcity and quality of local labour, and for other reasons. In July 1920 in Mesopotamia and Persia, coolies—Indian, Persian, Kurd, and Arab,— amounting in numbers to thirty-four thousand, were employed by the Mesopotamian Expeditionary Force, and these carried out such work as building, road-making, loading and unloading stores. As labourers the Kurds excelled, while as stevedores, as a whole, they would be difficult to rival. It is a common practice for a Kurdish porter to carry a weight of six maunds (480 lb.) and even eight on his back, and the output, in a loading or unloading sense, of a single man in an eight hours' day will amount to from four to ten tons. But even these figures, in a country where Trades Unions are as yet unknown, are sometimes exceeded by Arabs, who have been known to handle as much as twelve tons in a day.

But such cases are exceptional, and the Arab, being of a scheming nature, will, if allowed, do as little work as possible. The Indian, as a rule, is easier to handle, but as he lacks the sense of humour, which is highly developed in the Kurd and Arab, it is more difficult to rouse his enthusiasm for his work. Moreover, his want of stamina finds him a tired man when his day's work is done. On the other hand, the Arab will, when the hour for relaxation comes, be eager to take part in a looting expedition, while the Kurd will be as ready for the *chasse aux dames*.

As regards the state of our river defence, at the outbreak of hostilities there were four defence vessels in commission, fully armed and manned. Two of them were on the Tigris, one on the Lower and one on the Upper Euphrates. In addition, there were several vessels of similar type, three of which were used for towing on the Tigris and one on the Upper Euphrates, besides three laid up out of commission. On the 26th July I ordered these vessels to be mobilised, when it was brought to my notice that, except the four first-mentioned vessels, none of the remainder would be fit for service until they had been armed and their more vulnerable parts protected. With the exception of the vessel on the Upper Euphrates, where no dockyard for repairs existed, the remaining six were fitted out and provided with a 12-pr. gun, most of them also with a 3-pr. gun as well, and several machine-guns.

On the 27th, Commander C. H. Jones, who was passing through Baghdad on his way from Persia, offered me his services, subject to Admiralty approval, which was soon forthcoming, and I placed him in charge of the Mesopotamian Floating Defences. I desired him to arrange at once for the policing of that portion of the river which runs from Kadhimain, five and a half miles north of Baghdad, to Khirr Depot, which is the same distance below the capital. Both of these places are nearer to the centre of Baghdad by road than by river, but the Tigris has few straight reaches, and twists and turns to such an extent that distances along its banks are fully double those drawn from point to point. Baghdad was at this time undefended, and it was important to have an examination service after dark to control movements from one bank to the other, except by the Maude bridge, which was guarded. By the aid of several motor bellums and other craft, which were manned chiefly by machine-gunners of the 1st Battalion Rifle Brigade, this service was established, and remained in operation until the exterior situation had greatly altered for the better. A little later two other naval officers, Lieutenants Onslow and Cavendish, who were on their way home after serving in Persia under Commodore Norris, came under the orders of Commander Jones, and the trio relieved me of the task of closely supervising the floating defences of the country.

The Capital itself was the cause of some concern to me at this time. At Baghdad and Basrah, unlike India, where at military stations the European quarters are concentrated and comparatively simple to defend, there is no sanctuary for the white population, whose dwelling-places are fixed according to the dictates of their individual tastes, or, as more often happens, to the available accommodation. In order to protect in some degree the European inhabitants from an internal rising, a defence scheme had been in existence for some time which, by request of the Military Governor, could be put into operation at short notice; but to secure the city and its environs from external aggression was a far more difficult problem. Its inhabitants were known to number about two hundred thousand, many of whom were more or less disaffected, and were only waiting encouragement from outside to rise.

The problem, however, did not end there. Protection was essential for the Citadel, which is situated on the north side of the town, and which was in a somewhat dilapidated condition.

This ancient walled enclosure is unworthy of the sounding name of Citadel, for in 1920 it possessed no feature which resembled a work of such a nature beyond the remains of a ditch on its northern front, which was largely filled with rubbish, and here and there in its walls a few loopholes for rifle fire. It had been selected at the time of our occupation of Baghdad as a suitable place in which to store the greater part of the considerable quantities of gun and small-arm ammunition held in the country, as well as re-

serves of arms, and stores and workshops of all kinds.
No doubt it owed its selection to the great cost of constructing fireproof sheds elsewhere, and the impossibility of deciding where to build those sheds until the policy regarding the strength and location of the Mesopotamian garrison was settled. Owing to thefts of small-arm ammunition which had occurred, and the investigations regarding them which had been made, I was familiar with the Citadel. Its interior was overlooked on the east by minarets and houses at less than fifty yards' range, and it was situated several miles, and on the opposite side of the town, from the Baghdad garrison. Bricks, mortar, barbed-wire and canvas screens soon made the place reasonably secure and difficult of access, except through the open gates; and a garrison, which I could ill spare, under Major R. S. Hunt, 1st King's Dragoon Guards, who had served with me as a battalion commander in France, was given the task of holding it against attack.

But besides the Citadel there was a large number of establishments, such as depots and stores of all kinds (some highly inflammable), workshops, hospitals, railway stations, rolling-stock, a large electrical-power station, water-pumping station, and a military dairy. These establishments, which seemed to have been planted, as also at Basrah, on no considered plan, and more on the principle of a jungle than a garden, had sprung up and spread themselves over acres of ground, some of them at a considerable distance from the encampments of the troops, and actually in the middle of a town with a potentially hostile population. To attempt to concentrate them would have cost much time and money, but to protect them one and all was now essential.

In view of the reduction in the strength of the Mesopotamian Expeditionary Force, which it was proposed to effect towards the end of the year, the impossibility of sparing sufficient troops to guard the important military centre of Baghdad, and the necessity for economy, I had decided to take no steps in the matter beyond settling in my own mind, in general terms, how I would deal with the problem should the necessity to do so arise. I had, however, soon after I assumed command, ordered the aerodrome, which is situated on the opposite side of the river to that on which the troops were camped, and which covered a large space of ground, to be provided with suitable defences and guards, and it was owing to this precaution that an attempt, which I mentioned earlier, to burn down the sheds after the insurrection had begun, failed.

On the 26th and 27th July, accompanied by my Chief Engineer, Major-General E. H. de V. Atkinson, I fixed upon the approximate sites for a series of earthworks round the city. By the middle of August, thanks in great part to the tireless energy of Lieut.-Colonel A. V. Carey, Director of Military and Public Works, some forty brick blockhouses, which replaced the earthworks that had been constructed at short notice, had sprung up on a perimeter of sixteen miles, and as material became available the whole was enclosed by a continuous and formidable wire obstacle. Besides blockhouses round Baghdad others were built in the town to guard particularly vulnerable points such as bridges. The blockhouse system had a marked effect on the demeanour of the inhabitants, and served to diminish crime, not only in the city itself but in its immediate vicinity. Moreover, instead of requiring several battalions for the defence of the place, I was able to reduce the garrison considerably, and spare more troops for active operations.

In order as much as possible to restrict the area enclosed by the blockhouses, I terminated the tenancy of the Daurah cantonment, which was situated on the right bank of the Tigris some twelve miles below Baghdad, and opposite that at Hinaidi ; and in forty-eight hours shifted the many thousands of tons of stores there, ordnance and other, to safer quarters within the defended area.

The original idea as regards the quartering of the troops at Baghdad had been to purchase ground and construct cantonments at Chaldari, which site lies a few miles north of the city. Here were to be lodged an infantry division, a cavalry brigade, and army troops. In January 1919

Blockhouse No. 19, Baghdad.

Typical Mesopotamian scenery (one mile east of Baghdad).

the cost of the scheme, as put forward from Mesopotamia, lay between six and eight millions sterling, of which sum it was proposed during that year to expend one million pounds, an amount which, so far as I have been able to determine, did not include the price of the land to be acquired. Three months later a change of commanders led to a change of policy, and a proposal was brought forward to transfer the projected cantonment at Chaldari to sites south of the capital. Hinaidi, it was stated in the letter which explained the proposed change, would be better than Chaldari for many reasons, one of which was that at the latter place "all amenities of life would be tinged with the gloom of the circle of embankments," twelve feet high at least, which, on account of the rise of the river at certain seasons, would be necessary for the protection of the cantonment against flooding.

Thus it came about that, though no money had as yet been granted for the purchase of land, Daurah was in military occupation, and such troops as were quartered there were under canvas.

Both Daurah and Hinaidi had, prior to my arrival in Mesopotamia, been laid out in a manner which vividly recalled to my mind the ground plan of New Delhi, a city in embryo which I had the advantage of seeing in company with its distinguished designer. Wide avenues for motor-driven vehicles, bordered by narrower roads for transport carts and equestrians, formed part of the grandiose design, and in order to carry the power necessary for illuminating the roads, lighting the barracks, and working a tramway line, a tall row of steel standards would eventually spring up along the centre of the main approach. At intervals the straight line of these approaches was broken by circles which, if less spacious than the great *rond point* on which the Arc de Triomphe de l'Étoile at Paris stands, clearly betray a source whence the architect may have drawn his inspiration. In one of these circles it was proposed to erect a statue of Lieut.-General Sir Stanley Maude; and for others a cathedral and campanile with a peal of bells, a club and a soldiers' institute were planned. Although the whole scheme did credit to the imagination of its author, I trembled to think what, leaving everything else out of consideration, the metal alone necessary for the roads, which cover many miles and bear high-sounding names, would have cost the long-suffering British taxpayer.

Both of the projected cantonments are dreary, dusty, or muddy according to the season, and distant from human habitation; and from the point of view of amenities, for which they were to some extent chosen, seem to possess no advantage over Chaldari. It is true that in the proximity of Daurah, on the river front, there are some date-palm plantations, but beyond these there is nothing which is restful to the eye. The same remark might be applied to almost any part of Mesopotamia, for shade and grass, as we know them at home, are things almost non-existent. In course of time, however, when those same streets and avenues, fatiguing in their straightness, might be expected to be metalled and even shaded by the numerous but sickly saplings which at present border them, it is possible by a considerable stretch of the imagination to conjure up a picture less desolate and uninviting than in those regions now presents itself.

The price of the land at Daurah, approximately £500,000, was in my opinion prohibitive, and I gladly seized the first excuse to hand it back to its owners; while as regards Hinaidi, by transferring the site for cantonments a few hundred yards southwards, the ground, which was to have cost at least £132,000, was secured for nothing.

Having settled the question of Daurah, I arranged for the bridge of boats which connected the two cantonments to be moved closer to Baghdad, so as to allow of the quick transfer of troops from one bank of the river to the other, and make it possible to avoid the long circuit through the town and across either of the existing bridges.

On the 27th July I recalled from leave all officers except such as had been in Mesopotamia for two continuous years. This involved eleven per cent of the officers under my command, and created some heart-burning, as several of them had only arrived back in England a few days before the order came for their recall. The Indian ranks, too, were ordered to rejoin. In a country so far distant as Mesopotamia, probably the most remote of all our foreign garrisons, the replacement of officers, staff or other, or those who may be sick, absent or otherwise non-effective, is a lengthy process; and with the prospect of large reinforcements coming from India which would make heavy demands on the staff, and the weakness of my own units, to have delayed a day longer to recall the absent would have been unwise.

At this time I took certain steps to impress the inhabitants of Baghdad and the vicinity. These consisted in marching through the city and beyond from time to time variously composed contingents of troops, and in the despatch of small mounted columns in several directions to overawe marauding villagers. The Arab, as I mentioned earlier, is prone to exaggerate anything he sees; and as the city was frequented by visitors from without, I hoped by this procedure, which smacked of the stage with its reappearing supers, to engender and disseminate the belief that our forces were not so depleted as in reality they were. As the internal condition of the city was not satisfactory, military courts were established and proclamations issued prohibiting the holding of seditious meetings, and restricting movement in the streets after dark.

The position of Baghdad both within and from without, prior to the construction of defences, was highly dangerous. As I walked or drove daily through the principal street, accompanied by my British or Indian aide-de-camp, I could see scowls on the faces of the numerous truculent-looking Arabs, whose custom it is to sit on benches and drink coffee in front of the refreshment shops while discussing business, or more probably retailing to one another the latest news or gossip. With an assumed air of indifference or perhaps a smile on my face, I would look fixedly at them, when I generally noticed many nervously toying with the beads of the rosary which seems to be the habitual accompaniment of the mass of the Muhammadans of Iraq.

As the townsmen were in close touch with the leaders of the insurrection outside, and as combined action was far from improbable, I issued orders on the 26th July for the 53rd Infantry Brigade, less the 1/3rd Gurkha Rifles who were at Baiji on the line of communication to Mosul, to be sent to the Capital forthwith, where, as a general reserve, it would be more suitably placed.

I have referred before to the effect of moving troops from localities where the inhabitants had been accustomed to see them, and the danger of disturbance to which such a course was apt to lead. But the risk had to be accepted, as, with no prospect of reinforcements for some time to come, troops to keep in check the insurrection and prevent it from becoming general must be found. It was with some misgivings that I had almost stripped of guards the railway line to Shergat, for, should the rising spread to the tribes north of Baghdad or raids on the railway such as had occurred in May be repeated, the troops at Mosul would be cut off and left with supplies only sufficient to last for a few weeks. There was no prospect of my having sufficient troops with which to effect the relief of the Mosul garrison in the event of its being cut off, and to withdraw that force to Baghdad and so add to my reserve would have been an operation of such difficulty, and would have required so many troops to effect it, that, even if for military and political reasons it had been desirable, it could not be seriously contemplated. That this was so is due to the fact that from Shergat, some seventy miles south of Mosul, to Baiji, fifty-three miles nearer Baghdad, the railway and road beside it run at a distance of some miles west of the Tigris, from which they are separated by the Jabal Hamrin range, and pass through a waterless district. Unless therefore the railway be strongly guarded, troops cannot travel by that route, while along the river at the time of the insurrection there was no road suitable for wheeled traffic. This omission, I may mention here, has since been rectified, and a good motor road now runs from Baiji to Shergat. Not the least of the advantages of this alternative route from Mosul is that, between that place and Fathah on the Tigris at the southern end of the Jabal Hamrin, the population is sparse, and the colonies of Jubur tribesmen, which are scattered along both sides of the river, number only five hundred rifles on the right bank and three hundred on the left, and moreover are not likely to give trouble.

My readers will readily appreciate the nature of the situation in which we now stood. With long and easily assailable lines of communication, to guard which adequately troops were not available ; with garrisons scattered about the country and in possession of only small stocks of supplies, while the central force at Baghdad, when it arrived there, would suffice for little more than to defend that place, there was room for much anxiety. This situation had resulted from a too hasty reduction of the force after the Armistice, while the tribes were still dangerous and an unknown factor ; and I draw attention to it in order to furnish myself with an opportunity of laying stress on the fact that that situation was saved through the resolution and endurance of the troops under my command.

The supply situation at this time was one on which much depended, and in regulating which I was ably helped by Brigadier-General Hambro, who had a most efficient assistant in Colonel H. G. Burrard, who had only recently arrived in Mesopotamia, but had quickly grasped the difficult problem before him. Although a total of sixty days' supplies, which, during the insurrection was increased by War Office authority to seventy-five, was held for the whole force in Mesopotamia, each garrison or small detachment was not of course in possession of that quantity. It was now necessary to add as quickly as possible to the supplies at those places where a shortage, through the rupture of communications, was most likely to occur. This involved the reduction of the reserves maintained at Basrah and Baghdad to a low level, and at the last of these centres there was always the possibility of the inhabitants being thrown on my hands for their daily food. Orders were issued that at Mosul and Kirkuk, or wherever food and forage could be purchased, advantage should be taken of local resources to build up further supplies that would enable the garrisons to hold out for not less than six months. I was determined that there should be no repetition of the Kut episode, even on the smallest scale, and thanks to my administrative staff and the energy of those who effected the delivery of supplies, no garrison had to undergo the risk of almost certain death which a surrender would have carried with it, although one at least among the many that were besieged was forced to await relief for over eighty days.

Under normal conditions it takes a considerable time to replenish reserves of supplies, but in the situation that obtained the difficulty was increased by several factors :—

(a) The necessity of having to dispense with the Euphrates valley railway line from Basrah to Baghdad and rely solely on the river route to Kut, and thence by rail to Baghdad, involved an almost radical change in the supply arrangements. The small Supply Depot at Kut was suddenly called upon to deal with nine hundred tons a day. Barges had to be rapidly off-loaded there and the supplies transferred to trucks, which were not available on the single-line railway to the Capital in numbers sufficient to carry all that was required. On account of the low water at this time of year in certain reaches above Kut, even if the barges could be spared to proceed to Baghdad, they could not, owing to the question of draught, have taken full loads ; and to have despatched them up-stream with reduced cargoes would have been false economy.

(b) The daily feeding strength was suddenly increased by the arrival of large reinforcements, so that for a short period in September the reserves decreased, as the supplies being brought up river were not sufficient for the daily maintenance of the troops, and the truckage available could not cope with the required tonnage.

(c) The failure of the supplies normally purchased locally in affected areas, especially such bulky items as wood and forage, brought an additional strain on the carrying capacity of the barges and trucks. Not only had the consumption risen through the increased strength of the force, but the deficiency from the failure of local resources had to be made good from the Base.

(d) The movement of troops, ammunition, and important stores had to be given priority over everything else, so that, even though the supplies were at the Base ready to be transferred, several days' delay sometimes occurred in bringing them up-country.

Indeed if the Kut line had been interrupted during August and September the supply situation in Baghdad would have been critical; and yet for several months I was compelled to leave that line wholly unprotected.

Closely connected with the question of supply was another important matter. The main artery to Baghdad is the river Tigris, on which, as just mentioned, the feeding of the force depended directly the Euphrates line was cut. On this river plied the vessels of the Inland Water Transport, a great organisation built up for the supply of the forces which were kept at Baghdad and elsewhere in Mesopotamia. Could the safety of the railway line from Basrah to Baghdad have been guaranteed the reduction of this fleet of vessels—including several Thames penny steamboats which had made the adventurous voyage to Basrah —might for supply purposes have been dispensed with. But as was exemplified by the early cutting of the Euphrates valley railway, the Inland Water Transport, as Brigadier-General Hambro graphically put the matter to me, was " as essential to the Army as the Navy was to England." Indeed, if the safety of the hundred-mile-long railway line from Kut to Baghdad could not be ensured, it would be necessary to double the carrying power of the fleet, as the distance between these places by river is more than twice that by rail. In June 1920 this fleet, the personnel of which two years earlier had attained the huge figures of 799 officers and 42,169 other ranks, was carrying 316 tons per diem from Basrah to Kut and beyond, but under its able head, Brigadier-General R. H. W. Hughes, these figures, to meet the requirements of the additional troops coming to Mesopotamia, swelled to 590 per diem in July, 750 in August, and 878 tons in September. In addition to this tonnage, supplies of coal and oil fuel amounting to 400 tons, figures which include the requirements of the fleet itself, were borne daily on its barges. That this was possible was due to the opposition which was made soon after my arrival in Mesopotamia to the early sale of the vessels, at what were undoubtedly ruinously low prices, and I shall not readily forget the foresight of my adviser in the matter.

Before leaving the question of river transport, I must say a few words regarding the two main rivers of the country, for the water supply of the Euphrates and Tigris is one which gravely affected the administrative services of the army. Of these two rivers the Euphrates as a waterway for military purposes is negligible. I had been led to suppose that such places on its banks as Rumaithah and Samawah could be reached without difficulty by small steamers towing barges. As regards the first of these places, I had hoped to use, on the left flank of the force allotted to relieve it, one of the defence vessels from the Upper Euphrates. I found, however, that the information given me on the subject was incorrect, and that, on account of the various earth-dams laid across or partly across the stream, the project was impossible. Later on I was to find that, in the event of the inhabitants being hostile, the enclosed nature of the banks of the Euphrates, which is bordered in many places by groves of date-palms and other fruit trees, would make movement on the river, unless supported by troops on shore, who would have to fight their way through enclosed country, so difficult as to be out of the question. In fact the Euphrates has almost ceased to be a channel of commerce except for that carried on by small boats, and has become a great canal-like river, whose purpose is to furnish the necessary irrigation for the country near its banks.

On the other hand, the Tigris still serves as the main waterway of the country, and even when it is at its lowest, the narrowing of the channel causes the water to scour the silt which collects at the bottom and so maintains a depth sufficient for steamers having a draft of from three

to six feet. Yet in 1920 its waters fell to an abnormally
low level, and for some time I felt anxiety as to its carrying
capacity, for the narrowing of the channel by shifting
shoals and sandbanks made towage difficult, and caused
numerous vessels to run aground. But apart from that
feature of the river, its safety as a line of communication
is greatly diminished by the fact that, except during the
flood season—between January and June—its banks
usually overlook the stream by from twenty to twenty-
five feet, and at the curves of the river the channel for
steamers closely hugs the side. This would allow of ill-
disposed persons living on its banks firing on vessels as
they proceeded up or down, and as not one of our steamers
was bullet-proof, the transport of troops on barges would
have led to serious loss. Moreover, at the very season when
the river is at its lowest the tribes are most prone to give
trouble. But besides the chance of loss of life, even the
carriage of supplies would be precarious, as ships, liable to
be riddled by bullets and have their cargoes water-logged,
would in time founder, apart from the danger that their
personnel would run. In this respect the most dangerous
portion of the river is that known as the Narrows, which
extend for a distance of twenty-eight miles between Qalat
Salih and Ozier or Ezrah's Tomb. Between these places
the country on both sides is a swamp, and the whole region
is known as the Marshes. Navigation is difficult owing
to the shallow and sharp bends and shoals, which are liable
to change their size and situation. Fortunately in 1920,
although reports of possible trouble from tribes camped
along the banks were not infrequent, nothing beyond the
waywardness of the river occurred to interfere with navigation. On some sections of the river the pacific attitude
of the inhabitants was, it is believed, due to the fact that
they had realised that to join hands with the insurgents
meant the loss of all water for their flocks, which thus
would become hostages for the good behaviour of their
owners.

I will conclude this chapter of digressions by referring
to an incident which occurred on the 3rd August, and

which capped the various reports which came in from almost every quarter. Shortly after noon on that date volumes of black smoke, interspersed with flames, began to issue from a series of buildings on the right bank of the Tigris a little up-stream from General Headquarters. Which particular buildings were on fire no one for the moment could identify, but word soon came that the Advanced Mechanical Transport Depot, where almost all requirements for motor-cars and mechanical vehicles of all kinds were stored, was seriously involved. The inflammable nature of the contents was such that I question if even the presence of the London Fire Brigade could have done more than prevent the flames from spreading to the adjacent houses. By the efforts of their Baghdad prototype, aided by a river float, the fire was at length got under, when it was found, as had been anticipated, that all stores in the building had been destroyed.

How the conflagration arose was never ascertained, though searching inquiries were instituted by the military and police. It seems that the labourers, Indian and Arab, who were employed in the depot, where there were in force strict fire regulations, had left the building at noon, at which time nothing unusual had been noticed. A quarter of an hour later an officer, on entering the depot, observed smoke issuing from three sheds, and from the rapidity with which the fire, which had then taken a firm grip of its surroundings beyond possibility of extinction, spread, foul play was suspected.

The actual loss was a serious matter, as it threatened to paralyse all movement except by horsed vehicle, rail, or river. Fortunately some small consignments of mechanical transport stores had then arrived at Basrah, and a portion on its way to Baghdad had reached Kut ; so that with the exercise of the most rigid economy, the dangerous period was bridged over until replacements could arrive from overseas.

This fire, which had occurred in spite of careful preventative measures, so necessary in a country where rain does not fall for six consecutive months and the scorching

The Fire of 3rd August—Baghdad.

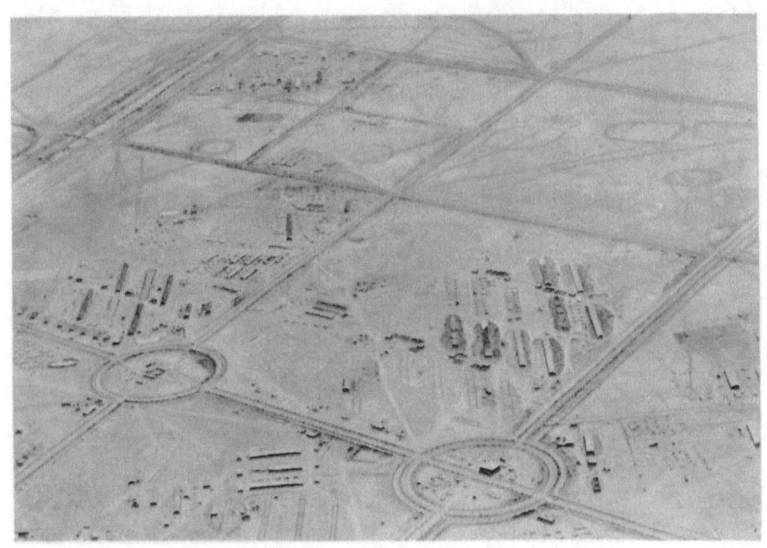

Part of Hinaidi Cantonment, looking east.

rays of the sun turn wood to tinder, was followed by attempts of incendiaries against the Supply Depots, which were frustrated. It is probable that such acts, which created a feeling of insecurity that lasted for some time, were instigated by the insurgent leaders; but when they proved to be unsuccessful they ceased. The golden rule of never keeping all one's eggs in the same basket was now more strictly observed, but an increased number of guards inevitably followed the greater distribution of stores.

A further precaution consisted in discharging all Arab labourers from Government employment throughout the country, and this, though it bore hardly on the majority, served as a warning which probably bore fruit. Shortly afterwards it was found necessary to re-employ skilled Arab labour, and in due course all Arabs were allowed to resume their work under the Government.

CHAPTER XII.

THE OPERATIONS AT HILLAH.

THE effect of the reverse of the 24th July soon made itself felt at Hillah, but fortunately not until the defences of the place were put in order. So far the number of tribesmen who had risen had increased to 85,000 armed men, of whom rather less than half carried serviceable rifles, of which one in ten was a modern small-bore weapon. Others now hastened to join the insurrectionary forces, and by the 30th August, when all who wished or had been forced to take up arms had done so, the numbers with which we had to deal were as follows :—

Armed men, 131,020.   Modern rifles, 59,805.

It must, however, be understood that the number of armed men does not actually represent those in the field, but the total strength of tribesmen who took part in the insurrection, all of whom, if not possessing modern rifles, carried old but serviceable weapons of that type.

The difficulty of keeping under arms a conglomeration of different tribesmen, even though bound together in some degree by religious feelings, must have been great, and so far as is known it was effected by the following means :—

The shaikhs were given glowing accounts of the assistance in arms and money which Turkey was said to have promised, and some of the more wealthy among them, as well as the saiyids,[1] provided cash for the upkeep of the *harbiyahs* or armies, and for the necessary purchases of arms and ammunition.

[1] Reputed descendants of the Prophet.

But the funds which were required came mainly, if not entirely, from Iraq, where every available means of raising them was resorted to by the insurgents. Some of the methods employed were the following :—

(a) After the political evacuation of a district the tax-farmers were summoned by the shaikhs and forced to surrender all taxes which had been collected. Thus Karbala alone handed over Rs. 70,000 (£8700 at this time).

(b) All existing tolls continued to be strictly enforced, and in many cases payment was accepted in kind in lieu of money.

(c) A heavy tax was placed on cereals carried to Najaf for the consumption of the populace, which exceeded 30,000.

(d) Public subscriptions were opened in various towns, and the Ulama of Karbala and Najaf exhorted the populace to contribute for religious and patriotic reasons.

Sometimes, when engaged at a distance from their homes, tribesmen received one rupee per day for subsistence. But this expenditure put too heavy a strain on the war-chest to last for long, and in certain cases the insurgents were fed by the inhabitants of that part of the country in which they happened to be operating.

We must now turn again to Hillah, which is about three miles south of the ruins of Babylon, and stands among date gardens on both banks of the river, here about one hundred yards wide, and crossed by a bridge of fifteen boats. The main portion of the town is situated on the right bank, and was formerly surrounded by a brick wall, sixteen feet high, of which it is difficult now to find any trace. The population, which numbered 30,000 souls, had begun after the Manchester affair to show signs of restlessness. In consequence a proclamation was issued whereby their freedom of action and movement was restricted; and a perimeter, six miles in extent, which included the town, railway station, resources' wharf and aerodrome, was held. Outside the town and south of it, on the Kifl road, the 2nd Euphrates Levy, with whom was Major C. A. Boyle, 11th (K.E.O.) Lancers, Inspector-General of

Arab and Kurdish Levies, had been doing useful work, besides ensuring the safe retreat of a number of stragglers from the Manchester column. By 6 P.M. on the 25th July the 2nd Battalion Royal Irish Rifles had arrived by train from Diwaniyah, and the garrison of Hillah now consisted of the following troops :—

   32nd Lancers (two squadrons).
   35th Scinde Horse (two squadrons).
   39th Battery R.F.A.
   67th Company (2nd Q.V.O.) Sappers and Miners.
   2nd Battalion Manchester Regiment (240 rifles).
   2nd Battalion Royal Irish Rifles (350 rifles).
   8th Rajputs.
   108th Infantry (3 British officers and 154 men).
   2nd Euphrates Levy.

Of these troops the 32nd Lancers had been withdrawn on the 15th July from Kirkuk in order to take part in the operations.

On the 26th July the detachment of the 108th Infantry and a section of sappers and miners were sent to strengthen the garrison of Jarbuiyah bridge; and on the 28th the 131st (How.) Battery R.F.A., and the 116th Mahrattas (two companies) arrived from Diwaniyah. After the 28th, it will be remembered, the cutting of the line south of Jarbuiyah prevented the evacuation of the force at Diwaniyah until General Coningham himself brought it in.

As, after the action between Hillah and Kifl, it seemed unlikely that I should be in a position for many weeks to move any troops to or beyond Diwaniyah, I had ordered that place to be evacuated, but the post at Jarbuiyah bridge was to be maintained. That bridge, a wooden structure, would, I was informed, take months to repair if seriously damaged, and the retention and protection of it by a force, so small that it could be spared without affecting major operations, would show the tribes that a return in that direction was intended. Later, as will appear in the narrative, I was obliged by circumstances to give it up.

THE OPERATIONS AT HILLAH

On hearing that Hillah was now strongly garrisoned I felt no further anxiety for the place; and in order to keep the troops in good spirits, more especially after what had occurred to some of them on the 24th, I ordered the defence to be carried out with activity. Nothing particular happened there until the night of the 27th/28th July, when a feeble attack was made. Four nights later, on the 31st July/1st August, fortunately after the arrival of an ammunition train—the last train to get through from Baghdad for some weeks—a more serious effort was made by the insurgents.

During this attack, which had probably been arranged in collusion with the townspeople, the tribesmen, being repulsed on the northern face of the defences, which was on the right bank of the Hillah branch of the Euphrates, forced their way about 4 A.M. into the south end of the town, between a piquet of the 8th Rajputs and another of the Levy.

The latter piquet became enfiladed, and was forced to retire, which it did in good order, being taunted for fighting on the Government side by insurgents of the same tribes from which it was recruited. For a time heavy firing went on in the town, until a portion of the 8th Rajputs, under Colonel L. H. Abbott, came up, whereupon a counter-attack was made which led to the ejection of the intruders and the restoration of the situation.

To judge by the noise and shouting, which are the customary accompaniments of the martial efforts of the Arab tribesmen, the attack had been made in considerable strength, and it was later ascertained that the assailants were followed by a reserve which remained behind in the date gardens in readiness to exploit success. It was conjectured that the loss on the side of the Arabs must have been heavy, for, although like all semi-savages, they will run considerable risks in order to transport from the field all evidence of failure, one hundred and fifty-six dead were found. Our own loss was insignificant.

CHAPTER XIII.

THE RETREAT FROM DIWANIYAH.

MEANWHILE the concentration of troops at Hillah was in progress, an operation on the successful issue of which I felt that our tenure of Mesopotamia and with it our position in North-West Persia hung. The necessity for avoiding delay had been expressly laid down, and had been conveyed in private communications, verbally, and by several telegrams to the G.O.C. 17th Division. I was prepared to sacrifice practically everything at Diwaniyah except those supplies which would be necessary for the force during its march to Hillah, and the ammunition, which could not be left behind. My anxiety to avoid the least delay was natural, and was due not only to the necessity for concentrating at Hillah, but to the danger which the troops might run through the marked predilection which the insurgents were showing everywhere for the destruction of railways. To have moved Brigadier-General Coningham's troops without the aid of the railway would have been impossible for the following reasons. The available road transport was quite insufficient to carry six days' rations for the whole force, which included 1120 railway personnel; while water amounting to 23,000 gallons, the sick, and a large quantity of ammunition, which would have filled three hundred carts and could not be abandoned to the Arabs, must be taken. Moreover, the lack of locomotives and rolling-stock due to the derailment of trains, and the temporary loss, for use between Baghdad and Diwaniyah, of everything of that description south of the latter place, was causing grave inconvenience in any troop or other movements which had to be carried out. Great as the task would be, it was within the bounds of possibility that the Arabs might tear up and damage the railway to such an extent that General Coningham's force might find itself marooned midway between Hillah and Diwaniyah, possibly at some waterless spot where the difficulty of further progress would, for much of it, be insuperable.

An axiom in war which I remember reading many years ago in Ropes's 'Waterloo Campaign' is that, "when there is any chance at all of the occurrence of an event which if it does happen will be fatal, it is folly to trust to the improbability of the case: every precaution should be taken; nothing that can avert a fatal calamity should be neglected, no matter how small may appear the chance of its happening." As the sequel will show, the event foreseen did actually occur, but fortunately not in so intense a form as it might have done.

Meantime more railway destruction had been going on south of Hillah through the activities of the Albu Sultan tribe, which had thrown in its lot with the insurgents; and on the 27th a train *en route* from Diwaniyah to Hillah, between which places six trains in all had been derailed, became isolated some twenty-eight miles north of the former place at Guchan station. An effort was made to reach it from Diwaniyah, but the construction train could not get through, and dropped food for the whole force at Khan Jadwal bridge post, which would be the halting-place at the end of the first day's march. Next day an attempt was again made to reach Guchan and bring the isolated train to Diwaniyah, where, owing to the mistake that had been made of pushing forward large quantities of ammunition and supplies, trucks were badly needed; but this again failed, though it was ascertained that the troops at the former place had with them rations for ten days.

On the same day Brigadier-General Coningham—who has since told me that had the urgent need for haste, which had been the feature of my telegrams on the subject of the move, been passed on to him, he could have marched several days earlier—received orders from the division directing him to withdraw to Hillah, bringing with him whatever he could load on the train which would accompany him.

Late at night he received my telegram, which ran, " Delay has jeopardised situation. Move at once with utmost rapidity consistent with preservation of order." This message had been repeated to his Divisional Commander.

At last the movement was on the point of beginning, and the withdrawal of the Assistant Political Officer, Captain W. F. Webb from Afaj—a small town on the Shatt-al-Dagharrah, near the remains of the ancient Sumerian city of Nippur—which was necessitated by the proposed evacuation of Diwaniyah, had been effected. On the 26th July it had come to his knowledge at his headquarters, which lay about twenty miles east of Diwaniyah, that a plot was being hatched to kidnap him and keep him as a hostage ; and on the same date, as I could not spare an aeroplane to bring him to Diwaniyah, he was ordered to make the best arrangements he could to escape. One of the messengers who carried the order to him was killed on the way, and the other arrived at 10 P.M. instead of 6 P.M. The head of the local police was ordered to get the ponies ready and arrange for an escort, but ten minutes later he sent the disquieting news that the five policemen, whom he had thought could be trusted, had deserted, and had informed the local shaikh of the intended departure of Captain Webb. Fortunately the ponies were quickly got ready and brought to Captain Webb's house, which was situated on the left bank of the river opposite the town, and which was later razed to the ground by the insurgents. No time was lost in making a start, for it was not possible for the refugee to carry any of his property with him in his flight. Information of the intended evasion had, however, probably through spies at Diwaniyah, reached certain tribesmen who purposed to waylay Captain Webb at the Yusufiyah canal ; but luckily before arriving there a man was met who disclosed the position of the ambush. Thus the Assistant Political Officer, who like others had pluckily

Diwaniyah and camp.

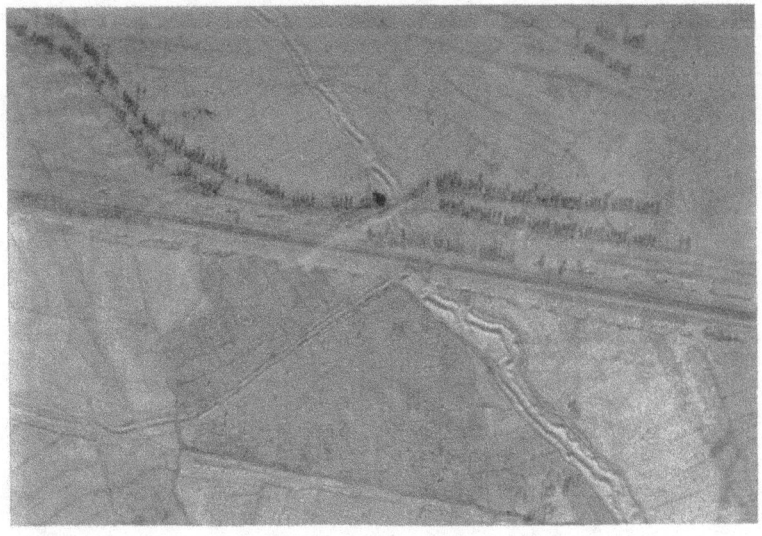

Brigadier-General Coningham's column between Ibn Ali and Guchan.

THE RETREAT FROM DIWANIYAH

remained at his post until the eleventh hour, succeeded in reaching Diwaniyah on the morning of the 27th.

On the 29th July truckage was allotted to each unit and department, besides the railway personnel and some thirteen Circassian and Armenian lady teachers; and a portion of the train was set apart as a hospital for sick and wounded. A few trucks with an engine were converted into a protected train carrying two armoured cars and two machine-guns, which was to accompany the rearguard of the force. By nightfall everything was completed, including the loading of six days' rations and as much water in tanks as could be carried.

The force under Brigadier-General Coningham was composed as follows :—

37th Lancers (two squadrons),
97th Battery R.F.A. (less one section),
131st (How.) Battery R.F.A.,
132nd (How.) Battery R.F.A. (one section),
45th Pack Battery,
61st Company, 2nd (Q.V.O.) Sappers and Miners,
45th (Rattray's) Sikhs,
87th Punjabis,
1/99th (Deccan) Infantry,
1/10th Gurkha Rifles,
and certain details.

It was reinforced as it proceeded north by the following troops :—

131st (How.) Battery R.F.A. (one section).
114th Mahrattas (one and a half companies).
1/116th Mahrattas (one company).
1/32 Sikh Pioneers (less one and a quarter companies).
108th Infantry (half a company).
86th Carnatic Infantry.

These troops were holding posts on the line of march, or were cut off in the isolated train at Guchan.

At 6.30 A.M. on the 30th the withdrawal from Diwaniyah began, at which hour two aeroplanes from Baghdad appeared and dropped bombs on some mounted Arabs. Some of the latter, about fifty in number, charged the protected train, not realising the sting which it carried in its tail, and few of these escaped alive. As the force moved off crowds of Arabs, keeping now at a respectful distance, showed themselves, and though a few of them fired into the column at intervals, no incident of importance occurred on this day's march. At 4.30 P.M. Khan Jadwal bridge was reached, and the force halted for the night.

So far the line had not been torn up, but on the 31st, soon after reaching Ibn Ali, after a march of nine miles, word was received that about one and a half miles further on there was a break of three hundred and fifty yards, and beyond that a badly-damaged bridge.

As the force moved north the difficulties increased daily, and on the 1st August the distance marched was only five miles. Hundreds of sleepers and many rails had to be removed by working parties from behind the rearmost train and carried forward to repair the gaps, a labour which, under the burning sun and frequent blinding duststorms, occupied many hours. Advantage was taken of the slow progress of the column to deal with several villages in the vicinity of the line, the inhabitants of which were known to be responsible for the damage. Some of these villages, those nearest the line, were burned, and others farther off were shelled. The work of repair was at this stage going on from two directions, as the isolated train at Guchan, from the vicinity of which the Arabs had cleared, was slowly working its way south.

By 8 A.M. on the 2nd August the two trains were only a mile apart, and under the able guidance of Major Lubbock of the railway staff numerous breaks, extending for a distance of four miles, were repaired, and the column with its trains reached Guchan at 4.30 P.M. Here the tanks were refilled, and early next day a force under Colonel M'Vean of the 45th Sikhs went forward, escorting a construction train which had orders to repair the line as far as possible towards the important Jarbuiyah bridge. Frequent reports of concentrations of Arabs reached General Coningham as he moved slowly northward, and though indications of an attack were seen, beyond some desultory fire, such as occurred daily and caused a few casualties, no engagement took place. Owing to the considerable number of tribesmen in the vicinity, Colonel M'Vean's column was ordered back, so that the whole force might be concentrated at night at Guchan; and to protect the now repaired line ahead during the hours of darkness, field and machine-guns were laid, and fired occasionally.

On the 4th the troops moved forward, the combined trains now covering a length of nearly a mile. The line beyond that part which had been repaired on the previous day was, as usual, greatly damaged, and, to add to the difficulties, the heaviest of the locomotives and some waggons left the track, and five and a half hours were required to replace them. The excessive heat and the rapidity with which the construction had necessarily to be carried out had caused the track to buckle, and so brought about the accident. The derailment of the engine proved to be more unfortunate than appeared at first sight, for the insurgents, taking advantage of the delay, tore up portions of the line ahead, which for a distance of some ten miles had not before been tampered with, and the advance of the column was consequently retarded by nearly forty-eight hours. Again advantage was taken of the delay to deal with the villages, and this day for the first time no casualties were suffered. Towards nightfall the force halted midway between Guchan and Jarbuiyah, a point where there is no water, as the river between those two places makes a wide bend, of which the railway is the chord.

On the 5th progress was slow, owing to the handiwork of the insurgents on the previous night, for much time was consumed in repairing the many breaks which occurred at intervals along the line. It was expected that the Arabs would make a stand on the south side of Jarbuiyah bridge, as, once beyond that point, no special obstacle would lie between the column and Hillah. Reports, which I suspected were exaggerated, had come in of an attack on the garrison at the bridge, which consisted of four British officers, six Indian officers, and two hundred and ninety-seven other ranks of the 108th Infantry and 32nd Pioneers, besides ninety-four followers, the whole under the command of Major H. S. Mitchell of the latter regiment. These reports, which seem to have been believed at Hillah, had caused a message to be sent to Brigadier-General Coningham directing him to send part of his force in advance of the remainder to the bridge, with supplies, of which the garrison was running short. A copy of the telegram had come to my headquarters, as, after the Manchester affair, the delegation of authority for movements of troops was much restricted; and as there was no proof of an Arab repulse, nor that, as was stated, the tribesmen had "no more stomach for the fight," I counter-ordered the instructions contained in it by wireless telegrams to Hillah and General Coningham.

What had actually occurred at Jarbuiyah was that an attempt had been made on the night of the 24th July to destroy the bridge by floating burning logs down the river with the intention of setting light to the wooden trestles. The garrison, who later stretched a cable up-stream of the bridge to prevent further attempts to damage it, had done well in defeating the evil purpose of the insurgents, more especially as the bridge, like other places on the line, was ill-sited from a defensive point of view. In this small affair, which became exaggerated into a serious fight, in which the ground in front of the post was stated to be littered with Arab dead, Major Mitchell, who behaved with creditable coolness, and seven of his men were wounded.

As General Coningham's force approached the bridge the cavalry reported that numbers of Arabs were holding the Jarbuiyah canal, which runs roughly parallel to and west of the line of march along the railway, and that several bunds or banks and a village on the eastern flank were held in force. Two hours of reparation work still remained to be done before the night camp could be reached, and

Jarbuiyah Bridge, looking down-stream.

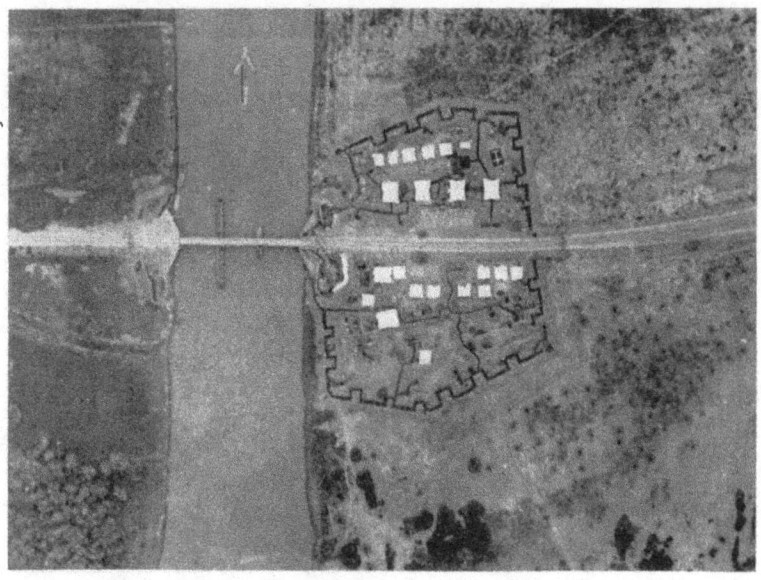
Jarbuiyah Post, 4th August 1920.

THE RETREAT FROM DIWANIYAH 135

in the meantime the enemy between it and the column must be driven off. The 87th Punjabis were now left to guard the train, and the remainder of the force was distributed as follows by its commander :—

One squadron 37th Lancers, the 45th Pack Battery, and the 99th (Deccan) Infantry were ordered to move under Captain O. Masters, 99th (Deccan) Infantry, along the Hashimiyah canal, and make good its junction with the bank at (a).

The 86th Carnatics were directed to form a right flank guard, and close on the advanced guard, which was under Lieut.-Colonel Scott, 1/10th Gurkha Rifles, and capture Shurufah village.

The advanced guard, consisting of the 1/10th Gurkha Rifles, two and a half companies of the 114th and 1/116th Mahrattas, was ordered to secure the river bend at (b) and the bank where it crosses the railway at (c).

The artillery was to assist the advanced guard and fire on all villages where the insurgents were reported to be concentrated; and the 45th Sikhs remained in reserve.

At 8.45 A.M. the advance began, and half an hour later Captain Masters reported that seven hundred tribesmen were closing on his left rear—the usual Arab tactics—and asked for artillery support, which was promptly given.

Meantime the advanced guard reached, without opposition, a point a thousand yards from the river, while the 86th Carnatics pushed on, being fired into from their right.

At 11 A.M. the advanced guard had secured the river bank, and the 86th Carnatics had occupied Shurufah village, when Captain Masters reported that he had surprised three hundred Arabs, and catching them at close range with Lewis guns, had inflicted on them seventy casualties.

The Mahrattas were sent at 11.30 A.M. to capture the bank at (c), which they effected an hour later. The 10th Gurkhas then crossed the river, and occupied the village of Diyar-albu-Said, killing some fifty Arabs in the process, while many more, flying before them, fell to the Lewis guns of the Mahrattas.

136   THE INSURRECTION IN MESOPOTAMIA

The Arabs were reported at this time to be concentrating at Imam Hamzah, and as soon as their movement towards that place seemed to be completed the field artillery opened fire on it with guns and howitzers, which caused the occupants to scatter, mostly towards the east. This terminated the action, our casualties being only fourteen Indian other ranks wounded; and the train was brought for the night close to Jarbuiyah bridge.

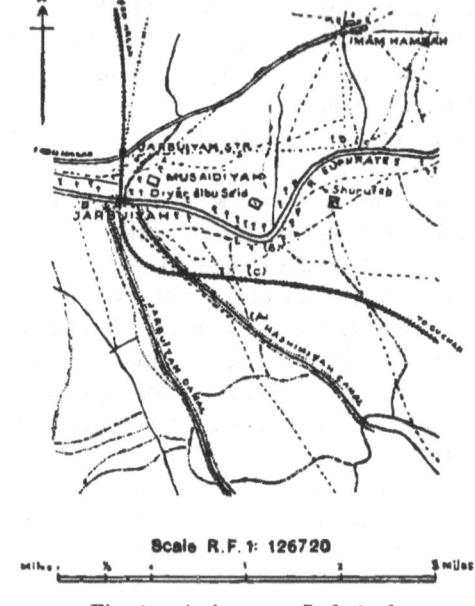

Fig. 4.—*Action near Jarbuiyah.*

On the 6th August five aeroplanes came overhead, and reported a concentration of one thousand Arabs one mile north-west of Imam Hamzah, on whom the guns shortly opened.

As Jarbuiyah bridge proved to be unfitted for carrying wheeled traffic, some time was occupied in laying the necessary sleepers, so that guns and other vehicles could cross to the left bank of the river.

In order to save time and get General Coningham's force

THE RETREAT FROM DIWANIYAH

back to Hillah as quickly as possible, I proposed leaving the train at Jarbuiyah, while he marched the thirteen miles between him and the former place with only sufficient transport to carry his supplies. But on an examination of the ground he came to the conclusion that a much larger force than could be spared to guard the train, the great length of which was unknown to me, would have to be left behind; and as a construction train was already working south, and repairs to the line from Hillah towards his force were in progress, the order was cancelled.

By 6 P.M. most of the impedimenta was north of the bridge, and the train reached Jarbuiyah station at 7 P.M., all railway personnel, under escort of the 37th Lancers and 1/10th Gurkha Rifles, being sent ahead to mend the line.

On the 7th the aeroplanes reported that no insurgents were visible, but that the line for seven miles north was broken up in many places. While repairs were going on the troops were despatched to burn all villages near Jarbuiyah, and the guns were employed to deal with a small concentration of Arabs which appeared to the north-east. At 3 P.M. the column moved forward, and at 5.40 P.M. reached a point five miles north-west of Jarbuiyah, where it camped for the night. Beyond this spot the line was reported to be badly broken.

At 1 A.M. on the 8th August the work of repairing began for the last time, and at 9.20 A.M. heliographic communication was established with a construction train and a column from Hillah, which were then about three miles distant. Much of the line had to be restored, as between the two trains nearly fifty per cent of the permanent way had been damaged or destroyed. As it was essential to get some of the troops back to Hillah without delay, two sections of the 131st Howitzer Battery, two of the 97th Battery, the 45th Pack Battery, the 32nd Pioneers, 87th Punjabis, and 116th Mahrattas and some details were ordered to continue the march. The remainder of the force advanced as repairs were completed, and by 4.45 P.M. the line to Hillah was restored, the trains, which now consisted of six locomotives and two hundred and fifty-one vehicles, reaching that place at 10.15 p.m. Next day the remainder of the column, which had halted for the night, continued its march to Hillah, where it arrived without incident.

The operation of withdrawal, owing to the time required for repairing the railway, had taken eleven days, an average of only five and a half miles being covered daily. The prolongation of the time allotted in the plan for the march might have proved serious, for only a supply of six days' rations for the whole force was carried, and an additional day's supply, as mentioned, had been sent to Khan Jadwal. But the delays which soon made their appearance showed that the food available must last for several days longer than was anticipated, and issues were at once restricted.

The weather had been most trying, shade temperature averaging 107 and rising sometimes several degrees higher; and as no cover had been carried for the troops, who were for some twelve hours daily exposed to the full glare of the sun's rays, it speaks well for their endurance that, under such conditions, the number of sick was small.

The withdrawal had been much helped by the daily appearance from Baghdad of aeroplanes which bombed the tribesmen who followed the column, and dropped information concerning concentrations which threatened it with attack, as well as the state of the railway ahead. The complete success of the operation, however, was mainly due to the resolution and resource displayed by its commander, and the confidence which all ranks had learned to repose in him. Even the Arabs seem to have been inspired by feelings of respect and awe. There were some among them who are credited with not having understood how the force with its trains a mile in length moved across the desert. Only tribesmen near the line had shared in the tearing up of the permanent way, and when these others saw the wide spaces innocent of rails and sleepers and heard that the train had crossed the desert, the man who led the column was regarded as a wizard.

My feelings at this time may perhaps be of interest to those who served in my command, so I record them here.

THE RETREAT FROM DIWANIYAH 139

From the date when the news was received of the disaster to the Manchester column until the message came announcing Brigadier-General Coningham's arrival at Jarbuiyah bridge, a period of twelve days, I can recall in my military career no cycle—and I use that word advisedly —of quite such tense anxiety, not that it cost me one single hour of sleep. From 1914 to the Armistice, except for an occasional brief spell of leave, I was never absent from the Western Front, and my troops often held ground which in the parlance of the time was called "unhealthy." But these twelve days at Baghdad in 1920, days that seemed like years, surpassed all earlier ones in the mental strain which they imposed. Presumably a soldier should possess a soul above anxiety, but I have never read or heard of such a being. One can steel oneself to hide one's real feelings and appear somewhat as Napoleon said a general should be—"neither elated by good news, nor depressed by bad." Even that is not always easy to achieve; but I think that beyond Brigadier-General Stewart, who knew my inmost thoughts at this most trying time, no one guessed the strain to which I was being continually subjected. Not only at this period but for several weeks the situation of affairs was critical, and visions of the siege and fall of Khartum sometimes flitted through my mind.

CHAPTER XIV.

THE RECOVERY OF THE HINDIYAH BARRAGE.

IN anticipation of the return of Brigadier-General Coningham's column to Hillah I had given orders for certain operations to begin directly that event occurred. With this object two columns were prepared as follows :—

55th Brigade Column, under Brigadier-General H. A. Walker, C.M.G., D.S.O.,
32nd Lancers (less two squadrons),
97th Battery R.F.A. (less one section),
131st (How.) Battery R.F.A. (less one section),
45th Pack Battery,
2nd Battalion Manchester Regiment,
8th Rajputs,
87th Punjabis,
Details of the 114th and 1/116th Mahrattas,
1/32nd Sikh Pioneers (one company),
    and certain details.

The second column was commanded by Lieut.-Colonel H. L. Scott, D.S.O., M.C., 1/10th Gurkha Rifles, and consisted of—

35th Scinde Horse (two squadrons),
97th Battery R.F.A. (one section),
131st (How.) Battery R.F.A. (one section),
1/99th Infantry,
1/10th Gurkha Rifles,
    and certain details.

Both columns contained troops taken from General Coningham's force, which was badly in need of a rest.

RECOVERY OF THE HINDIYAH BARRAGE 141

The situation, however, was one that admitted of no delay, and the first column assembled on the northern outskirts of Hillah on the afternoon of the 9th, the date on which General Coningham's column arrived at that place; that under Lieut.-Colonel Scott following in the same direction on the 10th.

I had decided to operate next in a northerly direction for the following reasons. I anticipated that the insurgents would conclude that my next effort would be the relief of the garrison of Kufah, which had been invested for nearly three weeks, and that they would not be found in strength north of Hillah. Kufah I knew had a fair supply of rations, and also, through the foresight of the Political Officer, Major Norbury, other comestibles, such as dates, which though possibly unpalatable after a time, would at least serve to keep the garrison alive until the troops arrived for its relief. I therefore felt no immediate anxiety for its safety, and had determined that, come what might, I would not start premature operations, but that when they began they must be carried on without fail to a satisfactory conclusion.

In another direction, that of Baghdad, the defences were still incomplete, and even after the arrival there on the 10th August of the first reinforcing battalion from India, the 2/7th Rajputs, which had landed at Basrah on the 6th, the Capital would be inadequately garrisoned. Frequent reports had come in regarding concentrations on the right bank of the Tigris, which, it was understood, were a prelude to an attempt to capture Baghdad; but I neither felt justified in hazarding my limited force at a distance from the Capital, nor in exposing the latter to the risks of a *coup-de-main*. It was essential, too, to repair and blockhouse the railway line from Baghdad to Hillah before putting into execution the plan for the relief of Kufah, as supplies of all kinds would be required at Hillah for that operation, besides a bridging train from Baghdad to ensure a passage across the Euphrates, which at Kufah is two hundred and fifty yards in width.

But the main reason which actuated my decision as to

the locality of the coming operations was the importance of securing the Hindiyah Barrage and the town of Musayib, which lies some eight miles further up the river. The capture of these two places, besides giving me water control, would secure command of two important crossings over the Euphrates, the possession of which had allowed the insurgents to conduct with impunity raids against the railway from the country which lies to the west of the river.

With regard to the first of these places, the Hindiyah Barrage, it is necessary at this point to make a somewhat lengthy digression. This great dam, which stands some sixteen miles north-west of Hillah, at the point where the Euphrates divides into two branches, which are known by the names of Hindiyah [1] and Hillah, was erected by the Turkish Government between 1910 and 1913 on the advice of Sir William Willcocks. Here, by a system of regulators, the waters of the Euphrates can be directed down either branch at will. I had been impressed with the desirability of maintaining a post at the bifurcation, so as to have control over the point where the water distribution was carried out by officers of the Irrigation Department; but, as I have already stated, this would have involved another detachment, and I received no encouragement from the civil administration, who may have imagined that military control might militate against the payment of revenue. When news came that the irrigation officers had been forced to leave their posts owing to the rising of the tribes, I made more inquiries as to any evil results that might follow, and was informed, correctly as it turned out, that the last thing the Arabs would do would be to damage the structure. Apparently the custom was for the water to be allowed to flow down each branch alternately for a week at a time, a routine which allowed of the crops of various natures along or in the vicinity of one branch of the river being irrigated, while those near the other branch sustained no damage until they in turn

---

[1] Sir William Willcocks identifies this branch as the Gihon mentioned in Genesis ii. 13.

Hindiyah barrage from the west.

Hillah from the south-east.

received their share of the water. On studying the ' Handbook of Mesopotamia,' however, I found it stated that "the branch could be deprived of all its water at any season by closing of the regulators." That is to say, by closing the regulators at the top of the Hillah branch, not only all the water could be cut off from the town of that name, but the stations on the railway thence to Baghdad would, through the drying up of the canals leading to them from the river, suffer equally. This was not all, for, if Kufah were to be relieved, the route that would be followed by the troops was watered by canals leading from the Hillah branch. The early recovery of the barrage was clearly most desirable, but it was thought by those who had knowledge of the subject that the tribes would, even in our absence from the regulators, continue to carry out the routine of water-flow to which they were accustomed. Both the Tigris and Euphrates were, however, very low in 1920, and it was not impossible that, in order to force the troops to give up Hillah, the tribes might sacrifice part of their crops, though the dissensions that would certainly have followed would have led to feuds among them.

Until the barrage was recovered alarming reports came in from time to time from Hillah as to the expected lack of water, or abundance which would break the river banks and flood the town and country. But neither of these evils occurred. There was a time, however, when I thought it possible that I might have to withdraw the garrison at Hillah and station it at Musayib, where it would be situated on the river and on the direct road between Baghdad and Karbala.

With the object then of recovering the barrage, the 55th Brigade Column moved on the 10th August to Khan Mahawil *en route* for Musayib, and next day the small force under Lieut.-Colonel Scott marched along the railway, repairing it and carrying out punitive measures, while it covered the construction of blockhouses at intervals of half a mile. Hillah was left with a garrison of two squadrons of the 37th Lancers, the 39th Battery, the 132nd (How.)

Battery, the 2nd Battalion Royal Irish Rifles, and the 45th Sikhs.

The movement of the two columns took place during the hottest season of the year—a season, be it remembered, during which no continuous operations in Mesopotamia

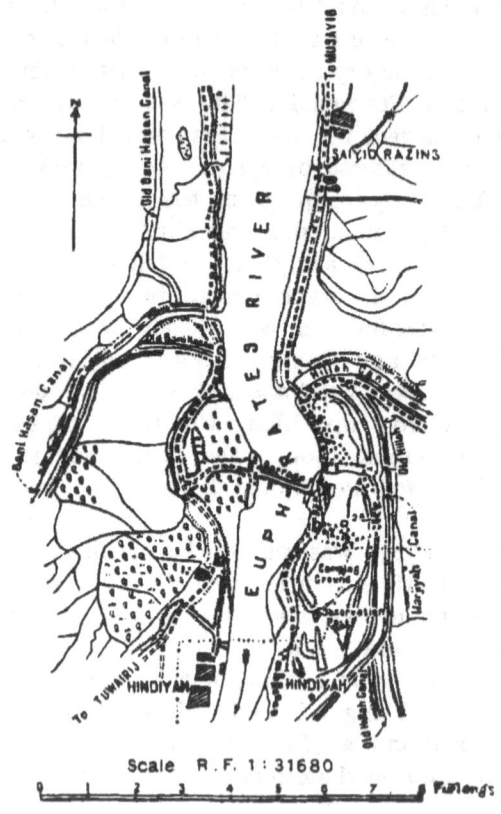

Fig. 5.—*Hindiyah Barrage.*

since our arrival there in 1914 had taken place. But the selection of the season did not lie with us, nor could the operations be postponed. These facts were evident to the troops engaged, and were accepted in the proper spirit. To add to the discomfort of the column on the first day of movement, it was found that the Arabs had cut off the

Bridge at Musayib from left bank.

Bridge at Tuwairij from right bank.

RECOVERY OF THE HINDIYAH BARRAGE 145

water west of Khan Nasiriyah, where the force passed a trying night.

On the 11th and 12th some opposition was encountered, but a bold advance by the 2nd Battalion Manchester Regiment, which, though weak in numbers after its trying experience on the 24th July, had been added to the column, forced the insurgents to retire with loss, and Musayib was occupied on the latter date.

Here, as before mentioned, is a crossing over the Euphrates, at this point two hundred to three hundred yards wide, consisting of a bridge of boats which is much used by pilgrims and others on their way from Baghdad to Karbala; and the town, which is surrounded by palm gardens, presents a pleasing aspect, which is due to the trees and its situation on both banks of the river. About one-third of the bridge of boats was found to be burnt, and as the passage here across the Euphrates was not required for military operations, repairs were not undertaken for some time, and orders were shortly after issued that all communication and the transmission of goods between the town and Karbala must cease.

At Musayib the 8th Rajputs were left as garrison, and on the 13th the insurgents, who stood between the column and the Hindiyah Barrage, were driven off, and that important place was occupied, the 2nd Battalion Manchester Regiment, with two 18-pr. guns, being allotted as garrison.

The position at the bifurcation of the Euphrates at Hindiyah was one of great strength for passive defence even before the barrage was constructed. But since that great work came into existence the double wet ditch on the eastern side, formed by the Hillah branch and the Jarjiyah canal, and the improbability of attack by a force armed with guns, made the site with a little labour impregnable. Few more favourable spots could be chosen for a double bridgehead, for on the eastern side the heaped-up spoil from the barrage excavation provided an elongated mound some thirty to forty feet in height, from which point of vantage the flat country for several miles on all sides is overlooked. The barrage itself, which would serve

K

to connect the defensive works on both sides of the Hindiyah branch, by which name the main river is called from this point for some distance southwards, is a broad brick dam and bridge combined, which could not easily be damaged or destroyed. The great advantage offered by the position was the ease and speed with which it could be made defensible, and the small size of the garrison required to hold it.

The necessary work was soon executed by the 2nd Manchester Regiment; infantry posts, which were protected by barbed wire, being held by a minimum of men by day, but at night in strength.

In addition to the two 18-pr. guns left with the defence, I sent later a 6-in. howitzer and a 60-pr. gun from the 5th Battery R.G.A. at Baghdad, a section of which battery did useful work in conjunction with the 15th Sikhs in the defence of the Diyalah bridge near Baqubah. These heavier weapons were employed to harass the insurgents and support the isolated post which was later made near the head of the Husainiyah canal.

As a place of temporary rest for troops fatigued with operations the barrage served a useful purpose, for the defence duties were light and the chances of attack remote; while the river, with its facilities for bathing and fishing, appealed equally to all ranks, British and Indian.

The occupation of Musayib and the barrage gave us control, as a means of communication between those places, of the broad embankment which follows the left bank of the Euphrates, and has a command of several feet over the surrounding country. This bank was made by the British between 1917 and 1919 with the object of keeping the river within bounds on its eastern side.

On the 14th August, the day following the capture of the barrage, punitive measures were undertaken along the left bank of the Husainiyah canal, which leaves the Euphrates three miles up-stream from that point. This canal carries water to Karbala, which is sixteen miles distant to the west on the edge of the Syrian desert, and the greatest of the Shiah centres of pilgrimage. Its chief shrine is that of Husain, the son of 'Ali, whose tomb, as well as that of his half-brother Abbas, is here. At Karbala, which is a hotbed of sedition, ten agitators, who included the son of the premier mujtahid,[1] Muhammad Mirza Taqi, had been arrested on the 22nd June, some infantry and a section of guns having been sent from Hillah to overawe the city while the police did their work.

As Karbala was responsible in no small degree for the insurrection, I was anxious to seize the regulator, which is some two hundred yards from the river, and make the inhabitants feel the discomfort of being deprived of water; but unfortunately it was considered that the force available was insufficient to admit of the detachment of even a platoon, and not until a month had passed was the regulator closed and guarded by blockhouses. When I inquired later as to the effect this action had produced I was informed that, by digging wells in the canal bed, sufficient water of a slightly brackish nature was obtainable, but that the inhabitants had felt some inconvenience and their supply of vegetables had suffered. Nevertheless, though my informants on the spot did their best to pooh-pooh my efforts to make their holy city "dry," I have strong reasons for believing that the effect of closing the regulator fell little short of my expectations. Apart from the hardships endured, the moral pressure exerted on the inhabitants by this demonstration of my power to deprive them of what was vital for their existence must have been considerable, for the posts guarding the regulator were attacked with determination on several occasions, on one of which Lieutenant G. H. Seater of the 8th Rajputs was killed. A small column, which operated on the 14th August on the right of the canal, in combination with the left-bank column, among the troops of which the 32nd Lancers did particularly well, met a considerable number of insurgents, who suffered so heavily that no attempt was made to interfere with the withdrawal of both columns.

Meanwhile Lieut.-Colonel Scott's force carried out daily

---
[1] Shiah religious leader.

operations of a similar nature while covering repairs to the railway and the construction and occupation of forty-five blockhouses.

From Baghdad also an organisation, under Brigadier-General G. A. F. Sanders, commanding the 53rd Infantry Brigade, which eventually comprised the garrisoning by five battalions of some three hundred blockhouses and twenty-five railway stations, distributed along two hundred and fifty miles of railway, began working on the 6th August on the Hillah line.

On an urgent appeal from the Assistant Political Officer at Mahmudiyah, a village and railway station on that route, twenty-five miles from Baghdad, which was followed by almost daily reports of an alarming and exaggerated nature, two companies of the 13th Rajputs had been sent on the 29th July to garrison that place. Further appeals were made for reinforcements, but they were not met. Gradually the blockhouses from both termini approached that station, and by the 19th August met at Khan Hiswah, when the trains—after a cessation for three weeks of all communication except by wireless telegraph or aeroplane —ran through from Baghdad to Hillah with a selection of the articles most needed. Shortly afterwards, as it came to my knowledge that propaganda, to the effect that Hillah and Kufah had been captured by the Arabs, was being spread among the Muntafiq to our disadvantage, it was arranged to run a train weekly for ordinary passengers from Baghdad to the former place and back.

On the 23rd and 24th August respectively the columns returned to Hillah, after having carried out punitive operations of a thorough nature, which included the destruction of thirty-three mud villages, all of which were known to have harboured insurgents and those who had cut the railway line.

Hillah in the meantime had, as before, not been left alone. It is a place which is difficult to defend, owing to the dense palm-groves and gardens, some enclosed within high mud walls, which surround it, and it was found necessary to make clearings of considerable extent. Eventually a defended perimeter, comprising thirty-two blockhouses connected by a wire entanglement, was constructed, and these, although frequently attacked, were never taken.

The principal effort of the insurgents had been made on the 21st August, when it became evident to the garrison that an attack in force was contemplated and impending. On the morning of that date, while the work of clearing the palm-groves was in progress to the south of the town on the left bank of the river, a covering party of the 45th Sikhs became engaged. At first only a few tribesmen opened fire, but in the afternoon they appeared in greater strength, and advanced with unusual boldness. The 45th Sikhs, however, with their customary stubbornness, held their ground, and as the Arabs offered good targets they were severely punished. Simultaneously an attack was delivered on that portion of the southern face of the perimeter which was situated on the right bank of the river, where only a few men of the 2nd Battalion Royal Irish Rifles were posted. Here also the insurgents, who were reinforced by others from the left bank when the attack there failed, made no impression, and were repulsed by gun, rifle, and machine-gun fire.

Besides their losses in this affray and those inflicted by the columns that had operated under Brigadier-General Walker and Lieut.-Colonel Scott, the Arabs south and north of Hillah would soon, through our possession of the barrage, begin to feel the inconvenience of the policy of water domination, for the rice crops of the considerable Shamiyah tribes could be deprived of irrigation and be ruined; while the Bani Hassan and Jarjiyah canals, which water the land west and east respectively of the Hindiyah branch, were blocked at the same central point. Along the railway line, too, the General Officer Commanding the 17th Division arranged that all canals, except the Khan Mahawil, were closed where they were commanded by the line of blockhouses on the railway, and the water was where possible diverted down the line. Thus all the country east of the railway, except that watered by the last-mentioned canal, whence supplies were being brought in by the inhabitants, was deprived of water.

I was now in a position to operate for the relief of Kufah, and from a purely military point of view I should have preferred to continue putting pressure on the insurgents who inhabit the country south of Baghdad, in which that place lies. Here it was clear that the focus of the insurrection was to be found. Events elsewhere, however, made it advisable and indeed imperative to transfer the troops to another area where I proposed to begin operating on the 1st September.

While preparations for this operation were in progress such troops as could be spared were given a few days' rest, and on the 26th August I moved the 34th Brigade Column, under Brigadier-General Coningham, from Hillah in a south-easterly direction. The column, which contained two battalions that had taken part in the operations which led to the capture of the Hindiyah Barrage and had only returned to Hillah two days earlier, was composed as follows :—

> 37th Lancers (less two squadrons),
> 39th Battery R.F.A.,
> 131st (How.) Battery R.F.A. (less one section),
> 67th Company, 2nd (Q.V.O.) Sappers and Miners,
> 45th (Rattray's) Sikhs,
> 1/99th (Deccan) Infantry,
> 1/116th Mahrattas,
> 1/10th Gurkha Rifles,
> 1/32nd Sikh Pioneers (one company),
> 17th Machine Gun Battalion (one section),
> 2nd Euphrates Levy (three troops),
>   and certain details.

It will be remembered that I had left a post at Jarbuiyah to protect the important railway bridge at that place; but I now found myself, not altogether unexpectedly, in no position to spare troops to hold it, nor was transport available with which to keep the post supplied with rations which would have to be sent to it from time to time. More-

RECOVERY OF THE HINDIYAH BARRAGE

over, the continued spread of the insurrection and the proclamation of a Jihad or holy war about the 6th August showed that this project would have to be deferred for some months. I therefore ordered the withdrawal of the post.

Brigadier-General Coningham's column found that the railway line had been still more damaged than was the case at the time of the withdrawal from Diwaniyah. The country at one point had been flooded, and the only road possible was the slight railway embankment, which had to be improved and used as a causeway. This resulted in delay, and it was not found possible to reach Jarbuiyah in one day. Some opposition was expected, as the Arabs well knew the value of the bridge, and doubtless hoped in time to starve its garrison into surrender. But no determined resistance was met with, and a force of some two thousand Arabs, which had thrown itself across the line of march, was outflanked by the cavalry, with which worked the three troops of the 2nd Euphrates Levy, and disappeared before the guns and infantry arrived.

On the 27th Jarbuiyah was reached, where it was found that the 86th Carnatics had at first been harassed by the insurgents, but, after causing them the loss of seven killed and four wounded, no further attacks had been made. On the following day a halt was made in order to deal with the large village of Imam Hamzah. This was attacked and captured with little difficulty, for the Albu Sultan tribe, in whose territory it lies, and who have some reputation as warriors, showed no keenness for the fray, and melted away before the fire of the artillery.

On the 29th the column arrived at Hillah, enlivening its march by dealing with the villages *en route*.

CHAPTER XV.

THE OPERATIONS NORTH-EAST OF BAGHDAD.

MEANWHILE the transfer of troops to which I have referred had begun, a transfer which necessitated the temporary suspension of active measures in the Hillah area.

On the 6th August signs of unrest in the area north-east of Baghdad had showed themselves. These were followed by attacks on the railway line, and from the 9th August the train service from Baghdad to Quraitu and Kingarban ceased. As the railway line at Baqubah had been cut, and the presence there of insurgents in some strength was reported, I sent from Baghdad, on the 10th, a small mixed column under Brigadier-General H. G. Young, commanding the 7th Cavalry Brigade, the despatch of which removed my last reserve from Baghdad.

The moment was an inopportune one for weakening the garrison of Baghdad, as reports, to which I have already alluded, had been received of possible attacks not only from the west but from the north. The police, too, had selected the 12th August for the arrest of certain agitators, and on the night of that date an outbreak was predicted, and the internal defence scheme was ordered to be put in operation. It was important, however, if possible, to nip in the bud the first signs of insurrection in an area which had so far escaped contamination.

Brigadier-General Young's column consisted of—

"A" Battery R.H.A., Chestnut Troop (one section).
1st King's Dragoon Guards (about one hundred sabres).
7th (P.R.) Dragoon Guards (about one hundred sabres).

OPERATIONS NORTH-EAST OF BAGHDAD

16th M.G. Squadron (one section).
50th Pack Battery R.G.A. (one section).
1st Battalion Rifle Brigade.
1/94th (Russell's) Infantry (one and three-quarter companies).

The concentration of this force at Baqubah—except the 1/94th Infantry, which was already there—was delayed owing to railway difficulties; but before daylight on the 12th August the column, less the 1st Battalion Rifle Brigade, which I ordered to be left at Baqubah Station, whence it was intended to entrain it again for Baghdad at 6 P.M., had started on its mission.

To the cavalry, under Lieut.-Colonel J. Williams, 1st King's Dragoon Guards, and a sub-section of the 16th Machine-gun Squadron, was entrusted the duty of destroying the offending villages, which proved to be eighteen miles distant from the railway. In rear, in support of the cavalry, followed the remainder of the troops under Brigadier-General Young, consisting of the section of the Chestnut Troop, the section of the 50th Pack Battery, one and three-quarter companies of the 1/94th (Russell's) Infantry, and a portion of a medical unit, whose destination was to be Marut, which is eleven and a quarter miles from Baqubah Station.

Doubts arose as to the trustworthiness of the guide, as difficulty was found in maintaining the proper direction, and the march was not to pass off without an incident which roused suspicions of an ambush. For, with four miles still to be accomplished and about an hour before dawn, some of that portion of the infantry which formed the rear of the column was fired into by a party of mounted Arabs. This was too much for the men's nerves; they became panic-struck, and caused the mules of the 50th Pack Battery to stampede through the ambulance and horse artillery, resulting in many other animals following suit with their vehicles. For a time, and until dawn at 4.30 when the column re-formed, there was almost complete chaos, the horse artillery being then able to move only by dismounting all detachments to replace teamhorses killed and missing.

Half an hour later a large volume of smoke was observed to the south-east, from which it was inferred that Colonel Williams's column had reached its objective and carried out its mission ; and at 5.30 A.M. some two to three hundred Arabs, mostly mounted, began to appear to the northeast and south. As they seemed to be gathering for an attack, and as the infantry had not recovered from its surprise and could not be relied upon, a message was sent by car for two companies of the Rifle Brigade to come up in support. But the guns of the section of the Chestnut Troop and the one serviceable pack battery gun now shelled the tribesmen with good effect, and by 7 A.M. they began to disappear. Brigadier-General Young then advanced, and came in touch with the cavalry, who, helped by the fire of the guns, joined him half an hour later. From Colonel Williams he learnt that on the return journey the mounted Arabs had closely followed up for eight miles, and that the cavalry had been constantly engaged with them. Meanwhile a search round the place where the stampede had occurred resulted in the recovery of a considerable quantity of material. By 8 A.M. the junction between the two small columns was effected, and Baqubah was reached at noon, the Rifle Brigade having been informed some time earlier that its support was no longer needed.

At 3 P.M., after the combined columns had gone to their bivouac across the Diyalah river, the road and railway bridge over which was guarded by the 1/94th Infantry, the local Assistant Political Officer reported that a heavy attack was imminent on Baqubah, which lies about a mile east of the river, and asked for help to protect the civilians there. This request was refused, as the troops were under orders to return immediately to Baghdad, and he was ordered to evacuate the town, which should have been done much earlier. This operation was effected with the help of the Rifle Brigade ; and all troops, except the bridge guard, which was left with rations for ten days, withdrew across the river by 7 P.M. An hour later the Rifle Brigade

Bridge over Diyalah river near Baqubah.

Baqubah—Railway station in foreground.

left by rail for Baghdad, other troops following as trains became available, while the cavalry and horse artillery returned by road, arriving on the 14th August.

The mishap which had occurred during the night march of Brigadier-General Young's column was known later not to be attributable in any degree to treachery on the part of the guide. It appears that a raiding party of some fifty Arabs, in ignorance that operations were in progress in the neighbourhood, was making its way to Baqubah in the hope of looting that place, and on suddenly meeting a body of troops opened fire on them. It is possible that had this night encounter not taken place the spread of the insurrection to the Diyalah district might have been delayed for a few days. As it was, however, it undid any good effect which the punishment inflicted by Colonel Williams's force might have brought about, and not only served to exasperate and encourage the tribes east of the Diyalah river, but precipitated the rising. The time at which the operation was undertaken could not, as I have pointed out, have happened more inopportunely, and the absence of troops from Baghdad caused me much anxiety, as the temper of the inhabitants was such that the forces left behind were quite inadequate to control them should an outbreak occur. Moreover, the large depots and stores on the right bank of the Tigris offered a temptation to the tribes in the neighbourhood, who for a long time gave annoyance by the numerous small raids they made in order to pilfer them.

Meanwhile the attempt to arrest several of the agitators to which I have referred proved a failure, and probably did more harm than good. I have been told that the intentions of the civil police were known not only to those whose liberty was threatened, but to many others in Baghdad. In consequence the police met with opposition, and there were a few casualties among the populace; and under cover of the disturbance those who were " wanted " made good their escape, and afterwards were constantly heard of in different parts of Iraq doing their best to keep the fires of insurrection burning.

By the 10th August the third infantry unit of the reinforcements from India—the 1/15th (Ludhiana) Sikhs—had landed at Basrah, and had been hurried by river to Kut, and thence by rail to Baghdad, where it arrived on the afternoon of the 13th. I had known this distinguished regiment on the North-West Frontier in 1897-8, and was particularly glad to have it under my command.

Early next morning it was sent to reinforce the small garrison at the railway bridge over the Diyalah near Baqubah, and protect the wireless station near that place. Here also was the large Assyrian refugee camp, which, in my despatch dated 8th November 1920, I credited with being in a far better position to take care of itself than I have since learned was actually the case.

Except two hundred modern rifles with only ten rounds apiece, there were no weapons at the camp beyond some hundreds of 1866 Winchester repeaters, which were of little practical value. Unfortunately the camp, which had a perimeter of nearly seven miles, and in which were living the officer in charge, Lieut.-Colonel F. Cunliffe-Owen and his wife, offered an easy target to the Arabs, who for three days harassed it on all sides with their fire, much of it at close range. In consequence, among the hospital patients alone there were from forty to fifty casualties, and many also among those guarding the animal camp, which had necessarily to be near the river, from the left bank of which much of the fire was directed. After three or four days a consignment of rifles and small arms ammunition was sent from Baghdad, but the insurgents derailed the train which was carrying it, four miles from the refugee siding west of Baqubah. Thereupon a mounted party under Lieut.-Colonel Cunliffe-Owen left the camp, and driving off the Arabs, prevented the ammunition from falling into hostile hands, and conveyed it safely back.

But the Assyrian riflemen repaid with interest all the unpleasant attentions which they and their families received. On one occasion, annoyed beyond endurance by the firing, a party crossed the river and took heavy toll of their tormentors, raiding four villages and bringing back two hundred and fifty sheep and seventy head of cattle. On the 17th August, too, when a train-load of Assyrians was on its way from the camp to Baghdad, it happened to draw up near a village which was friendly. But the Assyrians make no fine distinctions where an enemy or loot is in the wind. In a trice the train emptied itself, and no efforts could prevent men, women, and even children from making for the village, which, in retaliation for the firing into the camp and the fact that a train had at one time been derailed in its vicinity, was quickly cleared of all the portable property which it contained.

The unrest north-east of Baghdad now spread, and by the 25th August practically all the tribes north of the Diyalah became implicated in the rising, and lawlessness and disorder spread as far north as Kirkuk, and later on to Arbil. One of the results of this was that several of our outposts on the Baghdad-Quraitu line and the branch line to Kingarban were attacked and temporarily cut off. But this state of affairs was not allowed to continue without efforts being made to suppress it. Though troops were not available to check the rising in its initial stages, the energetic action of Colonel J. H. F. Lakin, the Officer Commanding the Persian Line of Communication, who made the utmost use of the very small force which he hastily collected, prevented the spread of the disorders beyond our border into Persia.

The disturbed condition of Mesopotamia in July began to reflect itself by increased uneasiness among the tribes within the Persian border. The new Governor-General of Kermanshah had signalised his appointment by following the time-honoured custom of discharging several subordinate officials and replacing them by others, who no doubt paid heavily for the privilege of serving him, and made those under them pay too. Ill-feeling had in consequence been aroused which spread to the tribes, and in the first week of August two isolated attacks had been made on convoys on the Hamadan-Kasvin road, which resulted in the death of several persons. But the prompt action of the British Assistant Political Officer at the former place, whereby the leader of the assailants and three others were killed and some taken prisoners, had a salutary effect on that area. The next part to be affected was that which lies west of the Kermanshah-Karind road, where it was reported that the wrath of the tribes might vent itself on the occupants of our camp at the latter place. Nothing came of this threat, and the trouble, as we have seen, now transferred itself to the route between Baqubah and the frontier. On the 18th August all rolling-stock north of that place was ordered to be collected at Khanakin Road and Quraitu, which, being a railhead for our troops in Persia, demanded special care for its protection.

Colonel Lakin now sent one of his staff, Major D. B. Edwards, Central India Horse, with seventy British and eighty-eight Indian ranks, three Vickers and two Lewis guns, to Khanakin Road, which was reached on the evening of the 14th. Here the Assistant Political Officer with his family arrived for safety, and no sooner had he left the town than it was sacked and his offices were burned. At the same time an attack on the engine-shed at the station was driven off.

Next day, while all the railway personnel that could be spared were being evacuated by rail to Quraitu, Major Edwards made a reconnaissance down the line, and after crossing the bridge, which had been badly burned, and entering a cutting, the train was fired on by a party of some forty mounted men, who were dispersed.

On the 16th August a body of tribesmen some two hundred strong, coming from the direction of Khanakin town, made a determined attack on the station. Two and a half hours of serious fighting followed, during which the Vickers gun teams of No. 2 Light Armoured Motor Battery and the Lewis gun sections of the 1st Battalion Royal Irish Fusiliers particularly distinguished themselves, and drove off the assailants, who left behind them fifteen dead.

But more troops were now approaching Quraitu. On the 18th August I had ordered the 1st Battalion Royal Irish Fusiliers to be sent from Kasvin in motor-lorries, and

OPERATIONS NORTH-EAST OF BAGHDAD 159

besides these troops Colonel Lakin had collected the 13th British Pack Battery from Karind, a section of which covered seventy-two miles in seventy-three hours, a creditable performance, as the heat was great. The Assistant Political Officer, too, at Kermanshah had placed at his disposal two hundred and fifty Sinjabis and two hundred Kalhur and Guran horsemen, who were concentrated for use on the Persian frontier.

When Colonel Lakin arrived at Quraitu on the 17th August, Kasr-i-Shirin town was in a state of panic, and the road crowded with refugees who were flying to the Persian hills. A column, under Lieut.-Colonel H. S. Gaskell, the Chief Engineer Officer on the line of communication, was at once formed, which consisted of the 13th Pack Battery R.G.A. (less one section), and the 79th Carnatic Infantry (four hundred rifles), and this force reached Khanakin Road without opposition on the morning of the 19th. Punishment was inflicted on the villages, the inhabitants of which had taken part in the previous attack, and repairs to the railway were begun. On the 20th Khanakin town was reoccupied by a small force, and the Assistant Political Officer reinstated. By the 23rd the small columns under Major Edwards and Colonel Gaskell were amalgamated into one force, under the command of the latter, to which was added the remainder of the 13th Pack Battery, the 65th Sapper and Miner Company, and some details.

Next day Colonel Gaskell, with two guns and two hundred and fifty rifles, marched to relieve Karaghan, where the railway from Baghdad bifurcates, one branch leading to Quraitu and the other to Kingarban. The post at Karaghan had been cut off for some days, and its state and that of other posts on the Kingarban branch had caused some anxiety, as the rising in that area had come with such suddenness that the garrisons were ill supplied to stand a siege.

Near Khanakin Road station a considerable body of tribesmen was driven off by Colonel Gaskell's column and severe punishment inflicted, with the loss of only two wounded to our troops; and later in the day the post at Karaghan was relieved and some additional rolling-stock which was recovered there sent back. The relieved garrison, consisting of one hundred and thirty rifles of the 1/94th (Russell's) Infantry, under Lieutenant J. H. D. Hunter, had made a fine defence, driving off repeated attacks by tribesmen in the neighbourhood, whose numbers were estimated at six hundred.

On the 25th a small force under Major R. M. Medill, Royal Artillery, in conjunction with two hundred and fifty Sinjabi mounted men under Captain J. B. Moore, Assistant Political Officer, made a night march and destroyed the stronghold of a local leader. On the same day, while a post to cover the bridge between Khanakin Road and Kizil Robat was under construction, two sections of the 65th Sappers and Miners were attacked by some three hundred tribesmen. Lieut.-Colonel Gaskell, who was present superintending the work, broke through the insurgents on an engine under heavy fire, and made for Khanakin Road, whence he brought back with him one hundred and thirty rifles. With these he relieved the little garrison of sappers who, under Captain Scott-Ruffle, had held their own for two hours, and the insurgents were driven off with forty casualties.

On the 27th, reinforced by part of the garrison of Karaghan, Lieut.-Colonel Gaskell advanced in two columns to Kizil Robat, where it was reported that the strength of the insurgents had greatly diminished. Although opposed, the town was reached and the railway repaired, after which the force withdrew.

On the 28th Lieut.-Colonel F. A. Greer, commanding 1st Battalion Royal Irish Fusiliers, who had arrived from Kasvin with part of his battalion, took command of the operations, which, though small in proportion to others, were of much importance, as, in conjunction with other operations about to be described, they served to open up the railway route to Persia.

On the 20th August the Acting Civil Commissioner had informed me that the forces in the disturbed area with which I should have to deal might soon rise to ten thou-

OPERATIONS NORTH-EAST OF BAGHDAD 161

sand men, that quantities of arms were being bought in Persia by the insurgents, and that the tribes across our border in that country would in all probability join forces against us.

As the situation was one which might conceivably involve the safety of the whole of the married families at Karind and Sar-i-Mil, or in any case create alarm locally and elsewhere, I ordered these camps to be concentrated at the former place, arrangements for defence to be made, and supplies to be collected locally. As regards defence there were one thousand British troops, mostly young soldiers, at Karind, and there was no cause for anxiety regarding supplies, which are readily obtainable in Persia.

It was in these circumstances that I decided to transfer the troops at Hillah and reopen the Persian line of communication, and defer the relief of Kufah. The plan, from a military point of view, was unsound, as it involved the postponement for some weeks of the despatch of troops to an area where their presence was essential as speedily as possible to wipe out the memory of the mishap of the 24th July. Moreover, early success south of Hillah would react to our advantage in other parts of Mesopotamia, and would help to stay the insurrection which still showed signs of spreading. Nevertheless, the shelving for a time of the Kufah operation was unavoidable, and fortunately the arrangements which were made to neutralise the ill effects of its postponement, and to which I shall presently refer, proved adequate.

While the necessary forces were being concentrated, Lieut.-Colonel Greer's troops began a forward movement. His column consisted of—

13th Pack Battery R.G.A.
1st Battalion Royal Irish Fusiliers (less two companies, which joined later).
79th Carnatic Infantry (one hundred and fifty rifles).
1/94th (Russell's) Infantry (three platoons).
15th Light Armoured Motor Battery (one section).
Fifty Irregular Horse (Persian Kurds).
Some sappers and miners and details.

L

Mirjanah was reached on the 1st September after some opposition, and useful work was done in the repair of the railway line.

The 1/15th Sikhs, in the meantime, under their energetic commander, Lieut.-Colonel H. S. E. Franklin, in anticipation of the arrival of the troops from Hillah, had occupied Baqubah and the railway station, expelling, after fighting under difficult conditions owing to the thick undergrowth, a number of insurgents who had taken possession of the palm gardens round the town.

On the 22nd August the construction of blockhouses between Baghdad and Baqubah and on the Baghdad-Kut railway was begun. The work on the latter line, which was my main line of communication, and which had already received attention in so far as the protection of the important bridge over the Diyalah river was concerned, was to begin simultaneously from both ends. This could only be carried out slowly at first, posts being placed at the railway stations, but, as troops arrived from India, I was able to allot for the work the 1/12th Pioneers, the 2/89th Punjabis, and the 2/96th Infantry.

I had hoped to begin moving from Baqubah by the 1st September, and, in order to help the administrative arrangements of the 17th Division, had sent some of my own staff to that place; but the single line of railway and the small amount of rolling-stock made the concentration of troops from Hillah, who had to detrain at Baghdad West, cross the river and entrain again, a painfully slow process. On the 5th September, however, the 34th Brigade column, under Brigadier-General Coningham, was assembled immediately south of the Diyalah railway bridge, and began its advance next day. It consisted of the following troops:—

32nd Lancers (less two squadrons),
35th Scinde Horse (less two squadrons),
97th Battery R.F.A. (less one section),
132nd (How.) Battery R.F.A.,
Bridging train (one section),
1/15th (Ludhiana) Sikhs,

45th (Rattray's) Sikhs,
1/99th Infantry,
1/10th Gurkha Rifles,
 and details.

A smaller column, the 75th Brigade column, under Brigadier-General G. A. H. Beatty, C.M.G., D.S.O., and composed of—

45th Pack Battery,
9th Company 2nd (Q.V.O.) Sappers and Miners,
3/9th (Bhopal) Infantry,
2/119th Infantry,
122nd (Rajputana) Infantry (a small detachment),
1/12th Pioneers (two companies),
 and details,

was entrusted with the care of the Persian line of communication within our border.

Of the tribes in the Baqubah - Quraitu area—generally called the Diyalah tribes, from the name of the river which waters the region they inhabit—it may be said that they had risen as the result of propaganda. Reports had been sedulously spread among them by agitators from Baghdad and elsewhere to the effect that the British had begun evacuating the country; and when Baqubah was left by the Political Officer on the 12th August, the truth of what they had been told seemed evident. The opportunity was one which promised loot, and was therefore not to be disregarded. The tribes in question are none of them large, and belong to no great confederation, as is the case with the Muntafiq, Shamiyah, Bani Lam, and others, and so lack the cohesion and fighting qualities of those in the Euphrates valley. Moreover, they are not so well armed as are the latter.

Before the advance began a proclamation had been issued calling upon them to cease hostilities, and whether this injunction, the fear of reprisals, or the knowledge of their inability to oppose a strong force actuated them, the resistance encountered by General Coningham on his march was almost negligible.

On the 8th, between Abu Jisrah and Sharaban, a force of six hundred insurgents was encountered who were holding the Marut canal, which carries a portion of the waters of the Diyalah to an area west of Balad Ruz. These, evidently thinking that they had only a small force to deal with such as had operated from the direction of Quraitu, began advancing from their position with some boldness. No sooner, however, had our main body come in sight than hesitation was displayed, and the 32nd Lancers, galloping forward, crossed the bridge, routed a portion of the force, and turned the flank of the remainder, who withdrew in haste.

The column now pushed on and reached Sharaban. That town had been attacked on the 15th August by a rabble, which included the villagers and tribesmen in the neighbourhood, the whole being led by an ex-Shabanah officer, who had some time before been dismissed for corruption. When the rising took place there was at Sharaban a small colony of Englishmen, the existence of which was unknown to me until after the incident which I am about to relate took place. The colony included an English lady, the wife of Captain Buchanan of the Irrigation Department; but through the non-reception of a return her name had not been entered in a lately revised statement of the wives of civil officials in Mesopotamia, and the Acting Civil Commissioner was unaware that she had left Baghdad, where she had been in June. The only troops at Sharaban consisted of a detachment of Levies,[1] numbering some fifty men, under the command of Captain Bradford, with Sergeant-Major Newton and Instructor Nesbitt. These were attacked by greatly superior numbers, whereupon the majority of the rank and file deserted; but the British officer in command, as well as the Assistant Political Officer, Captain Wrigley, the Irrigation Officer, Captain Buchanan, and the few men who remained faithful, gallantly defended the Qislah or old Turkish Barracks—the Levy quarters, which were situated a short distance to the north, being less suited for defence.

[1] The Levies were not at this time under my command.

Blockhouse and regulator of Ruz Canal.

Sharaban—Qishlah or old Turkish barracks in foreground.

The little force was assailed by hordes of yelling Arabs, among whom Captain Wrigley, it is said, recognised a local inhabitant of some consequence. Thereupon he called to him by name, and, accompanied by Captain Bradford, made as if to parley with him. For a brief space there was a pause in the fight, and it almost seemed as if the defenders of the Qislah were within an ace of escaping with their lives. Unfortunately some of the Levies of Kurdish origin, who may have failed to appreciate the situation, reopened fire on the Arabs, who, suspecting treachery, resumed the attack. They at length succeeded in forcing their way into the Qislah, where after a final stand all the Englishmen except one perished. The latter, who was severely wounded, and Mrs Buchanan, whose husband had been killed before her eyes, were removed to the house of a shaikh in the town, where they remained in captivity until the arrival of the relief column several weeks later.

It may be mentioned that on the date of this lamentable occurrence an aeroplane from Baghdad, which was making a reconnaissance over the freshly-disturbed area, flew over Sharaban, and on its return the observer reported that nothing unusual had been noticed there. Even if information of what was in progress had been forthcoming, no steps could have been taken that would have saved those at Sharaban from the fate which befell them; for the lack of troops, the danger of sending a column along an unguarded line as exemplified by the relief of Rumaithah, apart from the time necessary to organise and transport such a column to a point sixty-two miles from Baghdad, would have prevented the success of any attempt at rescue. It has been suggested that armoured-cars might have succeeded on this occasion in saving some at least of the British. The futility of their employment in a closely-cultivated and, in places, intricate country such as that which lies east of the Diyalah, has been more than once demonstrated in Mesopotamia with disastrous results. Moreover, as was mentioned earlier, the battery of these vehicles at Baghdad was unfit to move except on a road or prepared track.

But to resume the story of Brigadier-General Coningham's operations. On the 9th and 10th September the force halted, as Sharaban, being a centre of intrigue, a fine of rifles had to be collected and other punishment meted out. On the night of the 9th/10th an attack was made by the insurgents on the post at Abu Jisrah station, which demonstrated the necessity for erecting blockhouses at intervals along the line before the withdrawal of the married families from Karind could take place.

This procedure would lead to delay, but no risk could be taken where the lives of women and children were involved. In order to put into force this policy, part of General Coningham's force marched back to Abu Jisrah, and on the 12th blockhouse construction began simultaneously from Abu Hawa, Abu Jisrah, and the Marut canal. So quickly was the work carried out that in three days forty-five blockhouses were built between the station at Abu Hawa and the Balad Ruz canal.

In the meantime Colonel Greer's column, with which Brigadier-General Coningham's force was in communication, had been ordered to push forward through the gorge where the Diyalah traverses the low-lying Jabal Hamrin range; and on the 14th September the column entered it, and the latter officer advanced to meet him, leaving a battalion at Sharaban to cover the construction of blockhouses.

The railway line was repaired, but traffic could not be resumed throughout the length of the line owing to the damage to one important bridge, which took some weeks to restore. Posts, which were later replaced by strong blockhouses, were now established to guard the regulators at the heads of the several canals on the left bank and the Khalis canal on the right bank of the Diyalah, whence the waters are distributed by their agency throughout a very extensive area. By holding the regulators the supply of water could be completely cut off from the cultivators. As it happened, however, that the lands of some of the inhabitants who were well disposed towards us were situated some distance down-stream from the regu-

Table Mountain.

Quraitu railway station.

lators, while the possessors of those nearer the heads of the canals were hostile, the restriction of supply could not be placed on the latter without inflicting injury on the former.

By the 22nd September the first daily train of married families from Karind reached Baqubah. Elaborate and careful arrangements for their comfort had been made;

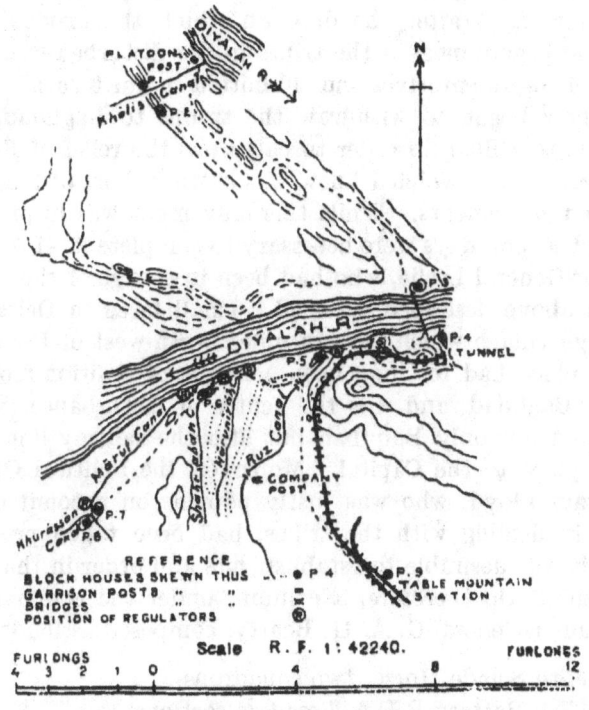

Fig. 6.—*Canal Head Defences near Table Mountain.*

but, owing to the centre portion of the large bridge just mentioned having been damaged with explosives by the insurgents, a change of trains was unavoidable. Quraitu, however, was left daily at such an hour as permitted the transfer of baggage from train to train to take place in the cool of the morning, and while this was going on breakfast was served. By 6 P.M. the train reached Baqubah, where bath, dressing, and dining tents were ready, and dinner shortly followed. Here the husbands met their wives, and accompanied them as far as Baghdad the same evening or next morning, according to whether the line on any particular date was considered safe for running trains by night or not. From Baghdad the journey was continued without change to Kut, and thence to Basrah and beyond by steamer.

A few days after the date on which the exodus from Karind began, most of the tribes in the disturbed area sent in their representatives and submitted to our terms.

I now began to withdraw the troops to Baghdad, and thence to Hillah, in order to carry out the relief of Kufah, the garrison of which I knew was getting short of food and other requirements. While this movement was in progress —and several days were necessary to complete it—I ordered Major-General Leslie, who had been in charge of the operations above described, to send a small force to Deltawah, a large village which lies ten miles north-west of Baqubah. This place had for long been a haunt of sedition-mongers from Baghdad, and was the centre of disturbances which affected not only Baqubah but also the railway line from that place to the Capital. Moreover, the Political Officer, Captain Lloyd, who was justly popular on account of his tact in dealing with the tribes, had been taken prisoner, and it was desirable to establish rule and order in the area. On the 24th, therefore, a column, under the command of Brigadier-General G. A. H. Beatty, composed as follows—

    35th Scinde Horse (two squadrons),
    97th Battery R.F.A. (less two sections),
    132nd (How.) Battery R.F.A. (less one section),
    9th Company Sappers and Miners,
    1/15th (Ludhiana) Sikhs,
    2/119th Infantry (two companies),
    1/12th Pioneers (two platoons),
       and certain details,

marched to occupy the place. The opposition met with was slight, and on reaching Deltawah due punishment was inflicted. There a detachment of two hundred Indian infantry was left to keep order, the government was again set up, and the submission of the tribes soon followed.

As a fortnight later indications of trouble showed themselves on the Tigris above Baghdad, the detachment at Deltawah was on the 15th October transferred to Sindiyah, where its presence was expected to have a salutary effect, and where, the rainy season being near, when movement across country becomes difficult, it could more easily be supplied from the Capital by river.

To keep order in the area from which I had withdrawn troops I left Brigadier-General Beatty with the undermentioned force, which included the garrisons of blockhouses :—

> 32nd Lancers (two squadrons and machine-gun section),
> 13th Pack Battery R.G.A.,
> 45th Pack Battery,
> 1/99th (Deccan) Infantry,
> 2/119th Infantry,
>> and some details, and also the detachment of the 122nd (Rajputana) Infantry, which shortly left to join its unit in the North Persian Force.

These troops, assisted by armed men of the Labour Corps, who held the blockhouse line and certain posts in the Jabal Hamrin, sufficed to keep the area in order, and furnished a small mobile column, whose headquarters was established at Sharaban. Baqubah, which had suffered much loss at the hands of raiders and even after Brigadier-General Coningham's advance, was constantly threatened with a recurrence of external attacks, was now defended by a circle of blockhouses, which were held by two companies of the 2/119th Infantry.

On the 17th September Lieut.-Colonel Greer's force had moved towards Kingarban, the branch railway to which place had been considerably damaged by the insurgents. The necessary repairs were effected, and on the 27th September a train reached Kingarban from Baqubah.

In order to maintain pressure on the inhabitants in and around Hillah during the absence of my main force north-east of Baghdad, I had ordered Brigadier-General Walker's 55th Brigade column to be maintained in that area, but in considerably reduced strength. The column thus was limited to the following troops :—

 37th Lancers (two squadrons).
 39th Battery R.F.A. (one section).
 131st (How.) Battery R.F.A.
 2nd Battalion Royal Irish Rifles.
 1/116th Mahrattas.
 17th Machine Gun Battalion (a detachment).
 39th Combined Field Ambulance (a detachment).

I considered that this force would, with the power that could be exercised by our possession of the Hindiyah Barrage, suffice to occupy the attention of the insurgents, and I further ordered that the Husainiyah canal, which supplies Karbala with river water and which had not been blocked when the barrage was occupied, should be closed and a post established at its head. To ensure safe access to Musayib from the railway and so facilitate supply, a line of blockhouses was constructed.

Brigadier-General Walker's column carried out some punitive operations against the tribes east of the railway who had interfered with the despatch of supplies to Hillah. These measures were successful, the shaikhs implicated surrendering unconditionally, and on the 23rd September the column returned to Hillah, having fully justified my hopes as to its utility.

Further north, on the Euphrates, the Zoba tribe, which for several weeks had trembled on the brink of insurrection, had risen on the 14th August, and two days earlier had murdered at Khan Nuqtah Lieut.-Colonel Gerald Leachman, the Political Officer of the Dulaim Division. On the 12th that officer had directed Shaikh Dhari of that tribe to meet him at Khan Nuqtah, which is one of two lonely caravanserai about midway between Baghdad and Fallujah. About 10.30 A.M. the shaikh arrived, accompanied by two of his sons, two nephews, and a few followers, and while waiting for Colonel Leachman sat smok-

Khan Nuqtah.

Baghdad from the south-west.

OPERATIONS NORTH-EAST OF BAGHDAD

ing in the doorway of the khan, which was occupied by shabanah or police. About 12.30 Leachman drove up in his car, having with him only his servant and driver, and joined Dhari at the entrance to the khan, discussing with him until 2 P.M. matters connected with crops and revenue. About that hour a motor-car with a party of Arabs arrived, and stated that they had been stopped and robbed about two miles from the khan in the direction of Baghdad. Leachman at once sent a shabanah officer and ten men, as well as five of the Zoba, to arrest the robbers, but ordered the party not to proceed further than two miles from the khan. During their absence Dhari and the remainder of his men left the khan, after, it is believed, a heated discussion regarding the reported robbery, for which the Zoba were considered responsible; but soon returned, when Dhari asked the sentry to grant him admission in order to speak to the Political Officer. Orders were given to admit him, upon which two of his followers, one of whom was his son Sulaiman, fired at and severely wounded Colonel Leachman. As he fell to the ground Dhari came into the khan, and Leachman asked him why he had shot him, as he had never done him an injury. Thereupon Dhari drew his sword and killed him.

The loss at this juncture of such a man came as a shock to every one, for he was possessed of great courage and resource, and had an intimate knowledge of the people and the country. From the action at Shaibah in 1915 until the surrender of Mosul by the Turks in 1918 he had been present at all the principal engagements, and had only escaped capture at Kut by leaving that place with the cavalry a few hours before it was surrounded.

The result of the rising of this tribe was to cut off from Baghdad the troops which held Fallujah and Ramadi. Although the garrison had, as already mentioned, been furnished with supplies, and Major J. I. Eadie, who had assumed political control, was doing admirable work in maintaining the *status quo*, I felt that some movement, however insignificant, towards reopening communication would, while my main force was north-east of Baghdad, occupy the attention of the tribes west of that place, who were still reported from time to time to be concentrating with a view to attempting a raid on our supply depots.

Moreover, in addition to the murder of the Political Officer, this area was responsible for one of the several mishaps which had occurred on one of the six days from the 10th to the 15th August. So closely did the Job-like reports of these mishaps, some of which have yet to be described, and all of which arrived from widely different areas, follow one another, that my equanimity was sorely tried. On the 10th came the news of the grounding of the *Greenfly*; on the 11th the ambiguous affair near Tel Afar; on the 12th the misfortune to Brigadier-General Young's column, the failure to arrest some extremists at Baghdad, and the murder of Lieut.-Colonel Leachman; on the 13th the loss of Khidhr railway station with two armoured trains and the isolation by land of Samawah and its garrison; on the 14th the massacre of the British at Sharaban, and on the 15th the loss of several vessels on the Upper Euphrates. Misfortunes seldom come alone, and those enumerated above, added to the disaster to the Manchester column ten days earlier, truly a heaping of Ossa on Pelion, were calculated almost to make one feel that the gods were not fighting on our side. Nevertheless, through having been in what are called "tight" places more than once before in my life, I not only felt confident that we should weather the storm, but could even sometimes laugh at the black clouds overhead. They had their silver lining in the recapture of the Hindiyah Barrage on the 13th, and in the fact, most vital of any, that my troops were not cut off at Diwaniyah as they might so easily have been.

As regards what had happened in the area where Colonel Leachman had held sway, Brevet Lieut.-Colonel L. G. Williams, 5th Cavalry, who was in temporary command of the 51st Infantry Brigade, being dissatisfied with the state of his forage rations, decided to send some steamers from Ramadi to Fallujah to supplement his stores at the former place. With this object three ships, including a hospital ship, left Ramadi at 6 A.M. on the 15th, and were fired on, first at five miles from that place, and again more heavily five miles further towards Fallujah, where there is much cover in the scrub on the river banks. No opposition had been anticipated, as on the 12th troops had moved by road and river along the same route without incident; but as a precaution a defence vessel, with a section of the 67th Company, 2nd (Q.V.O.) Sappers and Miners, under Lieut. A. W. H. Woods of that unit, on board, escorted the convoy, on two of whose steamers were five men of the 1/80th Carnatic Infantry.

About 7 A.M., when the firing opened for the second time, two of the steamers ran hard aground, and owing to the steersmen of the other two being hit by rifle fire, they also were carried by the current on to the mud, and could not move. Until ammunition ran short at noon, fire was maintained from the defence vessel, which, as well as the other steamers, was shortly boarded by some three hundred to four hundred Arabs. A few casualties occurred, but most of them probably earlier, for the marauders were bent on getting loot; and after securing it and setting fire to the vessels, made off, leaving the crews untouched.

Next day two squadrons 5th Cavalry, one section 96th Battery R.F.A., and two companies of the 2/6th Jat Infantry, under Major A. C. Norman, 5th Cavalry, marched from Ramadi at 4.30 A.M. to punish the villages whence the attack had come on the previous day. The enclosed nature of the ground, which at that season was overgrown with thick thorny scrub from three to five feet high, and intersected with deep irrigation channels, made movement for the troops difficult. Though opposed by the villagers, who took full advantage of the cover in the vicinity of their dwellings, the column carried out successfully the work assigned to it, and at 11.30 A.M. the return march began, Ramadi being reached some time later. Our casualties were three men slightly wounded, while of the insurgents seventeen, exclusive of those who fell from rifle fire, were bayoneted.

As mentioned earlier, the capture of the steamers, which were later salved, furnished useful propaganda among an ignorant population, and led them to believe that the British Fleet had been destroyed.

It was in view of the preceding circumstances, and in order to avoid an appearance of passivity west of the Capital, which was highly undesirable, that I directed Brigadier-General G. A. F. Sanders, who had ably carried out the arrangements for the defence of Baghdad and the construction of blockhouses along the several railway lines which diverge from it, to undertake the operation of reopening communication with Fallujah. So much work of this nature was in progress at this time, and the supply of troops so limited, that not until the 3rd September could any attempt be made to reopen road and rail communication. On that date the 11th Company Sappers and Miners, with a labour party, protected by the 2/116th Mahrattas, two pack artillery guns, and some armoured cars, began work. Opposition was met with daily at long range which caused some inconvenience, but only once did the insurgents come to close quarters during daylight, when they were punished by the mountain-guns. By the 20th September the party which had been reinforced by one 6-in. howitzer and two companies of the 1/12th Pioneers shifted camp from Baghdad to Khan Nuqtah, and next day the fort of Shaikh Dhari was razed to the ground, and all water cut off from his crops. This action led to the dispersion of the hostile elements in the neighbourhood, and facilitated the work on blockhouses. On the 24th Fallujah, which was already in communication with Ramadi, was reached by the armoured construction train, and the entire line was provided with blockhouses and garrisons by the 26th. Shortly afterwards I directed the troops at Fallujah to take over the garrisons of the blockhouses between that place and Baghdad, and to construct a post to command the regulators of the Saklawiyah canal. By securing control of this important point I should be in a position to prevent the insurgents from flooding, as the Turks had done in 1917, the country west of Baghdad, a procedure which would have caused considerable inconvenience, and made the movement of troops in

OPERATIONS NORTH-EAST OF BAGHDAD 175

that area impossible. The restoration of communication with the Upper Euphrates had a beneficial effect not only on the tribes of that area but also on those who were settled between Samarrah and Baghdad.

Three days earlier the last of one hundred and seventy-three blockhouses on the Kut-Baghdad line was completed, and as certain defences had by this time been constructed at important points on the Tigris, the main line of communication from Baghdad to the Base, after having been for three months exposed to the risk of being severed, could now be regarded as secure.

CHAPTER XVI.

THE RELIEF OF KUFAH.

THE town of Kufah has several times been mentioned in the preceding narrative, and the fact that a small garrison of regular troops was invested there. Though not included among the so-called sacred cities of Mesopotamia, this town was founded as far back as 638 A.D., three years after Iraq had fallen through conquest into the hands of the Muhammadans. The main interest of the place is due to the fact that 'Ali, the originator of the Shiah sect, and nephew of the Prophet Muhammad, was assassinated there in 661 A.D. The great mosque, which marks the traditional site of the murder, stands about a mile and a half from the present town on the way to Najaf, which lies seven miles to the south-east.

The story of how 'Ali came to be buried in the desert at Najaf, or rather where Najaf now stands, will, I think, bear repeating here. It is related that as he lay dying he said to those around him that, as a Badawin Arab, he desired to be buried in the desert, and gave instructions that after death his body was to be tied on the back of a camel which was to be free to wander and graze where fancy led him. Wherever the camel chanced to lie down to rest there was to be the burial place. The peculiar site of Najaf, which stands in the desert on a ridge of reddish sandstone, is accounted for by this story, which, like most traditions that have come down through the ages, has lost in accuracy but gained in interest. Thus the tale goes on to say that, when at the point of death, 'Ali had a vision from the Almighty, in which he was told that where the camel bearing his corpse should chance to rest, was the self-same spot at which Adam and Noah were buried.

The latter portion of the tale concerning 'Ali's death is known to few Europeans, but every true believer of the Shiah sect thinks that Najaf holds the tombs of the three patriarchs, and that when he makes his pilgrimage to the holy city and prays at the great shrine, he does so in the presence of their revered remains.

If 'Ali really gave vent in his dying hour to the utterance which is now attributed to him, he must have been one of the most far-seeing men who have trod this earth; but it is probable that the latter part of the tale owes its origin to the ingenuity and avarice of some Najaf holy men who were desirous of drawing pilgrims to their shrines from the rival city of Karbala.

Kufah, the houses of which are built mostly of stone and mortar, has a river frontage of from five to six hundred yards along the right bank of the Kufah channel of the Hindiyah branch, which forks at Kifl and forms two channels—the Kufah and the Shamiyah. The town, which is credited with a population of from three thousand to four thousand persons, is surrounded on all sides but the river front by date-palm plantations, and there are gardens on the left bank of the channel.

About the middle of June the garrison of Kufah, which was intended by its presence not only to overawe the inhabitants of the town but keep in check those of the surrounding country, consisted of two companies of the 108th Infantry (approximately four hundred and fifty rifles), under the command of Captain D. M. Dowling of that regiment. From this garrison, on the urgent representation of Major P. F. Norbury, the Political Officer of the Shamiyah Division, half a company was sent to Najaf on the 23rd June. This force was obtained by withdrawing to Kufah on the 20th two out of the three platoons which were at Abu Sukhair fort and village, a place which stands ten miles down-stream from Kufah and on the same bank of the channel. As the situation was one of growing and general unrest, and as the force at Abu Sukhair was very

M

small, it was strengthened on the 4th July by the despatch of a reinforcement of one hundred and six rifles, which had arrived at Kufah on the previous day. The Political Officer once more became importunate, with the result that Captain Dowling sent a platoon to Umm-al-Barur, which is twelve to eighteen miles from Kufah according to the route followed. At the same time Captain Dowling gave it as his opinion that such a force was totally inadequate to maintain order.

On the 8th July the Political Officer came to the conclusion that the detachment at Najaf was unnecessary, whereupon it was ordered to move to Kufah, at which place the hospital khan was occupied. Next day the Political Officer agreed to the concentration of all detachments at Kufah, but later advised against the withdrawal of troops from Abu Sukhair, where the defence vessel, *Firefly*, commanded by Lieutenant D. H. Stanley, arrived from the Upper Euphrates on the 13th.

Signs of hostility began to show themselves on the 14th, when a motor bellum on its way to Abu Sukhair with rations for the Levies, some of whom were also there, was heavily fired on, and only escaped capture through the intervention of the *Firefly*. On her return to Kufah next day, where work on the defences was in progress, she was continually under rifle fire.

As the withdrawal of the Abu Sukhair garrison now presented considerable risk, the Political Officer came to an agreement with the tribesmen, under the terms of which it marched to Kufah unmolested on the 18th. Two days later boats with supplies for the garrison of the latter place were attacked as they were coming down-stream and the guards overpowered, and on the 21st the investment may be said to have begun.

The relief of this beleagued garrison was the first and main object of the operations which were about to be undertaken from Hillah in a southerly direction. These would be followed by such action as would ensure the release of the prisoners taken on the 24th July, who were believed to be confined in Najaf; and the promoters of

Kufah from the south-east, 4th October 1920. (Buildings held by garrison are shown within white lines.)

Block of buildings held at Kufah by 108th Infantry. (Defence vessel *Firefly* on the left.)

THE RELIEF OF KUFAH

the insurrection and the inhabitants in and near the sacred cities would be overawed.

I was anxious to impress that part of the country in which the operations would take place with as great a display of strength as possible, and with that object in view the defence of Musayib and the Hindiyah Barrage was allotted to only one battalion, the 45th Sikhs, a unit which, though anxious to continue with the fighting column, would benefit by a brief rest. For a similar reason another unit, the 1/10th Gurkha Rifles, that, whenever it had been engaged, had won distinction, was left in charge of Hillah. To add still further to the force available and bring fresh troops on to the scene, the headquarters and two squadrons of the 5th Cavalry were withdrawn from Ramadi, and made their way by road to Hillah through Baghdad. The area on the Upper Euphrates, from which they came, had now become quiet, and on the 9th October the regular garrison of Hit, which post, as already mentioned, had been held by the loyal Dulaim tribe under their Shaikh, Ali Sulaiman, pending our ability to reoccupy it, was replaced.

Unfortunately it was necessary to leave troops northeast of Baghdad, where propagandists were reported to be busily engaged in trying to renew the disturbances, to continue the process of restoring order, and to ensure compliance with the terms that had been issued. For this purpose, and excluding the detachment at Deltawah, I left under the command of Brigadier-General Beatty the following troops, which included those necessary for guarding the railway line :—

32nd Lancers (less two squadrons),
13th Pack Battery R.G.A.,
40th Pack Battery,
1st Battalion Royal Irish Fusiliers and Machine-gun Company,
1/94th (Russell's) Infantry,
2/119th Infantry,
99th (Deccan) Infantry,
 and certain details.

The number of troops at my disposal was now, for the first time, sufficient to admit of operating simultaneously in strength in two directions, and by doing so it was expected that the insurgents would be led to divide themselves into two or more groups.

The plan of one of the forces, the 55th Brigade column, was to relieve Kufah and recover the prisoners. That of the other, the 53rd Brigade column, was to occupy Tuwairij, on the Hindiyah branch of the Euphrates, and threaten the holy city of Karbala, which lies thirteen miles to the west. The columns were composed as follows :—

55th Brigade Column—Brigadier-General H. A. Walker,

    35th Scinde Horse (less two squadrons),
    37th Lancers (two squadrons and Machine-gun Section),
    39th Battery R.F.A.,
    97th Battery R.F.A. (one section),
    131st (How.) Battery R.F.A.,
    45th Pack Battery (less one section),
    61st Company, 2nd (Q.V.O.) Sappers and Miners,
    67th Company, 2nd (Q.V.O.) Sappers and Miners (less one section),
    2nd Battalion Manchester Regiment,
    2nd Battalion Royal Irish Rifles,
    8th Rajputs,
    1/15th (Ludhiana) Sikhs,
    87th Punjabis,
    1/116th Mahrattas,
    108th Infantry (less detachment at Kufah),
    1/32 Sikh Pioneers,
      and certain details.

53rd Brigade Column—Brigadier-General G. A. F. Sanders.

    5th Cavalry (less two squadrons and Machine-gun Section),
    2nd Battery R.F.A. (less one section),
    132nd (How.) Battery R.F.A.,
    45th Pack Battery (one section),

THE RELIEF OF KUFAH

9th Company, 2nd (Q.V.O.) Sappers and Miners,
2nd Battalion East Yorkshire Regiment,
1st Battalion Rifle Brigade,
3/9th (Bhopal) Infantry,
13th Rajputs,
1/12th Sikh Pioneers,
and certain details.

As all operations that take place in Mesopotamia depend mainly on the supply of water, and as the troops moving along the Hillah-Kifl road would be forced to rely on what is carried by channels running westward from the Nahr Shah canal, which lies parallel to and from two to four miles east of the road, special arrangements had to be made. The little Hillah-Kifl railway of two feet six inches' gauge also depends for water on the same source, but the permanent way had been damaged by the insurgents, and as there was a deficiency of rolling-stock, it was of little military value. Either the tribesmen in July had cut off the water from the Kifl road at the time when the ill-fated advance towards that place was made, or the low level of the Hillah branch may have been responsible for the dried-up canals. In any case the result contributed in no small measure to the reverse suffered on that occasion. It was decided, therefore, that the Kufah force should march in two columns, one column along the bank of the Nahr Shah canal, which was to be the line of supply for the whole force under Brigadier-General Walker. The canal is navigable for country boats for some part of its length, and parallel and close to it a road with blockhouses at intervals would be made. These arrangements would ensure a supply of water running by side channels to the other column on the Kifl road, provided that the columns kept roughly abreast of one another. While following this road, which was a track superior to that along the canal, the column would be in a position to close the channels running to the westward of it, to the inconvenience of the inhabitants on that flank. The road itself passes through open country, which is intersected by numerous major and minor canals. All these are bridged, and thus make the road passable for all arms in normal times, but they form a series of excellent parallel defensive positions against a force moving either in a northerly or southerly direction.

Before, however, the date fixed for the advance on Kifl and Tuwairij, and while the troops required to move against the latter place were assembling from Baghdad and other places, a minor operation had to be undertaken. The necessity for it arose from the fact that the Nahr Shah canal takes off from the Hillah branch of the Euphrates two and a half miles below Hillah. On this stretch of the river the banks are covered with a dense belt of palm-trees, and the road to Diwaniyah lies close along the right bank of the river, which is here not more than fifty yards in breadth. Since July the insurgents had been in the habit of occupying these palm-groves in considerable strength, and it was certain that, unless they were driven from their stronghold, they would interfere with the passage of native boats from Hillah to the mouth of the Nahr Shah canal and the use of the road to the same point. The only means of ensuring the safety of the force and its supplies lay in the construction of a blockhouse line outside the belt of palms, and to a distance of three-quarters of a mile below the mouth of the canal. The advance on Kufah would be delayed by the work which would have to be undertaken; but the garrison, as it was afterwards known, though getting short of food, feared the possibility of a hasty and ineffectual attempt at relief, and raised no signals, when our aeroplanes made their periodical visits overhead, lest alarm should be caused regarding their condition.

On the 6th, when the troops moved out from Hillah, little opposition was met with, and it seems that the insurgents were taken by surprise. But on the 7th a considerable concentration of tribesmen from the surrounding country, who were confident of preventing us from reaching Kufah, collected, and held the numerous banks of old and new canals which branch off from the river south of Hillah. While columns of infantry worked their way down both

THE RELIEF OF KUFAH

banks of the river the engineers and pioneers carried out the construction of blockhouses and the erection of wire entanglements. The resistance offered was at first stubborn,

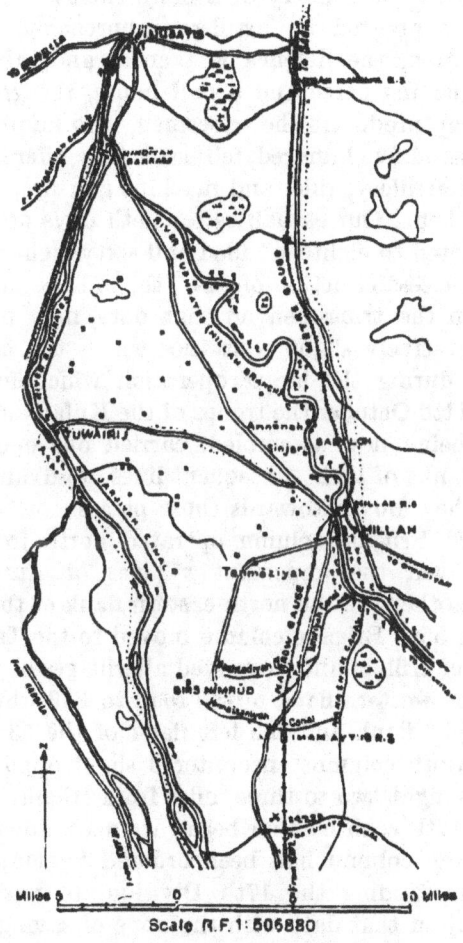

Fig. 7.—*Operations round Hillah.*

and the insurgents continued holding their strong positions until the infantry arrived at close range.

On the left bank the 2nd Battalion Royal Irish Rifles, with two companies of the 8th Rajputs, advanced without a check over the open plain outside the belt of palms along the river bank; while on the other bank the remainder of the 8th Rajputs, supported by the 1/15th Sikhs, was forced to traverse country of a more enclosed nature. As the force, supported by artillery, approached the insurgents' position, the defence weakened, and, after an engagement lasting three and a half hours, the ground they held was captured. As the tribesmen, who numbered some three thousand five hundred, fell back, they offered excellent targets for artillery, rifle, and machine-gun fire, and heavy toll was taken. Our casualties for both days of the operation amounted to eighteen killed and sixty-eight wounded.

To the successful action on the 7th, and the heavy losses inflicted on the tribesmen on that date, may be imputed the comparatively slight resistance which the column encountered during the larger operation which followed.

On the 11th October the troops of the Kufah and Tuwairij columns, being now assembled, carried out operations to clear the flanks of their subsequent lines of advance, and on the 12th they moved towards those places.

The 53rd Brigade column operated north from Hillah, and destroyed the important villages of Annanah and Sinjar and others on the north-eastern flank of the Tuwairij road. The 55th Brigade column moved to the Tahmaziyah area west of Hillah, and destroyed all villages of the Fatlah tribe on the western flank of the road to Kifl, thus clearing its own right flank and the left flank of the 53rd Brigade column. Both columns encountered slight opposition, and camped at night two to three miles from Hillah.

On the 12th each column began its main advance. The 53rd Brigade column had been ordered by Major-General Leslie, commanding the 17th Division, to push through to Tuwairij on that date with .the hope of saving the boat-bridge, which crosses the Euphrates there, before the insurgents had time to burn it. For the first five miles no opposition was met with, and blockhouse construction along the line of communication was carried out. Thereafter at two different lines of villages and the Jarjiyah canal, which runs parallel to the Hindiyah branch—on the right bank of

THE RELIEF OF KUFAH

which stands Tuwairij—and half a mile east of it, stubborn resistance was encountered. As the cavalry acting alone was unable to break through, the 2nd Battalion East Yorkshire Regiment and the 13th Rajputs, supported by artillery, were brought up. A heavy fire of guns and machine-guns was now brought to bear on the bank of the Jarjiyah canal, and the cars of the 6th Light Armoured Motor Battery, moving on in advance, crossed the canal bridge, and caused the tribesmen several casualties.

At Tuwairij a further stand was made by the tribesmen, who set fire to the boat-bridge; but the sappers and the 13th Rajputs, pushing on, extinguished the flames and occupied the town. Here Agha Hamid Khan, the former Deputy Assistant Political Officer at Najaf, who, as will presently be shown, had done good work in relation to our prisoners, was released, he having been taken to Tuwairij and kept in confinement, but not otherwise ill-treated. As an instance of the manner in which the tribal leaders kept up the spirits of their followers and of the lies with which they fed them, he relates that only two hours before his rescue he heard the people begin to dance and shout with glee in the streets of the town. On asking his guard what had happened, they replied that news had come of the capture of Mahmudiyah, which is on the railway to Hillah, nineteen miles south of Baghdad, by the Turks, and of the victorious advance of a Sharifian force from Ramadi.

In the action which led to the capture of Tuwairij aeroplanes co-operated with effect, as they had done on many similar occasions, attacking the insurgents as they streamed back to Karbala. The Arab loss this day in killed was estimated at two hundred. Our own was inconsiderable.

The following day the blockhouses on the Hillah-Tuwairij road were completed, and defences were begun at the latter place for a garrison of half a battalion.

As a result of the capture of Tuwairij the submission of the inhabitants of Karbala became imminent. Early in the insurrection a form of government had been set up at that place, and the eleven Arabs who constituted it were ordered to make formal submission for the town to Brigadier-General Sanders at Tuwairij, after which they would proceed to Baghdad, where the High Commissioner, Sir Percy Cox, who had replaced the Acting Civil Commissioner, Lieut.-Colonel A. T. Wilson, had arrived on the 11th October. Forty-eight hours' grace were given them in which to comply with the summons, failing which they were warned that the column would proceed to Karbala, from which river-water continued to be cut off. Ten of the eleven submitted on the 16th October, and were sent to Baghdad. The action of the insurrectionary government at Karbala was shortly followed by the submission of several tribes, whose representatives came in and complied unconditionally with our terms.

While these proceedings, which were the thin end of the wedge of general surrender to superior force, were taking their course, the 53rd Brigade column carried out operations in the neighbourhood of Tuwairij.

Turning next to the more important operation for the relief of Kufah, this was equally successful. On the 12th that portion of the column which marched along the Kifl road was opposed by a force of some two thousand Arabs, who were holding the Humaisaniyah canal, and who were driven off by the 87th Punjabis, the cavalry and guns working on their flank.

On the 14th a body of six hundred insurgents who held the canal bank north-east of Kifl was disposed of by the 1/116th Mahrattas, supported by the 6th Light Armoured Motor Battery, and the town was entered. Here the column which had constructed blockhouses along the Nahr Shah canal united with that which marched along the Hillah-Kifl road. To cover the construction of a bridge the 2nd Battalion Manchester Regiment was at once ferried across the Euphrates in pontoons, but the width of the river falsified reports, and was found to be considerably greater than was anticipated. Consequently all available bridging material which had been intended for Tuwairij, in case of the destruction of the crossing there, had to be despatched from Hillah on the 15th. It reached Kifl at

The cliff which gives Iraq its name.

Karbala from the east.

THE RELIEF OF KUFAH

2.30 P.M. on the same date, after an eighteen mile march, and by 5 P.M. the bridge was completed. By 9.30 A.M. on the 16th the whole force had crossed and resumed its march on Kufah.

At 8 A.M. on the 17th October the northern outskirts of the town were reached, and the insurgents were found to be holding them in strength; but the 35th Scinde Horse, making a wide turning movement to the west, cut the Kifl-Najaf road, and charging the insurgents sabred twenty-seven, and caused other casualties by Hotchkiss-gun fire.

Meanwhile the infantry advanced through the palm gardens, ably assisted by low-flying aeroplanes. In front the 108th Infantry, the balance of which regiment formed the beleaguered garrison, led, closely followed on its right by the 2nd Battalion Manchester Regiment, and on its left by the 1/15th Sikhs. The insurgents turned and fled, pursued by aeroplanes, and by 9.30 A.M. Kufah was relieved.

What had occurred there during the preceding months was briefly as follows. When the investment began the garrison consisted of the following:—

	British Officers.	British Other Ranks.	Indian Other Ranks.	Arabs and Persians.
108th Infantry	4	...	486	...
Police and Levies	6	3	...	115
Departments	2	12	102	...
D. V. *Firefly*	1	6	14	...
	13	21	602	115

As mentioned earlier, the hospital khan had been occupied on the 8th July, and as the probability of investment grew stronger the Assistant Political Officer's house and office, the barracks of the local police and certain other buildings, were held as a defensive position.

The miniature siege followed the usual course of such operations against a semi-savage enemy. At first the Arabs, who, here as elsewhere, were led by officers of some experience, made several attempts to expel the garrison by fire from the sheltered area which they held. Buildings were set alight, and the flames seriously threatened those which our troops were occupying. On one occasion the conflagration was so extensive that only with great difficulty and after several hours' work was the fire got under. During one of these attacks Captain J. S. Mann, Assistant Political Officer, while gallantly helping to save the police barracks from destruction, lost his life by rifle fire. This officer had not been long in the country, but his tact, ability, and personal charm had made a deep impression on all who had come in contact with him, and it was felt

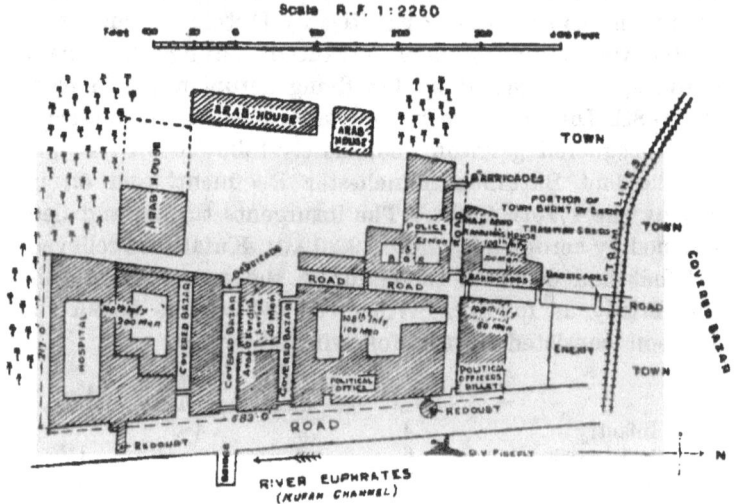

Fig. 8.—*Kufah Garrison, July-September* 1920.

that had he lived he would have risen high in the public service.

The next effort of the besiegers was to explode a mine, but this, like the attempts to burn out the garrison, was a failure. About the middle of August it was discovered that tunnelling was in progress at the north-west corner of the defences; but the work must have been of a perfunctory nature, for a burst of Lewis-gun fire caused the tunnel to collapse. Following this unsuccessful venture, an envoy from the leading shaikhs near Kufah arrived with a letter, in which the surrender of the garrison was demanded. But the defenders—over whose position aero-

THE RELIEF OF KUFAH

planes from Baghdad flew, according as they could be spared for the purpose, and from which encouraging messages, newspapers, and sometimes cigarettes were dropped, as well as bombs on the besiegers—knew that help, though long deferred, would be forthcoming, and the envoy returned empty-handed to his masters.

The mishap of the 24th July on the Kifl road had placed an 18-pdr. gun in the hands of the insurgents, and although the breech-block had been removed before capture, one of them managed to forge a rough substitute, and on the 17th August the gun opened on the *Firefly*. The first shot took effect and caused her to burn fiercely, so much so that it was feared that her magazine would explode and harm the garrison, for she was anchored close to the houses which were held. In consequence she was sunk by Lewis-gun fire, which perforated her plates. Her gallant commander had been wounded earlier and received some burns, and two days later died, while one British soldier of the crew was killed and another wounded.

Next day it was discovered that the field-gun had been removed to a point only two hundred and fifty yards distant from the defences. Concentrated Lewis-gun fire was turned on the spot, the gun was damaged, and the crew were annihilated. That night, under cover of darkness, the insurgents removed the gun; but the garrison had not seen the last of that weapon, for, at the end of August and early in September, some ninety shells were fired at them, causing, however, few casualties, while many were inflicted in return by rifle fire.

As the time of relief grew closer the besiegers seemed to slacken their efforts to overpower the garrison. On the 14th October it was known that our troops had taken Kifl, and on the 16th aeroplanes dropped the welcome news that on the morrow the defenders would regain their freedom. This, as has been seen, proved to be true, for on the 17th the column from Kifl arrived, and the siege of eighty-nine days' duration came to an end.

The good spirits which had been maintained throughout this weary trying time, during the last three weeks of which the garrison had subsisted on rice and horse-flesh, speak well for all who took part in the defence, and a special word of praise is due to the non-regular troops. Among the garrison were some Persian police and Arab Levies, who, resisting all appeals of the insurgents to desert and join what for long must have seemed to them the winning side, remained staunch to their leaders and true to their salt.

The casualties during the siege, which after a time involved itself into an attempt to starve the garrison, amounted to twenty-five killed and twenty-seven wounded.

When the relief force reached Kufah information was received that the British and Indian prisoners in the hands of the Arabs had been moved from Umm-al-Barur to Abu Sukhair, but it was shortly found that they had been transferred from the last place to Najaf.

On the 18th representatives of Najaf arrived at the headquarters of the 55th Infantry Brigade, and made submission for their town. They were then informed that the first condition of the terms was the surrender of the prisoners, and on the 19th October seventy-nine British and eighty-nine Indian prisoners were handed over.

At this point a few words regarding the vicissitudes of the prisoners may be of interest. The first news of them after their capture on the 24th July came through a Deputy Assistant Political Officer, Agha Hamid Khan, C.I.E., a first cousin of His Highness the Agha Khan. He had remained at Najaf, and in spite of the great risk to his life held his post there for some time after the insurrection began. He reported that the prisoners included about sixty-five British soldiers, who had been marched almost naked without socks or boots to Kufah, and had been disgracefully treated by the tribes on their way there. Hamid Khan added that he was sending these unfortunate men such clothes and comforts as he could procure, and that each prisoner would be given a small sum of money. A few days later a Muhammadan physician, who it was hoped would get through to the prisoners, was despatched from Baghdad to Karbala with necessaries and medical comforts for them, and it was learned with satisfaction shortly after that they were now at Abu Sukhair, nine miles southeast of Najaf, and were being better treated. The physician was not able to reach Najaf, where the prisoners, three only of whom were suffering from wounds, had been removed, as that city was in a highly-disturbed state; but Hamid Khan, who continued there for some time longer, did everything possible to alleviate their confinement. The notables of Najaf had been informed that all money spent by them on behalf of the prisoners would be refunded, and that any harm done to them would be visited with punishment in due course. About the middle of September the Assistant Political Officer of Musayib, who was in touch with Najaf, reported that some more prisoners had arrived there from Samawah, which proved that every one captured in the armoured train there had not been killed.

From that time onwards all news received regarding the prisoners was satisfactory, but, as was expected, the advance from Hillah to relieve Kufah caused them to be moved from Najaf, and a report was received that they had been transferred about the 9th October to Umm-al-Barur. They were, however, shortly afterwards brought back to their previous quarters, and, as stated, were handed over on the 19th October.

That in the end their treatment had been good was evident from their healthy and well-nourished appearance when released; and for their wellbeing credit is partly due to Company Sergeant-Major Mutter of the 2nd Battalion Manchester Regiment, the senior non-commissioned officer with them.

And here it may be mentioned that every endeavour was made to ascertain what had become of those reported missing after the fight of the 24th July on the Kifl road. From evidence found on the ground it seems probable that many men lost their way early in the retirement owing to a bend in the road, and, falling in with tribesmen near Birs Nimrud, where a tower which has incorrectly been credited as that of Babel stands, were captured and killed.

On the 20th October the 18-pdr. gun which had been lost on the 24th July, and which had fired altogether one hundred and thirty-five rounds into Kufah, sometimes at a distance of one hundred and fifty yards, causing the garrison considerable annoyance, was recovered from the left bank of the river near that place.

The 55th Infantry Brigade meantime was at Tuwairij waiting until our administration at Karbala was firmly established; but as some firing on the blockhouses round Musayib was reported, a part of it was sent northward to operate as far as the Hindiyah Barrage.

As in all cases of submission, the collection of fines and the execution of other terms lead to delay and demand the presence of troops, a commander soon finds himself with much of his force scattered about the country. Even then precautions, such as guarding lines of communication, cannot with safety be neglected; and though I was anxious that my troops should show themselves in every corner of the insurgents' country, which in some places was still unsubdued, such operations had for a time to be postponed.

CHAPTER XVII.

EVENTS IN THE RIVER AREA.

IT is now time to turn to the events that had taken place in the River Area, which, as mentioned earlier, roughly comprised all Mesopotamia south of a line running from Kut-al-Amarah to Nasiriyah and including both these places. This area, with the troops garrisoning it, was commanded by Brigadier-General H. E. C. B. Nepean, who also held the office of Inspector-General of Communications.

The disturbances which began at Rumaithah at the end of June spread quickly southwards, and displayed themselves mainly in the vicinity of Samawah and in attacks on the railway line north and south of that place.

At this time the only regular troops on the Euphrates between Jarbuiyah bridge and Basrah were the garrisons at Samawah, Ur, and Nasiriyah. At Samawah there were two and a half companies of the 114th Mahrattas, which were strengthened by some small detachments from other units, and at Nasiriyah three companies of the 2/125th Rifles. At Ur, the railway junction for the latter place and nine miles distant from it, was a company of the 2/125th Rifles, less one platoon.

I had every intention of withdrawing the garrison of Samawah, but to have done so before reinforcements arrived from overseas would almost certainly have precipitated events and led to other powerful tribes joining in the insurrection. Had this occurred, Basrah, which was my Base, and which, as stated previously, had, like Baghdad, its numerous establishments distributed over a wide area, and possessed a garrison inadequate for more than essential guard duties, would have been in danger of attack. And further, a rising of the tribes in the region between the Tigris and Euphrates on both banks of the Shatt-al-Gharraf, to which I shall refer more fully later on, would have led to disturbances on the Tigris, which would have imperilled my sole line of communication with the Base.

As reports reached General Nepean that trains were being fired upon, the railway being damaged and telegraph lines cut, a train, which carried as reinforcements one hundred men of the 2/125th Rifles under Major C. D. May, was despatched on the 2nd July to Samawah, which at that time was in the area of the 17th Division. On the same date No. 1 armoured train, manned by one hundred rifles of the 129th Baluchis, under Captain J. R. M. Hanna, was sent to patrol the line from Khidhr to Samawah. At the latter place was Major A. S. Hay, 31st Lancers, a capable and energetic officer, who had arrived there on the 27th June, and as senior officer assumed command of the garrison.

The next day, the 3rd July, as several tribes south of Rumaithah were reported to be disaffected, the *Greenfly*, one of the protected defence vessels, and another ship of the same type, known as F. 10, were ordered to proceed from Nasiriyah to Samawah. That place had been reached on the 3rd by Major May in face of opposition which caused five casualties to his detachment, and the armoured train, which was following, had its engine derailed about eight miles north of Khidhr. This mishap necessitated the construction of a diversion round it, and the train only reached Samawah on the 9th July, at which place it was berthed.

On the 3rd, too, seventy-five men of the 3rd Euphrates Levy, under Lieutenant C. E. Simpson, arrived at Ur, and marched next day for Khidhr. The railway station at that place happens to be the only point on the line between Nasiriyah and Samawah where the Baghdad-Basrah railway runs close to the river, and it is in consequence a point of considerable importance in that waterless area. On arrival there on the 4th July the situation was found to be quiet, and the stationmaster and his staff were enjoying

Basrah from the west.

Nasiriyah, looking up-stream.

the protection of the Albu Rishah section of the Juwabir tribe. As will presently be seen, the commendable behaviour of that tribe at this time did not prevent them six weeks later from firing into the backs of the retreating garrison of Khidhr and soon after committing the worst atrocity of the insurrection.

Meanwhile the *Greenfly*, which had arrived at Samawah, took part with F. 10 in minor operations which were engaged in by the garrison, but unfortunately on the 10th August, when on her way to Khidhr, she ran aground some five miles above that place. As the insurgents were then in control of the Hindiyah Barrage, and no more water could be turned down the Hindiyah branch, and as, to make matters worse, the river at this time was daily falling, all endeavours to refloat her failed. Efforts to haul her off the sandbank on which she was aground were made by another unprotected defence vessel, the *Grayfly*, and F. 11. These, as also another attempt made under heavy fire on the 15th August, during which the ships were riddled with bullets which caused several casualties, were unavailing. On the 20th August the last attempt to salve the ship was made. On that date the *Grayfly*, accompanied by two other vessels each carrying a company of Indian infantry, found that the insurgents had left the vicinity of the *Greenfly* to celebrate an annual festival, and in consequence it was possible to remove the wounded and replenish her supplies. Two days were spent by the flotilla near the stranded vessel in strenuous endeavours to extricate her from the sand, which through the action of the stream had silted up and held her like a vice. But all proved vain, and the flotilla, once more disappointed, turned down-stream and went back to Nasiriyah.

Between that place, which is fifty-six miles to the southeast of Samawah, and Basrah the line was rarely damaged, but on the section further north, between Khidhr and Samawah, which places are seventeen miles apart, rail-cutting and rail-repairing were an almost daily occurrence. The custom was for the armoured train to patrol daily from Samawah towards Khidhr, whence another similar train advanced to meet it, in the hope of keeping open the line between those places. This procedure had gone on uninterruptedly till the 12th August, when the track was so seriously damaged by the insurgents that the trains could no longer meet.

A few days earlier General Nepean had telegraphed that the tribes between those places were becoming more unruly, and that trouble of some kind was brewing. A later telegram added that a concentration of two thousand insurgents was reported to be near Khidhr, and he requested instructions whether that place should be reinforced or evacuated, the latter course being one strongly opposed by the local Political Officer.

The opposition of the latter officer to the proposed evacuation was natural, for the isolation of Samawah and the loss of Khidhr might well lead to an attack on the inadequately garrisoned town of Nasiriyah, combined with a rising by a considerable portion of the Muntafiq. As, however, Khidhr was too far from the *Greenfly* to assist her, was merely a point on the railway line to Samawah of no importance once that railway was closed for traffic, and to hold it would only add another to my isolated garrisons among which Samawah could now be counted, I, without hesitation, ordered it to be evacuated.

It may here be stated that Khidhr station is typical of such spots on the Mesopotamian railways, if those on the Baghdad-Samarrah line which were built by the Germans be excepted. These latter stations are solidly constructed of concrete blocks, and take the form of double-storied defensible barracks, within which are a well and pumping-engine for keeping the garrison supplied with water. Khidhr, on the other hand, possesses none of the usual attributes of a station in the European sense of that word, for nothing exists there beyond a small mud hut, which serves as an office and dwelling for the stationmaster, a few tents for the personnel, and a tower whence locomotives draw their water. Indeed such wayside stations would be flattered if they were classified as what are known at home as "halts."

Khidhr railway station on Basrah-Baghdad system.

Balad railway station on Baghdad-Samarrah system.

EVENTS IN THE RIVER AREA

The station at Khidhr had been occupied on the 4th July by three troops of the 3rd Euphrates Levy, under Lieutenant C. E. Simpson, and these formed the sole garrison of the place until its evacuation six weeks later. Nothing particular occurred there until the line north of it was reported to be seriously damaged. On the date of that occurrence, the 12th August, the armoured train on its return from a reconnaissance at 6 P.M. brought word that some three thousand Arabs had been seen fifteen miles to the north, and that they were moving in a south-easterly direction, with the evident intention of attacking the garrison.

At about 11.50 P.M. the insurgents, who by this time had arrived, opened fire, and the Levies, as well as the *Greenfly* with her 13-pdr. gun, replied. During the night the armoured train moved south, and engaged with its 13-pdr. gun large numbers of tribesmen, who soon worked round its flanks and compelled it to retire to the station, or run the risk of being isolated. About 9.30 A.M. next day the Ur Junction armoured train arrived, and its commander stated that the line to the south had not been damaged. Shortly afterwards my orders, transmitted through the General Officer Commanding the River Area, reached Lieutenant Simpson, and directed him to vacate the station.

As the Arabs were not far distant and kept up a hot fire, it was difficult to conceal the loading of horses, forty in number, besides kits and stores; but by the help of covering fire from the armoured train and the bravery and coolness of the garrison, the work was carried out successfully. In the absence of any competent railway personnel much shunting had to be done to marshal the trains in the order settled upon for the retirement, as it was necessary to have a rearguard composed of some armoured trucks and the 13-pdr. gun. The *Grayfly* and another unarmoured vessel, which were then engaged in helping to refloat the *Greenfly*, were desired to assist in covering the retirement until the trains had cleared the station. Owing to some misapprehension they failed to do so, and steamed to Nasiriyah without waiting for the operation to begin. In consequence the situation was gravely compromised, for the insurgents were able to come close to the station, and add greatly to the difficulty of getting the garrison and followers on board the trains.

About 3.30 P.M. the leading train, which was to be followed at five minutes' interval by the two armoured trains coupled together, left the station and proceeded slowly south. A few minutes later, for some unknown reason, the first armoured train charged the train ahead of it, and forced a number of trucks from the rails, or, according to another statement, some waggons which it was pushing were derailed. A scene of great confusion followed, which was not lessened by the fact that the Arabs were firing at close range, though fortunately with almost no effect. The derailed waggons so blocked the line that the two locomotives and the vehicles which they were drawing, and with them the 13-pdr. gun, had to be abandoned, but the personnel, crowding on to the leading undamaged train, left the scene in safety and reached Ur at 9.30 P.M. Unfortunately the regular troops, consisting of seventeen men of the 1/10th Gurkha Rifles who were occupying the waggon nearest to Khidhr, though it appears that they were warned to save themselves by jumping on to the undamaged train, failed to do so, and remained behind. What happened to these gallant soldiers is uncertain, but that they defended themselves until all were killed there can be no doubt, for when the Samawah relief column reached Khidhr several weeks after, their skulls were found laid out in a row at the village of that name. I have related this affair at length, as the behaviour of the Levies, who were unsupported by regular troops, except those on the armoured trains, redounds greatly to their credit.

During the six weeks which preceded the investment of Samawah several local expeditions were carried out by the garrison, which now approximated to the strength of one battalion, though composed of three different units, in retaliation for attacks made or threatened by the insurgents. Barbuti bridge, which is near the camp and was guarded by a platoon of only nineteen men, under a subadar, was attacked soon after midnight on the 2nd July, but was reinforced by a company at dawn, which only arrived in time to punish the aggressors as they retired. Some five hundred to six hundred Arabs had taken part in the attack, and although these succeeded in sacking and burning the camp in the vicinity they failed to reach the bridge. The defenders, who fought gallantly and whose commander was seriously wounded, suffered a loss of three killed and three wounded, while the tribesmen left twenty-seven dead on the ground. This attack was followed by other less serious affrays, for the Arabs have a rooted dislike to engage themselves against defences, and when our garrisons were besieged, generally preferred to expend their ammunition in firing from cover into the camp.

One of the minor expeditions referred to was undertaken against the village of Musa'adah, which is situated on the left bank of the river one mile north-west of the Barbuti bridge. This village, which was described to Major Hay by the Assistant Political Officer on the spot as "the property of a holy and pro-British saiyid," but which harboured some six hundred to eight hundred insurgents who had twice sallied forth to attack our troops, was dealt with in so thorough a manner that there was no question afterwards of its harbouring any living thing.

Another expedition treated in a similar fashion three villages which had formed the base for the raiders who had attacked Barbuti bridge, and a river expedition was undertaken by the *Greenfly* and F. 10 in order to create a diversion in rear of the insurgents who were besieging the garrison at Rumaithah. After these expeditions the troops at Samawah were left unmolested for a time; but unfortunately lost the services of the *Greenfly*, which, it will be remembered, while patrolling the river on the 10th August, ran aground some five miles up-stream from Khidhr.

Some time earlier I had been informed by Brigadier-General Nepean that the defences of Samawah were not in a satisfactory condition, and for this and other reasons that place was transferred on the 16th July to the River Area.

I had visited Samawah on the 12th April, immediately after the issue of a general order regarding the responsibility for defences, and found the garrison engaged in making a new camp at Barbuti bridge, which was manifestly the proper place to be held. And here I may mention that, although the Euphrates valley railway had been constructed at the time that the railways were in the hands of the military authorities, insufficient attention seems to have been paid to siting stations and constructing bridges with a view to easy water-supply or defence. In fact, throughout the country similar anomalies were noticeable, and places such as water regulators had been constructed quite regardless of military considerations which it would have been possible to observe. This omission was perhaps more marked at Samawah than at any other point on the Euphrates line, and had the station here been placed at Barbuti bridge, two miles from the town instead of close to it, the unfortunate loss of an armoured train and of several lives, an incident which will presently be described, could never have occurred.

The actual dispositions for defence at Samawah, which show a change in the arrangements that were in progress at the time of my visit—a change of which I was in ignorance until the incident of the armoured train—were as follows:—

No less than four different posts were held, which included the main camp, the supply camp, Barbuti bridge post, and the railway station post. At the last of these was No. 1 armoured train, which, under the arrangements of the General Officer Commanding the River Area, was berthed at Samawah, and patrolled thence towards Khidhr. After Major Hay took command of the place, the defences first began seriously to be made, and were sufficiently strong to withstand attacks by tribesmen. As firing into the camp increased, communication trenches were begun, and by the 29th August the garrison could move within the defences with comparative safety.

I have stated that I intended to evacuate Samawah, and the way in which the line had successfully been kept open for six weeks after the insurrection began induced me to believe that there would be no insuperable difficulty in doing so when the desired moment came. Moreover, my information led me to believe that the garrison could be extricated by the river route, and that that route would always enable supplies to be sent to the place. But the grounding of the *Greenfly* came as a distinct shock, and one which was not weakened by the failure of the *Grayfly* and other vessels sent from Nasiriyah to free her. It was evident that the garrison at Samawah would have to stand a siege. Their supply of food was sufficient to last until the middle of September, but that of ammunition was less satisfactory, as, in view of my intention to withdraw the troops, the retention of large quantities of either was inexpedient. On the 23rd the General Officer Commanding the River Area was ordered to send at once a month's supply by barge; and on the 1st September, by which date it had come to my knowledge that the supplies ordered had not all arrived and that there was a probability that the relief might be delayed, I ordered the garrison by wireless telegram to be placed on half rations.

On the 26th August a convoy, consisting of the *Grayfly*, *Sawfly*, *Stonefly*, and two steamers carrying troops and towing barges, on board of which were the supplies of food and ammunition I had ordered to be sent at once to Samawah, left Nasiriyah on a voyage which was to prove perilous. Heavy opposition was met with about eight miles above Darraji, which did not cease until Khidhr was passed. A few miles below that place one of the steamers, known as S. 9, appeared to be in difficulties, and was signalled, but replied that all was well, whereupon the defence vessel in rear steamed ahead, and joined the other ships in the vicinity of the *Greenfly*. As, however, an ominous cloud of smoke was noticed rising from the direction of S. 9, a defence vessel was detached to return to her lest she required assistance. On reaching her it was found that she had been abandoned and was in flames. Not a sign was visible of the crew or the platoon of Indian troops and two British officers who had formed her escort; and it was later gathered from the statements of a few survivors, who escaped to Nasiriyah, that the ship with her engines out of order had drifted up against the bank, where she was rushed by a large force of tribesmen. Except for the few mentioned above who were captured and escaped, all on board, including the two British officers, had been immediately massacred. At night the convoy, with the exception of the steamer and two barges, which had run aground, anchored in the neighbourhood of the stranded *Greenfly*. Next morning the defence vessel, *Stonefly*, was sent back to Nasiriyah, and the remainder of the convoy continued on its way to Samawah, all of the vessels being heavily engaged throughout the day. By 7 P.M. the *Grayfly* and her consorts reached their destination, but one of the two barges which were being towed, and on board of which were food and small-arm ammunition, grounded under heavy fire two miles short of Samawah, and had to be abandoned.

The commander of the little flotilla, Captain W. H. Suffolk of the Inland Water Transport, had shown gallantry and resolution in bringing his three ships to their goal under considerable difficulties, which might have daunted others similarly situated. For forty-eight hours the convoy, with inadequate protection, had been exposed to a galling fire of musketry at close range, which had caused heavy casualties, and the prospect of running the gauntlet with success seemed nearly hopeless. But he carried out his task, and not improbably saved the garrison of Samawah from surrender and all the horrors which that word conveyed. As a reward for his services he was forthwith given the Military Cross.

The same night as that on which the convoy arrived, the attack on the railway station camp began, and was pushed with great vigour by a large number of the insurgents. This was not altogether unexpected, for during August Major Hay had been told by an intelligence agent that many of the insurgents would disperse to their homes for the Muhammadan festival, known as the Id-adh-Dhuha, or, as it is called in India, the Baqr'Id, which would take place on the 25th of that month and following days. The same informant added that after it was over they would make an attack which would be directed first on the post known as the "railway camp."

Its defences consisted of a bullet-proof wall surrounded by a barbed-wire obstacle. These were sufficient to make it secure, and their condition had made marked improvement under Captain Oswald Russell of the 10th Lancers, who was in command of the post, and who a short time before, when with his regiment on the Upper Euphrates, had received the Military Cross for gallantry. The garrison under his command consisted of about seventy-five all ranks of his own regiment, and a similar number of the 2/125th Rifles under 2nd Lieutenant H. V. Fleming, as well as Captain J. W. Pigeon of the Indian Medical Service.

The regiment to which Captain Russell belonged having completed its tour in Mesopotamia, where it had done admirable work on the Upper Euphrates under Lieut.-Colonel Kemmis, was on the point of proceeding to India when the outbreak at Rumaithah occurred. A few days later, as the situation began to grow serious and every available man was wanted, I ordered the regiment, which had handed in its horses at Baghdad between the 28th and 30th June, to stand fast at Basrah. Thereafter it was employed, sometimes to provide the fighting portion of the crews of defence vessels and at other times to man armoured trains or any special point on the railway. Thus it happened that, on the 6th August, part of Captain Russell's squadron held a post at Barbuti bridge, while the balance replaced the personnel of No. 1 armoured train, who joined the garrison of the main camp. The train, which carried a 13-pdr. gun and crew, usually consisted of several ordinary iron trucks with loopholes cut in them, an engine, and a few other vehicles ; and, as stated earlier, was stabled at Samawah station. The water supply, which is alongside the railway line about two hundred yards north-east of the station, was still obtained by means of a pumping-engine connected with a pipe which ran to the river some distance away. Up to the time of the investment the question of water presented no difficulty, but the pumping-engine became damaged, and although apparently the pipe-line to the river was not cut, it became necessary to arrange a water store in all tanks and other receptacles that could be obtained. These were collected and for purposes of protection placed under a layer of earth.

The presence of the train at Samawah station was unknown to me, and I had no reason to suppose from the reports which came in periodically that the force at that locality was holding the ground otherwise than was projected when I visited the place in April. Had I heard what came to my knowledge too late to be remedied, I should unquestionably have ordered the station to be vacated and the gun on the train to be rendered harmless. Or as an alternative, if reports had come that the line was damaged, the train would more probably have been ordered to move to Barbuti bridge, and that post would not then have been evacuated. When the news arrived of the isolation of the station post with insufficient water and only eight to ten days' supplies, the danger of the situation was apparent, and no action but that which, as will be seen, was taken, was possible.

The site of the post, apart from its uncertain water supply, was faulty, as from the high wall of Samawah town, distant only about two hundred yards, fire of a slightly plunging nature could be directed on the camp, which not only exposed the garrison to loss, but caused many of the buried tanks to be perforated by bullets. In consequence of the loss of water that resulted, Captain Russell informed Major Hay that he would be forced to evacuate his ground if the investment exceeded four days, for the water from a well that had been dug proved to be brackish and unfit to drink. This report led to the preparation of a plan by which, in co-operation with aeroplanes from Baghdad, it was hoped to withdraw the garrison on the 3rd September. The plan it appears was as follows: As soon as the two aeroplanes appeared from Baghdad the defence vessel *Sawfly* was to fire a shot from her 3-pdr.

Samawah railway station and camp.

Samawah—The disabled armoured train.

gun at the pump-house near the station as a signal to evacuate. The supporting troops, consisting of two hundred rifles of the 114th Mahrattas, would then move from the main camp along the railway line to a point about four hundred yards from the station, while a detachment of thirty men sent from Barbuti bridge, which post was successfully evacuated during the larger operation, guarded against the risk of envelopment. Besides these troops fifty rifles were held in readiness as a reserve.

At first all went smoothly and in conformity with the plan. Thirty men of the 2/125th Rifles, under 2nd Lieutenant Fleming, who had been ordered to seize the pump-house and loading ramp adjacent to it while the station post was being cleared, carried out their instructions. Captain Russell himself, with his men and the Medical Officer, Captain Pigeon, who were to act as rearguard, climbed into the train, which then began to move. The small party under 2nd Lieutenant Fleming, seeing that the train had started, retired as ordered along the railway and passed through the covering screen of the Mahrattas. The train had gone about two hundred yards when the engine appeared to fail, or, as was later known, jumped the track, owing to a damaged switch. Immediately Captain Russell and Captain Pigeon were seen to jump out and run to each truck in turn, and survivors from the train relate that they were ordered to get out and make a bolt for safety.

What followed, so far as a careful study of all the evidence discloses, was that the Arabs, who were only two hundred yards distant and numbered from three to four thousand, rushed the train, hordes of them entering the waggons at one side and emerging on the other. Half of the occupants had not yet had time to leave it, and they were mostly killed, while a few were spared and made prisoners. Captains Russell and Pigeon remained with the train, doubtless unwilling to leave the sick and wounded who were on board, although had they chosen they could easily have escaped. The fight in which these gallant officers perished was short and sharp, covering, it is said, only a couple of minutes; but it is probable that in that short and tragic space they fought to bitter purpose.

As it became clear to the covering troops that no more survivors could be expected from the train, the retirement began. Thanks to the courage and coolness of Captain E. S. Storey-Cooper, 114th Mahrattas, whose adventures earlier in the insurrection have already appeared in 'Blackwood's Magazine,' and who received the immediate reward of the Military Cross on this occasion, it was carried out slowly and with great steadiness in the face of severe pressure by several thousand Arabs, many of whom were under one hundred yards away. It is impossible to be certain of the losses which were inflicted, but from information gained from many sources it is believed that from two hundred and fifty to three hundred of the insurgents were killed, and that their total casualties amounted to one thousand.

As soon as Major Hay, who from the main camp saw through his field-glasses most of what is above described, knew that two British officers and a large party of the 10th Lancers were missing, he collected every available man with the object of making a counter-attack towards the station. This idea, however, was soon abandoned when it became known from the three British officers, who were very close to the train, and the survivors from it, that it was impossible that any one could be left alive. This belief was strengthened by the fact that the morning was clear, with neither wind nor mirage, and no sound of firing was audible from the train.

It may be of interest here to summarise the reasons given later for the non-withdrawal of the garrison of the railway station post. They were as follows :—

(a) To have abandoned the camp would have resulted in the loss of large quantities of railway material, together with two trains.

(b) Although for two weeks the insurgents had threatened to attack they had not done so, and on the possibility of such an event, the abandonment of the station was not considered desirable. Moreover, from two independent sources information had come that if the attack were made,

EVENTS IN THE RIVER AREA 207

it would, if unsuccessful, not last more than four days. In some measure this information proved correct, for on the 2nd September many hundreds of the tribesmen left the neighbourhood of Samawah.

(c) Water sufficient for eight to ten days' consumption was stored at the station, and the perforation by bullets of the tanks was unforeseen. When the pumping-engine near the station was damaged, a water channel was dug to that point from Barbuti bridge, and on the 28th August

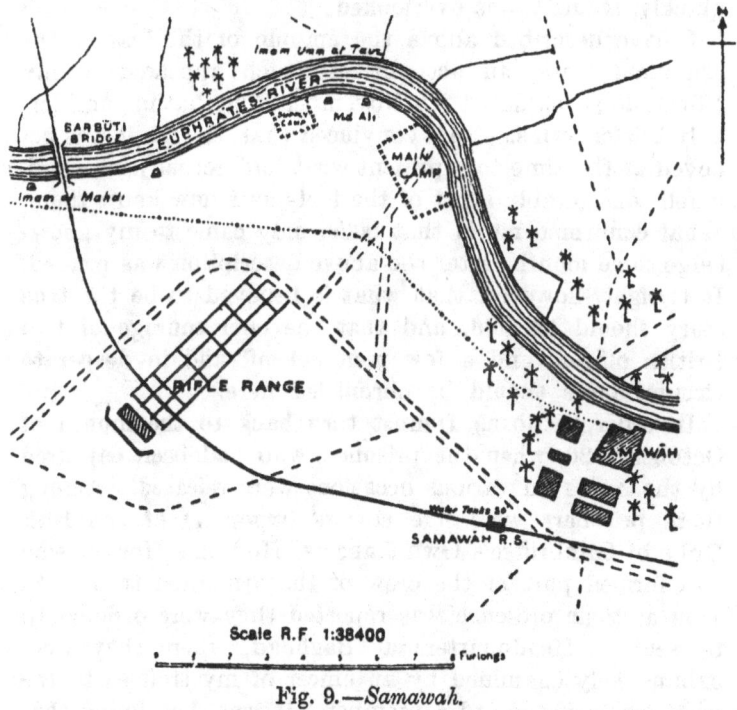

Fig. 9.—*Samawah*.

water had flowed into the channel for about half a mile from the river. Had the attack taken place forty-eight hours later, the large and shallow pits which existed between where the protected train stood and the station, and which had supplied the earth for the low railway embankment, would have been filled and have held several weeks' supply of water.

The obvious conclusion to which one is driven regarding this incident is that in unsettled or semi-settled countries railway construction and other work for which protection is sure to be demanded should not be undertaken without the approval, so far as defence questions are concerned, of the military authorities. In this case, as already mentioned, those authorities were responsible for the siting of the railway, its stations and its bridges, and it is evident that, in their desire to build this new line of communication quickly, security was overlooked.

I have described above the episode of the loss of the armoured train, an account of which appeared in my official despatch dated 8th November 1920, but in considerably briefer terms. I am convinced that, though it was believed at the time to represent what had actually occurred, it fell considerably short of the facts as I now know them. What confirmed me in that belief only came to my knowledge some months after the above description was penned. It is right, however, that what is believed to be the true story should be told, and that the cool courage of two British officers and a few men cut off and in desperate circumstances should be chronicled here.

In order to do so I must turn back to the month of October 1920, when the prisoners who had been captured by the Arabs on various occasions were released. Among these prisoners were five sowars (troopers) of the 10th Duke of Cambridge's Own Lancers (Hodson's Horse), who had formed part of the crew of the armoured train. As soon as their presence was reported they were ordered to be sent to Headquarters at Baghdad, where they were exhaustively examined by an officer of my staff as to the occurrences of the 3rd September. It was then found that three of them had been taken prisoners in an attempt to make their way to the camp after receiving an order to do so, and that the other two had been captured when the garrison of the train was overcome.

According to the story told by these two sowars, the train on the morning of the 3rd September was made up of several trucks and loopholed iron waggons, the gun-truck and gun having been detached and abandoned in anticipation of the withdrawal. In front of the engine and in the direction of the camp were two such waggons (those shown in the reproduced photograph), the greater portion of the vehicles being behind the tender and between it and the station. The Arabs soon surrounded the train, and after some heavy fighting overcame the occupants of several trucks, leaving alive only those who held the last two loopholed iron waggons which were nearest to the station. About 2 P.M. Captain Russell withdrew the few survivors into the end waggon, but left open the communication door between it and the waggon which he had previously been occupying. At this door he took his stand, and, from the great losses which the Arabs admit and with which he is associated, he must have used his machine-gun, rifle, and revolver with deadly effect. It was about this time, or probably shortly after, that the Arabs, finding that they could not capture the last waggon by direct assault, bethought themselves of burning out the occupants. In order to carry out this plan and to avoid exposure, which was inevitable if they attacked from the flank or the end of the train nearest to the camp, they made their way underneath the trucks towards the occupied waggon. Several of them were shot by Captain Russell, who remained at the door to prevent what was in progress, but about 4 P.M. he was wounded in the right side by a rifle shot. The communication door was now closed, and the Arabs were able to pour oil on the wooden sleepers underneath the carriage and set fire to them.

Fourteen men besides Captain Russell were in this waggon —possibly also Captain Pigeon, though it is believed that he fell earlier in the fight—and as the situation was evidently hopeless, he told them that the best thing to be done was to make a sortie and sell their lives as dearly as possible. The Arabs were all round, close to the carriage, when several of the men jumped to the ground and hurled themselves into the midst of them. As not one of these brave fellows, worthy successors of the brilliant soldier who raised their corps, was amongst the prisoners who were recovered later, it must be assumed that all of them lost their lives. Captain Russell, seeing what had occurred, remarked to those who were left that they might as well remain in the carriage, and he and they began firing again through the loopholes. But the Arabs, who were thirsting for the blood of the remaining few, had by this time made their way on to the roof of the waggon, and though several of them were shot, some succeeded by using crowbars in breaking in among the defenders, when the two remaining sowars were taken alive and their gallant leader was put to the sword.

Such was the account given by these two men of the grim struggle which had lasted for so many hours, and most of which had been fought out within the narrow limits of an iron waggon, where the terrible heat and lack of water must have been almost unbearable. It seemed to me to bear every evidence of truth, but was so substantially different from the earlier report which had been received that it was referred to the commander of the lately-relieved garrison of Samawah.

In his opinion, the evidence of the sowars was unreliable, and he remarked that " the stories of all of them are the stories of brave men who did all they could, but fear that they may be asked why they did not do more. They have been taken prisoners, and have got to account for it."

As I have stated earlier, three British officers and the numerous survivors, who included a subaltern and an Assistant Political Officer, were convinced that no one could be alive on the train, and no signs or sounds of any description which could have led to that belief were noticed in the camp throughout the day.

Soon after the occurrence, and before I knew that any one on board the train had been captured, I sent an Arab agent to Samawah to glean what information he could, as all that had so far reached me was extremely meagre. His researches, however, among the tribesmen and townspeople proved fruitless, for the Arab is notoriously careful not to commit himself lest retribution should follow any admission—and an amnesty had, of course, not then been declared—and it is equally rare for him to disclose anything that might react disadvantageously on his fellows.

Although I felt certain that Major Hay and his officers had given me an unvarnished account of the incident, as regarded from their point of view, yet the equally explicit and widely different tale of the sowars left doubts in my mind as to what had really occurred. As inquiries on the spot would certainly be unprofitable until some time had elapsed, I decided to wait.

In December 1921 my duties took me to Nasiriyah on the Lower Euphrates, and while passing through Samawah on my way there I inquired of the acting civil surgeon, Captain J. V. McNally, R.A.M.C., who was at the station, if he had heard any mention made by the inhabitants of the circumstances surrounding the capture of the armoured train. His knowledge of Arabic, he said, was slight, but he had gathered the impression that the fight had gone on until the afternoon, and that the Arabs had suffered heavily, owing to the gallantry of the officer in command. As I expected to pass through Samawah a few days later, I desired him to gather all the information he could on the subject, but knowing the suspicious nature of the Arabs, recommended him to be careful in prosecuting his inquiries. At Nasiriyah I was told by the Political Officer, Major Ditchburn, and also by one of his assistants, Captain Kitching from Suq-ash-Shuyuk, that from all they had heard on the subject the defence of the train had been a prolonged affair, and had been conducted with great gallantry. Indeed, the Arabs who were at Samawah at the time, of whom many had taken part in the capture, in which they had suffered heavily, had been so struck by the courage and determination shown by the commander of the train that they had conferred on him by common consent the title of " Abu sil Sillah " (Father of the chains), on account of the steel chains worn on the shoulders of his khaki jacket.

At last the evidence of the sowars seemed to be corroborated from the direction whence alone such corroboration could have come.

As I returned through Samawah Captain McNally added a few more details to what he had already told me. First-hand evidence was, however, necessary, and fortunately this was forthcoming. Travelling with me was Major W. J. Bovill, a special service officer of my staff, and a fluent Arabic scholar, as well as the Arab agent who had been sent previously to make the inquiries to which I have earlier referred. Both of them began questioning some of the local Arabs at the station, one of whom was armed with a rifle, and belonged to the railway police. To our surprise some half-dozen of them readily answered questions, more especially the policeman, who showed us the scar of a bullet wound in his left leg which he said he had received in the attack on the train. One and all spoke enthusiastically of the bravery of him whom they called " Abu sil Sillah," and how the fight had worn on till between 4 and 5 P.M., when he and some others were shot and the train captured. They particularly referred to an Englishman who was clean-shaven, and who may possibly have been Captain Pigeon. As the fight was drawing to a close this individual threw ten-rupee notes from the train, and when the Arabs rushed to pick them up he hurled bombs among them, causing ten, twenty, or more casualties at a time.

There was now no doubt in my mind that the defence of the train had been a desperate and protracted affair, in which all who remained on board had fought heroically, and shortly after I took steps to rectify my earlier report on the episode.

It may be thought strange that those in the camp at Samawah should have remained in ignorance of what was in progress a little more than a mile to the south. Regarding this point I have drawn attention to the explanation sent me by the commander there, who himself was rewarded for his gallant defence of the place. The atmospheric conditions in Mesopotamia are fruitful causes of deception, and I have several times noticed that peculiarity of the country, which is far more prominent during the summer months than when, as often in winter, the sun's rays are feeble and dust and wind are absent. The short distance which sound travels at times has been remarked on several occasions. As an instance of this I may quote the case of a squadron of Colonel Kemmis's regiment which reported that it had been under heavy fire, while he, though less than a mile distant, had not heard a shot. It must be remembered, too, that in the account above given, the fighting, after the first rush, took place at the station end of the train, and the Arabs were careful not to expose themselves to view.

Even if it had been known at the camp that a deadly struggle was proceeding within long-range rifle fire, the many thousands of armed Arabs round Samawah must inevitably have prevented the success of any attempt at rescue. Indeed, the Arab policeman who had been wounded volunteered a remark to the same effect, and added that the tribesmen would certainly have rushed the camp had the defenders made a sortie in force. That this was no idle boast is probable, and it is difficult to believe that with a diminished garrison the camp at Samawah could have held out, while its capture would inevitably have rallied to the insurgent standards a large section of the Muntafiq Confederation, besides throwing into the scale against us many waverers.

CHAPTER XVIII.

THE RELIEF OF SAMAWAH.

WHILE the operations in the Baghdad vilayat and those which led to the isolation of Samawah were in progress, the situation in that part of the River Area which is inhabited by the Muntafiq Confederation was steadily deteriorating. As the weeks went by and the prospect of an outbreak in this area trembled in the balance, Political Officers were ordered to withdraw, as otherwise their lives might have been forfeited. On the 6th August one of them, Captain W. F. Crawford, an Australian, a Rhodes Scholar and an Oxford Prizeman, was ambushed when returning to Qalat Sikar after dining with a friendly shaikh, but fortunately he and his escort escaped, though two of their horses were wounded. Thereafter he was removed by aeroplane to Nasiriyah, and though he manifested a desire to resume his charge when for a brief space the aspect of affairs improved, he was not permitted to do so.

Several times I was definitely informed that in the course of a few days some of the tribes were certain to revolt, and on one occasion the actual date was volunteered. Jihad was being preached with frenzied fervour by the numerous emissaries from the holy cities of Najaf and Karbala. Mirza Muhammad Taqi Shirazi, the chief mujtahid of the latter place, had offered prayers on the corpse of an Arab killed in battle—an act which he performed in public, and which conferred on the inanimate warrior the crown of martyrdom, free sepulture in supersacred ground, a passport to the celestial regions, and certain indulgences on arrival there. Parts of the country, stirred by the insidious propaganda, were in an uproar, and at any moment there might be thrown into the scale on the insurgents' side the majority of the tribesmen, who were credited with possessing approximately 43,000 rifles, of which over 30,000 were modern weapons.

So serious a menace was beyond my power to meet. Every man at my disposal was fully occupied in efforts to smother the insurrection further north, and, except the occasional despatch, for purposes of demonstration, of at most two aeroplanes—all that my limited resources in that respect allowed—nothing could be done to stay the growing trouble. Reinforcements from India were arriving, but the new situation which might arise at any moment had not been contemplated when demands for troops were made.

The possibility of serious friction with the Muntafiq had been brought to the notice of the War Office in my daily situation telegrams, in which communications I, however, carefully avoided anything that was calculated to create alarm.

On the 26th August the Secretary of State for War, Mr Winston Churchill, who with the Army Council was not only sympathetic but helpful, so far as resources and commitments in other directions than my own allowed, telegraphed as follows : " I take this opportunity of sending you my earnest good wishes for your success in the difficult task you are discharging. The Cabinet have decided that the rebellion must be quelled effectually, and I shall endeavour to meet all your requirements." He then went on to say what troops and air squadrons were coming to Mesopotamia, and concluded by inquiring if I had any further needs, which he would meet if possible.

Scarcely had I received and gratefully acknowledged this telegram than affairs in the territory of the Muntafiq went from bad to worse. On the 27th August the remaining Political Officer, who was stationed at Shattrah, where the first display of uneasiness with regard to British administration in the district in which it lies had shown itself, had to be withdrawn. That town, which has always been the barometer of the political situation on the Middle

Gharraf, possesses a long history of anarchy and plunder, and boasts, as a melancholy tribute to the past, a Turkish cemetery for Qaimaqams (in a civil sense, district officers), which is conveniently and somewhat suggestively situated close to the government offices. This uneasiness was due to the system of revenue collection which had been instituted by a Political Officer some time before during his period of office at Shattrah. The system in question was that of measuring the crops by chain; and when it is borne in mind that the Gharraf tribes for fifteen years prior to the arrival of the British had defied all attempts at the collection of revenue, it is hardly to be wondered at that a persistence in so bold a policy was not endured with the complacency which seems to have been expected.

About the 27th August also a report was received that some Kurdish tribes, who for long had been a menace, were on the point of breaking out, and were likely to be followed by others, on the principle that fighting is to be preferred to idleness.

On the 28th I telegraphed to the War Office that should these threats, now more marked than ever, come to anything, I should require forces from overseas—in addition to the troops in the country, on the way, or promised—amounting to two complete divisions, each with a cavalry brigade. A rising of the Muntafiq would imperil the Tigris line, my only means of communication with the sea, and from Basrah upwards the country would have to be reconquered. I added that I would do the utmost I could with the troops at my disposal to falsify my estimate of probable developments, and endeavour to reduce to order the areas which were then disturbed.

Three days later I followed up this telegram by another, in which I explained in some detail the gravity of the situation and the dangers with which we were threatened.

When these telegrams were sent I was fully aware what a great strain my demands would put upon the resources both of the United Kingdom and India. It is at crises such as these that a temptation may assail a commander similarly situated to myself. The authorities at home will probably have taken pains to impress upon him the fact that they are beset on all sides by demands for troops and war material, or that they are being urged with vehemence to effect drastic reductions in military expenditure. The commander consequently finds himself on the horns of a dilemma. If his requirements seem to be excessive—and it is difficult for those at a distance to put themselves in his place—they may be met with a refusal; nay, his command may be taken from him and given to another, or the enterprise on which he is engaged may be abandoned as too costly or beyond the military resources available. On the other hand, he may compromise with his conscience and ask for something less than he feels the circumstances necessitate, and trust to luck or a favourable change in the situation to bring matters to a successful termination. Should he be so unwise as to adopt this course, he may later discover that he has not only imperilled the safety of the troops entrusted to him and sacrificed his own military reputation, but has gambled with the honour and credit of his country.

For the commander who finds himself in such a quandary, come what may, there is one course, and one only: he must make a rigid examination of his conscience, and frame his recommendations strictly in accordance with military requirements.

The earlier of these telegrams produced another from the Secretary of State, dated the 31st August, which made me feel that, despite my daily telegraphic reports, the true state of affairs in Mesopotamia was only partly understood. His telegram, however, gave me an opportunity for removing such misconceptions as evidently prevailed. Certain comments were made and questions put to me, and the gist of my replies I give below, as they may help the reader to appreciate many points which bear on operations in Iraq.

Thus I stated that, owing to the situation on the Lower Euphrates, which might involve the Tigris line, I had only been able to bring to Baghdad three of the ten battalions which had so far come from overseas. I then went on to explain that since the outbreak of the insurrection, as may have been observed by those who have perused the preceding chapters, the operations had been carried on without a break. I pointed out that it was possible that I had failed to convey a clear picture of what had taken place—though reported every twenty-four hours—through the purposely moderate terms in which my telegrams had been couched. I then gave a summary of the previous operations, which had been carried out in a shade temperature sometimes exceeding 110 degrees, and which, on a conservative and carefully-checked estimate, had so far cost the insurgents at least six thousand casualties. Desirable as a decisive battle was—and no one recognised that fact more strongly than myself—the elusiveness of our adversaries, their great mobility, knowledge of the country, and power of quick assembly and dispersion, made such a consummation unattainable. It seemed possible that, with the capture and occupation of the Hindiyah Barrage, the tribesmen might be forced to quit their attitude of evasion and stand to fight; but that I doubted, for the Arab has no leaning for the attack of strong positions. I then explained that the difficulty of operating in Mesopotamia was largely due to the question of water, food supplies and fuel, and the necessity for guarding communications throughout their length, as otherwise a column became transformed into little else than a convoy, and in the open country a particularly vulnerable one. Movement was hampered by the numerous water-channels, wet and dry, which were passable only by single-track native bridges, and by the inefficient narrow-gauge railways and strictly limited amount of rolling-stock.

As I knew that Mr Churchill had experience of fighting in South Africa, I stated that "Mesopotamia is a vast plain devoid of features except the two main rivers and the old banks of disused and other canals, which afford strong positions for the Arabs. Campaigning in this country is not unlike the fighting in the later stages of the Boer War, with this difference, that then our forces were greatly in excess of those of our enemy, and we had large mounted

THE RELIEF OF SAMAWAH

forces, while here (in Mesopotamia) our forces available for operations are exceeded by those of the insurgents, and it is impossible to compare our mobility with theirs."

Before concluding I remarked that, " For a rebellion, such as is in progress, the country was totally unprepared, and in order to prevent great imperilment of the situation, much work, besides operations, has been necessary. As I have frequently pointed out, my resources debarred me from acting at more than one point at a time. This had led to the spread of the insurrection elsewhere before it could be dealt with. For penning in the enemy and cutting him off from water, other than his wells, my numbers are quite inadequate. If able to do so his submission, dismounting and disarming, could be effected. This would be a lengthy but a certain process."

On the 7th September the Secretary of State for War replied: " I have received your telegram with great satisfaction, as it makes it possible for me to obtain a clear view of the situation. Anything we can do to assist you we shall not hesitate to do."

These telegrams had the effect of clearing the air, and mutual understanding was established.

But to return to the River Area and its portentous possibilities. As Nasiriyah lies on one flank of the Muntafiq country, and from its situation seems to block the entrance from the west, it might be thought that to occupy that town would have served to keep that unruly confederation in check. Gladly as I would have adopted such a course and concentrated a strong force there, I felt debarred from doing so until its communication with Basrah could be made secure. To have assembled a force might have helped to keep the tribes in order, but should troops at a distance of one hundred and forty miles from Basrah become invested, their relief by land must be an operation difficult and slow, and one for which a force far exceeding my resources present or prospective would be essential.

I therefore made the place itself secure by strengthening the garrison, and on the 1st September ordered the defences of the railway line from Nasiriyah to the Base—the more important sections first—to be proceeded with. The line had already been cut south of Ur Junction on the 18th August, and again on the 2nd September, after which date, though threatened, it had been left alone.

For military reasons it proved fortunate that, unlike the tribes in other areas, those of the Shatt-al-Gharraf were much less under our administrative sway. There the Pax Britannica had not yet found its way to the same extent, nor had blood-feuds been compounded and the road made smooth for tribal combination. Indeed it may be said without fear of contradiction that it was very noticeable that, where British administration was most strict and, to our way of thinking, more efficient, tribal combination was most effective against us. On the other hand, in wilder districts, which were ruled with a lighter hand, such combination failed to materialise at all or proved ineffective.

Thus internal strife at length showed itself among the tribes of the Shatt-al-Gharraf, for which I felt heartily thankful. This was probably encouraged by the paramount shaikh of the Abudah tribe, Khaiyun al Obaid, a past-master in the methods by which the Turks had ruled the country. When on the 27th August the Assistant Political Officer, Captain B. S. Thomas, was forced to leave his post, he entrusted the interests of government to this personage, who deserves much credit for his good work with these tribes, over whom he wields great influence, especially round Shattrah and to the south. Khaiyun, who is a firm believer in Captain Thomas, I afterwards met on two occasions. He seemed to me to be little over thirty years of age, of somewhat striking appearance, strong, reticent, and not inclined readily to unbend. He displayed great force of character during the rising, for he refused to pay heed to all appeals to join in the Jihad, and, continuing to maintain a friendly attitude, kept his followers in order. The situation thus became alleviated, but the marsh Arabs who are to be found on both banks of the Euphrates south-east of Nasiriyah, and who had raised their banners on the 1st September, remained a menace to the railway thence to Basrah.

THE RELIEF OF SAMAWAH

It is indeed greatly to the credit of the Political Officers concerned that, along the whole line of the Tigris south of Baghdad, equilibrium was preserved, and this more especially on the Gharraf, where the tribes were in direct contact with the Diwaniyah insurgents.

Meanwhile Samawah was cut off, and the *Greenfly*, as mentioned, had run aground, and could not be extricated, and her crew of one British officer, four British and thirty Indian other ranks, was beset by hostile Arabs on both banks. When rations began to fail, food was several times dropped by aeroplanes, and at great risk a small proportion was picked up by the crew. The process of delivery was attended by such danger that after several aeroplanes had been damaged and one shot down and her pilot and observer murdered, I ordered that no further attempts to supply the crew in this manner were to be made, and that heavy bribes were to be offered to any Arab who would undertake to smuggle food on board. The relief force, but for disturbances on the north-west frontier of India, which delayed the arrival of troops and obliged me to postpone the advance for a week, could have reached the vessel in time to effect a rescue, for, so far as could be ascertained, she held out till the 2nd or 3rd October.

Several weeks earlier than these events, on the 24th July, I had telegraphed to the War Office for a Divisional General and Staff to command the troops which were arriving from India. As, however, their arrival was delayed, I selected my very able Chief Engineer, Major-General E. H. de V. Atkinson, to command the force which was to carry out the relief, and improvised a staff for him from many quarters. Although he had never commanded a force which approached in numbers those of a division, I knew his great organising qualities, and the speed and driving-power—so necessary and yet so often lacking east of Suez—which he would put into the work allotted to him.

As the actual fighting would devolve on a more junior commander, and as I knew nothing regarding the two brigade commanders who had come from India, except that neither had as yet led a brigade in actual contact with an enemy, I decided later to send Brigadier-General Coningham as soon as he could be spared from the operations north-east of Baghdad. He had proved himself to be cool-headed, courageous, and resourceful, and with the certainty before me of a Muntafiq or even greater rising should the operation fail, the risk of using untried leaders had to be avoided. I must admit that before taking this decision I reflected several days, as I was loth to hurt the feelings of those selected by the Commander-in-Chief in India, who, so far as I knew, may have possessed every qualification but experience of Arab warfare.

What actually decided me in the end, and I mention it as others in a similar position may find the example useful, occurred as follows :—

On the afternoon of the 14th September I happened to be reading, not for the first time, Lord Roberts's 'Forty-one Years in India,' and there I came across the following note, which I quote in full, regarding the commanders who took part in the Relief of Lucknow : " Sir Colin Campbell's selection of commanders caused considerable heartburning, especially among the senior officers who had been sent out from England for the purpose of being employed in the field. But as the Chief explained to the Duke of Cambridge, the selection had been made with the greatest care, it having been found that an officer inexperienced in war in India cannot act for himself . . . as it is quite impossible for him to weigh the value of intelligence . . . he cannot judge what are the resources of the country, and he is totally unable to make an estimate for himself of the resistance which the enemy opposed to him is likely to offer." Sir Colin wound up his letter as follows : " I do not wish to undervalue the merits of general and other officers lately arrived from England, but merely to indicate to your Royal Highness the difficulties against which they have to contend. What is more, the state of things at present does not permit of trusting anything to chance or allowing new-comers to learn except under the command of others."

The last sentence settled the matter in my own mind.

I at once walked over to Brigadier-General Stewart's house, which adjoined my own, and invited him to take his pencil and some telegraph forms. A telegram was sent to Major-General Atkinson, who was far from complaining at the change, and Brigadier-General Coningham with his staff, after replacement by Brigadier-General Beatty, was ordered to come to Baghdad by the 16th September with a view to his taking command of the relief force. The brigade commander, who was for this purpose solely superseded, was not forgotten, and a soothing message was sent to him. He later did good work in connection with the relief and in command of a column which carried out punitive measures.

Lest the opposition which might be met in the advance from the south should prove to be severe and a call have to be made for troops beyond those that were allotted— the number of which had to be limited by water facilities— I ordered that twelve of the twenty battalions, most of which had now arrived from overseas, should, if required, be at the disposal of the commander of the relief force. To have drawn to Baghdad the units not wanted in the first instance for the relief, though they would have helped in the operations in the vicinity of that place, might possibly have been followed by their forced return to the River Area, a transfer which would have involved considerable delay. As events turned out, the precaution of retaining them in the River Area proved to be unnecessary, but it is impossible to gauge the effect which their presence may have had there at so critical a time.

The arrangements to be made by Major-General Atkinson before it was possible to begin the movement on Samawah were numerous and demanded considerable forethought, but by the 23rd September they were completed. By that date, however, all the troops necessary for the operation had not arrived. The cause of the delay I have already mentioned, and this was aggravated by the fact that none of the units which arrived from India was fully equipped, and these had to be fitted out, as far as the stores in reserve at Basrah permitted, before they could take the field.

In order that no time should be wasted, and that the advance when it did take place should be carried out without pause, the construction of blockhouses from Ur —the junction for Nasiriyah—towards Samawah was begun, and as the first few miles of the advance would pass through an area which was not disturbed and is at a little distance only from the Euphrates, the work progressed satisfactorily. Indeed, it was found possible to establish an advanced railhead at Batha, which is some eighteen miles north-west of Ur Junction.

By the 30th September the force under Brigadier-General Coningham was assembled at Nasiriyah. It was composed as follows :—

    10th (D.C.O.) Lancers (less two squadrons),
    10th (How.) Battery R.F.A.,
    13th Battery R.F.A.,
    69th Company, 2nd (Q.V.O.) Sappers and Miners,
    8th Battalion Machine-gun Corps (two and a half sections),
    1st Battalion King's Own Yorkshire Light Infantry,
    3/5th Gurkha Rifles,
    3/8th Gurkha Rifles,
    1/11th Gurkha Rifles,
    3/23rd Sikh Infantry,
        and certain medical and other details.

Next day the column marched to Ur, where it was joined by Major-General Atkinson and his staff.

The troops which formed it were specially selected, and, as just stated, included two squadrons of the famous 10th Lancers (Hodson's Horse), under Lieut.-Colonel Kemmis, which had been mounted on artillery remounts at Basrah, and which were to take part in this, after a long spell in Mesopotamia, their final operation, before leaving for India. A portion of another unit, one and a half companies of the 114th Mahrattas, which had been specially brought from Hillah, joined the column shortly after Ur was left, so as to be in time to share in the relief of their invested comrades at Samawah.

THE RELIEF OF SAMAWAH

Before reaching this stage in the narrative, it will probably have been observed that I had been obliged, even in the case of the troops which were in the country when the insurrection broke out, to depart from the brigade organisation and form columns of such units as happened to be at the moment available. I had less compunction with the reinforcements from India in continuing this usually objectionable procedure, as I knew that, though on paper they possessed a brigade organisation, the units had never served together.

The line of communication in front of Nasiriyah and the defence of that place were in charge of Brigadier-General A. le G. Jacob, and from Ur to Basrah under Brigadier-General A. I. R. Glasfurd. As the railway line, which beyond Darraji station was known to require extensive repairs, is, except at Khidhr, at some distance from the Euphrates, the column was accompanied by two trains, each train carrying thirty thousand gallons of water in tanks, besides numerous other requirements. In addition, an armoured train, with a 13-pdr. gun, a machine-gun, and a searchlight, formed part of the column, as also a blockhouse train, which, based on Ur, carried sufficient materials for ten blockhouses, a number which it was intended daily to construct.

On the 3rd October a friendly shaikh reported that the crew of the *Greenfly* had surrendered owing to want of food. Next day, after the column had reached Darraji, where it was found that two thousand five hundred sleepers and a thousand yards of track had been removed, the same shaikh stated that the commander of the vessel and the British soldiers had been murdered some days earlier and the Indian ranks made prisoners. Cooped up in the unbearable heat of summer in what was little more than a tin box, with nothing to drink but the hot muddy water of the river, slowly to starve and not know that every effort was being made to relieve them, such was the fate of those on board. Rumours were for a time rife of treachery on the part of the crew, but though more than a year has elapsed since the incident, no absolute proof of this has been obtained. On the 6th, Khidhr was reached, a strong force of insurgents being driven off by the 3/5th Gurkha Rifles and 3/23rd Sikh Infantry, who inflicted upon them losses which included forty-seven killed. In this affair, in which our own casualties were only two killed and seven wounded, and daily throughout the march, aeroplanes dropped messages containing information for the column, while bombs and machine-guns were used from them against the insurgents whenever opportunity offered.

On the 7th, while the railway was being repaired and the débris from the two armoured trains, which had collided on the 13th August, was being removed, two squadrons of the 10th Lancers, two sections of artillery, two machine-gun sections, with the 1st Battalion King's Own Yorkshire Light Infantry and the 3/8th Gurkha Rifles, under the command of Colonel A. Paley, 1st Battalion Rifle Brigade, whom I had sent from Baghdad for work in connection with the relief, carried out punitive operations against numerous villages on the right bank of the Euphrates.

On the 8th punitive operations were continued on both sides of the Euphrates against the tribes who were known to be responsible for the ill-treatment of the crew of the *Greenfly*, and the 3/23rd Sikhs, under Lieut.-Colonel P. G. Carey, were sent to visit that vessel. She was found stripped of everything movable, and littered with dirt and débris. Both of her guns had been rendered useless, and all detachable parts had disappeared. One body, that of a European, probably one of the British soldiers, showing marks of three wounds, was discovered just forward of the bridge superstructure, and according to the opinion of the medical officer present death had occurred about eight days earlier. The ship was much scarred with bullets, but nothing remained to indicate what had happened to the crew.

On the 9th, the line ahead not yet having been repaired sufficiently for the advance to continue, search was made for railway material, and one village, where several thousand sleepers were found, was burned.

By the 12th the railway was repaired, and blockhouses

THE RELIEF OF SAMAWAH

were built as far as Hadbah, four and a half miles short of Samawah, which was reached that day by the column. The insurgents, in strength exceeding seven thousand men, were reported to be holding a strong position running through palm gardens and walled enclosures. It was evident that they did not mean to relax their hold on Samawah and the invested garrison without a final struggle.

On the 13th it had been intended to push through to that place, but the permanent way had been considerably damaged and every sleeper taken away. Moreover, as the troops advanced in battle formation, the insurgents, numbering from two thousand five hundred to three thousand rifles, were seen to be holding a position across the railway line. At 8 A.M. four aeroplanes arrived, and by their bombs and machine-guns caused considerable numbers to bolt and offer splendid targets for the artillery. The 1/11th Gurkhas, directed against the palm gardens near the river, whence a heavy fire came, and the 3/8th Gurkhas on their left, supported by the 1/114th Mahrattas, pushed forward, covered by the artillery, in the face of stubborn resistance. To help the advance the 1st Battalion King's Own Yorkshire Light Infantry was thrown into the fight on the right, and was fired on heavily from the palm gardens; but fortunately the insurgents' shooting was erratic, and the casualties were few. At 1.30 P.M. the troops nearest the river reported that large numbers still opposed them, and as the repairs to the line could not be carried out that day more than one mile further to the north, General Coningham decided that, after driving the insurgents from their position, he would camp for the night, and not enter the enclosed ground near Samawah until the following day. The infantry now continued the advance, and soon the insurgents were seen retiring in large numbers to the west under shell fire. Their losses included eighty killed, of whom twenty were drowned in an attempt to cross the river.

On the 14th October the column entered Samawah without opposition, only twenty-five Arabs and as many Jews being found in the town, and the repairs to the railway allowed the train to arrive at 11 P.M.

The work of the relief force, which, except on the 13th, met with less opposition than was anticipated, had won deserved success, for the arrangements both prior to the advance and during it were such that they worked with admirable smoothness.

From the 8th September to the 12th October, when a point one and a half miles south-east of Samawah was reached, two hundred and fifty blockhouses, some made of bricks and others of sandbags and gabions, had been constructed, and but for the considerable help given by the railway personnel and the expeditious manner in which they provided rolling-stock for construction trains and organised the traffic, so large an amount of work would have been impossible.

I had laid down the 23rd September as the latest date by which the blockhouses between Basrah and Nasiriyah were to be completed, and by the 20th all were ready.

The only unfortunate incident which can in any way be associated with the relief was the sad end of the British portion of the crew of the *Greenfly*. I have explained why they were not relieved before their food gave out, and the date of the letter, a copy of which will be found in Appendix V., shows that but for ill-fortune the lives of the gallant British who were on board would have been saved.

The casualties in the relief force from the 1st to the 18th October, and including those of the *Greenfly*, only amounted to—

	Killed or died of wounds.	Wounded.	Missing.
British officers . . .	...	1	1
British other ranks .	5	15	4
Indian officers . .	...	...	...
Indian other ranks .	6	14	24
Followers . . .	...	2	...
	11	32	29

As regards the garrison of Samawah, which, as mentioned earlier, was commanded by Major A. S. Hay, 31st Lancers, attached to the 1/114th Mahrattas, and numbered six hundred and seventy in all, they were found to be in good health and spirits, having suffered little by the two months' investment. Their casualties too were small.

The garrison had been strengthened on the 28th August by the escort of forty-five men of the 2/123rd Rifles, under Captain C. E. Norton, who had arrived with the river convoy on that date; while the presence of the *Grayfly* and the *Sandfly* exercised considerable moral effect on the insurgents. The garrison were therefore better able to withstand the attacks on the main camp which followed the loss of the armoured train. These attacks were invariably delivered at night, and preferably when there was no moon; and determined efforts were made to capture posts held by the piquets and destroy the barbed wire in their neighbourhood by men carrying bombs, who were supported by heavy fire from their flanks.

On three occasions the leader of the insurgents, Saiyid Hadi of the Bani Hachaim, sent in a letter in which he promised safe conduct for the garrison if carried by their own boats to Nasiriyah. His attempts to negotiate were ignored, and the investment ran its course, until the operations for relief liberated the garrison. These operations, which saved the third and largest of the invested garrisons from falling into the insurgents' hands, had at last given me freedom of action to deal with those who still opposed us when and where I chose.

It is fitting here that I should state that on the 18th October I received a telegram from Field-Marshal Sir Henry Wilson, Chief of the Imperial General Staff, who had been most sympathetic and helpful throughout a very trying period. It ran as follows:—

"Hearty congratulations on the relief of Samawah, which materially improves the situation, and reflects great credit on the troops, which have had to march and fight under such trying conditions."

This telegram, which was at once published for the benefit of the troops, was followed by one from the Secretary of State for War, Mr Winston Churchill, which began:—

"During these difficult months your patience and steadfastness have been of great value, and I congratulate you upon the distinct improvement in the situation which has been effected by you."

Previous to receiving either of the above telegrams I had informed the War Office that I should not require the additional reinforcements which, about two months earlier, it seemed possible would have to be sent.

CHAPTER XIX.

THE OPERATIONS NORTH OF BAGHDAD.

WHEN the insurrection broke out in the Euphrates valley there was a strong probability that it would spread north of Baghdad, where, as previously described, disturbances had occurred in May and June. At that time, by promises of gifts of arms and ammunition and other inducements, external propagandists had striven to incite the Kurdish and Jezireh Arab tribes to take hostile action against us, and it seemed certain that their efforts would shortly be repeated, as indeed they were. Fortunately the country lying north of Baghdad, and the district which is known as the Mosul vilayat, provide less material for the political incendiary than the regions further south, and it was hoped that the small force under Major-General T. Fraser, commanding the 18th Division, would suffice to maintain the area in order.

The considerable calls on the troops of that division which I had been forced to make in July and August for operations in the Baghdad vilayat necessitated a redistribution of the units left, which was arranged so as to hold the more important railway stations with detachments capable of dealing with minor raids, guard all posts on the Shergat-Mosul road, and retain at the latter place for offensive action as strong a reserve as possible.

July passed quietly but for the activities of small raiding parties such as are prone to make their appearance during the summer months. The immediate despatch, however, of aeroplanes and small columns either from Mosul or Tel Afar to deal with any concentration served to keep in check attempts to commit serious breaches of the peace; and this action, combined with a firm attitude, political and military, in the area produced at least a temporary settlement, and kept rebellion among Kurds and Arabs in suspended animation.

But on the 10th August the officer commanding at Tel Afar reported that two sections of the Northern Shammar, a nomad tribe whose annual movement north and south in a portion of the region which lies between the Tigris and Euphrates is a fruitful source of minor trouble, had crossed the Mosul-Sinjar road. As these sections had been implicated in the Tel Afar rising in June, they had been warned that, until the terms imposed on them had been complied with, they were prohibited from moving south of the above-mentioned road. Major-General Fraser had also laid down bounds at a little distance on either side of the railway, and trespass by the tribesmen within those limits would be punished by the speedy arrival of unexpected and unpleasant visitors in the shape of bomb-carrying aeroplanes.

On the 11th August a small column under Lieut.-Colonel G. B. M. Sarel, 11th (K.E.O.) Lancers, consisting of three squadrons of that regiment and a section of the 44th Battery R.F.A., left Mosul, and found the defaulting sections camped some eleven miles south-east of Tel Afar. The Assistant Political Officer of that place, escorted by a squadron, now rode forward some three miles, while the remainder of the column halted lest the knowledge of the presence of a force of such size should cause a failure in the negotiations.

While the Assistant Political Officer was discussing with the shaikh of one of the sections his breach of orders, the leader of the other section was observed to ride from the camp, followed by some mounted Arabs, who were headed off by a troop sent out from the squadron.

Hardly had this movement been successfully effected when heavy rifle fire was opened on the remainder of the squadron from the Shammar tents, and from a village which was close to the encampment. The squadron, which

THE OPERATIONS NORTH OF BAGHDAD 233

was under the command of Captain J. C. Hanwell, now found itself being fired into from three sides, whereupon it was withdrawn without loss of time to a position about eight hundred yards distant from the tents, on which fire was then directed. The remainder of the column had meantime ridden forward to cover the withdrawal of the squadron, and the guns which were unlimbered and in action opened fire.

As the Arabs in their usual fashion next began to work round the flanks of the column, Captain Hanwell was ordered to fall back and rejoin headquarters, being assisted in that operation by a troop of the second squadron. Eventually as the Arabs showed that they far exceeded the numbers of their opponents, and as the latter were some fourteen miles from Tel Afar, the column was withdrawn to that place.

Lieutenant A. L. Hanna, who came up with the reinforcing squadron, behaved with gallantry on this occasion, and was awarded the Distinguished Service Order. While passing over the open he saw a wounded sowar lying on the ground, who had been stripped of his equipment and clothing by the Arabs. While endeavouring to lift the man on to his own horse, the insurgents opened fire, and a bullet passed through his coat. However, he persisted in his intention to prevent the sowar from falling into hostile hands, and eventually carried him off in safety.

Further south the eloquence of two of the most troublesome agitators, Yusuf al Suwaidi and Saiyid Muhammad Sadr, who had escaped arrest at Baghdad on the 12th August, and who were traced to the Diyalah district, was giving rise to trouble at Samarrah. Here, some years after the death of the caliph, Harun al Rashid, known to most of us through the pages of the 'Arabian Nights,' stood for some sixty years the Capital of the Moslem world. Baghdad, which had earlier held that proud position, lost its supremacy owing to the civil wars which followed the death of the reputed hero of so many night adventures.

Of its successor, Samarrah, which is now a place greatly revered by shiahs, little remains but a walled city and a gilt-domed mosque, with some interesting remains to the north and east. Here local elements of the Azzah tribe, stirred by the propaganda which had reached their ears, concentrated, and on the 28th August sent a threatening message to the notables of the town. The townsmen, who, here as everywhere in Mesopotamia, are the most pusillanimous section of the population, and are incapable of protecting themselves and their belongings, terrified at the prospect of tribal lawlessness, begged the Political Officer, Major Berry, who displayed courage and good sense at a trying crisis, not to abandon them.

Early on the 30th Major E. T. W. McCausland, 1/3rd Gurkha Rifles, with two platoons of his battalion and a platoon of the 106th Hazara Pioneers—in all one hundred and twenty rifles with two machine-guns—arrived from Shergat to relieve Samarrah, in which were thirteen British soldiers under Lieutenant R. F. Garnons-Williams, 4th Battalion Royal Fusiliers, and some Indian and Burmese motor drivers, all of whom had recently arrived from Kirkuk with motor transport. The insurgents opened fire from trenches on our troops as they advanced from the railway station, which is on the opposite side of the river to the town. Two aeroplanes appeared from the direction of Baghdad, and their presence, combined with the rapidity with which the infantry pushed forward, caused the insurgents to fly, when the aeroplanes following them broke them up with bombs and machine-guns.

During the next fortnight the disturbed state of the country between Samarrah and Baghdad and a little to the north of the former place, which is seventy-six miles north of the capital, was a constant source of worry.

The line between those places and on to Shergat, over which trains for some months had run only by daylight, and which, for lack of men and labour, it was impossible to make secure by means of blockhouses, was of importance for several reasons, to explain which a lengthy digression is unavoidable.

In the first place, the question of the supply of the garrison of Mosul was a vital matter. The situation on

Fathah gorge, looking up-stream.

Samarrah from the east.

THE OPERATIONS NORTH OF BAGHDAD

the Euphrates and elsewhere was such that on the 14th July the Acting Civil Commissioner had put forward the idea of giving up the whole of the Mosul vilayat. His view was that the inadequate force in Mesopotamia and the time that must elapse before reinforcements from India could arrive would allow the situation in other parts of the country to become so aggravated that only the withdrawal of all troops from the north would suffice to secure the other two vilayats. He considered that, unless I could guarantee the supplies of Mosul for a period of from six to nine months, the prospects of relieving it were small.

On the date to which I refer matters everywhere bore an extremely serious aspect, and the advantages of adding to the small reserve at Baghdad were indisputable. Still, from a civil and military point of view—and my position compelled me to consider both—though the recommendation may have been in accordance with sound principles, I was loth to give up a square mile of the country for which I was responsible. I felt that the officer on the spot knew far better than I, brief as was my acquaintance with the country, whether such a withdrawal, if indeed it was advisable, was feasible, and even without a local opinion the difficulties seemed to be immense. As the Acting Civil Commissioner had telegraphed to the India Office on the matter I took similar action as regards the War Office, and was given a free hand to act as I thought best.

Before the answer from London came the commander of the 18th Division expressed his strong dislike to such an impracticable operation, and as my own inclinations were entirely in accordance with that view, the matter was put aside and the chance of isolation was accepted. Thus the necessity for pushing through to Mosul supplies and munitions of all kinds, to which I have referred in an earlier chapter, became of primary importance, and, as opportunity allowed, train after train was sent to Shergat, whence their contents were conveyed to Mosul by almost every kind of transport.

The next consideration which demanded the keeping open of the line was the repatriation of the Assyrian and

Armenian refugees, which was already under way when the insurrection began. The Armenians were sent to a spot near Basrah, whence if conditions allowed they would be shipped to their homes. On the other hand, the Assyrians, who numbered nearly twice as many as the Armenians, had to be transferred to the vicinity of Mosul, which involved a railway journey over a line liable to be cut and a march of seventy miles from its terminus at Shergat.

These refugees have been so frequently mentioned that some explanation as to their presence in Mesopotamia seems to be necessary.

As regards the Armenians, who were Turkish subjects from the Lake Van district, all was quiet in their area at the outbreak of the European war; but in the spring of 1915, when the Russians advanced towards the town of Van, the inhabitants severed their connection with their Moslem rulers, and threw in their lot with their fellow-Christians.

In June of the same year, when the Russians withdrew from Van and returned to the Caucasus, they were followed by the whole body of the Armenians. Two months later, however, when the Russians again advanced to Van, many of those who had followed them in their withdrawal accompanied them, intending to settle again in their deserted homes. But they had reckoned without the upheaval which had now begun in Russia, and which led to the evacuation of Turkish territory by their protectors. Slaves of circumstances, and fearing to remain with the cruel Turk, they turned their backs on their homes for the second time, and fled for refuge to their compatriots in Persia.

The Assyrians, or, as they are sometimes called, on account of the mountainous nature of the country of Hakkari in Turkish Kurdistan, the Hill Assyrians, to distinguish them from their brethren of the Plains, are the remnant of the oldest Christian body in existence. Prior to the war they numbered approximately one hundred thousand souls, and were distributed into tribal and subject people. The former, for the most part lawless shep-

Country near Shergat.

Mosul from the east.

THE OPERATIONS NORTH OF BAGHDAD 237

herds armed with obsolete weapons, lived in semi-independence in their rugged rocky fastnesses which are to be found near the upper waters of the Greater Zab, a tributary of the Tigris. They acknowledge no allegiance except to their Patriarch and their chiefs, and the Turks had no direct dealings with them. Their fellow-nationalists of the plains frequented a less inhospitable country, where they were subject to the control of their overlords, paid taxes, and provided recruits for the Turkish Army.

Both hill and plains-men lived on friendly terms with their rulers, as well as with their Kurdish neighbours, until the arrival of the Russians in Kurdistan in the summer of 1915. They were then persuaded to join in attacking the Turks, and when the Russians withdrew they were forced to quit their homes and fly to Persia.

But besides those Assyrians above referred to, there were others in Persia who formed a highly prosperous and peaceful community of agriculturists, and who, before the outbreak of war, had been for some years under Russian protection. These had also lived on good terms with their Moslem neighbours, but the arrival of their mountain brethren wrought a complete change in those relations. The Russians organised the hillmen during 1916 into bands of irregulars, who, under the leadership of Agha Petros, were used on various punitive expeditions against the Kurdish tribes on the Persian border, and who, from their racial traditions and martial temperament, required no urging on to raid, loot, burn, and kill.

Their leader, Agha Petros, is possessed of ability and force of character, but not overburdened with scruples. In earlier years he had to leave his village in Kurdistan on account of a blood-feud, which was probably the cause of his entering the American mission school at Urmia. After completing his education there and touring the world he returned to Urmia, having in the meantime become possessed of considerable wealth, and settled there as a trader. He now came into favour with the Turks, was made Vice-Consul, and gained considerable prestige in the country. In 1908, on the arrival of the Russian troops, he forsook his former masters, and after serving for a time with the Army was given a commission at the outbreak of war.

When the Russian Army broke up the Assyrians were visited by British and French delegates, and were induced by them to hold the Urmia front. Unfortunately, although arms and other war material were provided in plenty, the lack of foresight and want of capable European officers led to the non-seizure of the Russian base at Sharif Khana, on the northern shores of Lake Urmia, which would have made the Assyrians masters of the situation. However, for several months the Turks and Kurds were not only kept at bay, but several times defeated. The Persians now came on the scene, and on the Assyrians refusing to disarm, an attempt to compel them to do so by force was made. Disturbances followed in several places, and at Urmia, where the Christians routed the Persians and Kurds, the chief of the Shikah Kurds, Simko Agha, a well-known personage, sued for peace. A conference between both sides took place, at the conclusion of which the Assyrian patriarch and his followers were treacherously murdered. Retaliation speedily followed, for, as soon as the news of what had occurred reached Urmia, the Kurds there were massacred by the Christian population. The Assyrians next organised a force which defeated Simko and killed many of his people. Unfortunately for the peace of the country, where he continues to be a source of perennial trouble, Simko escaped to Khoi, and in conjunction with the Persian democrats massacred some four thousand Christians.

The Assyrians were now face to face with a combined force of Kurds, Turks, and Persians, which greatly outnumbered and threatened to annihilate them. An urgent appeal to the British was made, which resulted in an agreement that the Assyrians would meet the British mission at Sain Kala. There they would take over a convoy of Lewis guns, ammunition, and money, with which would be twelve British officers, who were detailed to accompany the Assyrians to Urmia, where they were to organise the troops. Owing, however, to the opposition of Turkish troops south of Lake Urmia, the meeting that had been arranged to take place at Sain Kala was delayed by one week, when Agha Petros marched there with his men. In the meantime, during his absence, the Turks had broken through the line and occupied Urmia town, which forced the Christians in the Urmia plain to leave their homes and make their way as best they could through hostile country to join the British. Of the Christians, some ten thousand, who may have been cut off and so failed to join in the general exodus, have not since been heard of, and it is conjectured that most of them were massacred. Pursued by the deadly enemies of their religion and an easy prey to the ferocity which recognises no distinction of age or sex, many more fell victims before Hamadan was reached. But from Sain Kala onwards the horrors of the journey were somewhat mitigated by the gallant efforts of the handful of British troops who met them, and day by day alone kept the pursuing Moslems at bay and covered the retirement of the remnant of the demoralised Assyrian army and the hordes of refugees.

But before the refugees could be placed in security many difficulties had to be overcome. The sudden arrival at Hamadan of tens of thousands of fresh mouths would have led to a grave food crisis, and the supply of the British on the long line from Baghdad to the Caspian Sea was alone a sufficiently intricate problem. The hordes had to be dealt with in detail, and spread as much as possible, and with that object in view speedy efforts were made to raise four battalions of Assyrians for employment in Persia under British officers. Others of them were formed into Labour Corps for work on the roads, while the remainder were despatched from Hamadan to Mesopotamia by stages in batches of a thousand. Supplies, local and other, were secured as quickly as possible, and were collected at the several stages, and as the refugees passed along the line rations were issued under the supervision of British officers.

Meanwhile Baqubah, thirty-three miles north-east of Baghdad, which is situated on the Diyalah river and on the rail and road routes to Persia, had been chosen as the concentration camp. Here, towards the end of August 1918, the refugees, exhausted by their march of many hundred miles, and suffering from a multitude of diseases, began to arrive. For two months the influx went on steadily, until about the end of October some forty-five thousand persons were accommodated in tents. The camp, which at first was organised and commanded by Brigadier-General H. H. Austin, who was assisted by a very limited staff of British officers, and British other ranks, covered an area of one square mile, and the utmost care was taken to secure the welfare, cleanliness, and discipline of the several sections into which it was divided. Not only were the refugees tended in every possible way, but many thousands of emaciated and sorry animals—ponies, mules, cattle, and donkeys, besides flocks of sheep and goats and one solitary camel—were cared for by the veterinary staff, and eventually discharged from the segregation camp and sent away for agricultural purposes, while the remainder formed the transport of the camp.

By Christmas 1918 the camp had reached the zenith of its organisation, and resembled a small town, complete with well-laid-out streets, a water supply, electric lamps, a bazaar, hospitals, churches, orphan schools and playgrounds for the children, a post office, labour bureau, and a railway station; while a club, a theatre, canteen, and Y.M.C.A. reading-room met the requirements of the British and Indian personnel. In June 1919 the camp, now fully organised and in smooth-running order, was taken over by the civil administration with a new headquarters staff, under Lieut.-Colonel F. Cunliffe-Owen, who carried on the good work of his predecessor.

During the time the camp remained at Baqubah I paid several visits to it, meeting the Patriarch and inspecting the armed men, boy scouts, and establishments. No sight more picturesque could well be imagined than a parade of the fighting men in their quaint garb, which seemed to be a combination of the dress of the pantomime harlequin and Joseph's multi-coloured coat. The rugged manliness

Assyrian warriors.

Arab levies.

THE OPERATIONS NORTH OF BAGHDAD

of their appearance, their handsome faces and military bearing, roused strong feelings of sympathy with a race which had gone through so fierce a struggle for existence, and seemed likely yet to have far to go before it reached a Promised Land.

As it had been decided that the repatriation of the Assyrian refugees to their former homes near Lake Urmia should be effected before the autumn, the movement to a camp some twenty miles north-east of Mosul had, as already mentioned, been begun. To ensure smoothness in the arrangements a steady flow northwards from Baghdad was essential, and this must evidently depend on secure rail communication.

The last and least important reason for endeavouring to keep open the Baghdad-Shergat line, was the moral effect which the refusal to accept the frequent interruptions by raiders as a cause for closing it to traffic for a time would have on the surrounding tribes. They must be taught that if the line could be cut it could also be repaired; and fortunately the more permanent nature of this, the first railway that was laid in Mesopotamia, and laid by the Germans in their usual thorough manner, was not so easily destructible as were our own more hastily constructed lines. Nevertheless the annoyance caused by the continual rail-cutting was considerable, and had it not been for the unremitting efforts of a detachment of the 26th Punjab Labour Corps under Lieutenant J. A. H. Devlin, the early resumption of the train service would not have been possible.

In the neighbourhood of Samarrah and between it and Baghdad the disturbed nature of the country, as has been said, was causing inconvenience. On the night of the 31st August a determined attack was made on Balad railway station, which is fifty-one miles north of the capital, by several hundred insurgents collected from both sides of the Tigris. After several hours' fighting they were driven off by the garrison of twenty-three men under a havildar of the 1/3rd Gurkha Rifles. Next day the line was reported to be cut at a point five miles north of Samarrah. Two platoons of the same regiment, under Captain T. A. Foster, were despatched from that place, and an armoured car detachment was sent to co-operate with them. The Arabs, who were firing from some villages between the railway and the river, were driven back, and left behind them several killed. Balad station was again attacked on the 1st and 4th September, but without success.

On the 31st August an armoured train and a train carrying Assyrian refugees had left Baghdad, and reached Sumaichah, forty miles to the north. Between that place and Balad station, about eleven miles further on, the line was damaged at intervals throughout its length, but by nightfall the latter place was reached. On the 1st September attempts were made to get through to Samarrah, but at Istabulat station, which is thirteen miles short of that place, it was found that the line immediately to the north had been seriously damaged. The trains now proceeded southwards, but found that the track behind them had in the meantime been cut.

That night a report came that the trains were isolated at Istabulat station, whither they had returned, that Arabs were holding trenches north and south of them, and that the passengers, who included a proportion of women and children, had practically no water. An armoured relief train was ordered to proceed at daylight to the scene, and an aeroplane which was also sent returned with the report that people had been observed standing on the ground beside the train. As troops were difficult to spare for the work of rescue, I ordered Colonel A. Paley, commanding the 1st Battalion Rifle Brigade, to take one company of his regiment, four hundred Assyrians (only one hundred and eighty actually entrained), and two field artillery guns, one of which was placed on a truck at the head of the train and the other at the tail, to proceed to the spot, drive off the insurgents, and withdraw the refugees and armoured train. Railway delays occurred, as usual, but at 3.45 P.M. the train of forty-three trucks and carriages —all the remaining rolling-stock that remained at Baghdad for work on the Shergat line—reached its destination.

THE OPERATIONS NORTH OF BAGHDAD 243

When Balad station, fifty-one miles north, was reached it was too dark to proceed further, and the train was halted and broken into two portions, which were placed for safety parallel to each other. Later, forty Assyrians were sent forward, and fortunately arrived at an important bridge in time to prevent its total destruction by a party of Arabs who had arrived before them.

Next day at 5.20 A.M. the train moved forward, and on reaching the bridge fifty minutes later it was found that, except for the girders, nothing remained of it, sleepers and rails having been thrown into the ravine below. At 8.25, the bridge having been repaired, the train started again, but a few minutes later encountered another breach, which had been effected by using teams of camels which hauled away the line by ropes. The armoured train from Istabulat station now arrived at the northern end of the breach, and it was ascertained that the officer in command, Captain W. H. Butcher, Royal Engineers, attached to the Mesopotamian Railway Service, who was mainly responsible for saving the refugees, and who was awarded an immediate Military Cross for his behaviour on this occasion, had made several attempts, under fire, to effect repairs, which, owing to extensive damage, had not been successful. His casualties at Balad and Istabulat had amounted to six killed and eight wounded.

The armoured train now moved north again to Istabulat station to fetch the refugees, and was to be followed by Colonel Paley as soon as the break between the trains was mended, when he would push on and cover the return journey. By 10.20 he was able to advance with fifty to sixty Assyrians skirmishing ahead on either side, twenty-five of the remainder having been left as a post at the bridge in rear.

A plan had been thought out in the eventuality of opposition being met, but on approaching the refugees it proved to be unnecessary. Both Arabs and Kurds have a wholesome dread of the Assyrian, whose drastic methods in dealing with his enemies recall those of Old Testament days. As soon as the train was found to have Assyrians and not supplies on board, the Arabs had sheered off and kept at a respectful distance from it. Thus at half-past ten, when Colonel Paley's train was moving in a northerly direction, and though the Arabs kept on firing, nobody was hurt.

The train, followed by the two which had been isolated, now proceeded to Balad station, where the truculent nature of the Assyrians displayed itself. Some time earlier two Arab men, two women, and a child had been captured, and, except one of the men who carried a revolver, they were ordered to be released. That man tried to escape, and was rightly shot by the escort. But a large number of the refugees saw the remainder of the prisoners moving off, and jumping from the train chased and killed the other man, and with considerable difficulty were prevented from killing the women.

This incident of the isolation of the refugees' train has been mentioned as one typical of the troubles on the northern line, which, had the Arabs proved tenacious, would have caused us considerable inconvenience.

The next incident on that line was a second attack on Samarrah, near which, on the right bank of the Tigris, a large body of Arabs was reported to be concentrating on the 11th. This was dealt with by the 1/3rd Gurkha Rifles and two aeroplanes, which were sent from Baghdad, and did good work in chasing fleeing insurgents, bombing and firing on them as they ran.

From that date onward no further disturbances occurred between Baghdad and Mosul, and it is probable that, as regards the southernmost section of the line, the absence of raids was due to the operations which were taking place north-east of the capital, and later to the occupation of Deltawah and Sindiyah.

Elsewhere, however, in the district, which fell within the command of Major-General Fraser, including the Kirkuk area, which was added to it on the 22nd August, the situation was unsatisfactory. The disturbances in the Diyalah Division had spread through the Kurdish tribes round Kifri, and communication between that place

THE OPERATIONS NORTH OF BAGHDAD 245

and Kirkuk was in danger. Kingarban station, which is the railhead and is about six miles distant from Kifri, was, like some other places, indifferently defended; and besides the fact that, owing to lack of compactness, the perimeter to be held by the garrison was almost two miles, the water supply came by a series of karezes or roughly-made tunnels from the pumping-station, which was distant from the camp about one thousand yards. The troops holding the place consisted of two and a quarter companies of the 94th (Russell's) Infantry and the 113th Infantry, besides some details, the whole being under the command of Major B. I. H. Adler of the latter regiment. As the protection and supply of two posts at important bridges on the railway line devolved upon that officer, the force at his disposal at Kingarban was liable to be reduced, and was so on the 17th August to only two platoons. The Political Officer, Captain G. H. Salmon, who with his wife was at Kifri, was pressed to move his quarters to the railway station on the 15th August, but he declined, as also did his wife, alleging, probably with good reason, that the moral effect of his presence among the inhabitants, who were hostile to the local tribesmen, was great, and that unless the situation became very grave he would not quit his post. Eventually on leaving the town to parley with some tribesmen on a hill close by he was captured, after which his wife came to the military camp. On the 28th he was killed by his captors, and on the day following a small column under Major N. F. C. Molloy, 32nd Lancers, consisting of five troops of that regiment, a section of the 49th Pack Battery, and a few details, reached Kingarban from Kirkuk, whence it had been sent to co-operate with the garrison against the Kifri insurgents. On the way there on the 27th Major Molloy, who met with opposition during his march, relieved one of the posts on the road at Tuz, which was held by a detachment of the 113th Infantry. This small post had been invested since the 18th August, and had sustained several attacks from a party of some two hundred tribesmen, who twice forced their way through the defences, and were driven out with bomb and bayonet.

Kifri was entered on the 30th with some slight opposition, but it was too late to save the life of Captain Salmon, who, like several other Political Officers, had gallantly remained at his post. The local shaikh was appointed governor, and a company of infantry was sent from Kingarban, after which Major Molloy returned to Kirkuk, which was reached on the 4th September.

The despatch of his small column had an excellent effect on the tribesmen in and around Kirkuk, and also on the Arbil and Sulaimaniyah areas. In the former of these areas the Political Officer, Major Hay, had been attacked in the Rowanduz gorge on the 12th August, but had escaped, and after that the whole of the area became unsettled. A plot by a small disaffected element at Arbil to set up a local government was discovered and frustrated, and the depredations committed by the Kurdish tribes effectually cooled the revolutionary ardour of the inhabitants.

On the 1st September the position was that the Surchi of the Akra district, a tribe possessed of strong proclivities for making trouble, having crossed the Zob and overthrown the government at Batas, were on their way to Rowanduz, where there was a small garrison of Levies. On receipt of the news of the events at Batas, Captain Littledale, the local Commandant of Levies, at once set off with thirty mounted and seventy footmen, relying on promises of help from a local leader. But no help was forthcoming, and the small force of Levies, who attacked alone and with gallantry, failed, and had to withdraw to Arbil, with a loss of eighteen men.

This repulse naturally reacted unfavourably wherever the news of it was borne. The position of the Assistant Political Officer at Keui at once became untenable, and on the 3rd September he was forced to evacuate that place, leaving the government in the hands of certain of the leading men. Even before the reverse at Batas the position at Rowanduz had become so critical that the small Levy garrison there had to be withdrawn, reaching Arbil without serious loss or adventure. Thereafter Rowanduz was

Arbil from the north-west.

Kirkuk from the west.

THE OPERATIONS NORTH OF BAGHDAD 247

attacked by the Surchi, and after some disorder a holy man was appointed, or appointed himself, governor.

In order to try and restore a semblance of order in the area, frequent bombing raids by aeroplanes were made from Mosul over Batas and other hostile villages, with the result that by the beginning of the first week in September the situation in Arbil appeared to be improving. The improvement there did not, however, continue, and at the end of the week matters grew so critical that the despatch of troops became necessary. Accordingly a small column under the command of Major G. B. Henderson (attached to the 52nd Sikhs), consisting of one squadron 11th (K.E.O.) Lancers, one section 8th Battery R.F.A., and fifty rifles of the 52nd Sikhs, left Mosul on the 11th September, and met at Arbil on the 14th half a squadron of the 32nd Lancers and one company of the 4th Battalion Royal Fusiliers from Kirkuk. The arrival of these troops had an immediate effect, and the area subsided into peacefulness.

In the Akra area hostile tribesmen were dispersed by bombing from aeroplanes the several villages west of the Greater Zab, where they were reported to be concentrating. On the 15th September about six hundred Surchi Kurds attacked an Assyrian repatriation camp at Jujar, where the refugees' animals were collected, thirty miles northeast of Mosul. The Assyrians, though heavily outnumbered, were better armed and disciplined, and made short work of the Kurds. With a loss of only four killed and eight wounded, they slew sixty of their opponents, and drove the rest back across the Zab, where one hundred and forty more are said to have been drowned.

But for this entirely fortuitous support it is possible that a large portion of the Mosul Division might have been swamped in the wave of anarchy.

This affair brought to a conclusion the operations in the 18th Divisional area, but during October small columns were sent wherever their arrival would have the effect of suppressing the first signs of disorder.

The possibility of the garrisons of Mosul and Kirkuk being cut off from Baghdad weighed on my mind, and caused me to order the women and children at those places to be withdrawn and sent to the capital. In the case of Mosul the regular route to the south was open, and provided special precautions were taken it was reasonably safe. On the other hand, the route by rail to Kingarban and thence by road to Kirkuk was closed, and access to the garrison of the latter place was only possible by traversing the disturbed area which lay between it and Mosul. The question of moving some of the women by aircraft was considered, but aeroplanes were not available for the numbers to be carried, which comprised eight women, some children, a few men seriously ill, and a quantity of baggage. The only means of withdrawing them, therefore, was by the waterless desert route to Tekrit on the Tigris, a run of seventy miles by motor-car, and thence by a track along the left bank of the river to Samarrah, near which town there is a ferry. The Arabs, through whose country the party would pass, had so far remained friendly, but others from a distance, should they get wind of the move, might constitute a danger. Secrecy therefore had to be maintained; and the commander at Kirkuk was told only to warn, late in the afternoon, those who were to move next day. The party, which would require several cars, would be escorted by British soldiers, and aeroplanes were ordered from Baghdad to proceed to Samarrah and patrol that part of the desert route which is nearest to the river. A hospital train, with an escort of an officer and fifty men, and an armoured construction train, were sent to Samarrah, where the journey by motor-car would terminate. At 7 A.M. on the 19th a start was made from Kirkuk, and a little later two aeroplanes left the Baghdad aerodrome. At the hour when an air report was expected to the effect that the convoy had been seen, word was received that the planes had failed to get any trace of it. Throughout the day information continued to be negative in character, and all that was known was that the party had left Kirkuk and had disappeared into space.

During the war on the Western Front we used to consider no news as bad news, but in the East I have found

THE OPERATIONS NORTH OF BAGHDAD 249

the contrary to be the case. There bad news travels fast, confirming the adage, "For evil news rides post, while good news baits"; and though I felt anxiety at the ominous silence, I was confident that nothing serious had happened.

Next morning, the 20th, word came that the convoy had lost its way in the desert, and had been forced to spend the night there with a minimum of water. By 10 A.M. it reached Samarrah, and by 3 P.M. was safe in Baghdad. It was the small escort of British soldiers with this convoy who a little later helped to make Samarrah secure.

CHAPTER XX.

THE OPERATIONS IN NORTH PERSIA.

ALTHOUGH Mesopotamia is at a great distance from North Persia, where our troops and those of the Bolsheviks were in contact, operations in both countries were in some measure interdependent. The distance, however, and the insecurity of the line of communication between Baghdad and Quraitu, removed all the advantages which the central position of the Capital of Mesopotamia might be imagined to possess, as the transfer of troops from one country to the other was an operation so prolonged as not to be lightly undertaken. Consequently, though frequent appeals came from Persia for help, I persistently, and as it turned out rightly, ignored them ; and in this connection I may mention that, it having come to the knowledge of the British Minister at Teheran that a division had been ordered to embark for Mesopotamia, he must have felt that a favourable opportunity had at last arrived to make me disgorge some more troops for use in Persia. On the 23rd August I received, with some amusement, a reiteration of the request for two more battalions, which, it was suggested, "in case of necessity, could be moved rapidly back to Mesopotamia." But I was then almost *in extremis* where man-power was concerned, and though at heart I sympathised, I could do nothing but turn a deaf ear to the east. It was clear that the decisive rôle must be played in Mesopotamia, a fact which was recognised by the General Staff at the War Office, who left me a free hand in the matter, and that on our success or failure there depended our position in North Persia.

THE OPERATIONS IN NORTH PERSIA 251

I have stated earlier that I had in June countermanded the order for two Indian battalions to join Brigadier-General Bateman-Champain's force, and soon after it was clear that, had I parted with those units, the situation in Iraq, where every man available was required, would have been compromised. The lesson was one which was not to be disregarded ; and although I wished to avoid the extreme step of ordering the evacuation of Persia, where the presence of my troops had a moral effect far out of proportion to their numbers, I did not hesitate later to draw on them for reinforcements.

I was confirmed in my decision by the knowledge of the indifferent quality of the troops opposed to us in Persia —little better than an armed rabble—and the excellence of my own ; and when Major-General Sir Edmund Ironside at my request was sent out at a later period to command the force, he expressed himself as more than satisfied that it would suffice for the work that was required.

About the middle of July I received a letter, dated the second of that month, from Brigadier-General Bateman-Champain, whose brigade headquarters were at Kasvin, in which he mentioned that he had paid a visit a few days earlier to Manjil. He stated that my inspection there in June had borne excellent fruit, and that those on the spot now understood the proper method of defence. The road was being defended well in advance of the bridge over the Safed Rud, and other arrangements to put in force my views were being made. He added that the 2nd Gurkha Rifles, who, as I knew, had been replaced by the 122nd Rajputs, were at Loshan, twelve miles behind Manjil, where they were preparing a second position covering the bridge at that place. There they were favourably posted to deal with any small parties of the enemy who might try to work their way over the hills with a view to cutting in behind the troops at the pass.

The sequel, however, proved to be disappointing, for on the morning of the 26th July a report was received at his headquarters that the position at Manjil was being attacked by some fourteen hundred Russians and Azerbaijanis, who had with them artillery and machine-guns. At the same time information arrived that a flank guard of one platoon from his force was engaged with a body of the enemy near Loshan, whose strength was estimated at three hundred men with two guns. The quality of the Russian troops, assuming that the numbers were not exaggerated, may be judged from the fact that on the arrival of a second platoon to aid the flank guard they were driven off.

On the 27th and 28th July the attack on Manjil, where our force seems to have acted in a purely passive manner, was continued, and was supported by a few guns. Reinforcements were asked for by Lieut.-Colonel P. C. R. Barclay, 122nd (Rajputana) Infantry, who was in command of the defence, but the system on which the North Persian Force was disposed did not admit of their despatch.

On the night of the 29th/30th a futile attack by five platoons of Indian troops was made, which resulted in a few casualties, among which were one British officer wounded and one man missing.

On the 30th a report, that came from a source which had so far always proved inaccurate, was received that two hundred Bolsheviks had been seen in the hills northwest of Kasvin. Troops were sent out to look for them, but they could not be found. On the same date General Bateman-Champain telegraphed to me to the effect that he was going to withdraw, to which I replied at once that he should not do so unnecessarily. Lieut.-Colonel Barclay, however, had already reported that he believed that the force in front of him had been reinforced, and numbered two thousand rifles, that it appeared to be working round his right flank, and that his left was also threatened. The surprising enterprise which the Bolsheviks were now stated to be displaying bore fruit in the orders which were issued by General Bateman-Champain for Manjil to be evacuated that night, and the troops to be concentrated at Kasvin, seventy miles to the rear.

The orders were duly executed, and our troops withdrew unobserved and unmolested, the bridge over the Safed Rud being blown up by the engineers after the rear-

THE OPERATIONS IN NORTH PERSIA 253

guard left. The dispositions now adopted consisted of a line of outposts round Kasvin, with a detachment placed on high ground near Kuhin, whence an advance of the enemy could be observed. In addition, the detachment which had been sent to Zinjan on the strength of rumours of an impending attack from that direction, and which consisted of one squadron of the Guides Cavalry and half a battalion of Indian Infantry, was ordered to remain and guard the left. Should circumstances compel a retirement from Kasvin, the detachment at Zinjan would act as a flank guard for the march to Hamadan.

The commander of the Persian Cossack Division on the 7th August offered to fill the breach, and arranged for an advance on Resht by three routes, requesting the assistance of our troops and guns. Brigadier-General Bateman-Champain, who expressed his anxiety to share in the enterprise, was, however, debarred by his orders from proceeding beyond the ground he had formerly held at Manjil, but he agreed to guard his colleague's line of communication to that point and repair the damaged bridge.

The Persian troops began their movement on the 17th, but three days earlier Major A. W. Van Straubenzee, commanding the detachment at Kuhin, was ordered to make a night march and try to surprise some hostile cavalry who were reported to be about to attack his position. The Bolsheviks, who were in greater strength than had been estimated, were found to be advancing by the main Manjil road towards Kuhin, which is twenty miles north by west of Kasvin, without the ordinary measures of protection. In consequence they were surprised with a loss of forty killed and wounded and forty-three taken prisoners. Six machine-guns were captured; and a 4·8-inch howitzer, of which half the team had been disabled by a Hotchkiss gun, made its escape, but fell into the hands of the Persian Cossacks. On this occasion we suffered no casualties, a proof of the skill with which the commander handled his force and the inferior quality of his opponent's troops. Even the Persian Cossacks were more than a match for the Bolsheviks, and so successful was their advance that by the 23rd August they had reached a point only nine miles from Enzeli, after killing many and capturing a number of prisoners, several machine-guns, and much booty. The Cossack Division commander now unwisely tried to reach Enzeli itself, but coming under the fire of several guns his troops retired to Resht, and thence in great disorder to Manjil. That place, which we had left on the 30th July, was now reoccupied, and as the Bolsheviks themselves were as demoralised as those they had driven back, it became possible to reorganise the panic-stricken Persian troops.

On the 2nd September they advanced again, supported by a troop of cavalry, a section of pack artillery, and a battalion of infantry from the North Persian Force, which troops took up a position north of the Manjil defile near Rustamabad. On this occasion the commander of the Persian Cossack Division, Colonel Starosselsky, moved in deliberate fashion, and occupied Resht on the 22nd September with scarcely any opposition.

As Brigadier-General Bateman-Champain had for some time been in indifferent health, and required a change of air, I had telegraphed to the War Office on the 8th August asking that, if possible, Major-General Sir Edmund Ironside might be sent to replace him. The latter officer was well known to me, having commanded a brigade of the 2nd Division, which formed part of my Corps for several months in 1918. Apart from his exceptional linguistic powers, his military knowledge, experience, sound judgment, and outstanding personality, he had gained, when in command at Archangel, an intimate knowledge of the Bolshevik troops, their methods, and their value in the field. Such a man was urgently required in Persia; and as General Sir George Milne was able to spare him from the post he held in the Black Sea Army, and the War Office approved of the appointment, he reached my headquarters at Baghdad on the 28th September, and next day left for Kasvin.

On the 23rd October he reported that the Persian Cossacks appeared to be in trouble, and that their commander was preparing to retire. This movement they had begun the day before, and by the night of the 25th/26th they were all collected behind the British troops. The Russian officers with them now engaged in active Bolshevik and anti-British propaganda, and the state of the force grew so serious that all were removed from their appointments and sent out of the country and overseas. The division was placed under the command of a Persian officer, who, helped by a few British officers, succeeded in introducing some order and discipline among the troops. But this régime was not of long duration, and during the following summer the connection of the British element with the Persian troops was severed.

The Bolsheviks, who had followed the Shah's troops, shelled our camp at 2 P.M. on the 26th, and a reconnaissance made by some armoured cars, the Guides Cavalry, and the 122nd Infantry, drove in their outposts, and found them holding an intrenched position. Their strength was estimated to be from twelve to fifteen hundred rifles, with cavalry, machine-guns, and four to six field-guns. But no offensive action could be taken against them, for on the night of the 26th they retired. General Ironside now pushed forward a covering force some twenty-five miles to the north, and arranged for the troops in rear to remain in winter quarters at Manjil. Several engagements with Bolshevik patrols ensued, in which they were invariably driven off with loss.

Our policy in North Persia, which, after the withdrawal from Enzeli, had, except for action by aeroplanes, been of a defensive nature, continued so throughout the severe winter which followed ; and when spring came the country was evacuated under orders from home, and the North Persian Force ceased to exist.

CHAPTER XXI.

THE DISARMING OF THE TRIBES.

THE main operations in Iraq came to an end when our troops entered Samawah on the 14th October. The next phase of the campaign may then be said to have been entered on—a phase which in every war, both great and small, makes a heavy call on both patience and determination, yet one which, like the pursuit after a battle, if carried out half-heartedly, is equivalent to throwing away most of the efforts that have preceded it. The tribes, without provocation worthy of the name, had chosen to risk the arbitrament of arms ; they had been overcome, and must be made to pass beneath the Caudine Forks. There could be no security for the future peace of Mesopotamia unless the punishment awarded were such as would discourage a repetition of this foolish outbreak either by themselves or by those who, through the wisdom or force of character of their chiefs, had on this occasion been restrained from actively participating. After that stage had been attained, when all hope of further resistance had been obliterated, then, and not before, the time for amnesty would come, and relations of a friendly nature could be established.

In other campaigns in which I had taken part I had had experience of the great difficulty of enforcing terms once the troops had turned their backs on the country where they had been operating. I had not forgotten the weary months spent at Peshawar in 1898 when waiting for the Afridis to hand in rifles, and how, in order to induce them to do so, every expedient, even that of making payments, was resorted to. I also remembered the long pause which

THE DISARMING OF THE TRIBES

followed the signing of the Armistice between the Russians and Japanese in Manchuria in 1905.

The situation in Iraq in the autumn of 1920 was, however, different, for there we were in occupation of the country, and the tribesmen could have no reason to conclude that there we should not stay indefinitely. But no sooner had the last garrison been relieved than I had been instructed from home to ensure that all the reinforcements which had arrived to help in quelling the outbreak were embarked to leave the country not later than the 31st March 1921. Before the date named I hoped not only to disarm and otherwise punish those who had fought against us, but to deprive of rifles all who possessed such weapons for self-protection and use in inter-tribal feuds, or who might rely on such means to coerce the Arab Government which was just about to spring into existence. Doubtless the early reduction of troops was desirable from the British taxpayers' point of view, and the situation both in Europe and India would not admit of locking up large numbers of troops in a country of secondary importance such as Mesopotamia.

The total number of rifles, modern and other, in Mesopotamia was computed in 1920 to amount to not less than 300,000, and of these the tribes who had participated in the rising possessed between 50,000 and 60,000. The opportunity of enforcing a general disarmament, when in 1918 and 1919 we had a vast force in the country, had probably for cogent reasons been allowed to pass. Then the weapons in the hands of the tribesmen were fewer than when the rising in 1920 came, but far more numerous than they had been when the campaign in Mesopotamia opened in 1914. From that date onwards the rifles and ammunition in the hands of the tribesmen had much increased, the main sources being as follows:—

    (*a*) Loot obtained by the tribesmen from battlefields.
    (*b*) Disarmament of fugitives and deserters of the opposing armies.

(c) The issue of arms and ammunition to friendly tribesmen by the British for employment against the Turks, or by Turks and Germans for use against the British.

(d) Consignments of arms and ammunition despatched for distribution among the tribesmen by anti-British organisations in Syria.

(e) The handing over by Turks, after the Armistice and during their evacuation of the country, of considerable stocks of munitions to the tribesmen.

(f) The increased wealth of tribal chiefs due to the influx of money and the boom in trade since the British occupation, which gave far greater opportunities for them to purchase rifles from the Persian Gulf and Syrian markets.

Not only had the number increased, but many obsolete weapons had been replaced by those of a modern small-bore type.

The possession of so large a quantity of arms was an undoubted danger to the maintenance of peace—a danger which was increased since our occupation by our method of rule, which set itself to settle blood feuds and paved the way for tribal combination. Yet the problem of total disarmament, however desirable, was one of great complexity. Indeed if it were possible to effect it, the open nature of the borders of Iraq, the impossibility of adequately guarding them, and the large profits and small risks attendant on the trade of gun-running, would speedily have caused fresh supplies to flow in and fill the vacuum which would be created.

So far as the insurgent tribes were concerned, it seemed possible by imposing heavy fines in rifles and ammunition to deprive them in great measure, if not entirely, of what they value above all other possessions. To do so would serve as an object-lesson to tribes in other parts of the country who had not risen, and would demonstrate the nature of the treatment which would be meted out should they at any time be tempted to take up arms against the

Government. Unfortunately the object-lesson would be
transitory, and would lose much of its value as soon as it
became known that the British garrison had been reduced
and had returned to pre-insurrection limits. Yet, beyond
setting an example to the non-insurgent tribes, no immediate
steps towards their disarmament seemed possible, for the
problem, as already stated, was a highly complicated one.

Thus we should have to deal with—

  (a) Tribes who had been friendly, and who had assisted
      during the operations.
  (b) Tribes who had remained neutral.
  (c) Tribes inhabiting inaccessible marsh country, whence
      they issue only for purposes of raiding.
  (d) Tribes who inhabit border regions where arms for
      their protection are necessary.
  (e) Nomad tribes who pass a portion of the year in
      Mesopotamia and then move their families, flocks,
      and herds beyond its borders.
  (f) The Kurdish tribes.

No two of these tribes could be considered under the
same heading, and each would require different treatment.
I consulted the High Commissioner on the subject, and his
opinion was that the question of general disarmament
must be left to the Arab Government, and that it would
be undesirable to extend my operations in that respect
beyond the actual insurgents.

As there still seemed a possibility of the insurrection
spreading beyond its present limits, should the idea prevail
that a general disarmament was in prospect, it was arranged
not to employ that terminology, but that when issuing
terms the fines inflicted should be such as to amount
practically to the deprivation of all serviceable arms and
ammunition. Where these were not forthcoming by specified dates, demands would be enhanced and punitive action
would follow; but in lieu of an unpaid residue, sums which
considerably exceeded the market value of the articles
would be accepted.

This procedure, in the case of tribes from whom more

than they possessed might happen to have been demanded, would encourage the surrender, in place of money payments, of arms and ammunition purchased from neighbouring tribes. Besides these terms, which tended towards disarmament, other and secondary demands, that included the restoration of and repayment for damage done to Government property and the refunding of unpaid revenue, would be made.

The time, however, though it had arrived in a few places and was imminent in others, was not yet favourable for a general declaration of the terms of submission, as the conditions governing operations had so far only admitted of limited areas being visited by our troops. No sooner therefore had the garrisons of Kufah and Samawah been relieved and full freedom of action been secured, than systematic operations on the Middle and Lower Euphrates were begun.

In the meantime some changes in commands had taken place, for Major-General G. N. Cory had arrived from home and relieved Major-General Atkinson on the 18th October in the command of the 6th Division; while Brevet-Colonel G. A. F. Sanders (temporary Major-General) had replaced Major-General Leslie in that of the 17th Division. Both of the new commanders were reminded that the weather was now favourable for operations, which should be more extended and carried out more quickly than was possible earlier in the year. Columns were ordered to be made as mobile as possible, and as small as was consistent with safety. Daily plans for their employment were to be thought out, and not a moment was to be wasted, so that more might be accomplished than in the great heat had been possible. Every one was urged to throw his heart into the work that remained to be done, and above all, to spare no efforts to ensure that it was done in a thorough manner.

Instructions regarding disarmament were issued on the 5th November (*vide* Appendix VII.), and in the following month, when it was found that the fines of rifles and ammunition demanded were not being paid as quickly as was

THE DISARMING OF THE TRIBES 261

desirable, I addressed each of the divisional commanders on the subject. I had noticed that in some areas where rifle fines had been laid down, difficulty was being experienced both in obtaining payment and ensuring that serviceable weapons were being handed in. Certain Political Officers, who, it must be remembered, have to live cheek by jowl with the tribesmen, and who no doubt felt that to impoverish them would react later against full payment of revenue, seemed to think that the fines imposed were excessive, and even surpassed what the tribesmen possessed in arms and ammunition. But as our estimate was based on information that had been furnished at an earlier date by the Civil Administration, I paid no heed whatever to their representations. Indeed I felt that if the question of payment of revenue was involved, there was a far better chance of its being paid if the attention of the late insurgents could be diverted from fighting to occupations of a peaceful kind, for so long as they were armed to the teeth the temptation to indulge in strife and loot would be irresistible. I pointed out that, under no circumstances, as had been suggested, was the payment of revenue to take precedence over or even equality with that of arms. The tribes in many instances had behaved with great brutality; the time for mercy had not yet come, and the pound of flesh must be exacted. I added that I was strongly opposed to extensions of the time laid down for the payment of fines, and if in that respect the Arab was given an inch he would assuredly take an ell. He must be made to understand that just as under Darius the statutes of the Medes and Persians were unalterable, so also at the present time the demands of the British Government admitted of no more favourable interpretation. Above all, it was to be remembered that we were amongst a people of whom it might be said with truth (I quote from memory)—

> "Use 'em kindly, they rebel;
> But be rough as nutmeg-graters,
> And the rogues obey you well."

Any display of leniency would be immediately attributed

by them to weakness, and justice, rhadamanthine in its inflexibility, would prove to be the best and quickest road to the desired goal. That this policy, though much more difficult and distasteful to enforce than were gentleness and brotherly love, proved right will presently be seen.

I will not attempt to describe in detail the movements of all the columns, some large, some small, which at one time numbered twelve, and which operated without pause not only in the Hillah and Samawah areas, but on the Upper Euphrates and east of the Tigris towards the Persian frontier. The object with which their movements were carried out was not only to ensure compliance with our terms, but to visit the areas where in the past neither we nor the Turks had been, and so prove to the tribesmen that no physical difficulty would prevent our troops from penetrating to their most inaccessible abodes.

The first places to be dealt with were the holy cities of Najaf and Karbala, on the inhabitants of which heavy fines of arms and ammunition were imposed. At first the latter city proved to be intractable, but the enforcement of a strict blockade, which added to the discomfort of the inhabitants, who were already suffering from lack of water, combined with the presence of considerable bodies of troops, portions of which swept the country in its neighbourhood and punished the inhabitants, had the desired effect. By the 8th November the fines were paid, and the blockading troops marched to Tuwairij, on the Hindiyah branch of the Euphrates.

Before this date, on the 27th October, a night attack had been made on the camp at Kufah, which failed completely, and caused the insurgents a loss of over one hundred killed and wounded. This proved to be their last serious effort in this area, for our advance on Kufah and Tuwairij, and the presence of large bodies of troops which dominated the holy cities, made their leaders realise that all combined action by the Arab tribes was futile, and that their power to continue the insurrection was at an end. If, however, visible proof were required to show their inability to withstand our arms and save their property from falling into

THE DISARMING OF THE TRIBES

our hands, it was provided also on the 27th October by the work of two columns, which swept an area between Hillah and Musayib. This operation, which came as a surprise, was entirely successful, and resulted in the capture of 800 prisoners, 3180 sheep and goats, 75 head of cattle, 35 ponies, and 40 donkeys.

The arrival from Constantinople some time earlier of a squadron of aeroplanes considerably altered the situation to our advantage, and helped the operations connected with disarmament. The insurgents, who after the attack on Kufah had moved out of reach of the 55th Brigade column, were now in a country which is much intersected by water-channels, where only a large force supplied by river could safely operate. It thus became necessary to bring the 53rd Brigade column from Tuwairij and Karbala with a fleet of mahelas (native boats), when both brigade columns could operate in conjunction, one column on each side of the river. To neutralise the temporary inaction of the 55th Brigade column, to remove which from the vicinity of Najaf was not yet desirable, aeroplanes operated daily between the 22nd October and the 5th November from Hillah and Baghdad with excellent results. The effect of their action was felt to within a few miles of the Capital, and by the 5th November most of the tribes who inhabit the country south of Hillah had surrendered, and had agreed to pay rifle fines which amounted virtually to disarmament.

By the 10th November the Hillah-Kifl light railway line had been repaired, and was in working order, and on the same date the two columns met; while the 53rd Brigade column, which had been divided, moved down both banks of the Hindiyah branch from Tuwairij and reached Kifl on the 12th.

The country through which the latter column passed was found to be deserted, but large quantities of Government property and many of the transport carts captured in the unfortunate affair of the 24th July were recovered.

Both brigade columns were now concentrated at Kufah, except a small column from the 55th Brigade, which occupied Abu Sukhair and Jaarah on the 13th, from both of which places the inhabitants had fled.

The number of troops was now sufficient to overawe the inhabitants of Najaf, and arrangements were made to deliver our terms on the 16th November. At 10 A.M. on that date the 2nd Battalion East Yorkshire Regiment, the 2nd Battalion Manchester Regiment, 2nd Battalion Royal Irish Rifles, 1st Battalion the Rifle Brigade, and the 1/15th Sikhs were drawn up facing the city from the east. Beside these infantry battalions stood three batteries of field artillery, and over the town circled ten aeroplanes. The 37th Lancers faced the Serai, where the representatives of Najaf were assembled and the terms read out to them.

On the same date the troops returned to Kufah, with the exception of a squadron of the 37th Lancers, two sections of field artillery, two companies of the 2nd Battalion Royal Irish Rifles, and two of the 1/15th Sikhs, which maintained a blockade over the town.

Punitive operations now ceased in the 17th Divisional area, as all the tribes therein had surrendered. As, however, it was important, in view of the desirability of releasing the reinforcements from India, to hasten the handing in of rifles, to confirm earlier successes gained and prove to the people of the Shamiyah that no portion of their intersected country was beyond our power to penetrate, movements of several columns were organised. The work of these forces required the construction of several bridges, some of them of considerable length, as the area is crossed everywhere by canals and channels, of which a few of the latter attain to the magnitude of rivers. The result of these operations was that every part of the country in which they were undertaken was visited, and most of the inhabitants for the first time saw and believed that the British were in strength in Iraq. The surrendering of rifles continued steadily, and the weekly reports sent to Baghdad showed satisfactory results. Najaf had only paid one-third of the quota due, and, like Karbala, was difficult to deal with, as, being one of the holy shiah cities, it had been exempted from suffering what on the North-West

Najaf from the east.

Announcement of terms of surrender at Najaf.

Frontier of India used euphemistically to be called "the destruction of the defences." The presence of two brigades there did not help the requirements of the case, so the majority of these were ordered to march back to Hillah between the 25th and 29th November; while two sections of field artillery, one section of the 61st Company Sappers and Miners, the 2nd Battalion Royal Irish Rifles, and the 1/15th Sikhs remained to ensure compliance with the terms.

The only areas of insurrection which had not so far been visited were the triangle, Musayib-Fallujah-Baghdad, and the Diwaniyah district. As regards the latter, the 6th Division was moving north from Samawah, repairing the railway as it advanced, and would eventually join hands with the 17th Division, which was preparing to work towards it.

To deal with the triangle above mentioned, the 77th Brigade group, under Brigadier-General B. E. C. Dent, C.M.G., D.S.O., was formed, and was mainly composed of the troops which, as the 34th Infantry Brigade under Brigadier-General Coningham, had operated to reopen the railway to Quraitu, and later had been given a rest in Musayib, at the barrage, in Hillah, and on the Diyalah. Relieved by the 55th Infantry Brigade, these troops marched from Hillah on the 2nd December, the column of which they formed part being composed as follows:—

    5th Cavalry (two squadrons),
    97th Battery R.F.A.,
    131st (How.) Battery R.F.A. (less one section),
    40th Pack Battery,
    61st Company 2nd (Q.V.O.) Sappers and Miners (less
        one section),
    2nd Battalion East Yorkshire Regiment,
    45th (Rattray's) Sikhs,
    108th Infantry,
    1/10th Gurkha Rifles,
    32nd Sikh Pioneers (two companies),
        and some details.

Its orders were to sweep wide to the flanks of the route

of its daily march, so that the whole area should be covered during its operations.

The weather had now turned bitterly cold, in contrast to the great heat of a few weeks earlier, and as tents and a double scale of kit had to be carried, the train would have been much increased had it not been possible to use river craft for transport and supply.

The force moved in two columns, one column following the river as far as the mouth of the Yusufiyah canal, fifty-six miles up-stream, where it joined the other column, which had marched along the Baghdad railway line as far as Mahmudiyah. As the advance of another force from the north to meet that coming from Hillah would have considerable moral effect on the late insurgents, a small column formed of troops of the 51st Infantry Brigade from Ramadi and Fallujah, under the command of Major T. McGowan, D.S.O., R.F.A., co-operated from Khan Nuqtah. It was composed as follows :—

5th Cavalry (one section) and machine-gun section.
96th Battery R.F.A. (one section).
67th Company Sappers and Miners (one section).
80th Carnatic Infantry (two companies).

The two forces came into touch with each other and reached Fallujah on the 10th December, no opposition having been encountered. The triangle had been swept in every part, except for a small tract fifteen miles south-west of Baghdad, and the results were soon shown by the way in which the surrender of rifles progressed.

By the beginning of December the tribes of the Diwaniyah area alone had not made submission. These had been the first to rise, and were believed to have done an immense amount of damage to the railway and Government property when Brigadier-General Coningham's troops withdrew on the 30th July.

So far as military operations were concerned I did not require the railway in order to deal with the Diwaniyah area from the north, and the repairs to it and the reconstruction of bridges would have involved much delay. The

THE DISARMING OF THE TRIBES 267

river, if sufficient craft could be secured, would serve my purpose equally well. The 53rd Brigade group, which had originally been under Brigadier-General Sanders, before he was appointed to the command of the 17th Division, was therefore ordered under its new commander, Brigadier-General A. T. Paley, to march from Hillah for Diwaniyah on the 1st December.

His force was composed as follows :—

    37th Lancers (two squadrons and machine-gun section),
    Arab Levies (two squadrons),
    2nd Battery R.F.A. (less one section),
    132nd (How.) Battery R.F.A.,
    45th Pack Battery,
    9th Company 2nd (Q.V.O.) Sappers and Miners,
    Detachment Bridging Train,
    1st Battalion Rifle Brigade,
    3/9th Bhopals,
    13th Rajputs,
    1/116th Mahrattas,
    1/12th Pioneers,
       and certain details.

For the first three days the column marched along both banks of the Hillah channel until the mouth of the Shatt-al-Dagharah was reached, where a pontoon bridge was thrown across the river, and the column on the left bank joined that on the right. After Jarbuiyah was reached the right bank column followed the railway, moving nightly to the river for supplies and tents, which were carried by native craft. Brigadier-General Paley had much trouble in keeping his force supplied, in spite of the fact that grain and fodder were procured locally. This was due to the strictly limited number of native boats and the difficulty presented by the Jarbuiyah bridge. The bridge had been burned by the Arabs after the post there had been withdrawn, and the obstruction caused by the fallen girders prevented all passage, and forced boats which were working below it to be towed up-stream and refilled at the bridge. The effect of the operations in other places seems to have told on the inhabitants in this area, for no opposition was met with, and the telegraph cable was only cut on two occasions, an incident which brought punishment on the nearest villages.

On the 6th December Diwaniyah was reached, where it was found that much wanton damage had been done by the insurgents to the railway station, Government buildings, electrical and other plant. The Diwaniyah and Dagharah tribes at once signified their wish to surrender, and on the 8th their formal submission was tendered, and the rifle fines which were ordered to be paid in by a certain date were announced.

Between the 8th and 22nd December the columns visited many places in the area, where they were received with every token of submission, and local supplies were obtained. A few houses and villages of the more prominent insurgents who had fled were destroyed.

On the 12th December connection was established at Imam Hamzah with a column of the 6th Division which had advanced north from Rumaithah, when a transfer of certain troops took place, the 1st Battalion Rifle Brigade and the 13th Rajputs, who were about to return to India, joining the 6th Division; while the 1st Battalion King's Own Yorkshire Light Infantry and the 3/70th Burmans passed to the 17th Division.

Although the civil administration had not arrived at a decision on the question of restoring the Euphrates valley railway, the relaying of that line, even for the purpose of removing it altogether, should that course be decided upon, would be a necessity. No sooner, therefore, had Brigadier-General Paley's column left Hillah, at which time the state of the country had become such as practically to guarantee the platelayers from interference, than work on the railway was begun. Almost every sleeper had been removed, and the embankment, such as it was, dug up in many places, but much of the necessary material was recovered from the Arabs and replaced by them *in situ*. Thus by the 12th December the railway was relaid as far as Jarbuiyah, where repairs could not be begun on the bridge until the 30th.

THE DISARMING OF THE TRIBES

This delay was due to the fact that the supply situation down-stream at Diwaniyah, which was carried out by boats, did not allow of the closing of the regulators at the Hindiyah Barrage in order to lower the level of the water for construction work.

A few days later heavy rain began to fall, which rendered operations difficult; and as the surrender of rifles was not as expeditious as was desirable, several small columns from the 55th Infantry Brigade at Hillah were despatched to the country of the defaulting tribes. This action had an immediate effect, and where the inhabitants continued to preserve a contumacious attitude as regards compliance with the terms, their sheep were seized and held as ransom.

But despite every measure that ingenuity could devise the policy of disarmament was not easy to enforce, and demanded unlimited patience, coupled with firmness.

In January the 17th Division continued operations, sending out eight columns, which were favoured by fine weather, but retarded as regards the carriage of their supplies by the abnormally low condition of the Euphrates. Far from showing signs of diminished vigour in their operations, the columns in this area, under their energetic divisional commander, continued to move from place to place with speed, and made frequent changes of camp, some of them being rewarded by the considerable number of rifles that were handed in.

West of Mahmudiyah, where the tribes had threatened an attack on Baghdad in August and interfered with the construction of blockhouses on the Hillah line, they had as yet only felt the presence of troops passing quickly through their territory.

On the 23rd January therefore a column consisting of—

7th Dragoon Guards (one squadron),
97th Battery R.F.A. (one section),
2/117th Mahrattas,
32nd Sikh Pioneers (one company),

under the command of Lieut.-Colonel E. W. Holmes, 2/117th Mahrattas, was sent to camp on the Yusufiyah canal, five miles west of Mahmudiyah, until the full fine of rifles was complete. As usual, the actual presence of troops had the desired effect.

Further south the Shamiyah tribes, which had been heavily fined in October at the time of the relief of Kufah, had fallen much into arrears in sending in their pound of flesh. As long as troops had remained in their area rifles were surrendered freely, but no sooner were they withdrawn than payment had grown less and less. This was most noticeable among the tribes in the Mishkab, as the lower reaches of the Kufah channel below Abu Sukhair are called.

The only remedy that could be prescribed was another visitation. This took the form of a column under the command of Brigadier-General P. W. L. Davies, C.R.A., 17th Division, which marched from Hillah on the 4th December, and was composed of some troops of the 55th Infantry Brigade and other arms, viz. :—

    Arab Levies (one squadron),
    39th Battery R.F.A. (one section),
    40th Pack Battery,
    67th Company 2nd (Q.V.O.) Sappers and Miners (less two sections),
    Detachment Bridging Train,
    8th Rajputs,
    2/96th Berar Infantry,
    32nd Sikh Pioneers (two companies),
    Machine-gun platoon of the 2nd Battalion Royal Irish Rifles,
    and some details.

Several other columns were at this time despatched from Kifl, Kufah, and other centres, on which places the troops of the Division were temporarily based. To assist them to march about the country more freely and to produce the civilising influence of good communications, roads fit for motor-cars at low river season were made by the tribes from Kufah in places where difficulty of movement had been earlier experienced. The columns from Kufah, three

Defence vessel *Blackfly*.

Types of Mesopotamian boats.

in number, left that place on the 17th January and moved
south, and roughly parallel to each other. They advanced
slowly, visiting every locality thoroughly, halting a few
days at each camp, and working at a distance from either
bank of the river. The Arabs, here as elsewhere, to whom
nothing but force appeals, helped in every way by closing
small canals and making roads for pack transport, while
the pontoons were used to bridge three or four broad canals
daily for the advancing column. By the 28th January
Turumah, which is twenty-six miles south of Kufah, was
reached.

No sooner did the tribes recognise that the troops could
move without difficulty wherever they desired, than rifles
which had been previously withheld were surrendered freely.

The progress of the operations may be judged by the
fact that in the 17th Divisional area, by the 15th January,
47,177 rifles had been handed in, and by the 31st these
numbers had increased to 52,769.

Throughout February disarmament continued, and by
that month the country had begun to resume its normal
peace aspect. Canals had been reopened, cultivation resumed, and individuals could move everywhere without
fear of molestation. Far from feeling any resentment at
the severity of their treatment, the opposite effect was
patent everywhere, and the relations which now existed
between the tribesmen and the troops were excellent.

In no instance was it found impossible to reach any
village in the large and difficult area of operations, and
no obstacle was allowed to interfere with the rationing of
troops or the carriage to outlying places of tents and the
winter scale of kit. Every form of transport had been
utilised, including both the metre and narrow-gauge railways, motor and other vehicles, paddle-steamers, and
native craft of all sizes, from the fifty-ton mahela down to
the marsh boat, capable of carrying only four men, and
going over flooded areas where the water was less than a
foot in depth.

Before turning to the operations of the 6th Division from
Samawah, the work done east and north-east of Baghdad

must be referred to. It will be remembered that Brigadier-General Beatty had been left in the Diyalah area, where, by the middle of October, the majority of the leading shaikhs had accepted the Government terms. Tribal control here was, however, weak, and besides the difficulty the shaikhs had in obtaining compliance with the terms, they were unable to prevent raiders from causing the district to remain in an unsettled condition.

On the 23rd October I issued orders for a scheme to be prepared for the march of a column, which it was hoped would lead to a better state of affairs, for the tribesmen in the area through which it would proceed had so far seen comparatively little of our troops. To strengthen Brigadier-General Beatty's force, " F " Battery R.F.A., one of the reinforcing units from India which I had brought to Baghdad directly it landed, and some details of other arms, were sent on the 26th and 27th October to Sharaban, whence the force would start.

A proclamation was issued to all tribes on the left bank of the Diyalah, which announced the forthcoming march, and directed supplies to be collected at certain places. In this proclamation it was pointed out that the operation was not of a hostile nature, and that if supplies were provided as ordered they would be paid for. On the other hand, should they not be forthcoming they would be seized and the tribe concerned credited with an act of hostility, which would bring punishment in its wake.

On the 29th October the column under Brigadier-General Beatty left Sharaban. It was composed as follows :—

75th Brigade Headquarters,
32nd Lancers (less two squadrons),
" F " Battery R.H.A. (one section),
13th Pack Battery R.G.A.,
1st Battalion Royal Irish Fusiliers,
2/11th Gurkha Rifles,
   and certain details.

Balad Ruz was reached on the 30th, where a halt was made, and next day the shaikhs of the tribes whose territory is watered by the Ruz and Marut canals met the Brigadier, and in his presence signed the Government terms, by which they undertook to pay a fine in rifles by the 16th November. The column continued its march on the 1st November, and returned to Sharaban on the 4th, having met with no opposition, and obtained all the supplies required.

As the state of feeling near Deli Abbas was unsatisfactory, a section of the 13th Pack Battery and the 2/11th Gurkha Rifles (less two companies)—which unit was a reinforcing battalion from India and one which I had brought direct to Baghdad—were sent there on the 17th, and remained for four days with good effect.

A considerable reduction in the number of blockhouses held on the Quraitu line became possible at this time, and the 99th Infantry was in consequence withdrawn for other duties.

By the 15th November it had become evident that compliance with our terms was not intended by the tribes on the left bank of the Diyalah, and a combined operation throughout the area was arranged.

On that date a column from Baghdad under Brigadier-General H. G. Young, commanding 7th Cavalry Brigade, consisting of—

> Headquarters 7th Cavalry Brigade,
> " F " Battery R.H.A.,
> 7th Dragoon Guards,
> 8th Hussars,
> 35th Scinde Horse (less two squadrons),
>   and certain details,

had moved to Mendali, where the townspeople were giving trouble. On reaching that place on the 20th it was found that all signs of hostility had vanished, and next day the members of the insurrectionary provisional government met Brigadier-General Young and signed the terms, but not without strong protest.

As by the 22nd very little effort had been made to comply with them, the destruction of the houses of two leading townsmen was ordered, but before the demolition preparations were completed, the sum demanded was produced; and as this represented the monetary equivalent of the balance of fines due that day, the sappers and covering force were withdrawn to camp. After the greater part of the column had marched through the town on the 23rd as a demonstration, considerable quantities of arms and money were handed in. Action of a nature somewhat similar to that taken on the 22nd had to be repeated on the 24th, after which the visit having terminated satisfactorily the column marched to Balad Ruz, where it came under Brigadier-General Beatty on the 27th in time to take its place in the combined operation.

His three columns were already in position, and their effect, combined with that of the force under Brigadier-General Young, at once hastened the delivery of fines. Many sheep were collected where rifles were not forthcoming, and in the case of the most troublesome and backward tribe, twelve aeroplanes sent from Baghdad led to the handing in of their full tale of rifles and ammunition.

By the 3rd December the operation was completed, all fines having been paid in with the exception of those due from two sections of the Bani Tamin tribe, which did not escape punishment.

The tribes on the right bank of the Diyalah next required attention, these having failed to comply with the Government terms in all respects. Early in November I had ordered preparations to be made for a march through this area and that east of Samarrah. A scheme had consequently been prepared, which involved a march through Deltawah and Dojman to Chai Khana on the left bank of the Adhaim. This river, which drains the lower hill country between Kirkuk, Sulaimaniyah, and Kifri, and in the dry season carries little or no water in the lower part of its course, runs into the Tigris in a north-easterly direction some forty-five miles north of Baghdad. The column, which was to be commanded by Brigadier-General Beatty, was composed as follows :—

THE DISARMING OF THE TRIBES

    32nd Lancers (one squadron),
    13th Pack Battery R.G.A.,
    11th Company 2nd (Q.V.O.) Sappers and Miners (one section),
    1st Battalion Royal Irish Fusiliers,
    2/11th Gurkha Rifles,
    and some details.

As the winter rains were shortly due it was desirable to begin the march as soon as possible, and in the meantime a proclamation was issued to the tribes that as they had failed to comply with the Government terms, to which they had signified agreement, they would now be punished by a fine of arms and ammunition. At the same time the date and place where payment would be accepted were announced.

As the column under Brigadier-General Beatty was not intended to pass through the territory of certain of the tribes on the right bank of the Diyalah, two small subsidiary columns were ordered to carry out that work. For this purpose the 2/117th Mahrattas and the 99th (Russell's) Infantry were employed.

By the 11th December the supply arrangements for Brigadier-General Beatty's column were completed, but on the night of that date rain fell heavily, and the move from Baqubah, where the troops were assembled, had to be postponed until the 17th.

Meanwhile the 2/117th Mahrattas and the 99th Infantry had been successful in collectiong the total fines due from the tribes into whose country they had been sent, on which they were withdrawn to Baqubah and Sharaban respectively.

Moving one day earlier than had been arranged, Brigadier-General Beatty's column arrived on the 18th at Dojman, which is situated on the left bank of the Tigris, five miles from the mouth of the Adhaim river. Chai Khana was reached on the 20th, and on the 21st aeroplanes sent from Baghdad were helpful in persuading the defaulting tribesmen to meet their obligations. After a two days' halt Brigadier-General Beatty, following the Adhaim and Tigris, marched to the railway line at Samarrah, which was reached on the 27th. Some trouble was experienced in collecting the fines imposed on certain of the tribes south of that place, and it was found that one shaikh had handed in, as his own contribution, rifles which had been collected from other sections who regarded him as their leader. The matter was adjusted, and towards the end of January the column as such ceased to exist, and the troops moved to Baghdad or other destinations. Its operations, under its energetic commander, had led to the practical disarmament of numerous small tribes who occupied a considerable area north and east of Baghdad.

CHAPTER XXII.

THE REOPENING OF THE EUPHRATES VALLEY ROUTE.

WHILE the disarmament above described of the tribes in the Diyalah and Samarrah areas and those on the middle Euphrates was in progress, the operations of the 6th Division continued further south. On the 22nd October I had informed Major-General Cory that I should require the 3/5th and 3/8th Gurkha Rifles and the 114th and 2/117th Mahrattas, which had been operating on the lower Euphrates, to be sent to Baghdad for work elsewhere. On the 24th I instructed him as to future plans. I directed him with the two British and seven Indian battalions and the other troops that would remain with him to continue such operations and punitive measures in the area within his reach as circumstances might require, and to inform me of his proposals. I stated that I was not yet in a position to deal with the Diwaniyah-Rumaithah area, for which purpose combined operations from the north and south would probably be necessary, and that until the Hillah and Shamiyah districts had been pacified these operations must be deferred. I added that the free use of aeroplanes to break the will and *moral* of the insurgents was advisable, and that machines in addition to those allotted to him would be sent at once from Baghdad on demand.

On the 15th October, prior to the issue of these instructions, and directly Samawah had been relieved, the 3/8th Gurkha Rifles, crossing to the left bank of the river, destroyed all villages to a distance of a mile below the town, and recovered from a mud fort the 13-pdr. gun which had been taken from the armoured train captured on the 3rd September.

As the tribes still gave no sign of responding to the proclamation calling upon them to submit, punitive measures were begun on the 17th, and the railway line was repaired and blockhouses were built to Barbuti bridge, which is about two miles north of the town. On that date, too, a column under Lieut.-Colonel H. J. Huddlestone, C.M.G., D.S.O., consisting of two squadrons of the 10th Lancers, two sections of field artillery, the 3/5th and 3/8th Gurkha Rifles, and the 3/23rd Sikhs, was despatched to resume the work which had been begun by the 3/8th Gurkhas two days earlier. This was effected with slight opposition, and the column returned to Samawah in the afternoon. Two days later another column under the command of the same officer, but differently constituted and helped by aeroplanes, worked northward, and returned at night, having seen signs of insurgents near Imam Abdullah bridge. It may be mentioned here that insufficient transport necessitated the nightly return to the main camp of the columns sent out from the 6th Division, a circumstance which undoubtedly diminished the effect of its operations as compared with those of the 17th Division.

On the 20th Brigadier-General Coningham, taking two squadrons of cavalry, four guns, and three battalions, carried out punitive measures, and reconnoitred that bridge, which was found to be badly damaged by fire. A considerable number of insurgents watched the operation, and maintained a heavy but ill-directed fire on the troops, which wounded two men of the 3/8th Gurkha Rifles. The withdrawal in the afternoon to the camp was a signal for the tribesmen to advance, but artillery and machine-gun fire soon dispersed them.

As the town of Samawah was deserted, it was desirable to encourage the inhabitants to return. In order therefore to afford them an opportunity of doing so, operations were suspended until the 27th, when they were resumed, and a large number of villages in its vicinity destroyed. As a rule, when the columns which were engaged in this work began their withdrawal to camp, the insurgents advanced with boldness and in considerable strength, and in all cases they suffered severely by coming under artillery fire, while our own casualties were inconsiderable.

Before the 6th Division began its advance northwards to come into touch with the 17th Division and cover repairs to the railway line to Jarbuiyah bridge, punishment was inflicted upon the Juwabir tribe which inhabits the neighbourhood of Khidhr, and which was responsible for the *Greenfly* incident and the murder of two officers of the Royal Air Force. Time had not permitted of this proceeding during the advance for the relief of Samawah, and now that a favourable opportunity had come, the insufficient transport with which the 6th Division was equipped unfortunately limited the range of action. The force which carried out the well-merited retribution was led by Brigadier-General A. le G. Jacob, commanding the 74th Infantry Brigade. Operations took place on the 6th, 7th, and 8th November, when much damage was caused to the property of the tribe in question, besides a loss of some thirty-five killed.

Meantime a column under Brigadier-General Coningham was preparing to advance northward. It was composed as follows :—

    37th Lancers (less two squadrons).
    17th Brigade R.F.A. (less 13th Battery).
    63rd and 69th Companies 2nd (Q.V.O.) Sappers and Miners.
    26th Railway Company Sappers and Miners.
    1st Battalion King's Own Yorkshire Light Infantry.
    3/5th and 1/11th Gurkha Rifles.
    3/23rd Sikh Infantry.

It was accompanied by a blockhouse, a construction, and a maintenance train ; and it was arranged that the 3/153rd Rifles should join the column on the 11th November.

By the 10th all was ready for the movement, and the troops were assembled north of the Barbuti bridge, the repairs to which were completed that day, while the line was laid beyond it for a distance of one and a half miles.

The day following had been fixed for this movement, and orders had been issued that it was intended to secure the damaged Imam Abdullah bridge, and occupy a general line beyond it, so as to enable repairs to be undertaken. The disposition of the troops was as follows :—

Advanced Guard . 3/23rd Sikh Infantry, supported by the 1/11th Gurkha Rifles (less one company), and some details, the whole under the command of Lieut.-Colonel P. G. Carey, 3/23rd Sikh Infantry.
Right Flank Guard . 3/5th Gurkha Rifles.
Left Flank Guard . 1/11th Gurkha Rifles (one company).

The cavalry was ordered to move west of the Shatt-al-Suwair.

In rear the remainder of the column was to follow.

At 5.50 A.M. the advance began, generally in a northerly direction, and as the Arabs seem to have been surprised by the comparatively early hour at which the force moved, the leading troops established themselves on the far bank of the river with very few casualties.

At 9.30 A.M. brigade headquarters and the main body reached the broken bridge, and an hour and a half later some two hundred Arabs made a counter-attack against the left of the position, but turned and fled when a company of the 3/23rd Sikhs, which had run short of ammunition, charged under their commander, Major R. N. B. Campbell. The right of the position was also attacked at 5.30 P.M., when three to five hundred insurgents tried to rush a piquet of the 3/5th Gurkhas, who were on the left bank of the river and posted so as to cover a ford. The attackers came under the fire of the troops of that regiment and two machine-guns on the other bank at a range of one hundred and fifty yards, and lost some seventy killed.

On the following day, as the insurgents showed no signs of submission, the villages in the neighbourhood were dealt

REOPENING OF THE EUPHRATES VALLEY 281

with, and large quantities of railway sleepers were recovered; the railway was repaired, and blockhouses were constructed as far as the south end of the bridge. Punitive action was continued daily, and on the 18th November, as

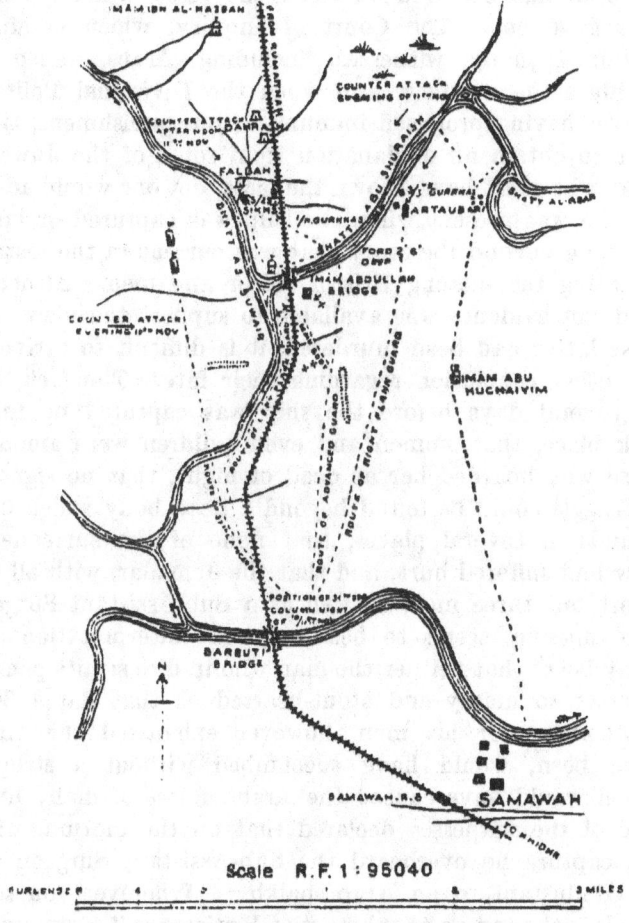

Fig. 10.—*Action at Imam Abdullah, 11th Nov. 1920.*

a proof of their desire to surrender, seventeen members of the crew of the defence vessel *Greenfly* were brought in by representatives of practically all the tribes in the Rumaithah area.

Three sepoys of the 2/123rd Rifles, who had formed part of the escort of the *Greenfly*, also rejoined, having escaped from their captors, and it was hoped to extract from them and the liberated members of the crew information regarding what had occurred on board the vessel when the supplies gave out. The Court of Inquiry, which carefully examined many witnesses, including Arabs, failed to elucidate the mystery, and when the Divisional Political Officer, having promised immunity from punishment, tried later to obtain an explanation from some of the Juwabir tribe, who must have known the facts, not one would admit that he was present when the ship was captured or knew anything beyond the story that was current in the district regarding the missing British officer and men. Although no direct evidence was available to support the view that these latter had been murdered, it is difficult to arrive at any other conclusion regarding their fate. The fact that for several days before the ship was captured no firing took place, that women and even children were amongst those who boarded her at dead of night, that no signs of a struggle could be found beyond a dead body which bore wounds in several places, that none of the surrendered crew had suffered hurt, and that the Jemadar, with all the escort but three men, as well as a Sub-Assistant Surgeon were missing, seems to bear only one interpretation. It is my belief that neither the man who in dire straits penned a letter so manly and stout-hearted as that dated 30th September, nor his men, however exhausted they may have been, would have succumbed without a struggle which would have caused the Arabs a loss of many lives. One of the witnesses declared that on the morning after the capture he overheard the Sub-Assistant Surgeon say in Hindustani to an Arab shaikh : " Wherever you send us, do not send us to where the British are," a statement which if true supports what has been said above.

The opinion held by the members of the Court of Inquiry was that the British officer and men were first rendered harmless by poison administered in their food, and then done to death ; but unless the escort and the surgeon make their way back to India, as was done by some deserters in Mesopotamia during the war, and are there captured, the actual facts must continue to remain in doubt.

I may mention here that before the Court of Inquiry had completed its researches, Major-General Cory wrote to me to say that one of the shaikhs of the Juwabir tribe who had surrendered told him that what had occurred was that, in the middle of the night, an Indian came ashore from the *Greenfly*. None of the tribesmen could understand his language, but by signs he induced one of them to accompany him. On arriving at the vessel it was seen that the British officer and the four gunners who were with him were dead. Thereupon the Arabs went in a body to the ship and looted her.

Since that time no inquiries made have added to our information regarding this unfortunate affair, but it is to be hoped that the long arm of Nemesis may some day overtake the guilty.

On the 26th November the repairs to Imam Abdullah bridge were completed, and the first train crossed it.

From that date until the 12th December, when, as mentioned, the 6th and 17th Divisions came into touch at Imam Hamzah, the tribesmen through whose country the 34th Brigade column passed became daily less hostile, and brought back railway sleepers, and, in the case of the Juwabir tribe, who signed terms on the 1st December, articles which they had looted from the *Greenfly* and elsewhere.

At Rumaithah, where the insurrection had begun, the Political Officer and the railway engineer were given a friendly reception, and rifles and about seven thousand sleepers were handed over.

On the 6th, when the column occupied that place, the leading townsmen and shaikhs of the neighbouring tribes made formal submission, and by that date all the tribes of the Rumaithah-Samawah districts had surrendered. On the 15th the 34th Brigade column returned to Rumaithah, the 53rd Brigade column of the 17th Division withdrawing to Diwaniyah on the same date.

On the 17th December I ordered the 6th Division to recall all troops from Rumaithah and from all places upstream of Nasiriyah except Samawah after the fines had been paid by the tribes. The retention of Samawah was only to be a temporary measure, as I had informed the High Commissioner that in the future I had no intention of maintaining troops in the Euphrates valley between Hillah and Nasiriyah. The occurrences in that area during July and August showed only too obviously the folly of retaining regular troops where their communications were unsafe, and I suggested that the Arab Levies were the proper force to guard the railway, which was of no value from a military point of view, the Tigris being my main and safer line of communication.

CHAPTER XXIII.

A MARCH ACROSS THE SHATT-AL-HAI.

FOR some time prior to the relief of Samawah the desirability of moving troops into the area between Kut and Nasiriyah, known as the Shatt-al-Hai, or Shatt-al-Gharraf, had become evident. The tribes there, whose inclinations for a time were distinctly bellicose, had been kept in check, and only in the vicinity of Nasiriyah incidents such as firing on blockhouses had taken place. Those among the tribesmen whose ill-feeling had been translated into hostile action could, through the medium of their Political Officers, be made to pay later for their temerity, but the mass of the inhabitants who lived at a distance had not laid themselves open to punishment. Yet, if in the future satisfactory relations were to be preserved between ourselves and the tribes of the well-armed Muntafiq confederation, it was essential that they should be made to see with their own eyes our military strength.

This I felt to be all the more important as the confederation in question held the position of a bogy, and the appearance of our troops within their borders at an earlier date had not enhanced our military reputation. What had then occurred I did not know fully until later, but it appears that towards the end of December 1915, when General Townshend's reports as to the urgency of relieving Kut became grave, the army commander decided that, although unready and deficient in many particulars, an advance must be made up the Tigris from Ali Gharbi at the earliest possible date. The Turks shortly after pushed their advanced troops down-stream to Shaikh Saad, and so increased the distance that lay between them and those engaged in the investment of Kut.

Prior to this movement the idea of initiating operations on the Shatt-al-Gharraf from Nasiriyah had been conceived, and with that object Major-General Gorringe left Qurnah for that place on Christmas Day.

On the 5th January, the date on which our troops suffered heavily at Shaikh Saad, he was ordered to advance at once in the hope of leading the Turks to believe that a strong attack was intended from the Euphrates valley, and so inducing them to weaken their main force by throwing out a detachment in his direction. Rain now fell, causing a delay in the collection of the necessary local transport, and not until the 14th January could a reconnoitring column leave Butaniyah, where the rest of the force had in the meantime been concentrated. The column in question consisted of some cavalry, a section of pack artillery, and a battalion, and marched towards Shattrah. On reaching Suwaij reports that had already been received of a considerable concentration were confirmed. Numbers of men mounted and on foot were seen in the distance advancing rapidly. The column soon became engaged, and fell back on Butaniyah, being helped in its retreat by two battalions from that place. Its casualties amounted to forty, and those of the Arabs were estimated at one hundred and eighty. On this date our troops were engaged with some three thousand men, among whom was a contingent of the Abudah section under their present redoubtable chief Khayun al Obaid, and that they intended to show fight if we entered their territory was clear. They had displayed their skill in manœuvring in their difficult country, which is so intersected by canals and small waterchannels as to make it resemble a gridiron.

The strength of the Muntafiq confederation and the natural difficulties of the advance by a regular force were such that it was decided not to attempt a further enterprise in their country. Orders were therefore given for the troops to remain at Butaniyah, between which place and Nasiriyah the tribes had shown no hostility, so that the fact of their presence might, through the medium of the Arabs, come to the knowledge of the Turks.

On the 7th February, it having been decided to withdraw the force at Butaniyah, which was then commanded by Major-General Brooking, all available troops at Nasiriyah were sent there to assist in the operation. The force consisted of one regiment and one squadron of cavalry, one field and one mountain battery, two British battalions (both much under strength), and two and a half Indian battalions.

No sooner had the baggage got clear of the camp and the rearguard begun to move than the Arabs appeared in force, and put into practice their customary tactics of working round the flanks. The numbers of the enemy kept on increasing, and the situation became grave, owing to the unsteadiness of the Indian troops. Hand-to-hand fighting ensued, and the force was only extricated with difficulty.

Subsequent reports, giving in detail the tribes who took part in the action, showed that before it terminated the numbers had increased from two thousand to about twelve thousand armed men. Our casualties numbered one hundred and forty-eight killed and thirty-five missing; those of the tribesmen were estimated to be one thousand.

In September 1916 the same tribes stubbornly resisted a force of two brigades, which was engaged in punitive operations in the neighbourhood of Nasiriyah.

The experiences of the Turks in this quarter were, however, even less encouraging than our own, for prior to the war they had sent several expeditions to subdue the tribes around Shattrah, and on each occasion had met with failure. In one expedition the force sent comprised seventeen battalions, each approximately three hundred rifles strong, but it had met with defeat, and was forced to make its way out of the area as best it could.

A peculiar feature of the fighting which had taken place in this portion of the country is said to have been the endeavour of the Arabs on all occasions to obtain possession of the invaders' guns. This object having been effected, the Turks would at once stop fighting, and a settlement be arrived at by the local leaders on both sides. Thereafter the artillery which had changed hands would be restored to its owners.

Such then was the country, whose tribesmen were now far better supplied with arms and ammunition than four years earlier, through which I was resolved to move. That there was little enthusiasm in my force to walk into such a possible wasps' nest is not surprising, for there still remained in it several officers who had been present at the engagement above described, and others who had served throughout the earlier campaigns in Mesopotamia.

Any operations in the Hai triangle must, however, necessarily be postponed until the flood season, as before that time neither craft for navigating the stream and carrying supplies nor water sufficient for the requirements of the troops and animals could be found. The difficulties of the operation were stated by those on the spot to be very great, and as time went on the obstacles to the scheme increased rather than diminished. But on Marshal Ney's dictum that "Some things are more difficult than others, but nothing is impossible"—an elaboration probably of Napoleon's more terse saying that "Can't is only to be found in the fool's dictionary"—I persisted in my determination to send troops through from Kut to Nasiriyah. I felt certain that, did I fail to carry out my plan, either I or others after me might have cause to regret the lost opportunity.

On the 24th November, after consulting the High Commissioner and obtaining his approval, I telegraphed my intentions to the War Office. I stated that the operation would probably not be concluded until the end of January, by which time all the arms that were likely to be collected throughout the areas in which the insurrection had taken place would have been handed in. The difficulties of the operation were expected to be such as are common to warfare in Mesopotamia, but in the Muntafiq area, apart from

Qalat Sikar.

Shattrah.

A MARCH ACROSS THE SHATT-AL-HAI 289

the question of the tribes themselves, who might or might not fight, the controlling influence, perhaps even in a more marked degree than in other parts of the country, was water. The river is prone to rise suddenly, and as suddenly subside, and troops dependent on water-borne supplies might find themselves forced to remain halted owing to the difficulty of movement of themselves and the animals and vehicles accompanying them. It was undesirable to move a small force through the area, as the inhabitants might not prove to be pacific, yet a large column might find itself immobilised and short of food. The country, too, being watered from the river along which the line of march must run, was intersected with innumerable canals of varying size, and the necessary bridging material, as well as the means of transporting it to the places where it would be required, could not be provided. In fact, so impracticable did the country seem likely to be at one point, that I was forced to give up the idea of marching a column through from Kut to Nasiriyah, and decided to content myself with arranging for the junction of a portion of the two columns which were to advance to meet each other from both those places.

The plan therefore resolved itself into the advance of a column under Brigadier-General Coningham from Nasiriyah to Shattrah (thirty miles by road), and another under Brigadier-General Dent from Kut-al-Amarah to Qalat Sikar (fifty-four miles by road). On reaching their respective destinations, which are twenty-nine miles apart, both columns would send a force to Karradi, which was to be the point of junction, and the column from Kut would transfer to that from Nasiriyah certain units. These units, which were due for return to India, would be sent from Nasiriyah to Basrah, which would be quicker than to march them back to Kut and thence convey them by river to the base. This proposed transfer of units was later cancelled, as it was found that it would give rise to administrative difficulties which were undesirable.

By the 14th January 1921 the following troops under

T

the command of Brigadier-General F. E. Cunningham were concentrated in a camp just north of Nasiriyah :—

37th Lancers (less two squadrons),
Composite Battery (two sections 18-pdrs., one section how.),
2nd Battalion Duke of Cornwall's Light Infantry,
3/8th Gurkha Rifles,
3/124th Baluchis,
2/125th and 3/153rd Rifles,
Half a machine-gun company,

while one company of sappers and miners as an advanced party, escorted by half a squadron and two companies of infantry from the column, moved to Lake Butaniyah. The water of the lake is brackish, and the supply there had to be improved before the main body arrived. Next day the column joined the advanced party, which was pushed on to Suwaij, nine miles further north, where the question of water again presented difficulties, the wells being thirty to forty feet deep and the amount obtainable small. In consequence the column was forced to halt at Lake Butaniyah on the 16th and 17th, while work on the wells proceeded. During this unavoidable delay all available waggons, carts, and cars in Nasiriyah were sent as a water-convoy to Suwaij to fill up the tanks there in anticipation of the arrival of the column.

On the 18th January the column, which had been joined by Shaikh Khayun al Obaid, the most influential man in the Shattrah district, whose good services in preventing the spread of the insurrection in the Hai have been referred to, and who brought with him some followers, marched to Suwaij, leaving a small post at Butaniyah. The preliminary arrangements at Suwaij proved so satisfactory that an ample supply of water was found there, but as a precautionary measure three more deep wells were dug next day, which proved to be greatly superior to the existing Arab wells.

On the 19th, leaving a small post at Suwaij, the troops followed the dry bed of the Shatt-al-Shattrah through

Shattrah town to a camp about two miles further north. During this march, as also that of the column from Kut-al-Amarah, aeroplanes made demonstration flights at certain times, the inhabitants of the towns and villages leaving their dwellings in large numbers to observe them and watch the troops as they passed. Supplies of certain natures had been arranged for in advance by the Political Officer, who accompanied the column, and these were satisfactorily delivered by the tribesmen, whose reception of the troops was generally of a friendly character.

Difficulties, which Brigadier-General Dent's column was meanwhile experiencing, necessitated a halt on the 20th and 21st of the column from Nasiriyah, during which the troops visited Shattrah, where their presence had a good effect.

On the 22nd Brigadier-General Coningham, leaving a small post at his camp, marched for Karradi, which was reached on the 23rd. Here the north and south columns joined hands, the large space covered by the camps of the united forces, and their combined strength, as also the aeroplanes which flew overhead, having a marked effect on the tribesmen. On the 24th Brigadier-General Coningham marched for Nasiriyah, which was reached without incident on the 30th January. The movement of his column had been carried out more easily than that from the north, which had to cover a greater distance, although, at first sight, the water-borne supplies on which the latter depended seemed to give it the advantage.

While preparations for the march to Shattrah by the column of the 6th Division were being made, those for the advance of the force from Kut-al-Amarah to meet it were in progress.

On the 24th December a preliminary reconnaissance was made by Brigadier-General Dent, who was to command the latter force. Accompanied by a staff officer and Major J. F. D. Jeffreys, the Political Officer at Kut, who possesses great influence with the tribesmen of Iraq, and who, like other officers on the Tigris, had done admirable work in keeping order during the insurrection, he reconnoitred the road to be followed as far as a point three miles south of Hai town, which is twenty-five miles south-east of Kut-al-Amarah. The road, or rather track, was found to be passable by all arms in fine weather, provided certain bridges were constructed.

On receipt of his report the constitution of the force, which was called the 77th Brigade column, was settled as follows :—

    5th Cavalry (one squadron),
    131st Battery R.F.A. (less one section),
    50th Pack Battery,
    61st Company 2nd (Q.V.O.) Sappers and Miners,
    1st Battalion Royal Irish Fusiliers,
    45th (Rattray's) Sikhs,
    1/94th (Russell's) Infantry,
    108th Infantry,
    1/10th Gurkha Rifles,
      and certain details.

These troops were moved by rail from Baghdad between the 6th and 12th January, and by the afternoon of the 13th were concentrated on the right bank of the Tigris opposite Kut.

By the same date two defence vessels and other craft, which included a hospital ship, were ready at Kut, and by next evening all native boats that were required for the carriage of supplies had arrived.

On the 15th fourteen days' rations, that were necessary for the column, which, less local produce, was to be self-supporting, and seven days' reserve rations, were loaded, the former on mahelas, the latter in iron barges.

On the 16th the column left its place of concentration, and on the 18th reached Hai town, the capital of the Bani Rikab ; and as the troops entered it aeroplanes which had arrived from Baghdad with commendable punctuality circled overhead, and added to the great impression presented by the spectacle of so many troops.

Not far from Hai river are some of the oldest mounds or remains of ancient cities in Mesopotamia, which were the abode of Sumerians or Southern Babylonians ; and as one of my staff, Lieut.-Colonel K. L. Stevenson, Royal Army Ordnance Corps, who is an amateur archæologist and can read the cuneiform writing, was about to proceed to Samawah for inspection duty, I arranged that he should travel to Karradi with Brigadier-General Dent's column, and then transfer himself to that of Brigadier-General Coningham. In company with the Political Officer, Captain Thomas, who earlier had done much good work in keeping the Muntafiq in check, he returned later from Nasiriyah and made some excavations at Umma, the constant rival and eventual destroyer of another ancient city, Lagash (about B.C. 4000), a report on which he sent to the British Museum.

Two days before Brigadier-General Dent's column left its place of concentration near Kut the river had begun to fall, with the result that at the end of the first day's march only one defence vessel had been able to proceed as far as the camp, and when Hai was reached all barges, as well as mahelas, were aground, and supplies had to be transferred to bellums.

To provide the smaller form of boat and to bring forward the reserve rations a halt of two days was necessary. To add to the difficulties of advance, a bar had now formed both at the mouth of the Hai and at a point four miles north of the town of that name, and an attempt to clear a passage through the latter obstacle by blasting proved unavailing. To this point the defence vessels, the hospital ship, and two other steamers had made their way, and Brigadier-General Dent arranged to form here an advanced base, guarded by a company of the 1/94th Infantry, where the rations from the two stranded barges would be collected.

On the 21st the column marched some fourteen miles further south, when another bar was encountered on which twenty-five boats became stranded. By the help of the Political Officer and a local shaikh, Arab coolies were procured and several of the boats refloated or lightened, hauled across the bar, and then reloaded. That night the force found itself with the minimum quantity of rations necessary to carry it to the point of junction with Brigadier-General Coningham's column and back again to Hai.

The march next day brought the force close to Qalat Sikar, where aeroplanes demonstrated over the town and then proceeded to meet the column coming from that direction. On the 23rd Karradi was reached, where one day's rations carried on bellums arrived, and on the following day the return journey began. The river, owing partly to a strong north wind, had by this time fallen 6¾ feet, and on the 27th, when the point where the advanced base had been prepared was reached, all native craft had to be abandoned. As animal transport for the whole force was not available it was divided into two groups. The first group, under Lieut.-Colonel M'Vean, 45th Sikhs, taking with it the transport of the other, made a march of twenty-four miles on the 28th, and reached the Tigris opposite Kut-al-Amarah on the afternoon of that date.

Rain, which had begun to fall at Baghdad and to the north on the 23rd, affected the Hai river on the 29th. By the following day it had risen two feet, and by 2.30 P.M. all vessels were afloat. The river continued to rise, and by the 1st February the second group of Brigadier-General Dent's column reached its concentration camp opposite Kut, all the river craft being assembled on the Tigris during the afternoon.

The combined operation carried out by the columns of Brigadier-Generals Dent and Coningham created a profound impression. Not only did it prove to the tribes distant from our main line of communication that we possessed troops, which by hostile propaganda they had been led to doubt, but that those troops were in considerable numbers; and the effect of seeing so many bodies of cavalry, infantry, and artillery, the long spaces which they covered on the march, and the size of the camps which they occupied, was much enhanced by the frequent coming and going of numerous aeroplanes.

As was to be expected, the arrival of our troops caused the prestige of those tribes of the confederation who had remained loyal throughout the insurrection to rise, and strengthened their faith in the wisdom and foresight of their leaders who had restrained them from following the evil example set by their neighbours. Several shaikhs of other tribes who before that time had excused themselves from accepting an invitation of the Political Officer to report themselves at Nasiriyah, alleging that they could not do so owing to the disturbed state of the country, now found no difficulty in complying.

As some twenty-five minor leaders in the area Butaniyah-Suwaij-Shattrah had earlier committed definitely hostile acts, and had for varying periods formed part of hostile concentrations during the insurrection, they were ordered to pay a fine of rifles, which they accordingly did. Several months later the Political Officer of the Division stated in a report that the Muntafiq fully expected to be disarmed at the time our troops visited their country, and regarded it as a sign of weakness that this course was not taken. My instructions from the High Commissioner in any case debarred me from taking such action, and it is open to question whether, had disarmament been ordered, it would have been possible, owing to the natural difficulties of the country and the warlike nature of the inhabitants, to have effected it before it became necessary to send back to India the reinforcements which had arrived to help in quelling the insurrection. The process would in any case have been a lengthy one, as the tribesmen are given to burying their weapons when the loss of them is threatened.

Immediately following the march through the Hai country, my attention was directed to Suq-ash-Suyukh (or Shaikhs' Market), a town of some twelve thousand inhabitants, which stands mainly on the right bank of the Euphrates, about twenty-seven miles down-stream in a south-easterly direction from Nasiriyah, and between that place and the Hammar Lake.

On the 1st July the Assistant Political Officer, Captain A. Platts, had held a race-meeting for the tribesmen of the district, which was largely attended. The sport was good and the diversion an entire success, yet within one hundred miles the tribes were gathering to destroy the railway and murder its officials. This fact must have been known to the Arab spectators, but was certainly not within the knowledge of Captain Platts nor of that of the several Europeans who were present.

Gradually the situation at Suq grew worse. The Jihad movement spread to that place, and the tribes began to think that the hand of Allah was against the British. The police took to deserting, and on the 1st September only one man who was guarding the prisoners remained. To attempt to control the situation now became impossible, and at midday on that date, the hour of the Arab meal, the Assistant Political Officer and some other Europeans embarked on a defence vessel, which had been stationed there for a few days when the unrest was approaching a head, and made their way in safety to Nasiriyah.

At that time river operations on the Euphrates had temporarily ceased, but as there was room for naval activity on the Tigris the two defence vessels at Nasiriyah were ordered on the 4th to run the gauntlet. This they successfully did, though fired on below Suq for one and a half hours. Being, however, well protected, the personnel escaped unscathed, while the insurgents were severely handled by the guns and machine-guns of the vessels. The Arabs had sunk a forage barge across the river, hoping thereby to block the passage, but the attempt proved to be abortive. The two vessels arrived in time to assist in covering the withdrawal of the dredger *Mudlark* from the Hammar Lake, where she was in danger of falling into the hands of the insurgents, as well as some other vessels which had been sent there to assist her in keeping open a passage through that shallow stretch of water when there seemed to be a prospect that the railway from Basrah to Nasiriyah might be severed. By the efforts of the *Mudlark*, manned by a scratch crew—for she was one of the vessels which, when the insurrection broke out, it was proposed to sell—a three-foot channel was kept open through the lake, which had allowed of the despatch for service on the Euphrates of four extra stern-wheelers with barges, besides permitting the defence vessels to pass freely between that river and Basrah for repairs. Indeed it may be said that the presence of the extra vessels which we had been able to place on the Euphrates helped to retard the spread of the insurrection round Nasiriyah, and also to assist Samawah.

During several months the attitude of the inhabitants of Suq and its vicinity had been such that it was highly desirable to make a show of force among them. Moreover, it was known that they were still incredulous regarding the relief of Samawah. When the news of our success there reached them it was thought that it might cool their hostile ardour, but, Arab-like, they declined to believe what they themselves had not seen, and sent a messenger to bear witness to the truth or otherwise of the report. When he returned and had been closely questioned, his account of what he had seen must have been but little to their liking, for it is said that with one accord they fell upon him and severely beat him.

On the 3rd February, therefore, a column, under the ubiquitous Brigadier-General Coningham, was sent to Suq; but the inhabitants had by this time come to their senses, and the visit, which had threatened to be stormy, passed off without incident.

Thus ended the operations which had been in constant progress for seven months, the seal on which may be said to have been set when a little later I received the following telegram from the Army Council :—

"The report that the operations in connection with the recent insurrection have been brought to a close has been received by the Army Council with much satisfaction, and they desire to offer their congratulations on the successful issue of a difficult task to you, to your staff, and to the troops under your command."

CHAPTER XXIV.

CONCLUSION.

The visit of the troops to Suq-ash-Suyukh brought to a conclusion all operations of a hostile nature, for after that, to the best of my belief, no shot was fired in anger on either side. But, as I have shown earlier, stationary and movable columns continued to collect fines in many areas, and teach the insurgents the price thay had to pay for throwing down the gauntlet to the British Empire. The punishment had of necessity to be exemplary; and besides the frequent visitations by the troops, which proved our power of moving where we pleased, and the casualties inflicted, which were considerable (see Appendix VIII.), the following fines were collected or extracted :—

>Rifles, 63,435—all serviceable—of which 21,154 were modern weapons.
>Small-arm ammunition, 3,185,000 rounds.
>Cash, Rs. 817,650—equivalent to about £54,112.

Prior to the insurrection, according to a carefully prepared but necessarily rough estimate, those tribes who took part in the rising were credited with possessing 59,805 rifles —figures which were regarded by the Political Officers in some areas, when the time came for levying fines, as excessive. That these figures should have been surpassed by several thousands, and in addition a sum of money equivalent to from five to ten thousand rifles should have been secured, are proofs of the thoroughness of the work of the several commanders, more especially those of the

17th Division, and of the assistance given them by their political advisers.

Earlier in my career I had taken part in three campaigns on the North-West Frontier of India, and I had not forgotten the weary months of waiting for the scanty quota of firearms—a few hundreds only—to be handed in, and these in most cases did not deserve the name of rifle. But here in Mesopotamia we had actually extracted from the tribesmen serviceable weapons, which exceeded in number those with which they had been credited. I confess to feelings of considerable satisfaction, to me more moving than those created by the rising figures of a political election, as the tale of arms, ammunition, and rupees reached me daily in a continually ascending scale.

The operations which had led to these results, and which were only undertaken with reluctance, involved a stern and protracted struggle. Indeed, from the beginning of July till well into October, as will have been apparent from the narrative, we lived on the edge of a precipice where the least slip might have led to a catastrophe. The vast area to be guarded by our limited numbers afforded many opportunities for such mishaps as those which made memorable the first half of August, all of which added fuel to the fire of insurrection, and any one of which might have had most serious results. But fortunately tribal combination, though in certain areas it existed and was encouraged by the incidents in question, was less widespread than might have been the case. Thus by the resolution, valour, and endurance of the troops, British and Indian, and those who led them in the field, it was possible to temporise and keep the situation to some extent in control until the reinforcements came from India.

In addition to the troops who operated in the open, those who were invested in blockhouses or elsewhere, the staff and the various ancillary services which helped to win success, I was much indebted to three other sources to which reference must be made. The first of these, the Royal Air Force, was directly under my command, and the other two were controlled by the civil administration.

As regards the Royal Air Force, I have stated earlier the number of squadrons available, and only during September did the first flight of a reinforcing squadron—the 84th —from Constantinople come into action.

Besides the limited number of machines that were available in July and for some time after, when the outbreak occurred the Royal Air Force in Mesopotamia was in process of being re-equipped with new aeroplanes and engines of which the personnel had little or no experience. Moreover, such is the summer heat of Mesopotamia that the question of the reliability of the engines was a cause of additional anxiety. This difficulty was overcome by designing and fitting extra water-cooling arrangements, so that some machines could be flown during the heat of the day until such time as tropical radiators, which are necessary in torrid climates, had arrived from home.

The work of the pilots and observers has been described at various places in the narrative, and as much of it was performed during the hottest hours of daylight with a limited number of machines, which were constantly being called upon to act at short notice, the strain on them was excessive.

But the less showy work of the air mechanics and others at the Aircraft Park which alone made flying possible was carried out, as I know from periodical visits, in corrugated iron sheds where the temperature was calculated to call up thoughts of Christian martyrs or the burning fiery furnace.

The man who above all others inspired what I may call the indoor and outdoor branches of the Royal Air Force in Mesopotamia, and kept his officers and men in trying conditions cheerful and unflagging in their work, was Wing Commander (now Group Commander) C. S. Burnett. I had learned his value in France in 1917, when for a time he commanded the 12th Squadron, which was attached to my corps, and helped materially during the stormy days which ushered in the battle of Arras and at other times. In 1920 I often undertook that what was called an " aerial holiday " should be granted, if only for twenty-four hours, to those whose work was of so strenuous a nature. During that period it was agreed that I should ask for no machine to leave the aerodrome, so that gradually a reserve might be built up. But for the first three months of the insurrection and until the arrival of the additional squadron that holiday remained a myth. Yet, with material which was constantly being damaged and sometimes lost —for eight machines fell into hostile hands and forty-one were injured by rifle fire—the Royal Air Force steadily pursued its daily risky task of co-operation with columns, reconnaissance, and dropping bombs; and at Rumaithah, and to some extent at other places, helped to prolong the existence of the garrison till rescue came.

I have touched upon the work of the Levies here and there in the narrative—a force which, like the Railway Service, was controlled by the civil administration, but acted from time to time with regular columns, besides carrying out their ordinary duties, which resemble those of an armed police.

In January 1920 and the months following the Levies were divided into what were called Police and Striking Force, their numbers amounting on the 1st April to 3687. With the Levies were a limited number of British officers and non-commissioned officers. The standard of training which the force had reached by June 1920 was not high, and until that month no unit had received instruction in mounted duties. The material was good, but, in order to raise it to a much higher state of efficiency, some additional officers, specially chosen for their military qualifications and possessing a knowledge of Arabic, were required.

No sooner had the insurrection broken out than the rank and file, especially those in the Middle Euphrates area, were assailed by blatant propaganda of every kind. In the bazaars and streets they were openly hailed as infidels and traitors; refreshments were denied them at the coffee-shops, and in several cases vessels from which they had drunk were ostentatiously flung to the ground and broken. Their female relatives were in the forefront of this campaign of abuse, and exerted all the pressure they could bring to bear to induce the men to desert assembling in clamorous crowds round the barracks and calling upon them to come to their protection. Those of the Levies who had been recruited from the countryside began to realise that to continue serving with the force meant the end of all relations with their tribe. But what perhaps strained their allegiance more than all else were the reports of assaults on their women-folk, who in some cases were stated to have been carried off or killed.

As time went on rumours were rife that a large Sharifian army was in the field and on its way to drive the British from Iraq. Then came the news of the disaster to the Manchester column, which had occurred in the very centre of the area where the 2nd Euphrates Levy performed its normal duties. The force, which had been trained substantially for mobile action, soon found itself sharing in a series of sieges or operations of a sedentary nature, and, as has been described in the case of Hillah, the men were greeted by cries from the insurgents to come and guard their homes and families.

At this period the British cause, so far as outward appearances showed, seemed to the men to be almost hopeless; and should that prove to be the case, the end of those who had stood firm beside the "infidels" in their need was one not pleasant to reflect upon.

I think in all fairness it may be said that in the annals of the British Empire no young force, a force in this case of only a few months' standing, has ever before passed through so high a trial. Deserters there were a few, for everywhere men of mean spirit will be found; but when the temptations to which the Levies were daily subjected, and which almost passed endurance, are weighed against those of them who proved faithless, the number is insignificant. Great credit is due to Major C. A. Boyle, the then Inspector-General of Levies, a gallant leader and a master of many Eastern languages, as well as to the officers and non-commissioned officers serving under him, that the force kept its allegiance and served with credit in many places during the insurrection. Like the regular troops, they had their share of losses, which amounted to one hundred and seven killed and wounded; while five Arab and Kurdish officers, besides ten other ranks, received rewards for gallantry and devotion to duty in the field.

Of the last of the three services whence assistance came I may seem to have written earlier in a captious and ungrateful strain; but perhaps I failed to appreciate fully the great and increasing difficulties with which it had to labour.

So much depends in war on assured and rapid movement that, when delays unforeseen and possibly avoidable occur which upset plans and cause the troops discomfort, it is no easy matter to maintain a strictly impartial attitude.

Throughout the whole of the disturbances, in areas in which the railway continued to function, the first warning of attacks or anticipation thereof generally emanated from the railway staff. It is true that reports were often exaggerated, but it must be remembered that the station staff of outlying places were isolated and their lives frequently in imminent danger. Normally their only source of protection lay in the presence of local Shabana; and the devotion to duty shown by the railway employees in the face of repeated attempts at looting and destruction of property was as remarkable as it was praiseworthy. Not only railway staff but permanent-way gangmen and others similarly isolated on the several lines were exposed to treatment of that nature, and many suffered considerable hardships. Engine-drivers also and train staff ran grave risks throughout the operations in the execution of their duties in extremely difficult circumstances both from actual attack and from damage to the road, and several among them lost their lives.

It is interesting to note that on the 30th June the total route-mileage under full traffic was 867 miles, and on the 2nd July 286 miles of the through route were closed to all but urgent military traffic. About two months later 636 miles were closed to all ordinary traffic, and some 324 miles of railway line were in the hands of the insurgents; while by the beginning of October, when the tide was turning in our favour, 184 miles of railway, with all the plant involved, were still in hostile possession; and on all lines, except that from Kut to Baghdad, which was never cut, nothing more than a precarious service could be maintained.

The casualties among the railway personnel of this civilian service up to the 30th September speak for themselves. They amounted approximately to twenty-three killed, fifty wounded, and forty-one missing; and on that date eight locomotives and about one hundred and fifty vehicles of our limited rolling-stock were in areas in which the insurgents still predominated.

The punishment which had been inflicted on the insurgent tribes had consisted mainly of fines in rifles and ammunition, for except sheep and cattle they possessed little else of value. But even the imposition of such fines was unsatisfactory—a fact which had begun to show itself at the time that the troops marched through the Shatt-al-Hai area. Reports of the difficulties which column commanders, who were operating in other parts of the country, were experiencing in extracting rifles were frequent, and it was becoming apparent that the day of disarmament by force in Mesopotamia had departed when the mass of troops left after the Armistice. As I write these words nearly a year after the insurrection was at its height, and am aware that those whom we deprived last year of their most valued possession have already not only rearmed themselves but acquired weapons of more modern type than those they handed in, I perceive the vanity of what we undertook, necessary and unavoidable as it was. Though the lesson given was salutary and will be effective for a time, it is clear that in a country such as Mesopotamia, with its borders open practically on all sides, it is folly to think, not in one year but even in many years, to draw the teeth of its inhabitants.

While dealing with the subject of disarmament I may refer to certain factors which seem to me to occupy an important position with relation to it. I allude to a system which, as already mentioned, I instituted in certain districts during the insurrection, and which, I have since learned,

CONCLUSION 305

prevailed in Egypt with somewhat similar objects under the Pharaohs thousands of years ago. The system in question is based on the supply of water, which is essential for the operations of the cultivator, and was applied in the Diyalah area and at the Hindiyah Barrage, where small garrisons were so placed as to maintain complete control of the regulators on the canals.

Since that time I have urged the extension of the system, and several large effluents and canals are now being protected by blockhouses at those points near the main stream of the Tigris where the regulators have for some time been in course of construction or are completed. The proximity of the blockhouses to the river, whence the canals draw their water supply, make it possible for defence vessels to reach them at all times, so that the garrisons cannot be cut off or besieged. Some of these canals carry vast quantities of water—one of them, it is estimated, swallowing up half the volume of the Tigris—and irrigate areas which maintain populations amounting to hundreds of thousands. Consequently by the mere control of a brick dam with regulators, half a dozen men can be placed in a position to deny a recalcitrant tribe what is essential for its daily bread. But this is not all, for through the presence of the small garrison the payment of revenue could be enforced, and even the peaceful surrender of arms might be effected. Than this it would be hard to find a more striking exemplification of the great principle of economy of force.

Unfortunately the system is not applicable to the Euphrates, as that river in its middle and lower reaches has been practically reduced to the condition of an irrigation canal with numerous subsidiary branches. Indeed, its further degradation is inevitable, unless its future as a trade route can be assured by some grand and costly scheme, such as that propounded by Sir William Willcocks, which, amongst other works, includes the construction of a barrage whereby the excess water of both the Tigris and the Euphrates could be stored in certain natural depressions of the land which are to be found somewhere north-west of Baghdad. During the insurrection gun-vessels and other steamers were able to proceed as far north as Samawah, but this is no longer possible. The Arabs near Suq-ash-Suyukh have complained that the Mezlaq channel, which was opened for navigation early in 1917 and which carries the Euphrates into the Hammar Lake, robs them of water to the detriment of cultivation. In consequence the dredging of the channel, whereby defence vessels could enter the river and proceed, even at low water, for over one hundred and twenty miles northward, has been stopped, and the time is at hand when only Arab vessels of shallow draught will be able to ply on its waters.

Another feature of this subject is that many of the irrigating pumps in Iraq—and their numbers are increasing—are driven by means of oil-engines, the supply of the fuel for which can readily be controlled. It will be obvious that these pumps afford a means, beyond that provided by regulators, of maintaining pressure where circumstances may render it advisable.

Regulators, however desirable from a military point of view, cannot be constructed where fancy alone dictates, or a serious situation may easily be created. The question concerning them is a complicated one, which has puzzled experts and given rise to differences of opinion. In fact, in dealing with the matter of irrigation in a country like Iraq, it would be unwise to begin with a purely local project based on the requirements of a particular district and planned without reference to a general scheme for the whole country. Still, something can be done in the required direction without harmfully affecting the problem as a whole, for irrigation is the crying need which surpasses all the other requirements of Iraq.

Another factor which, if the experience of other countries is to be relied on, should have a civilising effect on the tribes, and not only benefit them but the Arab nation, is the provision of medical assistance in an easily accessible form. Before I left England in 1920 Sir John Hewett made a strong point, when talking to me on the subject, of the necessity for peripatetic ambulances together with the requisite personnel. Statistics of any value are not available, but I have been assured that some seventy-five per cent of the children born annually in Iraq do not arrive at maturity—an appalling loss of life, which is due to climate, absence of sanitation, and other causes. In the towns the loss is less, but the rate of infant mortality is a very high one. The following figures, which cover a period of three years, show the mortality per thousand births at Baghdad as compared with that of England and Wales:—

Baghdad.	England and Wales.
1918—353	1918—96
1919—408	1919—89
1920—293	1920—80

In the towns there are civil medical establishments, which would no doubt be extended were money forthcoming; but unless the tribesmen bring their sick to such places, they are dependent on their own antediluvian curative measures, which resolve themselves into the survival of the fittest. Were help such as suggested forthcoming, the rivers provide a ready means of transporting the necessary personnel and material for combating the last enemy of mankind; and as the tribesmen, whether shepherds or cultivators, dwell for the most part in the vicinity of the waterways, they could easily be reached and receive such treatment from physicians of either sex as their several maladies might require.

Unfortunately, like many more civilised beings, they look upon doctors with suspicion, and have an innate horror of amputation. I remember seeing at Rumaithah an Arab lad who had lost the sight of one eye from trachoma, and was threatened with total blindness within a year. He had been treated for a time by a British civil surgeon, but the process of cauterisation was necessarily prolonged and somewhat painful, and rather than continue it he ceased to visit the hospital, and wasted his money on nostrums prepared by the local quack in the bazaar. Another case at the same place was that of a boy with a tubercular knee whose parents refused to consent to an amputation, whereby his life might have been saved.

The treatment of Arab women presents great difficulties, as no male physician is allowed to approach them; and there are some who will not even tolerate examination by a foreign female doctor. Time, however, will no doubt break down the barriers of century-old convention, and induce the ignorant to take advantage of Western knowledge.

Two marked instances of how medical science can exert a pacificatory influence came under my notice some time after the insurrection was suppressed, and of such importance do I regard this subject that at the risk of being accused of prolixity I will mention them here.

In July 1921 an incident took place in the desert midway between the Euphrates and Syria such as is of common occurrence in these regions. A shaikh of the Amarat section of the Anizah tribe, who was encamped with his followers near some wells, was attacked by a certain doughty raider, who had come across from the Syrian side on one of his customary summer expeditions. The Amarat succeeded in driving off their opponents with the loss of a goodly number of camels, but in the fight their shaikh received a severe wound. It chanced that a few hours later a reconnoitring party of British officers, which included a Political Officer from Ramadi, arrived on the scene of the fight. The officers were returning to Amman by car after having completed the pioneer journey from that place to Baghdad. The shaikh's wound was dressed and further aid promised; and at the end of the next stage the party of British met the aeroplanes which had left Cairo for Baghdad that same morning. To make a long story short, under the guidance of Air Commander (now Air Commodore) R. Brooke-Popham, R.A.F., the wounded shaikh was transported on a Vickers-Vimy machine to Baghdad, where he was soon restored to health and rejoined his tribe.

The sequel to this incident occurred about a week later, when owing to an accident to an aeroplane in the desert several other machines had to be sent from Baghdad to assist. Towards sunset, as the air party were settling down to spend the night in the desert, five Arabs mounted on camels rode up, and after some futile attempts to explain their intentions, took up an outpost line round the aeroplanes, where they remained till dawn, when they rode silently away. It was subsequently ascertained that this party belonged to the wounded shaikh's tribe, and that they had come to show their gratitude for what had been done for their leader by ensuring that no attempts were made during the night to molest the airmen.

But the good effect of the action taken by the Royal Air Force was not confined solely to the pleasing gratitude shown by this small party of tribesmen, for I have been assured by several officers of that force that whenever it has happened that an aeroplane flying between Baghdad and Cairo has been obliged to land in the desert, the Arabs everywhere have displayed marked friendliness to the occupants. And what is still more satisfactory, the land route between those two places, which at one time was far from safe, can now be traversed with little fear of molestation.

The second instance only came to my notice as I was about to leave Mesopotamia on the termination of my appointment there. Having a few spare days at my disposal while waiting for my successor to arrive, I visited the oil-fields of the Anglo-Persian Oil Company at Maidan-i-Naftun, where, and at other places in the company's hands, I received the utmost kindness and attention from my hosts. One of the points which interested me particularly were the admirable arrangements for dealing with sick employees, over which Dr M. Y. Young, the chief medical officer, presides. During the past year some 20,000 cases were treated either in the hospitals, in quarters, or in field dispensaries. But the work did not end here, for I was informed to my astonishment that besides sick employees, over 60,000 cases had passed through the hands of the medical officers, making in all a grand total of 80,382. The result of the far-sighted and generous action of the company in providing free medical assistance to all and sundry—and many cases, both men and women, travelled hundreds of miles over difficult country to the hospitals—is that the Bakhtiari area, which was at one time notoriously unruly, has now subsided into quiescence, a condition which must be highly satisfactory to the shareholders in the admirably administered and ever-growing oil-fields of the Anglo-Persian Oil Company.

Before leaving the subject of the benefits that accrue to a community through medical science, and perhaps more noticeably if it be still in the semi-civilised stage, I must refer to yet another case which has come under my observation.

When attached to the Japanese Army in Manchuria in 1904-5 during the war with Russia, I could not help noticing how markedly friendly the Chinese peasant was to the British military attachés, and on making inquiries was informed by Dr Christie, the head of the Scottish Medical Mission at Mukden, that the attitude in question was mainly due to the appreciation which the Chinese felt for the labours of the Mission on their behalf. The fact, too, that unlike similar eleemosynary enterprises from other nations, those from the United Kingdom were known and recognised to be devoid of political significance, tended not a little to foster the confidence of the Chinese.

What is done in Manchuria, a country in the increase of whose population, I imagine, we have no overpowering interest, could be repeated on a larger scale in Mesopotamia; but the missionary element, if there were any idea of proselytising the inhabitants, would have to be eliminated. Perhaps some day those at home who take a keen interest in child welfare may turn their attention and devote their money to that problem in Iraq. The tribesmen see but little return for the large sums which they contribute annually to the revenue; and if medical facilities and increased irrigation could be provided—the two great factors which together would solve the problem of restoring the pristine agricultural greatness of Iraq—there would inevitably follow an era of prosperity and in its train civilisation, and possibly a reign of peace.

I have talked to King Faisal and others on these subjects; and on the question of disarmament it seems as reasonable to hope to dam Niagara—an operation doubtless more possible than when that well-worn synonym first was used—as to attempt wholly to disarm the tribes. This can only be effected by measures such as I have suggested, which would divert the mind of the Arab into unwarlike channels. His mental outlook must submit to change, gradual no doubt at first, a matter which is feasible through his fondness for money and all it brings, so that he may in course of time learn to acquire by legitimate methods and not by loot and murder, those things which at the present time he covets. In other words, he must be taught to forget

> ". . . the simple plan,
> That they should take who have the power,
> And they should keep who can."

There are those alive who knew Japan when the swashbuckling Samurai terrorised the towns and villages; and how different is that country now! She does not, of course, offer a true parallel to Mesopotamia, where amongst other difficulties the problem, owing to nomad tribes, is greatly complicated, but serves as an example of how a change in thought may, in a few decades, effect what force without annihilation could never do. All countries in their evolution have gone through the stage at which the brand-new kingdom of King Faisal finds itself, a kingdom which has often in the past been the scene of bitter strife; and it seems plain that if that evolution is to be hastened, all measures which may tend to kill the idea of the armed retainer, and may lead to his early disappearance in favour of a regularly constituted force for the maintenance of law and order and the safety of the borders, must be introduced. The Arabs may aspire some day, as others have before them, to become a nation in arms, but an armed horde of tribesmen is another matter, and such must disappear.

Whether that consummation will be attained, or whether forces from beyond the borders may renew the strife of old, I cannot pretend to prophesy. It must, however, be remembered that we are now garrisoning Mesopotamia, which has certain local forces little past the state of embryo, with about one-fourth of those that held the country eighteen months ago, but which have been replaced by the Royal Air Force, and that, as I have stated, the inhabitants are better armed than ever.

Those inhabitants, though they are not formidable except in overwhelming superiority, are distinguished by their treachery; and "that which is crooked cannot be made straight." Their cruel methods of dealing with their prisoners are notorious, and recall the most horrible of those described in Foxe's 'Book of Martyrs.' Yet so little are these facts known or recognised by some at home, that I recently read a statement by a distinguished officer, who was referring to the Arab of Mesopotamia, that "Arabs are very highly civilised and fight as gentlemen always." The Arabs of Iraq respect nothing but force, and to force only will they bend; and little as I know of them, I am certain of that characteristic. It is strange, however, among such a people, who seem to follow the Old Testament precept of "an eye for an eye and a tooth for a tooth," and more if possible, that their power of feeling, or it may be showing, resentment is small or wears off quickly. Although in the summer of 1920 no European could travel in most areas without taking his life in his hands, some months later the inhabitants of those same areas, which meantime had been repeatedly visited by troops and swept from end to end, would receive the British soldier with outward tokens of respect and manifestations of goodwill. Since then, when moving about the country, I have met no trace of such ill-feeling as one might expect to find as the result of the damage, material and other, which was inflicted on them. They seem indeed to accept the situation, admit that they were beaten, bow to superior force, and bury the hatchet till a good chance comes of paying off the score.

In my numerous journeys—and I have visited nearly every corner of Iraq—I have met and harangued hundreds of shaikhs, including those who stood by us during the insurrection, and others, a far greater number, who took up arms against us at that time. I can count among those with whom I have conversed, through the medium of my excellent intelligence officer and interpreter, Major Bovill, every shaikh whose name appears in this narrative of the disturbances. I have enjoyed their princely hospitality, and on one occasion spent an afternoon snipe-shooting with Shaikh Sha'alan Abu, whose arrest on the 30th June 1920 was the ostensible beginning of the insurrection. Amongst others I have met Yusuf al Suwaidi, a handsome courtly old gentleman, and rallied him on his modesty in repelling my advances to make his acquaintance (*i.e.*, arrest him) in August 1920, and his passion for foreign travel ! With all his faults, I confess to a strong liking for the Arab, and I regret that on my arrival in Mesopotamia I was too much occupied with military matters, and too ill-informed regarding the political problem to go among the people with advantage. Whether I might have been able to effect anything towards staving off the trouble which soon followed I hesitate to say ; but the Arab, with all his innate respect for force, seems to me to be highly susceptible to tactful and sympathetic handling. A Middle Euphrates shaikh, when speaking to me of his fellow-countrymen, said with conviction, " The Arab is a slave, and requires a hard master ; give him the stick first, then the sugar." The method he advocated is probably correct, and the employment of any other would be accepted as weakness.

But to pass on to a characteristic which has particularly struck me, one which is not attributable to self-interest but comes under the head of magnanimity. It is noteworthy how on some occasions certain Arab shaikhs at risk to themselves would intervene to save the lives of British officers, while in other cases the quality of mercy was not strained on their behalf. I have given examples of this in an appendix ; and I may mention, principally for the information of those who benefited by their captors' magnanimity or whatever it may be called, that every one who during the insurrection did us a service or showed concern for the welfare of prisoners or intervened to save their lives, was rewarded in such a manner as seemed most appropriate to his position and the particular circumstances of the case.

That the Arab, with his strangely subtle mind—a being so vain, so given to exaggerate, and so susceptible to propaganda, in spite of the fact that he is credited with believing only what he sees—is extremely difficult for a European to understand, will probably be admitted even by those who know him best. One of them, an Arab of Arabs, Ibn Saud, Sultan of Najd, in a letter which I read some time ago and noted, remarked, "As regards the tribal leaders and notables of Iraq from whom you want the improvement of the country, they do not wish that the people of Iraq should be quiet, and that there should be law and order in the land. It is impossible to change their nature, as this has been their policy of old and continues so to-day. Their whole idea in life is to stir up the people in order to gain profit from the Government. It may be accepted as an uncontrovertible fact that it will be impossible to manage the people of that country except by strong measures and military force. Never forget that the feelings which animate them are expressed in the saying, ' He who even dips his pen in an inkstand on behalf of a Christian, that man becomes a Kafir.' "

The writer of this letter may possibly be prejudiced in some degree, but his words contain much that will be admitted to be true.

The future of Iraq is not a matter easy to foresee, and apart from my ignorance of Arabic, my experience of the country is too short to warrant the expression of an opinion. That future, as we should say, lies on the knees of the gods, or, as the Arabs would put it, " Wa Allah 'alam," which, being interpreted, means " God is all-knowing."

APPENDIX I.

MESOPOTAMIAN EXPEDITIONARY FORCE.

ORDER OF BATTLE.—1st JULY 1920.

General Officer Commanding-in-Chief—Lieut.-General Sir Aylmer Haldane, K.C.B., D.S.O.
Brig.-General, General Staff—Brig.-General J. H. K. Stewart, D.S.O.
Brig.-General, i/c Administration—Brig.-General P. O. Hambro, C.B., C.M.G.

17TH DIVISION.

General Officer Commanding—Major-General G. A. J. Leslie, C.B., C.M.G.

34TH INFANTRY BRIGADE.

Commander—Brig.-General A. G. Wauchope, C.M.G., C.I.E., D.S.O.

    2nd Bn. Royal Irish Rifles.
    1/99th Deccan Infantry.
    108th Infantry.
    114th Mahrattas.

51ST INFANTRY BRIGADE.

Commander—Brig.-General F. E. Coningham, C.M.G., D.S.O.

    *2nd Bn. York and Lancaster Regiment.
    2/6th Jat Light Infantry.
    1/80th Carnatic Infantry.
    1/10th Gurkha Rifles.

52ND INFANTRY BRIGADE.

Commander—Brig.-General H. W. Wooldridge, C.M.G.

    4th Bn. Royal Fusiliers.
    45th Sikhs.
    1/94th Russell's Infantry.
    1/113th Infantry.

---

* In Persia as reinforcements to N.P. Force.

DIVISIONAL TROOPS.

19TH BRIGADE R.F.A.
39th, 96th, 97th, 131st (How.) Batteries.

13TH PACK ARTILLERY BRIGADE.
13th (British), 31st, 45th, 49th (Indian) Batteries.

17TH DIVISIONAL SIGNAL COY.
9th, 61st, 64th, 67th Field Coys. 2nd Sappers and Miners.
1/32nd Sikh Pioneers.
17th Machine-Gun Battalion (less one Coy.).

Attached: 5th Cavalry (less 2 Sqns.), 32nd Lancers (less 2½ Sqns.), 37th Lancers (2 Sqns.).
6th and 7th Lt. Armd. Motor Batteries.

18TH DIVISION.

General Officer Commanding—Major-General T. Fraser, C.B., C.S.I., C.M.G.

53RD INFANTRY BRIGADE.

Commander—Brig.-General G. A. F. Sanders, C.M.G.

2nd Bn. Manchester Regiment.
8th Rajputs.
86th Carnatic Infantry.
1/87th Punjabis.

54TH INFANTRY BRIGADE.

Commander—Brig.-General M. R. W. Nightingale, C.I.E., C.M.G., D.S.O.

2nd Bn. Northumberland Fusiliers.
1/39th Garwhal Rifles.
52nd Sikhs, F.F.
1/7th Gurkha Rifles.

55TH INFANTRY BRIGADE.

Commander—Brig.-General G. M. Morris, C.B., D.S.O.

1st Bn. Rifle Brigade.
3/9th Bhopal Infantry.
*13th Rajputs.
1/116th Mahrattas.
1/3rd Gurkha Rifles.

---

* Relief stopped.

APPENDIX I.

DIVISIONAL TROOPS.

   13TH BRIGADE R.F.A.
   2nd, 8th, 44th, and 160th (How.) Batteries.

   2ND PACK ARTILLERY BRIGADE.
   14th (British), 25th, 34th, 40th, and 50th (Indian) Batteries.

   18TH DIVISIONAL SIGNAL COY.
   2nd, 6th, and 8th Field Coys. 1st Sappers and Miners.
   106th Hazara Pioneers.
   17th Machine-Gun Bn. (1 Coy.).
   Attached: 11th Lancers and 35th Scinde Horse (2 Sqns.).
      8th and 14th Lt. Armd. Motor Batteries.
      30th Squadron R.A.F. (1 flight).

   7TH CAVALRY BRIGADE.

Commander—Brig.-General H. G. Young, D.S.O.

   1st King's Dragoon Guards.
   7th Dragoon Guards.
   16th (Composite) Machine-Gun Squadron.
   8th Field Troop 2nd S. & M.

HEADQUARTERS, R.A.F.

   6th Squadron R.A.F.
   30th Squadron R.A.F.

ARMY TROOPS.

   5th Battery R.G.A.; 9th Co. 2nd S. & M.; 132nd, 133rd, and 138th Railway Construction Coys.; 7th Lt. Armd. Motor Battery; 1st Ry. Armd. Motor Battery, and some Signal and Bridging units.

   BAGHDAD DEFENCES.

   2/9th Delhi Regiment.
   2/119th Infantry.

   RIVER AREA.

   Line of Communication Troops.

Commander—Brig.-General H. E. C. B. Nepean, C.S.I., C.M.G.

   37th Lancers (less 2 Squadrons).
   83rd Wallajahbad Light Infantry.
   2/125th Napier's Rifles.
   2/129th Baluchis.
   124th, 134th, and 140th Ry. Construction Coys.

REINFORCEMENTS FROM INDIA AFTER 1st JULY 1920.

6TH DIVISION.

General Officer Commanding—Major-General G. N. Cory, C.B., D.S.O.

74TH INFANTRY BRIGADE.

Commander—Brig.-General A. le G. Jacob, C.M.G., C.I.E., D.S.O.

    2/7th Rajputs.
    1/15th Sikhs.
    3/123rd Outram's Rifles.

75TH INFANTRY BRIGADE.

Commander—Brig.-General G. A. H. Beatty, C.M.G., D.S.O.

    2/96th Infantry.
    2/116th Mahrattas.
    3/70th Burma Rifles.

76TH INFANTRY BRIGADE.

Commander—Brig.-General G. I. R. Glasfurd, C.M.G., D.S.O.

    3/23rd Sikhs.
    2/89th Punjabis.
    2/117th Mahrattas.

DIVISIONAL TROOPS.

"F" Battery R.H.A.
17th Brigade R.F.A.
26th, 92nd, and 10th (How.) Batteries.
11th, 63rd, and 69th Coys. 2nd S. & M.
1/12th Pioneers.
8th Machine-Gun Bn. (2 Coys.).

ADDITIONAL UNITS.

2nd Bn. East Yorkshire Regiment.
2nd Bn. Duke of Cornwall's L.I.
1st Bn. Yorkshire L.I.
3/153rd Rifles.
2/5th Gurkha Rifles, F.F.
2/11th Gurkha Rifles.
Kapurthala Infantry.

APPENDIX I.

77TH INFANTRY BRIGADE.

Commander—Brig.-General B. C. Dent, C.M.G., D.S.O.

    63rd Palamcottah L.I.
    3/124th Baluchistan Infantry.
    3/8th Gurkha Rifles.
    1/11th Gurkha Rifles.

Note—As stated in the narrative of operations, the brigade organisation of infantry units from India was not adhered to in Mesopotamia.

NORTH PERSIAN FORCE.

36TH INDIAN (MIXED) BRIGADE.

Commander—Brig.-General H. F. Bateman-Champain, C.M.G.

    "A" Battery (The Chestnut Troop) R.H.A.
    Guides Cavalry.
    31st Indian Pack Battery.
    *1st Bn. Royal Berkshire Regiment.
    *2nd Bn. York and Lancaster Regiment.
    1st Bn. Royal Irish Fusiliers.
    1/42nd Deoli Regiment.
    †1/67th Punjabis (2 platoons).
    122nd Rajputana Infantry.
    1/2nd Gurkha Rifles.
    19th Co. 3rd S. & M.
    48th Div. Signal Coy.
    15th Lt. Armd. Motor Battery.

Attached: 30th Squadron R.A.F. (1 flight).

PERSIAN L. OF C.

Commander—Colonel J. H. F. Lakin, 7th Gurkha Rifles.

    2/26th Punjabis.
    64th Pioneers.
    79th Carnatic Infantry.
    7th, 52nd, and 65th Coys. Sappers and Miners.

---

* Sent as reinforcements from Mesopotamia.
† At Tabriz.

APPENDIX II.

ADVENTURES OF OFFICERS.

Capture of Flying Officers G. C. Gardiner and Herbert.

As these officers were returning to Baghdad on the 14th July, after taking part in a bombing raid, they were forced to land near Dagharah, which is in what was at that time a thoroughly hostile area. Five minutes later some fifty Arabs arrived, attempts to keep off whom failed owing to the Lewis gun becoming damaged when it was hastily forced from its mounting on the aeroplane. The officers were overpowered and stripped of their arms and other possessions, and roughly handled by women who plucked at their throats. After paying them a good deal of unpleasant attention the mob next occupied themselves with the machine. Two apparently well-disposed Arabs, taking advantage of the distraction, dismounted and made the officers understand that if they remained where they were they would be drastically treated. These Arabs made signs to the officers to mount their horses, and all four galloped off for some miles to the tents of a section of the Albu Sultan tribe. Here the Shaikh Faris al Jaryan, hearing that the officers had been ill-treated, rode off with some forty horsemen and recovered their arms and other belongings, but refused to allow them to return to the aeroplane.

Next day the officers were escorted at dawn on horseback thirty-five miles to the house of the shaikh's brother, who is the paramount shaikh of the Albu Sultan. He treated them well and sent them by motor-car to Hillah.

Capture of Flying Officers G. R. Gowler and H. G. W. Locke, R.A.F.

About 8 A.M. on the 12th October 1920, these officers were obliged, through engine trouble, to make a forced landing near Kifl, which is not far from the at that time invested Kufah.

APPENDIX II.

Almost immediately some twelve horsemen and two armed Arabs on foot arrived on the scene and demanded bakhsheesh. The officers' personal belongings and coats were taken from them, and they showed their captors the printed card in Arabic and Persian, signed by the High Commissioner, offering a money reward—approximately £500—in return for their safety being ensured. This card each officer of the Royal Air Force in Mesopotamia carries when flying as a safeguard, but it has not always proved efficacious. The officers tried to explain that if taken to Kufah the Political Officer there would give a reward, and the Arabs seemed to understand. An argument followed among the Arabs, who by this time numbered fifty to sixty, as to who should take charge of the officers, and while this was going on their helmets, shoes, and socks were removed.

They were next each tied to the head of a horse, which started off at a trot in a south-westerly direction. After running about a mile and suffering considerable pain and discomfort from the camelthorn which covered the ground over which they passed, they were both tied to the same horse, and the pace was changed to a sharp walk until Kifl was reached. For the last three miles of their journey they skirted north of Kifl and just east of some date gardens. Thence the inhabitants emerged and brandished, and prodded them with, their knives, some hitting them on the head and striking them with rifles. In this unpleasant horseplay the women and children bore a leading part, spitting in their faces and throwing stones at them, while the horsemen made no attempt to interfere on their behalf.

About 1.30 P.M. Kifl was reached, and they were led before Shaikh Umran, the chief of the Bani Hussain, who immediately ordered the ropes which tied them to the horse's head to be undone. He then took them to the bazaar and sent for a Hebrew interpreter, who remained with them until they were removed from Kifl. Umran offered the officers food, gave them tea and cigarettes, and inquired what had become of their helmets, shoes, and socks. On the crowd, who were looking on, being asked if they had any of the missing articles, a helmet was at once produced, and a man was ordered to take off his shoes and give them to F.O. Gowler, for whom a pair of socks of Government pattern was shortly produced from the bazaar. The officers showed Umran their printed cards offering a reward, but these he treated with apparent contempt. The interpreter thereupon explained that Umran had said that he did not want a reward from the Government, but that his own reputation, which was worth more than any money, would ensure their safety, and added that the shaikh was a very rich and influential man.

Umran next suggested that they should inform the commander at Hillah that they were safe and well cared for, and this was done by letter. Later in the day he said that he had decided not to keep them at Kifl, but would take them to his own house, where

x

they were transferred. On the 14th they were pushed out of the hut in which they were by the Arab guard, the door was locked from inside, and they made their way to Kifl, where they joined the troops of the 55th Brigade column who had arrived there.

Capture of Flying Officers Bockett Pugh and Macdonald at Khidhr.

On the 22nd September 1920, these two officers were in an aeroplane which was shot down from a height of a few hundred feet. These officers with others were engaged in trying to drop supplies for the British and Indian personnel on board the defence vessel *Greenfly*, which was aground in the Euphrates. Their plane crashed in the river about one mile above Khidhr and turned over. An observer of another machine noticed the occupants, neither of whom had apparently suffered damage, scramble out on to the bank. It was also observed that, when the machine came down to within a few hundred feet of the ground to see if it were possible to help, neither of the two officers who had crashed looked up. Arabs state that on reaching the shore one of the two officers was shot at once by insurgents of the Juwabir tribe. As regards the other officer, it is said that he offered a large sum of money provided he were given safe conduct to the *Greenfly*, but the headman of some villages in the vicinity came on the scene and shot him.

Officers of the Royal Air Force think that the bomb-racks, to which the rations were attached, failed to act, for the aeroplane continued to fly for some time at a low altitude, thus offering an easy target for the insurgents.

Adventures of Four Officers of the Royal Air Force.

On the 1st November 1920, after leaving Hillah to carry out a reconnaissance of the railway towards Diwaniyah, one of two machines of the 55th Squadron began to leak. The pilot, F.O. P. D. Maxwell, after watching to see if the water continued to escape, and finding that it did so, decided that it would be wise to turn back. He was by this time about twelve miles from Hillah, and the water, having probably all run out, had ceased to flow from the leak, the engine had become noisy, the revolutions were decreasing, and clouds of smoke were coming from the exhaust. As the engine appeared to be on the point of "seizing," he landed far from any signs of habitation and as much to the west as he could manage to go. The other machine, piloted by F.O. D. Lloyd-Evans, M.C., D.F.C., which was following, observed F.O. Maxwell turn back and fly in a north-westerly direction, and when the latter landed, the former, who believed that the area in which they were was hostile, did so also, and ran

APPENDIX II.

his machine to a position near that of his companion, so as to be able to pick up, if necessary, both him and the observer, F.O. Groom.

As it was not certain whether the area was unfriendly or not, and as for a single machine to start in the soft sand and lift four passengers presented considerable risk, the pilot decided to wait, while a good look-out was kept in all directions, which was possible as the country was level.

Meantime, about ten minutes after landing, F.O. Groom was endeavouring to remove the Lewis gun from his machine, which was about a hundred yards from the other, when a mounted Bedouin appeared round the corner of a bank some three hundred yards distant. F.O. Groom had only time to put the Lewis gun out of action by removing a portion of it, after which he ran to F.O. Lloyd-Evans's machine, during which time he was fired at by the Bedouin, who was followed by some twelve more mounted Arabs. F.O. Groom at once climbed into the back seat of the sound machine, joining there Aircraftsman Hughes, F.O. Lloyd-Evans's observer, while F.O. Maxwell lay down on the port lower wing alongside the fuselage.

Regardless of the difficulty of starting a machine on soft sand, and accepting the very apparent risk of a crash with so heavy a load, the courage and skill of F.O. Lloyd-Evans saved the situation. The machine took off well from the ground in spite of its heavy freight, and the leading Bedouin, who was only about twenty yards away, did not fire again, probably because his horse shied. F.O. Lloyd-Evans was able to bring back his machine in safety to Hillah, and made an excellent landing with his heavy freight.

Shortly afterwards a report came in from a pilot of another squadron that he had seen F.O. Maxwell's machine in flames as he passed over the spot where it had landed. It had been set on fire by Arabs, which caused the bombs it was carrying to explode and inflict casualties among the onlookers.

The courage shown by F.O. Lloyd-Evans, for which he received the immediate reward of a bar to the Distinguished Flying Cross, probably saved the lives of two flying officers at the risk of his own and that of his observer, for in the area where the machines landed the chance of being made prisoners and not being murdered was small.

It is interesting to note that during a bombing expedition to Rowanduz on the borders of Kurdistan on the 5th May 1921, the machine which was being piloted by F.O. Maxwell, and which also carried an Assistant Political Officer, Captain Dickinson, was shot down near Batas in hostile country. On this occasion F.O. V. E. Groom, D.F.C., who with an observer was also taking part in the operation, seeing what had occurred, at once landed and rescued the two officers from the disabled machine. For this gallant action he received the immediate reward of a bar to the Distinguished Flying Cross.

APPENDIX III.

RESPONSIBILITY OF OFFICERS.

13TH AUGUST 1920.

On two recent occasions, on the advice or recommendation of a political officer, risks quite unwarrantable from a military point of view have been taken by officers in command of troops. Unfortunate results have followed, not only as regards the losses incurred, but in increasing our difficulties at the present juncture and in greatly encouraging the rebels in their hostile attitude, and so leading to the spread of the rebellion.

The General Officer Commanding-in-Chief impresses on all officers in command of troops the responsibility which they incur should they act in a manner not strictly in accordance with sound military principles, more especially in a country such as Mesopotamia, where the climate is in itself our greatest enemy. Political like other information is often untrustworthy and must not be blindly accepted; and to keep his division quiet at all costs is with the political officer a natural and paramount instinct.

The G.O.C.-in-C. does not wish in any way to cramp the initiative of officers, but there is a wide distinction between initiative and rashness. The present situation is such that the least set-back must have harmful results, and it is every officer's duty to reflect before acting, and realise how great a responsibility he accepts if he is not certain in his own mind that he can fully justify his action.

APPENDIX IV.

STRENGTH OF TROOPS IN MESOPOTAMIA AND PERSIA.

	British.	Indian.	Followers.
Total strength (approx.)	12,000	61,000	60,000
Non-combatants	3,000	23,000	60,000
Balance of combatants	9,000	38,000	
Deduct—			
Sick	700	1,000	
In transit	600	1,000	
In Persia	3,500	6,000	
Total reduction	4,800	8,000	
Balance of combatants in Mesopotamia	4,200	30,000	
Composed of—			
Sabres	...	2,900	
Bayonets	2,900	23,700	
Gunners	1,300	3,400	
	4,200	30,000	
Non-combatants consisted of—			
R.A.S.C. and S. & T. Ordnance Works	1,800	20,000	
Med. Vet. Remounts Accounts, Mil. Police Camps and Depots, and Miscellaneous	850	2,400	
Labour	200	580	
I.W.T.	150	20	
	3,000	23,000	
Followers include—			
R.A.S.C.	8,600		
Medical	7,000		
Ordnance	1,100		
Works	7,000		
Veterinary	700		
Remounts	1,600		
Labour	17,500		
I.W.T.	11,000		
Regimental and miscellaneous	5,500		
	60,000		

APPENDIX V.

LETTER FROM THE CAPTAIN OF THE *GREENFLY*.

D.V. *Greenfly*,
Septr. 30th, 1920.

POLITICAL OFFICER,
NASIRIYAH.

SIR,—I am in receipt of your communication dated 20th instant. You will no doubt have seen my letter to the G.O.C., which was sent to the G.O.C. by Shaikh Wannas of El Bab, and left yesterday.

Food is the great question on board; but if your arrangements are successful, I expect we shall be able to hang on. The condition of the crew is really very good considering the very severe shortage of rations that we have all experienced. Our spirits are still "up," altho' at times we have felt very depressed. To get your letter and to know that things are happening helps us all very much indeed. I have lost one Indian and I have one B.O.R. (British Other Rank) severely wounded; besides these casualties I have one Indian wounded and 3 or 4 men sick owing to weakness—lack of food. Since I have been on board I have only been able to procure 4 bags of rations and 2 small packets of biscuits dropped from aeros. This has lasted us for the 34 days on board. And these were got on board under very heavy fire, and all praise is due to the men who volunteered to go and procure what little rations we have received. Sniping from the left bank has been continuous during my stay here. The last two days no shots have been fired.

Small attacks have been made occasionally, but nothing serious has happened; only we've practically all received slight flesh wounds. One point I would like to say, and that is that we have no medical stores on board. At times, and at present, my port side is practically on a dry bank, and this is separated from the land by only a stretch of water a few feet deep (2 or 3).

My letter of yesterday suggested, and I hope explained, the condition of things on board; and I would again like to point out that we are all here to hold on as long as it is possible, but we must have food.

There are 31 Indians, and you know the number of B.O.R.'s on

APPENDIX V. 327

board. Give us rations and we will have the heart and spirit to stick out until the last.

My G.O.C.'s (Brigadier-General Hughes, Inland Water Transport) esteem is highly appreciated by all on board, and in return we wish to thank him for his appreciation of our duties and to confirm the fact that what we have endured in the past can be endured in the future until the troops arrive. It's very pleasing to know that help is on the way.

Send us rations by aeros more often if possible, as we only get 25 per cent of what is dropped; and I should like to state that rations should be dropped at our stern, so as to float down on us.

You have probably interviewed Shaikh Wannas of El Bab to-day, and you will know what to make of his idea as regards *Greenfly* better than I; but there is something at the back of it all I feel certain. Only, if we can be sure of Shaikh Wannas of El Bab as our friend, then we shall feel better. Try and win him over for us; he holds a lot of power in this district. I spoke him yesterday and he seemed to be quite friendly. El Bab promised us some food yesterday, but it has not arrived, and will not be sent until S. K. (shaikh) returns with the G.O.C.'s orders for me. This to me seems extraordinary, as, if he intended to give us food, there's no need to await his return from Nasiriyah before he does this kind action.

I don't know if your agents have got to work already, but I have managed to get in touch with an Arab on shore, and he has brought me a little—only it means my baksheeshing him heavily. If I knew the agent, this would not be quite so necessary.

We can still hold on (and more so if El Bab are our friends) provided we get food and no heavy casualties; and I would again like to say that we are all willing, and have both spirit and heart (although perhaps not strength at present) to stick out as long as possible—and that is to the very last.

We all thank the garrison for its kind feeling, and hope we shall see you all soon. This is a great strain of watching and waiting. I have painted signals "Rations" 6 ft. letters on my canvas, but I don't think they have been seen. Tell aeros I will also use No. 1 Signal Book and exhibit signal on my barge alongside.

Thanking you for your cheerful letter, and again assuring you of our all performing our duties to the best of our ability.

I have the honour to be, sir, your obedient servant,

ALFRED C. HEDGER.

Note—Shaikh Wannas al Sachit is the chief of the Juwabir tribe whose following were responsible for the attack on *Greenfly* and shooting down an areoplane, which was followed by the murder of the two officers who were with it.

APPENDIX VI.

CHRONOLOGICAL TABLE SHOWING TOTAL STRENGTHS, BY AREAS, OF TRIBES WHICH PARTICIPATED IN 1920 INSURRECTION.

Area.	Date.	Number of armed men.	Rifles.		Remarks.
			Modern.	Old but serviceable.	
Lower Euphrates	30/6/20	2,500	500	1,000	
"	2/7/20	16,300	2,500	6,200	
Middle Euphrates	20/7/20	16,500	2,200	6,000	
"	24/7/20	48,100	4,630	19,795	
"	30/7/20	16,270	800	3,000	
Lower Euphrates	30/7/20	4,350	680	1,600	
Diyalah Division	9/8/20	1,600	200	100	
Baghdad - Fallujah-Mufraz Area	12/8/20	7,500	900	2,050	
Diyalah Division and Kirkuk-Kifri Area	12/8/20	14,300	2,800	2,990	
Samarrah Division	24/8/20	600	175	75	
"	30/8/20	3,000	1,245	365	
Grand Totals		131,020	16,630	43,175	

APPENDIX VII.

MEMORANDUM REGARDING DISARMAMENT.

1. In the operations conducted in this country since the 1st July, the principle of concentration of force as opposed to dispersion has been rigidly and successfully followed.

The General Officer Commanding-in-Chief proposes to adhere to this principle until those tribes at least who have been, or may still be, hostile to us are completely disarmed.

Because disarmament may be difficult, the General Officer Commanding-in-Chief is none the less determined to enforce the policy to the last rifle and round of ammunition, and if all ranks are animated by the same firm purpose the process of depriving the tribes of their weapons will be considerably facilitated and the stay of troops in the country proportionately shortened. The onus and odium of carrying out this policy lie with the General Officer Commanding-in-Chief and his subordinates, and it must be understood that except in so far as to help in carrying it out, Political Officers have no voice in the matter.

2. The General Officer Commanding-in-Chief intends to operate as follows:—

(a) Area of maximum force.
(b) Areas of minimum forces.

(a) AREA OF MAXIMUM FORCE.

In such an area the General Officer Commanding-in-Chief will concentrate every atom of force which he can spare from other areas. It will be the duty of the Divisional Commander in that area to apply the force allotted to him in such a way as to bring about disarmament as quickly as possible. The inhabitants in that area will be informed by proclamation or otherwise that having borne arms against the government, it has been decided that they are no longer to possess arms; that the military forces will remain in that area until such time as all rifles and ammunition are handed in; that the inhabitants will be held individually and collectively responsible that rifles and ammunition are handed in, and that if, hereafter, any individual is found with a rifle or round of ammunition in his possession, not only will he be dealt with with the utmost severity, but the village where he resides will be destroyed.

The number of rifles demanded should fully cover the number of all kinds that tribes are believed to possess.

£T/20 per rifle and 1/- per round may be accepted as a security for the subsequent surrender of any short paid in within a specified period. The object is to obtain rifles, not money.

The date by which rifles and ammunition are to be handed in will be fixed by the Military Commander, and if by that date effect has not been given to his orders the area concerned will be treated as rebellious. Thereupon military action will be taken deliberately, villages will be razed to the ground, and all woodwork removed. Pressure will be brought on the inhabitants by cutting off waterpower and destroying water-lifts; efforts to carry out cultivation will be interfered with, and the systematic collection of supplies of all kinds beyond our actual requirements will be carried out, the area being cleared of the necessaries of life.

Trees—except as a last resort, and if definitely belonging to insurgents and where they interfere with view as regards defence work—will be spared; the Royal Air Force will be available for bomb-dropping both by day and by night. During these proceedings roads should as far as possible be improved, so as to facilitate the rapid movement of small columns for punitive work.

(b) AREAS OF MINIMUM FORCES.

Such areas are those where only sufficient force can be left to maintain pressure upon the inhabitants, who having been hostile during the insurrection have since submitted. Here the carrying out of the policy of disarmament will continue so far as resources will allow. The Royal Air Force will assist with such aeroplanes as can be spared from the area in which maximum force is being applied. The principles guiding the collection of arms and ammunition will be the same as in area (*a*).

As regards proclamations, their nature will be to inform the tribes what is required from them, and that non-compliance will result in treatment similar to that meted out in area (*a*).

5*th November* 1920.

APPENDIX VIII.

BRITISH AND INDIAN CASUALTIES.

FROM 2ND JULY TO 17TH OCTOBER 1920.

	Killed.	Wounded.	Died of Wounds.	Missing.	Prisoners of War.	Died while Prisoners of War.
British officers	19	43	2	5	—	—
British other ranks	28	57	5	136	79	1
Indian officers	7	39	4	4	—	—
Indian other ranks	243	1040	100	278	74	—
Followers	15	49	2	28	11	—
	312	1228	113	451	164	1

Grand Total, 2269.

Most of the missing were killed, a few only rejoining.

ARAB CASUALTIES.

It is impossible to give the Arab casualties with any approach to exactitude, but they have been estimated at 8450 killed and wounded. Careful and conservative estimates based on the number of dead counted, reports from various sources, hostile and other, and the register of burials at the holy cities of Najaf and Karbala, were made. It was ascertained that 3500 free burials were registered at Najaf, and it is probable that a considerable portion of these were killed in action. Shaikh Abdul Wahid, of the Fatlah tribe, who remained hostile to the last, estimated that 2000 corpses of men who fell during the insurrection were buried at Najaf. As this Shaikh fought against us, it is improbable that he exaggerated the Arab loss.

At Karbala 167 corpses, which are known to be those of insurgents who were killed in action, were given free burial, but near that city there was no fighting such as took place in the neighbourhood of Najaf.

In areas other than those of the Upper and Middle Euphrates the Arab casualties have been estimated to be 550.

APPENDIX IX.

NOTES ON MODERN ARAB WARFARE BASED ON THE FIGHTING ROUND RUMAITHAH AND DIWANIYAH, JULY-AUGUST 1920.

Characteristics.

The Arab is most treacherous. He will overpower a small detachment, and when a larger force appears he will put up white flags and be found working peacefully in his fields—incidentally with his rifle within easy reach. It is sometimes of advantage to let him continue this rôle of peaceful cultivation, as, for instance, when a large convoy is proceeding with a small guard; but the fact must always be remembered that he will become an active enemy directly he sees his chance. The white flags and peaceful cultivator's rôle must not prevent the enemy from being punished later at our convenience.

The Arab insurgents may be met with in any number up to 10,000. Between Hillah and Rumaithah in the recent fighting 5000 have been the maximum numbers. One in four are usually mounted, and one in three armed with modern rifles. The remainder represent the supply and medical services of a regular army, bringing up ammunition, food and water, and removing the dead and wounded; they also act as a reinforcement, as they take over the rifles of the wounded and dead.

They flock to the banner of their Shaikh and then to the sound of the guns, moving and collecting with a rapidity little short of marvellous. A large concentration consists of a great number of banners each with its group of followers. When they intend to attack they work themselves up to the necessary pitch of frenzy, with much shouting and waving of banners.

In the present rising they are directed by skilled brains, well versed in the power of the modern rifle (their weapon) and in the limitations and weak points of our modern army. They make very skilful defensive dispositions, and show considerable cunning in the selection of time and place to interfere with water supply, railway, or line of march.

However, owing to their lack of organisation and discipline they can rarely alter plans once made or make new ones to meet a new

APPENDIX IX. 333

situation, unless it is one which visibly appeals to each man individually, such as the withdrawal of our forces, when each independently would swarm after them. During the relief of Rumaithah, finding that in their plans for a direct endeavour to stop our advance they had undertaken more than they liked, they dispersed during the night and early morning and made no attempt to harass our flanks and transport, which might have successfully delayed our march.

Their ammunition is limited, and each round purchased costs them about eight annas. They are consequently very careful in its use, and seldom fire unless it is a target they have a very good chance of hitting and from which they hope to gain something. It is a pity a practical scheme cannot be evolved under which our own men pay for their ammunition or some share of it; it would improve the fire discipline of some units beyond recognition. The Arabs boldly risk their lives to strip our dead of rifle and ammunition while a fight is still going on; these therefore should be removed if possible. They must be considered good shots. The comparative immunity of a large camp from sniping may be put down to their shortage of ammunition, and to the fact that they have nothing to gain by it personally in the shape of loot of rifles or ammunition.

Although there have been exceptions, prisoners and wounded cannot safely be left in their hands. They are liable to be tortured and murdered.

They are ever on the look-out for a chance of wiping out an isolated detachment or odd man in the hope of getting rifles, ammunition, and loot. They seem to appear from nowhere with astonishing rapidity.

They have an inherent dislike of getting killed, though some of their attacks show they can still be worked up to a state of fanatical frenzy—probably on promises of much loot.

Like all semi-savages, they will boldly follow up a retiring force and take any opportunity of closing with it such as afforded by the dust (raised by the column itself) in the case of the Rumaithah relief column on the 22nd July, and by the darkness in the case of the Manchester column on the 25th July.

They have shown a great dislike to artillery. On the 30th July, 3rd August, and 5th August, very large concentrations advancing to attack were completely dispersed by gun fire.

A large concentration cannot maintain itself for more than three or four days, but must disperse for more food and ammunition if there has been any fighting. Except for the bolder spirits, they are loth to fight far from their own villages, particularly in another tribal area. This was very noticeable in the withdrawal from Diwaniyah; at the boundary between the Diwaniyah and Hillah divisions the tribes of the former stopped dead and the fighting was continued by the tribes of the latter.

It was very noticeable that the Arab liked his night's rest and afternoon siesta.

Country.

In the area of recent operations the country is dead level, but intersected at varying intervals by irrigation channels which are occasionally serious obstacles impassable for all arms except at regular crossings. They run to a width of 90 feet, a depth below ground level of 15 feet, and a bank of 35 feet above ground level. They form natural positions for the Arab, out of which he can only be turned by a flanking movement or heavy expenditure of gun ammunition. They interfere with the movement of guns and transport on a wide front, and when met with, in order to avoid undue lengthening of the column, a halt must be made while the transport is brought up and packed on the near side, passed over the canal, and packed again on the far side,—this may mean an hour's delay.

Villages are scattered about irregularly and are favourite haunts for snipers. When shelled the latter take cover in the irrigation channels.

There are many shrines which form the usual assembly centres when the local inhabitants go out to war.

The river is lined in places with palm groves dotted with villages and intersected by high walls. They are best dealt with by bombs and rifle grenades.

Generally speaking, apart from the palm gardens and the bigger canals, the country is, or can easily be made, passable for all arms. During the withdrawal from Diwaniyah the road was only followed for the first ten miles. During the hot weather it cuts up into very fine dust, which rises in clouds, forming a serious handicap to any column by limiting the visibility. After rain the country may be considered impassable off the roads, which themselves become very heavy.

Water is limited to the river and irrigation channels. The latter can very easily be bunded by the Arab, as has been done on several occasions, which may leave a force in a precarious position, particularly as he will do his best from the opposite bank to prevent the river being made good.

Principles.

These are the same as in dealing with any savage tribes. Security first and self-confidence are the secrets of success. But the former is of course purely passive, and the latter, unless combined with the former, is a sure road to disaster.

However peaceful the situation may seem, and however deserted the landscape, precautions must never be relaxed. All-round defence is essential.

In deciding on a course of action, every possible way in which it can go wrong should be considered and measures taken accordingly. In dealing with savage tribes, regrettable incidents or failure to complete what one sets out to do have political effects out of all pro-

APPENDIX IX. 335

portion to their military importance. "Legitimate Gambles" are not to be thought of; a sound straightforward course of action should be followed, even though promising less brilliant results.

The golden rule is to keep the men well in hand, whether at rest or on the march. Long extended lines are a danger and should be avoided.

It is essential to success that the men should have full confidence in their superiority, and feel that they are individually and collectively more than a match for the Arab.

Formation Adopted.

Bearing the above principles in mind and the characteristics of the Arab given earlier, the following formations were adopted by the Rumaithah Relief Column and during the withdrawal from Diwaniyah, on each of which operations a railway train formed part of the column.

At rest by night.

The protection of the long train made a proper continuous perimeter impossible.

Every use was of course made of any natural cover and natural obstacles, and the transport was always parked on the least exposed side of the train.

In the open, in the absence of any modifying features of ground, piquets were normally posted on the perimeter of the camp at about fifty to hundred yards' interval, consisting each of a platoon. The number of course varied, and on occasions admitted of no reserve being kept in hand.

This method of strong concentrated piquets ensured the men being well in hand under the eye of a responsible commander, and gave them the extra confidence to withstand any sudden rush. Unless properly entrenched and wired small piquets are a danger; they can be easily rushed, and the men are liable to get their nerves shaken. It is better to have gaps and strong piquets which can support each other with cross fire, and can be relied on to hold their own than be weak everywhere.

Any canal bank or other point offering snipers a good opportunity was treated in two ways. Either the camp was put right on the top of it so that it formed part of the perimeter, or else the camp was moved sufficiently far away to counteract its value as a sniping post.

Detached piquets are a weakness, particularly when situated on the rear side of the camp in a withdrawal. It is better to face being sniped within reason than to have to extricate a piquet in the morning.

On the night of 5/6th August, when three detached piquets appeared essential, two on a canal bank were made two companies strong; the third in a village was only one company strong, but was closely supported from the perimeter.

336 THE INSURRECTION IN MESOPOTAMIA

Night lines were invariably laid out by the artillery in every direction whence attack or heavy sniping was probable.

Machine-guns were also in position where they could best deal with any serious attack.

Little or no notice should be taken of sniping. If it becomes unpleasantly hot a couple of shells from a howitzer usually stops it.

At rest by day.

It was found that guns were sufficient to keep the Arab at arm's-

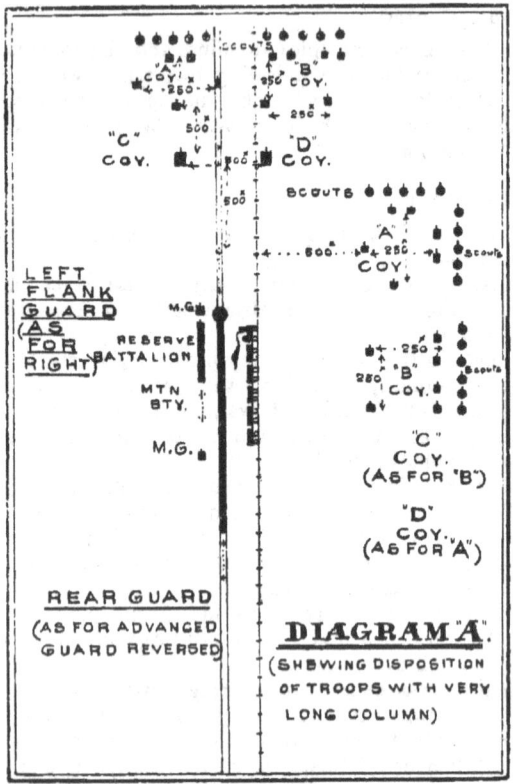

length. All that is required, therefore, is that the surrounding country should be thoroughly watched. This may require certain important points to be held; these detached posts, even though they may have only to find two sentries, should be sent out in the first instance strong enough to hold their own without calling on the main camp for more than artillery support; two companies is a reasonable strength.

In a dust-storm night dispositions must be adopted.

APPENDIX IX.

Dispositions on the march: Column Formation.

With five or more battalions a diamond formation was invariably adopted, whether advancing or withdrawing, with the train and transport in the centre. One battalion formed each point of the diamond, and the balance was left in reserve in the centre.

With only four battalions, as in the first day of the withdrawal from Diwaniyah, a triangular formation was adopted with the base

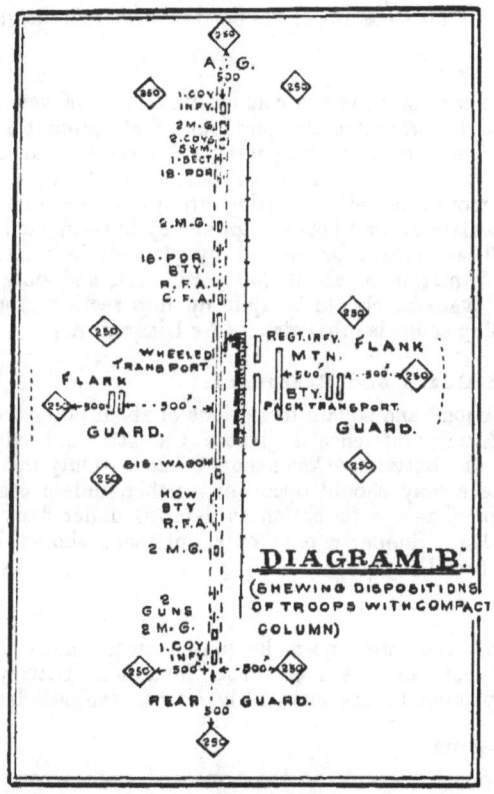

towards the most threatened face, in this case the rear. A central reserve is essential, and if the diamond formation had been adhered to, could only have been obtained by breaking up battalions.

Under normal conditions the distance of these outer battalions from the main body was laid down so as to be not more than five hundred yards from the outer edge of the main body to their inner point; but this distance had to be varied to suit the ground,—for instance, on the 5th August when approaching Jarbuiyah the left battalion, which had to follow the Hashimiyah Canal, was more than a mile from the main body; and in several cases owing to the proximity of the river to the railway, the river battalion had to close right up to the main body.

Battalion Formation.

The formation to be adopted by the battalions was left to the discretion of Battalion Commanders, on whom the necessity was impressed of keeping their men in hand and working them in groups. This also admits of supporting fire from behind.

Flank Guards.

Owing to the length of the column, flank guards were frequently called upon to protect a distance out of all proportion to their strength. The danger of being weak everywhere in an attempt to watch this whole length had to be avoided. Under these conditions battalions moved in self-supporting groups of companies, covering the intermediate ground between groups by fire—in fact, as mobile piquets. These companies moved by platoons in either diamond or square formation of about 250 yards side, and only the other platoon or platoons should be split up into section groups, unless heavy sniping compels otherwise. (*See* Diagram A.)

Advanced Guard and Rearguard.

Both diamond and square formations of about 500 yards side are suitable, though preference is given to the latter as leaving a larger reserve in the Battalion Commander's hand. Only the companies nearest the enemy should open out further, unless compelled by heavy sniping, and a formation as detailed under flank guards is recommended. Similarly only outer platoons should be further split up. (*See* Diagram A.)

Artillery.

Half the guns were normally placed at the head of the main body and half at the rear. The Mountain Battery normally marched parallel to the main body on the exposed flank.

Machine-guns.

These were invaluable on the armoured train accompanying the rearguard during the withdrawal. The train remained behind at each canal or bund until the infantry was well clear, and then rapidly overtook it.

Other machine-guns were placed at each end of the main body either on the train or on pack mules. They could thus deal with any enemy coming in between the advanced guard or rearguard and the flank guards.

A sub-section with A.G. or R.G. when available is also of great value.

APPENDIX IX.

Cavalry.

Cavalry was normally employed with the advanced guard and flank guards, particularly after the experience of the 22nd July, when the correct rapid withdrawal of the cavalry to the next position contributed towards the temporary confusion of the infantry. This rôle in the withdrawal from Diwaniyah was played by the armoured train.

Sappers and Pioneers.

Invariably accompanied the advanced guard to open up and improve communications.

Dispositions in Action.

These can best be exemplified by actual examples. Two will be chosen :—
  (a) The attack on Jarbuiyah on the 5th August.
  (b) The actual withdrawal from Diwaniyah on the 30th July.

Attack on Jarbuiyah, 5th August.

The column with five battalions was advancing in the usual diamond formation, except that the left flank battalion, reinforced by a squadron of cavalry and mountain battery, was one mile from the main body following the line of a canal, vitally important tactically.

As soon as the Advanced-guard Commander reported the enemy in position ahead in strength greater than he thought he could deal with, the two flanking battalions were ordered to move up their H.Q. and two companies on the flanks of the advanced guard, their other two companies to close up towards the front half of the flanks they were protecting; the rearguard battalion was ordered to take over protection of the rear half of the flanks.

The whole attacking line then pushed forward steadily to within 1000 yards of the enemy's position, under cover of the guns, which had all come into action.

From this point patrols were sent forward and reported the enemy to be in no great strength.

The whole attacking force then advanced in lines of skirmishers, and marched, with few casualties, without another halt straight into the line held by the Arabs.

An attack on an Arab position differs little from the usual form, but is handicapped by the necessity of making the guns and transport secure from every direction during its progress, thus preventing full use being made of the available infantry.

Withdrawal from Diwaniyah, 30th July.

Four battalions and an armoured train were available.
The operation was divided into two distinct periods—
Period A, getting clear of the town itself ; period B, the subsequent withdrawal.

Period A consisted of three phases :—
  (1) Getting transport, &c., out into the open while the town was held on each bank by one battalion.
  (2) Withdrawing battalion from left bank under protection of battalion on right bank.

The battalion from the left bank then moved into a position to
  (3) cover the final withdrawal of the right bank battalion—greatly assisted by the armoured train.

When successfully withdrawn the right bank battalion formed up and became the reserve for period B.

During period B the work of the rearguard was made easy by the armoured train, which remained at each successive position, keeping the Arabs back until the infantry was well clear. Then the armoured train rapidly rejoined the infantry.

A proportion of artillery was always ready to give the rearguard immediate assistance.

A very large concentration which later threatened one of the flanks was kept off by gun fire assisted by machine-guns from the train; the flank guard was temporarily reinforced by two companies from the reserve battalion.

In the absence of the armoured train, as small a detachment as possible, supported by guns, machine-gun and rifle fire, was left to cover the withdrawal, and itself then rapidly withdrawn under cover of gun, machine-gun, and rifle fire.

Conclusion.

In conclusion, attention is drawn to the following excellent advice in "Notes on Warfare against Arabs in Mesopotamia," issued by 17th Indian Division, May 1919 :—

"Do not get rattled by his unexpected appearance.
  Keep your eyes open, and your men in hand and ready for action.
  Control your fire and look after fire discipline.
  Keep your (lines straight) formation regular and with proper intervals and distances.
  So long as the troops are well disciplined and remain steady, there is nothing to be feared from the Arabs as an enemy. But if the men become excited and unsteady when the Arabs collect and attack in overwhelming numbers, a disaster may easily occur."

NOTES ON DEALING WITH VILLAGES.

The main principles are :—
  Firstly—To provide for the safety of your own flanks.
  Secondly—Envelop the flanks of the village.
  Thirdly—Advance scouts from your centre straight towards or into the village, being careful to provide for strong covering fire for these scouts in case of necessity.

APPENDIX IX.

Fourthly—Provide for a strong assaulting force to be ready to attack the village without delay, and under all covering fire possible, if the scouts are fired on.

Fifthly—Cover withdrawal as strongly as possible and from flanks.

Apparent hesitation or delay encourages the Arab, and a few men in the average village could inflict many casualties on attacking troops.

The troops should therefore be allotted their tasks and formed up into suitable formations at a long distance, out of rifle range if possible, from the village, and then advance as quickly as possible.

For the purpose of outflanking the village, and as scouts to approach it at first, cavalry is the most suitable arm.

It can gallop back out of range if the enemy suddenly opens fire, but infantry should be detailed to take up these duties if the cavalry is so checked.

Artillery should work at close range, 1500 to 2000 yards. There is usually no time for the laying of telephone lines, and unless the movements of our cavalry and infantry can be clearly observed from the battery positions the guns cannot assist with accurate fire.

Infantry should be in groups (platoon groups seem most suitable). This formation helps the artillery and others to distinguish our men from the enemy. It assists covering fire, enables the cavalry to retire through the infantry without masking the latter's fire and without breaking the latter's formation. Above all, it has a very steadying effect in case of a surprise attack by the enemy.

The assaulting troops must pass right through the village and take up a covering position beyond it.

Separate parties should be detailed for firing the houses, digging up and burning the grain and bhoosa, looting, &c.

The main difficulty usually is caused by the gardens and palm groves which often surround the villages.

To work in these cavalry must dismount.

When such enclosed ground is met, mixed groups are useful to form the outflanking parties. The cavalry finds out whether the gardens or groves are held, while the infantry, supported by guns if necessary, penetrates and holds them.

In the case of villages on or near a river the flanking groups, if they push forward to the river bank quickly enough, can often catch the enemy trying to escape across the river at the last moment.

Rifle bombs are of great value. The Arabs hate them, and the infantry acts much more boldly when it can fire a bomb or two into a village, house or fort, or into a piece of thick cover.

The first men who get into such places are always nervous, and more so if they have been fired at from them.

During recent operations the enemy has never done more than fire a few sniping shots from villages attacked by infantry and guns. Thereafter he ran away.

Twice he stood up to cavalry alone. In each case resistance ceased as soon as the cavalry had got machine-guns well round each flank and well into action.

At Mahmud Effendi the cavalry acted in this manner and caught 40 to 50 enemy crossing the river under close machine-gun fire and caused 20 to 25 casualties.

In dealing with villages as advocated above it is impossible to avoid dispersing one's force. This cannot be helped, and must be accepted. One must simply try to ensure that every group of infantry can be supported on its flanks by the effective fire of other groups of infantry or cavalry.

Cavalry must always be prepared to clear away rapidly if in serious trouble beyond support, but it has the right to expect the infantry or its own Hotchkiss guns to cover its rear and give it a rallying-point.

When it is a question of entering palm groves or thick gardens the troops concerned must look after themselves, but provision must be made for covering their exit should they have to evacuate under attack.

Burning a village properly takes a long time, an hour or more according to size from the time the burning parties enter.

When small groups of troops are hidden in thick cover and firing is going on and no reports can be obtained, this long wait is trying to a commander's nerves. However, it is no good trying to hurry the operation.

The Officer Commanding the cavalry with the column in the recent operations lays special stress on the advantages which can be gained by utilising the mobility of the cavalry to the full. It can scout far forward and to the flanks, and if it meets with serious opposition can gallop out of the enemy's range.

Infantry must, however, understand this manœuvre, and not allow itself to be shaken by the cavalry riding hard back on to its support.

APPENDIX X.

DEMANDS FOR REINFORCEMENTS.

(SUMMARY OF TELEGRAMS SENT TO THE WAR OFFICE AND REPEATED TO INDIA.)

1920.

8th July.	An infantry brigade and a field battery required to be ready for despatch to Basrah.
15th July.	Despatch as soon as possible troops asked for on 8th July. A full division will probably be required.
18th July.	A full division required, but should not be embarked till demanded.
25th July.	Despatch of troops urgent. They should (brigade first asked for), to save delay, embark without transport.
26th July.	A second division may be required.
30th July.	Full division should be despatched at once, and preparations made to send a second division.
3rd August.	If second division is not available, request large drafts for divisions now in Mesopotamia, and earliest possible despatch of full proportion of British units.
(The British units of the division were, owing to danger of moving them through the Persian Gulf in summer, being withheld temporarily.)
13th August.	A fourth Indian battalion should be sent for each reinforcing brigade. (The brigades would then have one British and four Indian battalions.)
17th August.	The three British battalions destined for the relief of similar units in Mesopotamia should now be sent.
28th August.	War Office warned that under certain circumstances reinforcements considerably exceeding those ordered to be sent might be required. (This demand was cancelled after Samawah was relieved.)

APPENDIX XI.

STATEMENT OF COMBATANT REINFORCEMENTS RECEIVED FROM INDIA.

Unit.	Total Combatant Strength.	Date of arrival.	Where sent to on Disembarkation.
2/7th Rajputs . . .	807	6th Aug.	Baghdad
2/123rd Rifles . . .	642	10th Aug.	Nasiriyah
1/15th Sikhs . . .	618	10th Aug.	Baghdad
10th Howitzer Battery .	164	16th Aug.	Nasariyah
1/12th Pioneers . .	736	17th Aug.	Kut-Baghdad L. of C.
2/96th Infantry . .	782	17th Aug.	Kut-Baghdad L. of C.
3/23rd Sikh Infantry .	699	18th Aug.	Nasiriyah
2/117th Mahrattas . .	649	20th Aug.	Nasiriyah
11th Field Coy. . .	183	23rd Aug.	Baghdad
63rd Field Coy. . .	160	23rd Aug.	Baghdad (but sent back to Basrah)
69th Field Coy. . .	169	23rd Aug.	Nasiriyah
2/116th Mahrattas . .	511	25th Aug.	Baghdad
2/89th Punjabis . .	750	26th Aug.	Baghdad-Kut L. of C.
3/70th Burmans . .	540	31st Aug.	Basrah
"C" & "D" Coys. 8th M.G. Bn. . . .	330	2nd Sept.	Baghdad and Nasiriyah
13th Battery R.F.A. .	143	7th Sept. and 14th Sept.	H. Q. 17th Brigade R.F.A. and 1 battery ordered to Nasiriyah. Two 18-pdrs. to Baghdad (subsequently retained Basrah)
26th Battery R.F.A. .	140		
92nd Battery R.F.A. .	145		
1st Bn. K.O.Y.L.I. . .	574	8th Sept.	Nasiriyah
"F" Battery R.H.A. .	210	9th Sept.	Baghdad
2/153rd Rifles . . .	780	18th Sept.	Basrah
63rd Palamcottahs . .	635	18th Sept.	Basrah
3/124th Baluchis . .	730	18th Sept.	Nasiriyah
2nd D.C.L.I. . . .	673	23rd Sept.	Basrah
2nd East Yorkshire Regt.	707	23rd Sept.	Baghdad
3/5th Gurkhas . .	656	24th Sept.	Samawah relief column
3/8th Gurkhas . .	495	24th Sept.	Samawah relief column
1/11th Gurkhas . .	570	24th Sept.	Samawah relief column
2/11th Gurkhas . .	826	28th Sept.	Reserve for Samawah relief column
Kapurthala Infantry .	410	29th Sept.	Basrah

INDEX.

Abadan island, 7.
Abbott, Colonel L. H., 127.
Abdul Wahid, Shaikh, 331.
Abu Hawa, blockhouse construction, 166.
Abu Jisrah, affair at, 164; attacked, 166.
Abu Sukhair, garrison of, 177; strengthened, 178; withdrawn, 178; occupied, 264.
Adler, Major B. I. H., 14; at Kingarban, 245.
Aerodrome, defence of, at Baghdad, 16.
Aeroplanes, 55; over Sharaban, 165; over Kufah, 189; rescue Political Officer, 214; at Samawah, 234, 244; from Constantinople, 262; available for columns, 277; carry wounded shaikh, 308.
Afaj, 20, 130.
Ahwaz, 54.
Albu Kamal, 10, 33.
Albu Sultan joins insurgents, 129; defeated, 151.
Aleppo, 19.
'Ali, 30; tradition regarding, 176.
Ali Sulaiman, Shaikh, loyalty of, 105.
Altun Keupri, occupation of, 19.
Amarrah, 9.
Anah, 20, 33.
Anglo-Persian Agreement, Arab suspicion of, 27.
Anglo-Persian Oil Company, works of, 7; visit to works of, 309; medical help from, 309; efficiency of, 310.
Anizah, 33.
Aquaidat, 33.
Arabs, thefts by, 12; classes of, 22, 23; qualities of, 27, 28, 89, 309, 311, 313; efficiency as labourers, 108; exaggerative habits of, 115; dislike of strong places, 199; mobility of, 219; dislike of Assyrians, 243; notes regarding, 332 et seq.
Arbil, disorders at, 157.
Area, river, events in, 193 et seq.
Areas of command, 11.
Armenians, expense of, 58; safety of, 72; sent to Basrah, 236; vicissitudes of, 236 et seq.; camp of, 240.
Arms, tribes with, 257; handed in, 271, 298.
Army Council, 60; congratulations from, 297.
Assyrians, expense of, 58; losses in camp, 156; truculency of, 157, 244; vicissitudes of, 236 et seq.; camp of, 240; repatriation of, 241; adventure to, 242; defeat Surchi, 247.
Atkinson, Major-General H. de V., 112; commands Samawah relief operations, 221; arrangements of, 223; joins force at Ur, 224.

Baghdad, 10, 11, 12; hostile meetings at, 35, 36; disturbed country north of, 241.
Baiji, 11; raid on, 43.
Baku, 48.
Bani Hachaim murder two R.A.F. officers, 22, 73; negotiate at Samawah, 229.
Bani Hassan, 22, 31.
Bani Lam remains loyal, 106.
Bani Rabia remains loyal, 106.
Balad Ruz, column visits, 272; Young's column reaches, 274.
Balad station, attack on, 241.
Baqubah, 146; railway cutting at, 152; in danger, 154; refugee camp near, 240.
Barbuti bridge, attack on, 198.
Barclay, Lieut.-Colonel P. C. R., calls for reinforcements, 252; alarm of, 252.
Barlow, Major J. E., murdered, 42.
Basrah, extent of, 8, 10, 12, 15.
Bateman-Champain, Brig.-General H. F., troops under, 46; at Enzeli, 47, 51, 55; orders troops to retire seventy miles, 252; anxiety to advance, 253; invalided, 254, 319.
Bazian Pass, 14.
Beatty, Brig.-General G. A. H., commands column, 163, 168, 169; troops with, 179; operations in Diyalah area, 272 et seq., 318.

INDEX

Bedouins, 22.
Berry, Major, 234.
Birs Nimrud, 191.
Bisitun, 49.
Blockhouses, at Baghdad, 112; organisation for, 148; begun on Kut line, 162; on Quraitu line, 166; at Baqubah, 169; to Musayib, 170; to Fallujah, 174; Kut line completed, 175; to Nahr Shah Canal, 182; to Tuwairij, 185; ordered for Nasiriyah line, 219; ordered to be made north of Ur, 224; fewer held, 273; to Barbuti bridge, 278.
Bockett-Pugh, Flying Officer, murdered, 322.
Bolsheviks, 13, 27; land at Enzeli, 47; fighting value of, 253.
Bovill, Major W. J., 212.
Boyle, Major C. A., Inspector-General of Levies, 125; good services of, 302.
Bragg, Captain H. V., commands at Rumaithah, 75.
Bradford, Captain, killed, 164.
Bridging train, 162, 186, 267, 270.
Brooke-Popham, Air Commander, rescues wounded shaikh, 308.
Brooking, Major-General, 287.
Buchanan, Captain, killed, 165.
Buchanan, Mrs, prisoner, 165.
Bunting, Major T. E., 54.
Burnett, Wing Commander C. S., excellent work of, 300.
Burn-Murdoch, Major I., 51; areoplane adventure, 55.
Burrard, Colonel H. G., deals successfully with supply problem, 117.
Butcher, Captain W. H., gallantry of, 287.

Campbell, Major R. N. B., makes gallant charge, 280.
Carey, Lieut.-Colonel A. V., energy of, 112.
Carey, Lieut.-Colonel P. G., visits *Greenfly*, 226.
Cars, armoured, at Tel Afar, 40, 41; unsuitability of, 69, 158; Sharaban garrison and, 165; engaged, 185, 186.
Caspian Sea, 10.
Cash extracted from tribes, 298.
Casualties, British, Indian, Arab, 331.
Cavendish, Lieutenant, joins force, 110.
Chai Khana bridge, column reaches, 275.
Chaldari, camp site at, 112, 113, 114.
Chelmsford, Rt. Hon. Lord, interview with, 6.
Christie, Dr, at Mukden, 310.
Churchill, Rt. Hon. W. S., interview with, 13; telegrams from, 215 *et seq.*; congratulations from, 229.
Coningham, Brig.-General F. E., 57; commands Rumaithah relief force, 81; as a leader, 83; attacks insurgents, 85; serious situation of, 86;

effects relief, 87, 88; tactics of, 89; isolation of force under, 97; ordered to march, 130; at Jarbuiyah, 134, 135, 136, 139; marches to relieve Jarbuiyah, 150, 151; his force assembles, 5th September, 162; ordered to command Samawah relief force, 223; reconnoitres Imam Abdullah bridge, 278; advances, 280; commands Shatt-al-Hai column, 290, 291; takes force to Suq-ash-Suyukh, 297, 315.
Connop, Major H. E., gallantry of, 102.
Cory, Major-General G. N., arrives, 260; orders to, 277, 318.
Cowans, General Sir John, hints from, 3.
Cox, Sir P. Z., at Teheran, 45, 51; arrives at Baghdad. 186; views on disarmament, 259, 295.
Crawford, Captain W. F., ambushed, 214.
Crops, survey of, 29, 30; measuring of, 30, 31, 216.
Cunliffe-Owen, Lieut.-Colonel F., recovers ammunition, 156; in charge of refugees, 240.

Dair-al-Zaur, 13, 20, 32, 33, 50.
Daly, Major C., 73, 74.
Daurah cantonment, 113, 114.
Davies, Brig.-General P. W. L., commands column, 270.
Deering, Sergeant A. V., gallantry of, 102.
Defence vessels, condition of, 109; lost, 201.
Deli Abbas, column visits, 273.
Deltawah, column sent to, 168; detachment left at, 168.
Dent, Brig.-General B. E. C., commands column, 265, 291, 298 *et seq.*, 319.
De Roebeck, Lieutenant, gallantry of, 102.
Devlin, Lieutenant J. A. H., good work of, 241.
Dhari, Shaikh, murders Lieut.-Colonel Leachman, 170; his fort razed, 174.
Dhawalim, 73, 74.
Dickinson, Captain, adventure of, 323.
Ditchburn, Major, 211.
Disarmament, instructions regarding, 260; High Commissioner and, 259, 295; Memorandum on, 329, 330.
Distances, 10, 14, 16, 37, 45, 70.
Diwaniyah, 20, 36, 73; stores at, 128; reoccupied, 268.
Diyalah bridge, 146.
Diyar-albu-Said village occupied, 135.
Dohuk, supply of, 43.
Dojman, Beatty's column reaches, 275.
Dowling, Captain D. M., commands Kufah garrison, 177; opinion of, 178.
Dulaim, arrangement made with, 105.

INDEX

Eadie, Major J. I., wisdom of, 106; valuable work of, 171.
Economy of force, exemplification of, 329.
Edwards, Major D. B., reaches Khanikin Road, 158; his column, 159.
Effendi, 23, 24, 25, 26.
Enzeli, 10, 27, 45; Bolsheviks at, 47.
Euphrates, 10; operations on, 13; raids on, 35; as irrigation canal, 120; peculiarity of, 305.
Extravagance, 65, 66, 67, 68.
Extremists, attempted arrest of, 172.

Fadghami, forces at, 39.
Fahad Beg, Shaikh, loyalty of, 33, 105.
Faisal, H.M. King, 26; opinion on disarmament, 310; kingdom of, 311.
Fallujah, isolation of, 171; communications to, reopened, 174; columns meet at, 266.
Families, soldiers', 59; number of, 72; arrangements for, 61, 167; removal of, 248.
Fao, 10.
Faris-al-Jaryan, Shaikh, magnanimity of, 320.
Fathah, 117.
Fatlah tribe, village destroyed, 184.
Firefly, at Kufah, 178; sunk, 189.
Fires at Baghdad, 122.
Fleming, Lieutenant H. N., 203, 205.
Foster, Captain T. A., 242.
Fraser, Major-General T., view *re* Zakho, 57; ordered to send troops, 79; small force of, 231; lays down bounds, 232, 315.
Frost, Colonel F. B., Director of Labour, 108.

Gowler, Flying Officer G. R., adventure of, 320.
Gardiner, Flying Officer G. C., adventure of, 320.
Garnons-Williams, Lieutenant R. F., 234.
Garrisons, security of, 16; of Mesopotamia, 64, 105, 106, 107; relief of, 141, 143.
Gaskell, Lieut.-Colonel H. S., column under, 159; bold action of, 160.
Glasfurd, Brig.-General A. I. R., commands section of communications, 225, 318.
Goltz, General von der, 10.
Gorringe, Major-General, 287.
Grayfly attempts to refloat *Greenfly*, 195.
Greenfly, sent to Samawah, 194; runs aground, 195; murder of British crew of, 225; part of native crew rejoins, 281; story of captain of, 282, 283; letter from captain of, 326.
Greer, Lieut.-Colonel F. A., commands operations, 160; forward move of, 161; in touch with Coningham, 166; moves to Kingarban, 169.
Grehan, Lieutenant S. A. J., 4, 48.
Groom, Flying Officer V. E., adventure of, 323; gallantry rewarded, 323.
Guchan, 129; isolated train at, 131, 132; halt near, 133.
Gun, captured, used, 189; recovered, 192, 277.

Hadithah, 19.
Hamadan, 48, 49, 54, 55.
Hambro, Brig.-General P., 9; arrangements for families by, 61; arranges supplies, 117, 315.
Hammond, Major T. E., athletic accomplishments, 55.
Hammar Lake, 295, 296, 306.
Hanna, Lieutenant A. L., gallantry of, 233.
Hanna, Captain J. R. M., commands armoured train, 194.
Hanwell, Captain J. C., 233.
Haqqi, Ismail, captured, 19.
Hardat, sepoy, gallantry of, 77.
Hardcastle, Brevet Lieut.-Colonel R. N., commands column, 94, 95, 98; retires force, 100; difficult situation of, 103.
Harper, E. W., gallantry of, 77.
Hashimiyah canal, 135.
Hay, Major A. S., commands at Samawah, 194, 206.
Hay, Major (Political Officer), at Rowanduz, 246.
Healey, Lieutenant J. J., 74.
Hedger, Alfred C., letter from, 327.
Henderson, Major G. B., proceeds to Arbil, 247.
Henderson, Captain G. S., gallantry of, 101.
Herbert, Flying Officer, adventure of, 320.
Hewett, Sir John, information from, 3, 306.
Hillah, 11, 36, 37, 124; attack on, 127; garrison of, 143; train reaches, 148; defence of, 148, 149; operations around, 182, 183, 184.
Hinaidi, 10; roads at, 68, 113; nature of cantonments, 114.
Hindiyah Barrage, 17; erection of, 142; recapture of, 145; defences of, 145.
Hinxman, Sergeant E., gallantry of, 102.
Hit, regular garrison replaced at, 179.
Holmes, Lieut.-Colonel E. W., commands column, 268.
Huddlestone, Lieut.-Colonel, commands column, 278.
Hughes, Brig.-General R. H. W., head of Inland Water Transport, 29.
Hughes, Aircraftsman, adventure of, 323.

INDEX

Humaisaniyah canal, insurgents at, 186.
Hunt, Major R. S., commands at Citadel, 111.
Hunter, Lieutenant J. H. D., gallantry of, 160.
Husainiyah canal, 146; head of, blocked, 170.
Hyatt, Lieutenant P. T., 73, 74; good sense of, 84.

Ibn Ali reached, 132.
Ibn Saud, Sultan of Najd, letter of, 314.
Iman Hamzah reached, 78, 82; Paley's column and 6th Division meet at, 268.
Inland Water Transport, 9, 119.
Iraq, explanation of name, 19; impatience in, 26; tribes of, 27; future of, 314.
Irrigation, question of, 305, 306.
Ironside, Major-General Sir Edmund, arrives, 254: proceeds to Kasvin, 254; effect of presence on troops, 255.

Jaarah occupied, 264.
Jabal Hamrin, 117; traversed by Greer's column, 166.
Jacob, Brig.-General A. le G., commands section of communications, 225; punishes Juwabir tribe, 279, 318.
Jarbuiyah bridge, importance of, 105; defence of, 106, 132, 133, 136; post at, 150; line repaired to, by 12th December, 268.
Jarjiyah canal, 145, 149; opposition at, 184.
Jeffreys, Major J. F. D., influence of, 291.
Jones, Commander C. H., joins force, 109; commands floating defences, 110.
Juwabir tribe, treachery of, 195, 283.

Kabur river, 39.
Kadhimain, Shiah holy city, 26, 27, 109.
Kapurthala, H.H. Maharajah of, sends troops, 107.
Karaghan, relief of, 159, 160.
Karbala, Shiah holy city, 26, 37; water supply of, 146, 147, 170; submits, 186.
Karind, visit to, 45, 48, 61; soldiers' families' camp at, 60; description of, 61, 62; safety of, 161.
Kasvin, situation of, 37; isolation of, in winter, 45; headquarters of British forces at, 46, 51.
Kemmis, Lieut.-Colonel A. W. M., good work of his regiment, 203.
Kermanshah, 48, 55.
Khalis canal, head guarded, 166.

Khan, H.H. the Agha, travel with, 4; remarks of, 31.
Khan, Agha Hamid, rescued, 185; his care of prisoners, 190.
Khan Hiswah, 148.
Khan Jadwal, rations at, 129.
Khan Mahawil canal, 149.
Khan Nasiriyah, camp at, 145.
Khan Nuqtah, murder at, 170; column from, 266.
Khanikin Road station, 158; insurgents near, 159.
Khayun-al-Obaid, character of, 220, 290.
Khidhr railway station lost, 172; situation of, 194; description of, 196; hostile concentration near, 196; order to evacuate, 196; attack on, 197; vacated, 197.
Khirr depot, 109.
Kiernander, Major, engaged with insurgents, 74.
Kifl, 91.
Kifri, disturbances at, 244; arrival of troops at, 246.
Kingarban, railway to, closed, 152, 159; situation of, 245.
Kirkuk, 11, 14, 37; disorder at, 157.
Kitching, Captain, 211.
Kizil Robat, 160.
Kufah,'Ali assassinated at, 30; detachment at, 91; rations at, 141, 143; relief of deferred, 161; arrangements for relief, 168; relief of, 176 *et seq.*; founded, 176; description of, 176; plan of march to, 181; relieved, 187; garrison of, 187; attack on camp, 262.
Kut-al-Amarah, 9, 11; supply depot at, 118; railway to, 119.
Kurdistan, 11, 13, 14, 35.
Kurds as labourers, 108.

Labour Corps, 108; holds blockhouses, 169.
Lakin, Colonel J. H. F., troops under, 46; energetic action of, 157; sends out column, 158; arrival of, at Quraitu, 159, 319.
Lawlor, Mr, murder of, 42.
Leachman, Lieut.-Colonel Gerald, murder of, 171; serious loss, 171.
Leslie, Major-General G. A. J., commanding 17th Division, ordered to go to Hillah, 105; ordered to send column to Deltawah, 168; commands Kufah and Tuwairij operations, 184; replaced by Brig.-General Sanders, 260, 315.
Levies, 78; good work of, 125, 126, 127, 150, 151, 190, 197, 198, 246; at Sharaban, 165; at Khidhr, 197, 198; with Paley's column, 267; with Davies' column, 270; staunchness of, 301, 302; losses of, 303; rewards earned by, 303.
Littledale, Captain, gallantry of, 246.

INDEX 349

Lloyd, Captain, prisoner, 168.
Lloyd-Evans, Flying Officer D., adventure, 322; gallantry rewarded, 323.
Locke, Flying Officer H. G. W., adventure of, 320.
Lubbock, Major, good work of, 132.
Lukin, Colonel R. C. W., 93.
Lutyens, Sir E., 6.

Macdonald, Flying Officer, murdered, 322.
Macintyre, Major F. P., 51.
MacMunn, Major-General Sir G., 5.
Mahmudiyah, 148; columns meet at, 266.
Maidan-i-Naftun, visit to, 309.
Manchester Column, 94; transport carts recovered, 263.
Manjil Pass. strength of, 47, 52, 53, 54; Bolsheviks near, 48; visit to, 51; exaggerated reports of movement against, 252.
Mann, Captain J. S., killed, 188; gallantry of, 188.
Marriott, Lieutenant, attacks Albu Hassan, 75.
Marut, 153; blockhouse construction near, 166.
Masters, Captain O., 135.
May, Major C. D., takes detachment to Samawah, 194.
McCausland, Major E. T. W., relieves Samarrah, 234.
McGowan, Major T., commands a column, 266.
McNally, Captain J. V., 211, 212.
M'Vean, Lieut.-Colonel D. A. D., resolution of, 78, 132.
Maxwell, Flying Officer P. D., adventures of, 322, 323.
Medill, Major R. M., commands a column, 160.
Mendali, Young's column moves to, 273.
Merriman, Lieut.-Colonel A. D. N., assists rearguard, 90.
Mezlaq Channel, 306.
Mirjanah occupied, 162.
Mitchell, Major H. S., commands at Jarbuiyah, 134.
Molloy, Major N. F. C., relieves Tuz and Kingarban, 245.
Moore, Captain J. B., 160.
Morris, Brig.-General G. M., 316.
Mortality of children, 307.
Mosul, 11, 35, 38, 39, 43; supply of, 234; suggested evacuation of, 235.
Mudlark, 296.
Muhammad Mirza Taqi, son arrested, 147; declares Jihad, 214.
Muhammad Sadr, 233.
Muhammarah, Shaikh of, 54.
Munro, General Sir C., visit to, 5; offer of, 107.
Muntafiq, 106; propaganda among, 148; armed men among, 215; march through country of, 285 *et seq*.

Musayib, importance of, 142; column advances on, 143; occupied, 145; advantage of, 146; blockhouse line to, 170; operations near, 263.
Mutter, Company Sergeant-Major, care of prisoners, 191.

Nahr Shah Canal, blockhouses to mouth of, 182.
Nahr Umar, port at, 8.
Najaf, holy city, 26, 27, 36; 'Ali buried at, 176; half-company sent to, 177; half-company withdrawn, 178; submits, 190; fine paid, 262; display of force at, 264; terms read, 264.
Nalder, Colonel, sagacity of, 57.
Nasiriyah, 11, 36; troops at, 193; important situation of, 219; Samawah relief column at, 224.
Nepean, Brig.-General H. E. C. B., commands River Area, 193, 317.
Nesbitt, Instructor of Levies. killed, 164.
Newton, Sergeant-Major, killed, 164.
Nightingale, Brig.-General M. R. W., 316.
Nisibin, 38.
Norbury, Major P. FitzG., foresight of, 141; urgent representations of, 177.
Norman, Major A. C., commands a column, 173.
Norman, H., H.B.M.'s minister at Teheran, 50.
Norris, Commodore D., arrives at Kasvin, 54, 110.
Norton, Captain C. E., 229.
Nuttall, Flight-Lieutenant, killed, 57.

O'Donovan, Captain M. J. W., 54.
Officers, military, responsibility of, 324.
Onslow, Lieutenant, joins force, 110.
Organisation, brigade, departed from, 225.

Paley, Brig.-General A., carries out punitive operations, 226; rescues isolated Assyrians, 242; his column marches to Diwaniyah, 267; difficulties encountered, 267.
Petros, Agha, leader of Assyrians, 237.
Persia, 13, 27, 37; distances in, 45; withdrawal from, 55.
Physicians, necessity for, 307.
Pigeon, Captain J. W., 203, 205; self-sacrifice of, 209.
Platt, Captain A., 295; escapes, 296.
Political Officers, inexperience of, 20, 21, 25, 29; efforts of, 35; interviews with, 36.
Prisoners, British and Indian, number of, 102; movements of, 190; surrender of, 190; treatment of, 190, 191.
Prisoners, Turkish, guards for, 11, 72; number of, 58; shipped to Constantinople, 107.

INDEX

Proclamation to Diyalah tribes, 163.
Propaganda, 174, 185.
Pulley, Major, urges military action, 93.
Pusht-i-Kuh, 9.

Qalat Sikar, 20.
Qislah at Sharaban attacked, 164; captured, 165.
Quiyarah, ambush near, 44.
Quraitu, 37, 45, 48; train service to, 152.

Railways, inefficiency of, 11, 70, 71, 80; shortage of rolling-stock, 162; re-opened to Quraitu, 167; reopened to Kingarban, 169; siting of stations, 200; Hillah-Kifl line repaired, 263; repairs on main Basrah line begun, 268; repaired north of Samawah, 278; good work of personnel, 303, 304; loss of personnel, 304.
Ramadhan, 43, 56.
Ramadhan-al-Shallash, 32.
Ramadi, troops at, 11; operations near, 13; isolation of, 171; communication with, restored, 174.
Raqqa, in Aqaidat country, 32.
Refugees. (See "Assyrians" and "Armenians.")
Regulators on rivers, 142, 166, 174, 305, 306.
Reinforcements, demands for, 343; received, 344.
Resht, Bolsheviks at, 48; reoccupied, 254.
Roads, nature of, 14, 15, 69; at Hinaidi, 68; Baiji-Shergat, 116.
Robertson, Brevet Lieut.-Colonel D. E., attacks ambushed Arabs, 44.
Robinson, Flight-Lieut. F. L., adventure of, 55.
Rowanduz, occupation of, 20.
Royal Air Force, strength of, 70; assists Rumaithah garrison, 77; raid by, 80; assists at Samarrah, 234; assists columns, 131, 132, 136, 137, 138, 185, 227, 275; excellent work of, 300, 301; rescues wounded shaikh, 308; prestige of, 309; rewards offered by, 321.
Rumaithah, outbreak at, 73; submission of, 283.
Russell, Captain O., defends railway post at Samawah, 203, 205; gallant conduct of, 209, 210; killed, 210.
Rustumiyah canal, camp on, 98.

Saklawiyah canal, blockhouse at head of, 174.
Salmon, Captain G. H., murdered, 246.
Samarrah threatened, 234; Beatty's column at, 276.
Samawah, disturbance at, 73; isolated, 172; troops at, 193; defence of, 199, 200; supplies sent to, 201; attack on begins, 202; relief of, 227; garrison during siege, 228; attacked again, 244.
Sanders, Brig.-General G. A. F., in charge of blockhouse scheme, 148, 174; commands Tuwairij column, 180; appointed to command 17th Division, 260, 316.
Sarel, Lieut.-Colonel G. B. M., commands a column, 43.
Sar-i-Mil, 36, 48; headquarter camp at, 62; safety of, 161.
Sarim-ud-Daulah, Prince, 48.
Scott, Lieut.-Colonel H. L., initiative of, 86, 89, 135; commands a column, 140, 143, 147, 149.
Scott-Ruffle, Captain, relief of, 160.
Seaton, Lieut. G. H., killed, 147.
Sha'alan Abu, arrest of, 73, 84.
Shamiyah, visit to, 264.
Shammar, 40; give trouble, 232.
Sharaban, affairs near, 164; reached, 164; massacre at, 165; punishment of, 166; Beatty's column leaves, 272.
Shattrah, 20; bad reputation of, 215, 216.
Shergat, road to, 15; capture of, 19, 35, 37, 39.
Shiah, origin of, 30.
Shurufah occupied, 135.
Simpson, Lieut. C. E., arrives at Ur, 194; arrives at Khidhr station, 197.
Sindiyah, detachment at, 169.
Stevenson, Lieut.-Colonel K. L., 293.
Stewart, Colonel A. C., commanding Guides Cavalry, 53.
Stewart, Brig.-General J. H. K., senior G. S. officer, 48, 51; value of, 104, 139, 315.
Storey-Cooper, Captain E. S., gallantry of, 206.
Stuart, Captain, murdered, 42.
Suffolk, Captain W. H., Inland Water Transport, gallantry of, 202.
Sulaimaniyah, 14.
Sunni, origin of, 30.
Supplies, 117, 118, 119.
Suq-ash-Suyukh, column sent to, 297.
Surchi, disturbances among, 35, 246; attack Rowanduz, 247; attack Assyrians, 247.
Sweet, Lieut.-Colonel E. H., commands at Manjil Pass, 52.
Syria, 19, 26.

Tabriz, troops at, 54.
Tak-i-Girrah Pass, 48.
Tanks, suitability of Iraq for, 15; asked for, 70.
Taq-i-Bostan, 49.
Teheran visited, 14, 46, 48, 51.
Tekrit, garrison of, 11.
Tel Afar occupied, 20; incident at, 38, 39, 40, 172; column reaches, 43, 50.
Temperature, 63, 98, 138, 144, 218, 266, 300.

INDEX

Thomas, Captain B. S., good work of, 220, 293.
Tigris, 11; delta of, 15, 43; main artery, 119, 120, 305.
Townshend, Major-General Sir C., 2, 285.
Tozer, Captain, accompanies Manchester Column, 96, 97.
Trains, armoured, patrol, 195; two lost, 198; lost at Samawah, 205; isolated, 242.
Transport, natures of, used, 271; shortage affects operations, 278.
Tribes engaged, 124; Diyalah, characteristics of, 163; Diyalah surrender, 168; Kurdish, restless, 216; presence of troops, effect of, 294; gratitude of, 309; characteristics of, 312; magnanimity of, 313; strength engaged, 328.
Troops, endurance of, 299; strength of, 325.
Turumah occupied, 271.
Tuwairij, movement on, 184; bridge saved at, 185; garrison left at, 185.
Tuz isolated, 225.

Umma, excavations at, 293.
Umm-al-Barur, prisoners at, 178.
Umran, Shaikh, magnanimity of, 321.
Units—
British Cavalry :—
1st King's Dragoon Guards, 80, 152.
7th Dragoon Guards (Princess Royal's), 80, 152, 273, 269.
8th King's Royal Irish Hussars, 273.
Indian Cavalry :—
5th Cavalry, 105, 173, 179, 180, 265, 292.
10th Duke of Cambridge's Own Lancers (Hodson's Horse), 203, 209, 210, 224, 226, 278.
11th King Edward's Own Lancers (Probyn's Horse), 43, 44, 247.
32nd Lancers, 126, 140, 147, 162, 169, 247, 272, 275.
35th Scinde Horse, 54, 93, 94, 98, 101, 102, 140, 162, 168, 180, 187, 273.
37th Lancers (Baluch Horse), 54, 78, 81, 131, 135, 137, 143, 150, 170, 180, 264, 267, 279, 290.
Queen Victoria's Own Corps of Guides (Lumsden's), 46, 52, 53.
British Artillery :—
"A" Battery R.H.A. (Chestnut Troop), 46, 53, 152, 153.
"F" Battery R.H.A., 272, 273.
2nd Battery R.F.A., 180, 267.
8th Battery R.F.A., 247.
10th (How.) Battery R.F.A., 224, 279.
13th Battery R.F.A., 224, 279.
26th Battery R.F.A., 279.
39th Battery R.F.A., 93, 94, 99, 100, 102, 150, 170, 180, 270.
44th Battery R.F.A., 232.
92nd Battery R.F.A., 279.
96th Battery R.F.A., 173.
97th Battery R.F.A., 81, 86, 131, 140, 162, 168, 265, 269.
131st (How.) Battery R.F.A., 126, 131, 137, 140, 150, 170, 180, 265, 292.
132nd (How.) Battery R.F.A., 81, 131, 143, 162, 180, 267.
5th Battery R.G.A., 146.
13th Pack Battery R.G.A., 159, 161, 169, 272, 275.
45th Pack Battery R.G.A., 78, 81, 131, 135, 137, 140, 163, 169, 180, 267.
50th Pack Battery R.G.A., 153, 292.
British Infantry :—
4th Batt. The Royal Fusiliers, 247.
2nd Batt. The East Yorkshire Regiment, 181, 185, 264, 265.
2nd Batt. The Duke of Cornwall's Light Infantry, 290.
1st Batt. The Royal Berkshire Regiment, 53.
1st Batt. The King's Own Yorkshire Light Infantry, 224, 226, 227, 268, 279.
2nd Batt. The Manchester Regiment, 79, 94, 98, 104, 126, 140, 145, 146, 180, 187, 264.
2nd Batt. The York and Lancaster Regiment, 53.
2nd Batt. The Royal Irish Rifles, 78, 81, 83, 90, 126, 144, 150, 170, 180, 183, 264.
1st Batt. The Royal Irish Fusiliers, 53, 161, 179, 272, 292.
1st Batt. The Rifle Brigade, 110, 153, 154, 264, 267, 268.
Indian Artillery :—
40th Pack Battery, 179, 265, 290.
Engineers :—
9th Coy. 2nd Queen Victoria's Own Sappers and Miners, 163, 168, 181, 267.
11th Coy. 2nd Queen Victoria's Own Sappers and Miners, 174, 275.
61st Coy. 2nd Queen Victoria's Own Sappers and Miners, 81, 131, 180, 265, 292.
65th Coy. 2nd Queen Victoria's Own Sappers and Miners, 159, 160.
67th Coy. 2nd Queen Victoria's Own Sappers and Miners, 126, 150, 173, 180, 276.
69th Coy. 2nd Queen Victoria's Own Sappers and Miners, 224.
26th (Railway) Coy. Sappers and Miners, 279.
Indian Infantry :—
2/6th Royal Jat Light Infantry, 173.

INDEX

2/7th Duke of Connaught's Own Rajputs, 141.
8th Rajputs, 126, 127, 140, 145, 150, 183, 184, 270.
3/9th Bhopal Infantry, 163, 181, 267.
1/12th Pioneers, 162, 163, 168, 181, 267.
13th Rajputs, 148, 181, 185, 267, 268.
1/15th Ludhiana Sikhs, 146, 156, 162, 168, 180, 184, 187, 264.
3/23rd Sikh Infantry, 224, 226, 278, 279, 280.
1/32nd Sikh Pioneers, 93, 101, 131, 134, 137, 140, 150, 180, 265, 269, 270.
1/39th Royal Garhwal Rifles, 44.
45th Rattray's Sikhs, 57, 78, 79, 82, 83, 86, 87, 88, 90, 131, 135, 144, 150, 162, 179, 265, 292.
52nd Sikhs (Frontier Force), 247.
1/67th Punjabis, 54.
3/70th Burma Rifles, 268.
79th Carnatic Infantry, 159, 161.
86th Carnatic Infantry, 131, 135, 151.
87th Punjabis, 79, 81, 90, 131, 137, 180, 186.
1/89th Punjabis, 162.
1/94th Russell's Infantry, 153, 154, 160, 161, 179, 245, 292.
2/96th Infantry, 162, 270.
1/99th Deccan Infantry, 75, 77, 78, 81, 131, 135, 140, 150, 162, 179, 273, 275.
106th Hazara Pioneers, 234.
108th Infantry, 126, 131, 134, 180, 187, 265.
1/113th Infantry, 245.
1/114th Mahrattas, 74, 75, 76, 77, 131, 135, 140, 193, 227, 277.
1/116th Mahrattas, 79, 81, 86, 87, 126, 135, 137, 140, 150, 170, 180, 186, 267.
2/117th Royal Mahrattas, 268, 275, 277.
2/119th Infantry, 163, 168, 169, 179.
122nd Rajputana Infantry, 163.
3/124th Duchess of Connaught's Own Baluchistan Infantry, 290.
2/125th Napier's Rifles, 193, 194, 290.
2/129th Duke of Connaught's Own Baluchis, 194.
3/153rd Rifles, 279, 290.
2nd King Edward's Own Gurkha Rifles, 52.
1/3rd Queen Alexandra's Own Gurkha Rifles, 116, 234, 241, 244.

3/5th Royal Gurkha Rifles (Frontier Force), 224, 226, 277, 278, 279, 280.
3/8th Gurkha Rifles, 224, 226, 278, 290.
1/10th Gurkha Rifles, 80, 81, 83, 86, 87, 88, 131, 135, 137, 140, 150, 162, 179, 265, 292.
1/11th Gurkha Rifles, 224, 279, 280.
2/11th Gurkha Rifles, 272, 275.

Van Straubenzee, Major A. W., commanding Chestnut Troop, R.H.A., 53; routs Bolsheviks, 253.

Walker, Brig.-General H. A., commands a column, 140, 170; recaptures Barrage, 146, 149; exerts pressure in Hillah area, 170; returns to Hillah, 170; commands Kufah relief column, 180.
Walker, Sergeant, murder of, 42.
Wannas-al-Sachit, Shaikh, 327.
Water, dominating question, 17; Kufah column and, 181; carried on trains, 225.
Webb, Captain W. F., escape of, 130.
Willcocks, Sir Wm., associated with Hindiyah Barrage, 142; his irrigation scheme, 305.
Williams, Lieut.-Colonel J., destroys villages, 153, 154, 155.
Williams, Brevet Lieut.-Colonel L. G., despatches convoy of vessels, 172.
Willis, Sergeant J., gallantry of, 102.
Wilson, Lieut.-Colonel Sir A. T., Acting Civil Commissioner, 10; his task, 24, 25; anticipates trouble, 36, 37, 50, 51, 56, 160; replaced, 186.
Wilson, Field-Marshal Sir H., congratulations from, 229.
Woods, Lieut. A. W. H., escorts convoy, 113.
Wooldridge, Brig.-General H. W., 315.
Wright, Mr and Mrs, visit to, 49, 55.
Wrigley, Captain, killed, 164.

Young, Brig.-General H. G., commands a column, 152, 153, 154, 155, 273, 317.
Young, Dr M. Y., excellent work of, 309.
Yusuf-al-Suwaidi, 233.
Yusufiyah canal, march to, 266; Holmes's column camps on, 269.

Zakho, 10, 39, 43, 50.
Zingan, 54.
Zoba tribe revolts, 170; murders Lieut.-Colonel Leachman, 170.

www.ingramcontent.com/pod-product-compliance
Lightning Source LLC
Chambersburg PA
CBHW011717220426
43662CB00019B/2408